AS/A-LEVEL

FIFTH EDITION

UK GOVERNMENT AND POLITICS

Philip Lynch
Paul Fairclough
Toby Cooper

Editor: Eric Magee

HODDER
EDUCATION
AN HACHETTE UK COMPANY

Hachette UK's policy is to use papers that are natural, renewable and recyclable products and made from wood grown in sustainable forests. The logging and manufacturing processes are expected to conform to the environmental regulations of the country of origin.

Orders: please contact Bookpoint Ltd, 130 Park Drive, Milton Park, Abingdon, Oxon OX14 4SE. Telephone: (44) 01235 827720. Fax: (44) 01235 400454. Email education@bookpoint. co.uk

Lines are open from 9 a.m. to 5 p.m., Monday to Saturday, with a 24-hour message answering service. You can also order through our website: www.hoddereducation.co.uk

ISBN: 978 1 4718 89233

© Philip Lynch, Paul Fairclough, Toby Cooper and Eric Magee 2017

First published in 2017 by

Hodder Education,
An Hachette UK Company
Carmelite House
50 Victoria Embankment
London EC4Y 0DZ

www.hoddereducation.co.uk

Impression number   10 9 8 7

Year   2021 2020

Photos reproduced by permission of: **p. 2** Topfoto, **p. 4** Topfoto, **p. 13** Topfoto, **p. 16** Wiktor Szymanowicz/Alamy, **p. 22** eye35/Alamy, **p. 27** Andy Buchanan/Alamy, **p. 31** Homer Sykes Archive/Alamy, **p. 35** Topfoto, **p. 38** Victor Moussa/Fotolia, **p. 45** Tupungato/Fotolia, **p. 48** Newsphoto/Alamy, **p. 50** Topfoto, **p. 59** Pete Maclaine/Alamy, **p. 63** Corund/Fotolia, **p. 64** Roger Pilkington/Fotolia, **p. 67** Topfoto, **p. 68** Topfoto, **p. 70** Josemaria Toscano/Fotolia, **p. 75** Mark Kerrison/Alamy, **p. 82** Mark Kerrison/Alamy, **p. 84** Topfoto, **p. 87** Kirsty Wigglesworth/AFP/Getty Images, **p. 100** UK Parliament/Jessica Taylor, **p. 108** WENN Ltd/Alamy, **p. 117** Simon Dawson/Bloomberg/Getty Images, **p. 129** Reuters/Alamy, **p. 142** Reuters/Alamy, **p. 146** Reuters/Alamy, **p. 152** Topfoto, **p. 158** Reuters/Alamy, **p. 165** Evgesha/Fotolia, **p. 168** Gary Lucken/Alamy, **p. 170** David Levenson/Alamy, **p. 173** Jelle van der Wolf/Fotolia, **p. 178** lazylama/Fotolia, **p. 182** wronaphoto.com/Alamy, **p. 186** Patrick Hertzog/AFP/Getty Images, **p. 195** BasPhoto/Alamy, **p. 196** Tommy London/Alamy, **p. 202** 7razer/Fotolia, **p. 208** Adrian Buck/Alamy, **p. 218** Topfoto, **p. 224** Vibrant Pictures/Alamy, **p. 229** Charles Stirling/Alamy, **p. 234** Steve Morgan/Alamy, **p. 249** Oli Scarff/AFP/Getty Images, **p. 254** Bonzo/Alamy, **p. 259** PjrNews/Alamy, **p. 273** Mark Richardson/Alamy, **p. 277** Jeff J. Mitchell/Getty Images, **p. 281** Jon Jones/Sygma via Getty Images, **p. 286** Ian Forsyth/Getty Images, **p. 293** AFP/Getty Images, **p. 295** The Conservative Party Archive/Getty Images, **p. 298** The Conservative Party Archive/Getty Images, **p. 302** Jonny White/Alamy, **p. 310** Paul Bevitt/Alamy, **p. 315** Topfoto, **p. 319** Trinity Mirror/Mirrorpix/Alamy, **p. 324** Rupert Rivett/Alamy, **p. 326** Jack Taylor/Alamy

Typeset in Bliss light 10.75/13.5 pts by Aptara Inc.

Printed in Dubai

A catalogue record for this title is available from the British Library.

Get the most from this book

This new edition of our best-selling textbook covers the key content of the government and politics specifications for teaching from September 2017.

Special features

Key questions answered
Key topics covered in each chapter.

Synoptic links
Links between concepts that occur in more than one area of the specification.

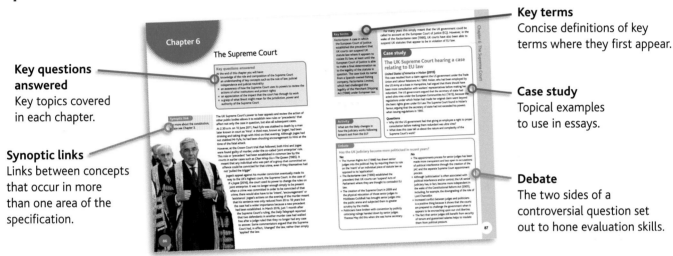

Key terms
Concise definitions of key terms where they first appear.

Case study
Topical examples to use in essays.

Debate
The two sides of a controversial question set out to hone evaluation skills.

In focus
Key concepts explained.

Distinguish between
A clarification of the difference between commonly confused concepts or institutions.

Exam-style questions
Practice exam questions at the end of each chapter.

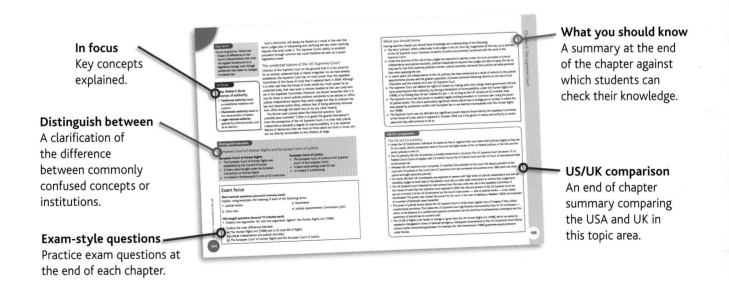

What you should know
A summary at the end of the chapter against which students can check their knowledge.

US/UK comparison
An end of chapter summary comparing the USA and UK in this topic area.

Contents

Section 2   Political participation in the UK

Answers to the exam-style questions at the end of each chapter can be found at:
www.hoddereducation.co.uk/UKGovernmentandPolitics

INTRODUCTION

Chapter 1

Historical context of the UK political system

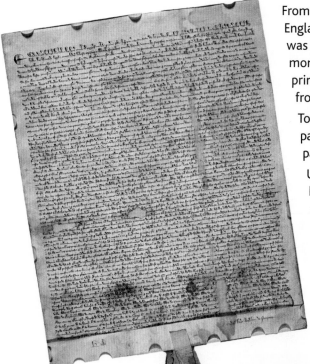

From 1066 until 1215, when Magna Carta was introduced, England was effectively run as an absolute monarchy. The king was sovereign and held all power. Scotland had its own absolute monarchy, while Wales and Ireland were ruled by a series of princes and chieftains, with nominal oversight and domination from England.

Today the monarchy is limited and sovereignty, or power, has passed to parliament, while the separate nations have become part of a United Kingdom.

Unlike many nations, there is no single point at which the UK became the modern democracy it is today. Instead, the system of government and politics in the UK has evolved over time, thanks to its **uncodified constitution**, resulting in a number of unusual features.

An understanding of this historical evolution will help you to grasp many of the issues faced by the UK today, such as devolution, relations with the EU, the idea of parliamentary sovereignty and the nature of parliamentary democracy.

Magna Carta established the first formal limits to the power of the monarchy and paved the way for the creation of parliament

Key term

Uncodified constitution This describes a constitution where the laws, rules and principles specifying how a state is to be governed are not gathered in a single document. Instead, they are found in a variety of sources — some written (e.g. statute law) and some unwritten (e.g. convention).

Synoptic links

Constitutions

A constitution is the set of rules that set out how a country is to operate. Among other things it establishes links between the different parts of the political system and the rights of the citizens. Many constitutions are created in one go, usually after a revolution, and are therefore set out in one document. The UK constitution has evolved, rather than been created, and its various elements are not collected in one place. You can find out more about this in Chapter 3.

Table 1.1 The development of the UK constitution

Date	Event	Date	Event
924–1066	Development of the witan (the council of the Anglo-Saxon kings), trial by jury and habeas corpus	1800	Acts of Union create the United Kingdom of Great Britain and Ireland
1066	Norman invasion of England and building of Westminster Hall begins	1832	Great Reform Act
1215	Signing of Magna Carta Beginning of the House of Lords	1867	Second Reform Act
1275	Beginning of the House of Commons	1872	Ballot Act
1327	Edward II removed as king by parliament	1883	Corrupt and Illegal Practices Act
1534	First Act of Supremacy	1885	Redistribution of Seats Act (Third Reform Act)
1559	Second Act of Supremacy and the introduction of the Oath of Supremacy	1911	Parliament Act reduces the power of the Lords
1603	James VI of Scotland becomes James I of England	1918	Representation of the People Act gives all men and some women the right to vote
1642	Start of the English Civil War	1921	Anglo-Irish Treaty leads to an independent Ireland and the establishment of the United Kingdom of Great Britain and Northern Ireland
1649	King Charles I tried and executed by parliament	1928	Representation of the People Act gives all women the right to vote
1660	Restoration of the monarchy	1949	Parliament Act further reduces the power of the Lords
1688	Glorious Revolution	1969	Representation of the People Act lowers voting age to 18
1689	Bill of Rights	1972	European Communities Act
1701	Act of Settlement		
1707	Act of Union creates the United Kingdom of Great Britain		

Anglo-Saxon institutions

Key terms

Habeas corpus A process in law which means a person can appeal to the courts against unfair or illegal imprisonment.

Trial by jury The idea that a group of twelve peers would hear the evidence in a case and decide if the accused was guilty.

Trial by ordeal The medieval practice of putting the accused through an ordeal to determine guilt, such as burning their hand and waiting to see how well it healed.

As England came into existence from a series of smaller kingdoms under the Anglo-Saxons, three key elements emerged that would have profound effects on the development of politics in the UK:

- the witan
- the principle of **trial by jury**
- **habeas corpus**

The witan was a council that advised the king on taxation and military matters. Although not a parliament as we would understand it today, it established the principle that the king of England should consult with the lords before taxing and commanding the people. It was also the job of the witan to decide who should be king.

The principle of trial by jury was the Anglo-Saxon legal principle that any noble accused of a crime should be tried a jury of peers. The king would determine the sentence, but guilt was decided by the deliberation of his fellow lords. Elsewhere in Europe, guilt was often determined by a decision of the king or through **trial by ordeal**, but England was governed by law and the power of the monarch was limited.

The principle of habeas corpus meant that a prisoner had the right to appeal to the courts against unfair or illegal detention. This meant that even the lowest ranked citizen could appeal to the law about unfair punishment and imprisonment. In this sense, the weakest in society were protected by the rule of law against unfair treatment by the strongest.

Although these three aspects of Anglo-Saxon society were challenged and ignored in the years immediately after the Norman Conquest, they became the underpinning of the revolt of the barons in 1214 and later still became the founding principles of the UK constitution when it emerged.

Norman and Angevin rule

Under the feudal system nobles had to swear an oath of loyalty to the king

From the Battle of Hastings in 1066 until the signing of Magna Carta in 1215, England was run as a feudal system. This meant the king effectively owned all the land and everyone had to swear an oath of loyalty or 'fealty' to him. The king would give land to the nobles who would use knights to manage it for the king. In return, the nobles would supply an army to the king if the country needed it. Over time, rather than supply an army, the nobles began to supply cash instead. To work out what the nobles owed, the king's chancellor would use a huge chequered mat (like a giant chess board) to calculate the amount of money owed, hence the title the '**chancellor of the exchequer**'.

Key term

Chancellor of the exchequer The government official responsible for calculating, collecting and distributing government funds through taxation and duties.

As well as being king of England, most kings — from the Norman Conquest of 1066 until the end of the Angevin empire with the death of King John in 1216 — were also lords in France, owning Normandy, Anjou and Aquitaine. As such, the kings were often absent and would leave their nobles — chief ministers — to run England while they were away. These chief ministers were nothing like modern prime ministers, but they helped to establish the principle of royal powers being exercised by someone nominated by the king.

Finally, the absence of the king meant he could not be relied on to preside over court proceedings and dispense justice. To combat this, he would appoint justices of the peace, or judges, who would travel the country and hear cases on behalf of the crown. This marked the beginning of the English legal system, and many of the common-law principles that were established then continued to exist in UK politics until fairly recently.

Magna Carta

Unlike his immediate predecessors, King John (1166–1216) was seen as a ruthless and ineffective king. The English nobles resented him raising money in England to fund wars in France, as well as his abuse of royal powers, his conflict with the Church and his arbitrary abuse of the justice system for his own ends.

By 1214, these issues had come to a head and the barons of England revolted against the king. The nobles referred to the Anglo-Saxon principles of the witan and habeas corpus as limits on the power of the monarchy. They even went so far as to offer the crown to Prince Louis of France. This revolt led to the defeat of the monarchy and John was forced to sign a great charter, or 'Magna Carta', at Runnymede in Berkshire.

Key provisions of Magna Carta

Magna Carta guaranteed the freedom of the Church from royal interference (Clause 1) and curbed the powers of the king:

- The king could not raise a tax without the consent of the people (Clause 12).
- The right to due process in the law was guaranteed (Clause 29).
- The right to trial by jury was guaranteed (Clause 39).
- Justice had to be free and fair (Clause 40).
- The nobles could select a committee of 25 to scrutinise the actions of the king (Clause 61).

Magna Carta was the first time since 1066 that the powers of the monarch had been limited and it was an acknowledgement that the rights of the lords had to be respected. There were 63 provisions in total, mostly concerning the rights of the nobles to be consulted about taxation and about the legal protection they had from the power of the monarchy. By consolidating these Anglo-Saxon principles into a formal legal document, the lords created the first part of the UK's constitution and established the first formal limits to the power of the monarchy. Magna Carta also paved the way for the creation of parliament.

The creation of parliament

Key terms

House of Commons The chamber where elected members of the UK Parliament sit.

House of Lords The second, unelected, chamber of the UK Parliament.

Palace of Westminster Originally the royal palace attached to Westminster Hall, today it is the seat of government and comprises Westminster Hall, the House of Commons and the House of Lords.

parler A French term meaning to speak or converse.

Parliament The British legislative body that is made up of the House of Commons, the House of Lords and the monarchy.

Westminster Hall A large chamber in Westminster where the early Norman kings would meet with the nobility.

The right of the nobles to be consulted on the king's demands for tax to defend England, the right to air their grievances to the king and the right to have a committee to scrutinise the actions of the monarch meant the nobles had to be consulted regularly — this was effectively the creation of the **House of Lords**.

In 1275, King Edward I required money to fight against Scotland. Knowing the lords would object to this, he sent out writs demanding that each shire and each town elect two representatives from among the knights and burgesses (town officials) to join with the lords in voting to authorise the king's demands for taxation. The knights agreed and they, too, were regularly consulted by the monarch. Not being noble, the knights and burgesses were classed as 'commoners' — this was effectively the creation of the **House of Commons**.

Both the Lords and the Commoners met to *parler* with the monarch at **Westminster Hall** in the **Palace of Westminster**. Therefore, the Palace of Westminster became the **parliament** where the lords and the representatives of the knights met to discuss their grievances with the monarch and confirm or deny the monarch's requests for tax reform. This is where the concept of parliamentary democracy began.

In 1327, following a period of civil war, King Edward II was formally removed by parliament on the basis that his personal faults and weak leadership had led to disaster in England. Parliament chose to replace him with his son, Edward III. This established the principle that the government, in the form of the monarch, was answerable to parliament and could be removed by parliament.

The journey towards parliamentary sovereignty

Most legislative chambers in the world have powers over taxation but few hold **sovereignty** in the way that the UK system does today. Sovereignty usually resides in the constitution, especially if it is a **codified constitution**. While the lack of a codified constitution explains why the UK does not have a sovereign constitution, it does not explain why parliament should be sovereign.

The idea of parliamentary sovereignty began with King Henry VIII. To justify his break with the church in Rome and change religious practice across England and Wales, Henry used legislation, or **Acts of Parliament**, saying that the changes had been approved by the will of the people and should therefore be respected. Henry forced the members of parliament to pass the Acts he wanted but his repeated statements that parliament — as the representatives of the people — had the power to approve the actions of the king established the idea of parliamentary sovereignty. This became a major issue during the English Civil War.

The monarchy and parliament clash: the English Civil War

Between 1603 and 1642, tension increased between the monarchy and parliament over who held power. This came to a head in 1642 when the king declared war on parliament. There were many factors at work during the English Civil War but the main ones concerned the nature of power and the resulting conflicts between King Charles I, who believed that he had a divine right to run the country as he wanted, and parliament, whose members believed the monarchy had to consult them and listen to their grievances following Magna Carta and Henry VIII's use of parliament to justify his actions.

The English Civil War was won by parliament when the royal forces were defeated at Naseby. Parliament put King Charles I on trial as a traitor and ruled that he was guilty and should be executed, thus establishing the supreme authority of parliament over the monarchy. From 1653 to 1658, England was ruled as a republic under the strict military rule of Oliver Cromwell. This nature of rule proved unpopular, so when Cromwell died and his son failed to be an effective leader, parliament elected to restore the monarchy with limited powers.

The Bill of Rights

The year 1660 saw the restoration of the monarchy, initially under Charles II and then under his brother, James II. The restoration was passed by parliament, meaning it had decided to accept Charles II as the legitimate king of England. However, Charles and James both attempted to rule as absolute monarchs with a divine right, which created tensions with parliament.

Key term

Declaration of Rights A statement of the rights of the subject which also declared that the monarch could not act without the consent of parliament.

In 1688, the invasion of William of Orange, who claimed the English throne through his wife Mary, became known as the Glorious Revolution. Faced with this and mounting opposition, King James II resigned the throne.

As MPs debated a replacement for James, William of Orange threatened to abandon the country if he was not made king. A Convention Parliament was called and it drafted a **Declaration of Rights**. This was presented to William and Mary when they were offered the crown and the declaration was read aloud at their coronation.

The Declaration of Rights was modified in 1689 and placed on the statute book as the Bill of Rights (see Table 1.2). The bill was heavily influenced by the political philosopher John Locke, who believed that government existed as the result of an agreement between the people and the monarch. Far from the monarch having absolute power, Locke believed the people were entitled to freedom from the government and that this should be protected by law.

Table 1.2 Key provisions of the Bill of Rights, 1689

Provision	Effect
The suspension or execution of laws, without parliamentary consent, was made illegal.	Only parliament could pass or remove laws.
The levying of money for the crown through prerogative and without consent of parliament was made illegal.	Only parliament could raise money for government expenditure.
Subjects were given the right to petition the king.	People could complain to the monarchy through parliament.
Raising or keeping an army in peacetime, unless by the consent of parliament, was made illegal.	Only parliament could raise and maintain an army during peacetime.
Members of parliament must be elected in free elections.	The principle of free elections away from government influence was established.
The impeachment or questioning of debates and proceedings in parliament was made illegal in any court or place outside of parliament. Freedom of speech was protected.	The parliamentary privilege of being able to say things in the chamber of the House of Commons without fear of prosecution was established, in order to allow for full and open debate.
Imposing excessive bail or excessive fines was made illegal. Cruel and unusual punishments were made illegal.	The judicial power of the monarchy was limited and the court system could not be abused by the executive.
Parliaments were to be held frequently.	The monarch could not simply ignore parliament by refusing to call it.

Synoptic links

The UK and US constitutions

The framers of the US Constitution modelled many of its features on the British constitution. Key elements of the American Bill of Rights (the first ten amendments to the Constitution) were based on the English Bill of Rights.

Study the American Bill of Rights and try to identify which clauses were based on the English Bill of Rights. Were there any other principles from the English political system that the USA may have tried to replicate? Why do you think this?

The Bill of Rights was a major milestone in the development of the UK's constitution.
- It removed royal interference in elections.
- It placed limits on the use of the royal prerogative.
- It established the legal position of the army.
- It established key principles of rights or freedoms from the government.
- It formally established the principle of parliamentary sovereignty.

However, there were also problems with the bill:
- The rights were vague and could be easily reinterpreted.
- The precise definition of 'free elections' was unclear.
- As a statute law it held no higher legal authority and so could be easily repealed or replaced by a future parliament.
- There was no formal procedure for removal of the monarchy.
- The monarch still held enormous powers over war, the peaceful running of the kingdom and foreign policy.

The Act of Settlement 1701

The Act of Settlement in 1701 marked another step in the changing relationship between the crown and parliament. When it became clear that neither William III nor his heir, Queen Anne, would have any children, the succession should have gone to one of the heirs of James II or Charles I. However, these heirs were Catholic and the Protestant Westminster parliament objected to a Catholic monarch. The Act of Settlement was passed to settle the succession problem and parliament decided to offer the throne to George of Hanover. While there were nearly 50 closer relatives to Queen Anne, George was chosen as the closest relative who was not a Catholic, despite having never been to England and not being able to speak a word of English.

So when George I became king in 1714 it was the result of an Act of Parliament, not through any divine right of inheritance. In addition to granting parliament the power to choose the monarch, the Act of Settlement also established several principles that had been suggested during the debates over the Bill of Rights:

- Judges could not be removed without the consent of parliament.
- Royal pardons were to be irrelevant in cases of impeachment.
- The monarch could not take England into a war to defend their home country, without the consent of parliament.
- In governing Britain, the monarch could not make decisions alone and had to consult the full **Privy Council**.
- No foreign-born man could join the Privy Council, sit in parliament, hold a military command or be given lands or titles in Britain.
- The monarch had to be a member of the Church of England.
- The monarch could not be Catholic or married to a Catholic.

Key term

Privy Council A group of senior political advisors who have the job of advising the monarch on the use of the royal prerogative.

The Act contained a provision that, after the death of Queen Anne, 'no person who has an office or place of profit under the king, or receives a pension from the Crown, shall be capable of serving as a member of the House of Commons'. Had this clause not been repealed by the Regency Act of 1706, the UK would have seen a strict separation of power and the idea of cabinet government would not have become established.

After the Act of Settlement, anyone appointed to the cabinet had to resign their seat in the House of Commons and stand in a by-election, a practice that continued until 1918. This meant the power of the monarch, and then the prime minister, to appoint cabinet ministers was limited by the fear of losing a by-election.

The Act also established the principle that the monarch could only choose ministers who could command a majority of support across both Houses of Parliament. This meant the king had to choose a 'king in parliament' who could control both chambers, rather than appointing the minister of his choice.

Debate

Did the Bill of Rights and Act of Settlement mark a significant change in the power of parliament?

Yes

- The monarch was now of parliament's choosing, rather than ruling through divine right.
- They established the principle of regular and free elections.
- They restricted the monarch's ability to interfere with laws.
- They meant taxation could only be passed by parliament.

No

- Parliament remained only advisory in nature.
- The monarch remained the dominant force in British politics.
- Parliament itself only represented the wealthiest 2% of the country.

The creation of the United Kingdom

England and Wales had developed as one country since the conquest of Wales by Edward I in the 1270s. Wales still retained its own language and customs for many years, but politically it was run from Westminster and was often referred to as part of England, though, more accurately, England and Wales together were 'Britain'. Scotland remained an independent kingdom until 1707, with its own monarch, laws and institutions.

In 1603, King James VI of Scotland became King James I of England. The two kingdoms were still legally separate but they now shared the same head of state, which brought a period of peace and stability to Anglo-Scottish relations.

In 1155, Pope Adrian IV had offered the crown of Ireland to King Henry II if he could bring the Irish under control. Following his own break with Rome in the sixteenth century, King Henry VIII began a more formal subjugation of Ireland, first by persuading the Irish Parliament to pass the Crown of Ireland Act in 1542. This formally made the Kings of England also Kings of Ireland.

Therefore, by the start of the eighteenth century, the same monarch ruled the three separate kingdoms, but England (and Wales), Scotland and Ireland all had separate parliaments, laws and customs, and were still separate countries.

The Acts of Union

1707

The Act of Settlement allowed the English Parliament to decide who should be the monarch in England and there was a real possibility that the Scottish Parliament might choose a different monarch to rule their country. This would lead to the breakup of the informal union between the two kingdoms and the possibility of future wars.

In 1698 and 1699, Scotland attempted to establish its own colony in Panama in the Gulf of Darien. The expedition proved disastrous and effectively bankrupted the country. Urged on by King William III, the Scottish Parliament was forced to accept terms from the English

Parliament that would give Scotland a limited voice in Westminster, or face the threats of financial disaster, internal division, commercial blockade and war.

The Scottish Parliament passed an Act accepting the union with Britain in January 1707 and the British Parliament passed its own Act of Union in March, accepting jurisdiction over Scotland and Scottish representation in parliament. These Acts of Union dissolved the Scottish Parliament and, when the first unified parliament met in Westminster on 1 May 1707, the new country of Great Britain was formally recognised by statute.

1800

In 1782, Ireland had gained effective legislative independence from Great Britain with its own constitution. However, only Protestants could hold political power, meaning the Catholic majority was largely excluded. This led to a Catholic uprising in 1798 and an appeal to the French to invade the country. The uprising was brutally suppressed, but with the continuing threat of invasion, the Great British Parliament and Protestant Parliament of Ireland agreed to form a formal political union to guarantee future security.

On 2 July 1800, the Westminster parliament passed the Union with Ireland Act. This was followed by the passage of the Act of Union (Ireland) by the Irish Parliament on 1 August. The Acts came into effect on 1 January 1801 and saw the introduction of 32 Irish peers to the House of Lords and 100 new Irish MPs, all of whom had to be Anglican (i.e. members of the Protestant Church of Ireland). These Acts created the new United Kingdom of Great Britain and Ireland.

The Anglo-Irish Treaty, 1921

Following years of pressure for Irish Home Rule and a civil war in Ireland, the British parliament passed the Government of Ireland Act in 1920 to create two Irish regions with 'Home Rule' — the six northeastern counties formed Northern Ireland and the rest of the country (the larger part) formed Southern Ireland. In 1921, the Anglo-Irish Treaty was signed by the British prime minister, David Lloyd-George, to formally create the Irish Free State. The six counties of Northern Ireland opted to remain part of the United Kingdom and so the United Kingdom of Great Britain and Northern Ireland was established.

The Parliament Acts

1911

From the time of the Act of Settlement until the mid-nineteenth century, the Lords had been the dominant force in UK politics, seen as a moderating force between the crown and the House of Commons. Most prime ministers had sat in the House of Lords, as had most leading statesmen. However, the rise of democracy in the UK meant that the status of the Lords as the 'upper' chamber was being increasingly challenged:

- Lord Salisbury stepped down as prime minister in 1902, becoming the last person to serve as prime minister while sitting in the Lords.
- In 1888, the Lords had lost power to the new county councils, which took over the role of running the shires.

- Opposition grew over the fact that the Lords had an inbuilt Conservative majority, thanks largely to hereditary peerages, and could block any measures taken by reforming parties.
- The Lords defeated the Liberal Party's 'People's Budget' in 1909 because revenue was to be raised by taxes on land and inheritance in order to fund welfare programmes. This would have impacted directly on the Lords.
- In January 1910, the Liberals appealed to the country and won a decisive general election based on their financial measures. The 'People's Budget' was accordingly passed by both chambers.

Synoptic links

Prime minister, cabinet and parliament

The reduction in powers of the House of Lords means there is no effective check on the power of the House of Commons. Is it better to have an all-powerful House of Commons that can get things done, or to have an effective second chamber that can act as a check on governmental power?

To prevent the Lords from ever again rejecting a proposal that had popular support in the democratically elected House of Commons, and in order to establish the primacy of the Commons through statute law rather than via a convention, prime minister Herbert Asquith introduced a bill in 1910 that would:

- give the Commons exclusive powers over money bills
- allow the Lords to delay a bill for 2 years only
- reduce the duration of a parliament from 7 to 5 years

Another general election was held in December 1910 and the Liberals again secured a majority and went on to pass the Parliament Act in 1911.

A government needed the Lords to vote for an Act of Parliament in order for it to be passed. Any reform of the upper chamber meant that the Lords would have to vote to restrict their own powers. This did not look likely until Asquith persuaded the king to threaten to create enough new Liberal peers to flood the chamber and create a Liberal majority. The threat did the trick and the Lords passed the Parliament Act by 17 votes, confirming their lack of power over money bills and to veto legislation.

While the restriction in the powers of the Lords was a step forward for democracy in the UK, the removal of an effective second chamber created the opportunity for elective dictatorship, where a party with a clear majority would have no institution able to withstand it.

1949

The 1949 Parliament Act resulted from a conflict between the Labour government of Clement Attlee and the Conservative-dominated House of Lords. The Lords had voiced strong opposition to the nationalisation programmes of Attlee's government. To prevent the Lords from blocking the Iron and Steel Act, the Labour-controlled Commons attempted to pass a new Parliament Act in 1947 which would reduce the time by which the Lords could delay legislation from 2 years to 1 year, or two parliamentary sessions. The Lords voted against the Act and, after 2 years, the Commons invoked the 1911 Parliament Act to bypass the Lords and force through the legislation.

Unlike the 1911 Parliament Act, which had been passed by the Lords, the 1949 Act did not have the consent of the Lords. In 2004, this led to a legal challenge by the Countryside Alliance, which claimed the 1949 Act was invalid on the common-law principle that a delegate cannot enlarge his power (*delegatus non potest delegare*). This was rejected by the judiciary as the 1949 Parliament Act is statute law and therefore takes priority over any other form of law.

The two Parliament Acts marked the formal shift in power in UK politics from the House of Lords to the House of Commons. The removal of the Lords' power to veto primary legislation introduced in the Commons, its loss of power over money bills, and the reduced time for delaying legislation have made the Lords a much weaker second chamber.

The European Communities Act

The European Communities Act of 1972 was passed by parliament in order to allow the UK to join three European institutions:
- the European Economic Community (EEC) (the Common Market)
- the European Coal and Steel Community
- the European Atomic Energy Community

The Act also allowed EEC law to become part of domestic law in the UK, with immediate effect. This meant that laws passed by the EEC (and later the European Union (EU)) would take effect automatically in the UK, without the need to pass new statute laws and therefore without parliamentary approval. The Act also stated that no UK law could conflict with European law. This meant that EU law had priority over UK law and that the court system could strike down statute laws passed by parliament.

The European Communities Act therefore marked the first time since Queen Anne vetoed the Scottish Militia Bill in 1708 that another institution took priority over parliament. The challenge to parliamentary sovereignty covered several aspects:
- The European Communities Act was, effectively, binding on future parliaments.
- EU law could take priority over statute law.
- Statute law could be struck down by the courts if it was incompatible with EU law, a principle confirmed by the *Factortame* case in 1991.

Despite this, it can be argued that parliament has remained sovereign since:
- The European Communities Act was itself a statute law passed by parliament.
- Parliament chose to accept the primacy of EEC (EU) law, which meant that parliament had chosen to pass sovereignty to the EEC (EU).
- Court rulings to strike down UK law are passed based on UK statute law.

Synoptic links

The European Union

For more information and details about the EEC (EU) and how membership has affected democracy in the UK, refer to the chapters on democracy (Chapter 9) and the European Union (Chapter 8).

Debate

Did UK membership of the EEC (EU) end parliamentary sovereignty?

Yes
- EEC (EU) law takes primacy over UK law.
- UK law must comply with EEC (EU) laws.
- The courts can strike down statute laws if they are incompatible with EEC (EU) law.

No
- Parliament can repeal the European Communities Act.
- Parliament chose to pass power to the EEC (EU).
- Membership of the EEC (EU) has limited the sovereignty of parliament but it was a limit that parliament chose to impose on itself and can choose to remove through repeal of the European Communities Act.

The rise of democracy in the UK

From 1832 until 1969, Britain saw a huge growth in democratic representation

While much of the political history of the United Kingdom has been about the transfer of power from the monarch to parliament, it was not until the nineteenth century that issues relating to democracy and representation became prominent. Before 1832, the Lords was clearly the dominant house, with the Commons representing less than 2% of the population. There were elections, but these were often undemocratic affairs, with rotten boroughs, multiple votes and only the wealthiest of landowners entitled to vote for members of the House of Commons.

From 1832 until 1969, Britain saw a huge growth in democratic representation, with the electorate growing from 2% to full universal adult suffrage (see Table 1.3). This growth in democracy led to the shift in power from the Lords to the Commons.

Table 1.3 Reforms to extend the franchise

Extension	Who could vote	Size of the electorate (as a percentage of the adult population)
Great Reform Act 1832	Anyone who owned property worth more than £10 (the middle classes)	8%
Second Reform Act 1867	Anyone who paid rent worth at least £10 a year or owned a small plot of land (the urban working classes and rural middle classes)	16%
Redistribution of the Seats Act 1885 (Third Reform Act)	Extended the franchise to agricultural labourers (the rural working class)	28%
Representation of the People Act 1918	All men aged over 21 and women aged over 35	74%
Representation of the People Act 1928	All men and women aged over 21	96%
Representation of the People Act 1969	All men and women aged over 18	97%

Furthermore, the nineteenth century also saw significant reforms to the way elections were held and seats were allocated, making representation across the UK fairer (see Table 1.4).

Table 1.4 Reforms to the conduct of elections

Reform	How it changed British democracy
Great Reform Act 1832	Rotten boroughs were abolished and more seats were allocated to the new industrial towns.
Ballot Act 1872	Introduced the secret ballot to prevent voter intimidation and reduce corruption.
Corrupt and Illegal Practices Act 1883	Rules were established for how much a candidate could spend and what they could spend the money on in a campaign, in order to reduce bribery in elections.
Redistribution of Seats Act 1885	This reallocated 142 seats from the south of England to the industrial centres of the north and Scotland, breaking the traditional dominance of the south of England in Westminster politics.

What you should know

- British politics is rooted in its history. For more than a thousand years it has developed and evolved into the modern system of constitutional monarchy and a sovereign parliament that we have today.
- Many of the key principles of British politics have been present to some degree throughout its history. The idea of a group of representatives of the people who meet regularly, discuss what is best for the common good and advise the monarch has been present since Anglo-Saxon times.
- The principle of the rule of law with trial by jury and habeas corpus has curbed the power of tyrannical monarchs and ensured judges have had a role in protecting rights and liberties to some degree for much of British history.
- Even the idea of people choosing their representatives has been present, in some form, for much of this history.
- As such, the ideas of representation, parliamentary power, scrutiny of the government and, above all, a society governed by laws, have existed in Britain since Anglo-Saxon times.
- These core principles have been present throughout British history but several things have changed dramatically over time: the way the core principles are exercised, the balance of power between different aspects of politics, the way the core principles are interpreted, and the very makeup of the United Kingdom itself.
- Sovereignty has passed from the monarchy to parliament and then been shared, to some degree, with other institutions. The monarchy today has very little power. The Lords is no longer the senior House in parliament, as the Commons takes the lead in representing the people.
- Perhaps the greatest and most important change has been the development of democracy and representation. The debates, decisions and actions of parliament and the government are now public and the process of elections has become more free, more fair and far more open to ordinary men and women.
- The people who choose their representatives are no longer a small group of wealthy and privileged men, but almost everyone over the age of 18, regardless of wealth, race or gender, making the UK a modern democracy, despite its traditional institutions.
- An understanding of this history, and the continuity and changes that have occurred, will help you to appreciate the way in which modern politics works, the United Kingdom's unique institutions and the issues which lead to many of the ideological, constitutional and social debates of today.

Further reading

Bryant, C. (2015) *Parliament: The Biography (Volume I: Ancestral Voices)*, Black Swan.

Bryant, C. (2015) *Parliament: The Biography (Volume II: Reform)*, Black Swan.

Butler, D. and Kitinger, U. (1996) *The 1975 Referendum*, Palgrave Macmillan.

Colley, L. (2014) *Acts of Union and Disunion*, Profile Books Ltd.

Field, J. (2006) *The Story of Parliament: In the Palace of Westminster*, Third Millennium.

Jones, D. (2014) *Magna Carta: The Making and Legacy of the Great Charter*, Head of Zeus.

Keates, J. (2015) *William III & Mary II (Penguin Monarchs): Partners in Revolution*, Penguin.

The Constitution Unit: www.ucl.ac.uk/constitution-unit

Parliament: www.parliament.uk

Chapter 2

The UK political system

In December 2016, the Supreme Court heard an appeal from the UK government against a High Court ruling that it could not trigger Article 50 of the Lisbon Treaty, and thus begin the process of leaving the European Union, without the authorisation of parliament. The Supreme Court ruled in January 2017 that triggering Article 50 did not fall within the prerogative powers of the executive but required an Act of Parliament.

In the same month, the Court of Session in Edinburgh ruled that the Scottish government could implement its policy to set a minimum price for alcohol of 50p per unit. This is a devolved power in which the Scottish Parliament has primary legislative authority, but legislation passed 4 years earlier had not come into force because of legal challenges by alcohol producers.

Both of these cases illustrate the complex relationships between the three branches of government in the UK — the executive, the legislature and the judiciary — as well as the impact of devolution and of leaving the EU.

Pro-Brexit supporters gathered outside Parliament in November 2016 to oppose the recent High Court ruling to give MPs the final decision on the matter

What is politics?

Before starting to study UK government and politics, it is helpful to define our subject matter. A student of English literature or chemistry may have little difficulty in offering a definition of their chosen subject, but it is harder to explain precisely what politics is. This is not surprising, given the range of definitions and interpretations in common usage.

Definitions of politics

One of the most memorable and effective definitions of politics is found in the title of a book by US political scientist Howard Lasswell: *Politics: Who Gets What, When and How* (1935). Politics is, in essence, the process by which individuals and groups with divergent interests and values make collective decisions. It exists because of two key features of human societies:

- **Scarcity of resources.** Certain goods, from material wealth to knowledge and influence, are in short supply, so disputes arise over their distribution.
- **Competing interests and values.** There are competing interests, needs and wants in complex societies, as well as different views on how resources should be distributed.

Power or conciliation

There are two broad perspectives on the conduct of politics:

- **Politics is about power. Power** is the ability to achieve a favoured outcome, whether through coercion or the exercise of **authority**. The study of politics thus focuses on the distribution of power within a society: who makes the rules and where does their authority come from?
- **Politics is about conciliation.** Here the focus is on conflict resolution, negotiation and compromise. Politics can be a force for good, a way of reaching decisions in divided societies without resorting to force.

Key terms

Authority The right to take a particular course of action.
Power The ability to do something or make something happen.

In focus

Power

Power is the ability to do something or make something happen. It can be subdivided into four forms:

- **Absolute power** is the unlimited ability to do as one wishes and this exists only in theory.
- **Persuasive power** is the ability to persuade others that a course of action is the right one.
- **Legitimate power** involves others accepting an individual's right to make decisions, perhaps as a result of an election.
- **Coercive power** means pressing others into complying, using laws and penalties.

In a democracy, governments exercise legitimate power, with elements of persuasive and coercive power.

In focus

Authority

Authority is the right to take a particular course of action. The German sociologist Max Weber (1864–1920) identified three sources of authority:

- **Traditional authority** is based on established traditions and customs.
- **Charismatic authority** is based on the characteristics of leaders.
- **Legal–rational authority** is granted by a formal process such as an election.

Only parliament has the authority to make and unmake laws in the UK. This legal–rational authority is legitimised through free and fair elections.

Authority and power may be held independently of one another: a bomb-wielding terrorist may have power without authority; a teacher might have authority without genuine power; and a police officer in a tactical firearms unit may have power and authority.

Politics, government and the state

The most common perspective on politics sees it take place primarily within the state. The state is the set of institutions that exercise authority over a political community within a territory. It includes the institutions of **government** that determine the common rules of a political unit. The state has a monopoly on the legitimate use of force and its institutions include those that enforce order, such as the police, courts, military and security services. The remit of the state expanded in the twentieth century as it took on a greater role in the economy and developed an extensive welfare state. But its role has shrunk in the last 30 years as some of its economic and social functions have been contracted out to the private sector, and functions have been transferred to international or regional organisations. This marked a shift from top-down government, in which decision making was conducted within central government, to **governance**, in which a wide range of formal and informal institutions and networks are involved in decision making.

Politics beyond the state

Politics is found in various spheres of human activity that lie beyond the state:

- **Civil society.** Politics is found in civil society — that is, the realm of autonomous groups and associations found between the state and the individual. Civil society thus includes pressure groups, businesses, trade unions, churches and community groups.
- **All collective social action.** In *What is Politics? The Activity and its Study* (2004), Adrian Leftwich argued that politics is present in all collective social activity, whether formal or informal, and in all human groups and societies. This perspective rejects the notion of a public–private divide in which politics is only present in the public sphere. Although the focus is still on power and conciliation, it shows how politics pervades our everyday lives — for example, 'who gets what, when and how' in the family or school.

British politics

The rest of this chapter provides a brief overview of key features of the British political system, examining continuity and change in the relationship between its institutions, and the character and health of British democracy. These issues are then explored in greater depth in the rest of the book.

The **Westminster model** is the traditional way of understanding British politics. It focuses on the constitution and major institutions of the British political system, and reflects the long-standing British experience of strong, centralised government run by disciplined political parties. Key features of the Westminster model include:

- The constitution is uncodified and can be easily amended.
- The doctrine of parliamentary sovereignty concentrates authority at the centre.
- The **executive** and **legislature** are fused, and the former is dominant.
- Government ministers are bound by collective responsibility and party discipline is imposed in parliament.

Key terms

Governance A form of decision making which involves a wide range of institutions, networks and relationships.

Government (a) The activity or system of governing a political unit. (b) The set of institutions that exercise authority and make the rules of a political unit.

Key terms

Executive The branch of government responsible for the implementation of policy.

Legislature The branch of government responsible for passing laws.

Westminster model A form of government exemplified by the British political system in which parliament is sovereign, the executive and legislature are fused and political power is centralised.

Key terms

Judiciary The branch of government responsible for interpreting the law and deciding upon legal disputes.

Rule of law A legal theory holding that the relationship between the state and the individual is governed by law, protecting the individual from arbitrary state action.

- An independent **judiciary** upholds the **rule of law**, but cannot strike down laws made by parliament.
- Sub-national government is largely absent and local government is weak.
- Single-party government is the norm given the operation of the single-member plurality electoral system and the two-party system.
- A system of representative democracy means that government is held accountable through elections, which are the key form of political participation.

Debate

Is the Westminster model a desirable political system?

Yes

- Government is representative and responsible. It is accountable to parliament for its actions and accountable to the people through elections. Collective responsibility means that parliament can force the resignation of the government. Individual ministerial responsibility means that ministers must account for their actions in parliament.
- Government is strong and effective. The electoral system produces single-party governments with parliamentary majorities. Executive control of the legislature ensures that governments deliver the commitments they made to voters.
- Voters are presented with a clear choice between the governing party and the opposition party.
- The rule of law defends basic **civil liberties** and ensures that power is not exercised arbitrarily. Ministers and officials are not above the law.

No

- There are insufficient checks and balances. Parliamentary sovereignty, the single-member plurality electoral system and executive dominance of the legislature allow the government to do whatever it wants. This can produce **elective dictatorship**.
- The concentration of power at the centre means that decisions are not taken close to the people.
- There are limited opportunities for political participation.
- There is not a strong rights culture: governments can use ordinary legislation or executive powers to restrict the rights of citizens.

Key terms

Civil liberties Fundamental individual rights and freedoms that ought to be protected from interference or encroachment by the state.

Elective dictatorship Where there is excessive concentration of power in the executive branch of government.

In focus

Elective dictatorship

This refers to the excessive concentration of power in the executive branch. It implies that the only check on the power of government is the need to hold (and win) general elections at regular intervals. Beyond this, the government is regarded as free to do as it wishes because the constitution concentrates power in the executive branch and does not provide effective checks and balances.

Majoritarian or consensual democracy?

Dutch political scientist Arend Lijphart located liberal democracies on a spectrum with majoritarian democracy at one extreme and consensual democracy at the other (see Table 2.1).

In a majoritarian democracy, political power is concentrated at the centre and there are few limits to its exercise. Common features include a flexible constitution, a plurality electoral system, a two-party system, a dominant executive and a unitary state. In a consensual democracy, political power is diffused. Typical features are a rigid constitution, proportional representation, multiparty politics, the separation of powers and a federal system. There are also important differences in political culture. Politics is adversarial in a majoritarian democracy, characterised by conflict between two main parties with opposing ideological positions. Power sharing is the norm in a consensual democracy.

The UK Westminster model is the archetypal majoritarian democracy, while Switzerland is a leading example of consensual democracy. The Blair governments' constitutional reforms introduced elements of consensual democracy (e.g. devolution and the Human Rights Act), while multiparty politics and coalition government have also become more apparent. But the UK is still close to the majoritarian position. Parliamentary sovereignty remains the guiding constitutional principle, the fusion of the legislature and executive has not been disturbed greatly, and the first-past-the-post (FPTP) electoral system is still used for Westminster elections.

Questions
- What are the main differences between a majoritarian and a consensual democracy?
- Is the UK still a majoritarian democracy?

Table 2.1 Majoritarian and consensual democracy

Aspect of political system	Majoritarian democracy	Consensual democracy
Constitution	Flexible constitution is easily amended	Rigid constitution can only be amended through special procedures
Executive–legislative relations	Executive is dominant and controls the legislature	There is a balance of power between the executive and legislature
Judiciary	Courts cannot challenge the constitutionality of legislation	Constitutional court can strike down legislation
Territorial politics	Unitary state with power concentrated at the centre	Federal system with power divided between tiers of government
Electoral system	Majoritarian system produces single-party government	Proportional representation produces coalition government
Party system	Adversarial two-party system	Cooperative multiparty system

Activity

Using the information in Table 2.1 and the rest of this chapter, assess the extent to which the UK has moved from the majoritarian democracy extreme towards the consensual democracy end of the spectrum.

Key term

Constitution The laws, rules and practices which determine the institutions of the state, and the relationship between the state and its citizens.

The constitution

The British **constitution** is highly unusual as it is uncodified. This means that the major principles of the political system are not found in a single, authoritative document. Instead they are located in various Acts of

Parliament, in decisions of the courts and in conventions. The uncodified nature of the constitution has important implications for British politics:

- The constitution does not have the status of fundamental or higher law — it has the same status as other law made by the legislature.
- There are no special procedures for amending the constitution — it can be amended by an Act of Parliament in the same way as other laws.
- Parliament, rather than a constitutional court, determines what is permissible under the constitution — there is no definitive criterion for determining what is unconstitutional.

Parliamentary sovereignty

Parliamentary sovereignty is the cornerstone of the British constitution. It states that the Westminster parliament is the supreme law-making body. **Sovereignty** means legal supremacy: parliament has ultimate law-making authority. This legislative supremacy is constructed around three propositions:

- **Parliament can legislate on any subject of its choosing.** There are no constitutional restrictions on the scope of parliament's legislative authority.
- **Legislation cannot be overturned by any higher authority.** The courts cannot strike down statute law as unconstitutional.
- **No parliament can bind its successors.** All legislation is of equal status: legislation that brings about major constitutional change has the same status as, say, animal welfare law. It is not entrenched: one piece of legislation can be amended in the same way as any other.

The reality of parliamentary sovereignty is rather different from the legal theory. As the executive dominates the legislature, it is the government, rather than the House of Commons, that has the greatest influence over legislation. But there are formal and informal constraints on what it can do: a government that systematically ignores public opinion will see its **legitimacy** undermined. In recent decades, several important developments have challenged parliamentary sovereignty.

Membership of the European Union

European Union (EU) law has precedence over domestic British law. In the event of a conflict between the two, EU law must be applied. This challenges the notion that no higher authority can overturn Acts of Parliament, but parliament retained ultimate decision-making authority as it could decide to leave the EU. The extension of the EU's policy competence, the removal of the national veto in many policy areas, and the strengthening of the European Parliament have also restricted the powers of national governments. Withdrawal from the EU (Brexit) will end the supremacy of EU law in the UK and restore decision-making powers to the nation state. But political constraints on sovereignty will remain as cross-border challenges such as migration and climate change cannot be tackled effectively by any one state in isolation.

The Human Rights Act 1998

The Act incorporated the rights set out in the European Convention on Human Rights (ECHR) into UK statute law. All new legislation must be compatible with these rights and the UK courts decide cases

Key terms

Legitimacy Rightfulness: a political system is legitimate when it is based on the consent of the people and actions follow from agreed laws and procedures.

Sovereignty Legal supremacy or absolute law-making authority.

The use of referendums to settle constitutional issues marks a shift from parliamentary sovereignty to popular sovereignty

brought under the ECHR. The courts cannot automatically strike down laws: if they find legislation to be incompatible with the Act, it is for parliament (i.e. ministers) to decide whether to amend the law or launch an appeal.

Devolution

The Scottish Parliament, Welsh Assembly and Northern Ireland Assembly have primary legislative authority on devolved matters such as education and health. Westminster can no longer makes laws in these areas, but has sole authority over 'reserved matters' such as the UK economy, foreign policy and the constitution. The Scotland Act 2016 states that the Scottish Parliament and government are permanent institutions which cannot be abolished without approval in a referendum. Some commentators regard the devolution legislation as de facto 'higher law' given the difficulties Westminster would face if it sought to abolish the devolved institutions without their consent.

The increased use of referendums

Governments have used **referendums** to settle constitutional issues such as devolution, electoral reform and EU membership. This marks a shift from parliamentary sovereignty to popular sovereignty. In most cases, referendums are advisory rather than binding but the legitimacy of parliament would be damaged if it ignored referendum outcomes.

Changes to the traditional constitution are examined in detail in Chapter 3.

> **Key term**
>
> **Referendum** A vote on a single issue put to a public ballot by the government.

The parliamentary system

> **Key terms**
>
> **Constitutional monarchy** A form of monarchy in which the monarch is head of state but in which powers are exercised by parliament and by ministers.
>
> **Fusion of powers** The intermingling of personnel in the executive and legislative branches found in parliamentary systems.
>
> **Head of state** The chief public representative of a country, such as a monarch or president.
>
> **Separation of powers** The principle that the legislative, executive and judicial branches of government should be independent of each other.

The constitution establishes a parliamentary system of government. The key features of a parliamentary system are:

- **The executive and legislative branches are fused.** There is a **fusion of powers** due to overlap between membership of the two branches, with the government consisting of members of the legislature.
- **The legislature can dismiss the executive.** The government is accountable to parliament, which can remove the government through a vote of confidence. The government can dissolve parliament by calling a general election.
- **Parliamentary elections decide the government.** Governments are formed according to their strength in parliament. The person who commands a majority in parliament, usually the leader of the largest party, becomes prime minister.
- **Collective government.** The executive branch is led by a prime minister who chairs a cabinet of senior ministers. Collective responsibility requires ministers to support government policy once it has been agreed.
- **Separate head of state.** The head of the executive branch (the prime minister) is not the **head of state**. The UK is a **constitutional monarchy** in which the monarch is head of state. The modern monarchy has a primarily ceremonial role but does retain prerogative powers such as choosing the prime minister and assenting to Acts of Parliament.

Presidential government is the main alternative system to the parliamentary system. Here, there is a clear **separation of powers** between the executive and legislative branches, and the executive is dominated by a single individual (the president) who is directly elected by the people.

Distinguish between

Parliamentary and presidential government

Parliamentary government
- The executive and legislative branches are fused — government ministers must be members of the legislature, and are responsible to it.
- Parliament can dismiss the government through a vote of confidence; the government can dissolve parliament by calling a general election.
- Power is exercised collectively within the executive branch. The prime minister is the head of a cabinet.
- The prime minister is the person who can command a majority in parliament following a general election.
- The head of the executive is not the head of state.

Presidential government
- There is a clear separation of powers between the executive and legislative branches — members of the executive cannot be members of the legislature.
- The legislature cannot dismiss the president, except in special circumstances, and the executive cannot dissolve the legislature.
- Executive power is concentrated in the office of the president.
- The president is directly elected by the people.
- The president is also head of state.

The executive

The executive is the branch of government concerned with the formulation and implementation of policy. In the UK, it consists of the prime minister, the cabinet and its committees, and government departments. The prime minister is the head of the government and his or her role entails:

- **Political leadership.** The prime minister decides the political direction taken by the government, setting its priorities and determining policy on key issues.
- **National leadership.** The prime minister is communicator-in-chief for the government and provides national leadership at times of crisis.
- **Appointing the government.** The prime minister appoints and dismisses ministers.
- **Chairing the cabinet.** The prime minister chairs the cabinet and steers its decisions. He or she creates cabinet committees and holds bilateral meetings with ministers.
- **Managing the executive.** The prime minister can restructure government departments and the civil service.

The power of the prime minister also depends on their leadership skills and the wider political context — policy success, popularity with the public and a large parliamentary majority will strengthen their position. Some commentators argue that the greater authority of, and focus on, the individual who holds the office of prime minister have brought elements of presidentialism into the UK parliamentary system. The nature of prime-ministerial power, and claims that the office of prime minister has become more presidential, are examined in depth in Chapter 6.

Collective government through cabinet had been the norm until the latter part of the twentieth century. The cabinet consists of senior ministers and is responsible for discussing and making decisions on major issues, ratifying decisions taken in its committees, and settling disputes between government departments. In practice, many decisions are not taken in cabinet but in meetings of the prime minister and his or her key advisers and ministerial allies. But without the support of their senior ministers, a prime minister's ability to achieve his or her objectives is reduced.

The legislature

Government takes place through parliament. Proposals for new laws must be approved by parliament, while parliament also scrutinises the policies and actions of the executive and holds it to account.

The UK has a bicameral legislature consisting of the House of Commons and the House of Lords. The Commons has been the predominant chamber for more than a century. Key elements of the primacy of the Commons include:

- **Legitimacy.** The Commons has greater legitimacy than the Lords because it is directly elected and accountable to voters, whereas members of the upper house are either appointed or have inherited their title.
- **Exclusive powers.** The Commons has the right to insist on its legislation — the Lords can only delay bills for 1 year and cannot delay or amend money bills (bills that relate to taxation, public money or loans). Only the Commons has the power to dismiss the government through a vote of confidence.
- **Conventions.** By convention, the Lords should not oppose bills implementing manifesto commitments (a convention known as the Salisbury Doctrine), unduly delay government business or reject secondary legislation.

The composition and functions of the two houses of Parliament are explored in detail in Chapter 5.

Executive–legislative relations

As we have seen, the executive and legislative branches are fused rather than separated. The relationship between the two branches is unequal, with the executive having various institutional advantages:

- **Control of the legislative agenda.** Most bills are proposed by the government and it controls the legislative timetable (e.g. it can limit debate on bills). This means that most government bills become law.
- **Secondary legislation.** This gives ministers the power to amend some existing legislation without requiring another Act of Parliament.
- **Prerogative powers.** These are powers exercised by ministers, on behalf of the Crown, that do not require parliamentary approval. They include making and ratifying treaties, and deploying the armed forces overseas.

The government usually benefits from a parliamentary majority and party cohesion. The single member plurality electoral system often delivers a parliamentary majority to the party winning most votes in a general election — but did not in 2010 or 2017. Collective responsibility requires ministers to support the government and the whips enforce party discipline. Governments are rarely defeated on major votes in the Commons.

Activity

Use the UK government website (www.tinyurl.com/jyjaw5h) to identify the key personnel and offices of government.

Activity

Use the www.legislation.gov.uk website to identify new pieces of legislation.

Legislative–executive relations are not only shaped by the institutional resources of each branch, but also by the political context. The larger a government's parliamentary majority, the less likely it is that the other parties will be able to amend government bills and the more likely that any dissent within the governing party can be absorbed.

Despite the institutional advantages enjoyed by the executive, there has been a rebalancing of the relationship between parliament and government in recent years. Parliament has become more effective because of the following developments:

- **Select committees.** Departmental select committees scrutinise the policy and administration of government departments. Many recommendations made by select committees are taken up by government. The election of committee chairs and members has further enhanced the independence of select committees.
- **Backbench business.** The creation of the Backbench Business Committee (BBBC), which allows non-government MPs to select issues for debate, and the increased use of 'urgent questions' to ministers have weakened executive control of the parliamentary timetable.
- **Backbench rebellions.** Backbench MPs from the governing party are more likely to rebel than was the case in the early postwar period. Rebellions, or the threat of rebellions, have forced governments to withdraw or amend policy proposals on issues such as tax, counter-terrorism and air strikes in Syria.
- **Weakening of prerogative powers.** Parliament, rather than the prime minister, now decides whether there should be an early general election, and there is an emerging convention that the UK does not engage in armed conflict overseas without the consent of the Commons.
- **An assertive House of Lords.** No party has a majority in the Lords, and the Lords has become more assertive since the removal of most hereditary peers in 1999. Government defeats in the Lords have become more frequent and, on many occasions, have forced the government to rethink its legislation.

The judiciary

The judiciary is independent of the executive and legislature. The UK does not have a single legal system — for example, Scotland retains a separate system. The UK Supreme Court, which began its work in 2009, is the highest court for all but Scottish criminal cases. Its creation brought about a clearer separation of powers between the judiciary and the legislature and executive because, prior to 2009, the Law Lords in the House of Lords had acted as the highest court of appeal. There was an overlap of powers because the lord chancellor was a Law Lord, speaker of the House of Lords and a government minister.

As the highest court and last court of appeal, the Supreme Court resolves cases that have constitutional significance. It also determines cases concerning the relative powers of the devolved institutions and the UK government. The uncodified constitution and doctrine of parliamentary sovereignty mean that the UK Supreme Court, unlike the US Supreme Court, cannot strike down Acts of Parliament.

The creation of the Supreme Court is just one way in which judicial power has become more significant.

Activity

Use the UK parliament website www.parliament.uk to research the structure and role of the Westminster parliament.

The Human Rights Act 1998

The Act incorporated the articles of the European Convention on Human Rights (ECHR) into UK law, allowing citizens to pursue cases under the ECHR through the UK courts rather than having to take them to the European Court of Human Rights (ECtHR) in Strasbourg. The Supreme Court can now issue a declaration of incompatibility where an Act of Parliament is found to have violated the rights that are guaranteed by the Human Rights Act. Again, the Supreme Court cannot strike down the offending legislation, and parliament is not required to amend it. But, in most cases, parliament has done so. The contents and impact of the Human Rights Act are examined in depth in Chapter 7.

European Union membership

European Union (EU) law has precedence over national laws. Where national law conflicts with EU law, it is the former that must be changed — as happened in the 1990 *Factortame* case when the Merchant Shipping Act 1988 was disapplied. For as long as the UK remains a member of the EU, British courts decide cases on EU law.

Extension of judicial review

The Human Rights Act and EU membership have extended **judicial review**. This is the power of the courts to determine whether the government and public authorities have operated beyond the bounds of their authority under the law when making decisions (i.e. acted ultra vires). Tensions between the judiciary and executive have been apparent, with ministers criticising judicial decisions on cases concerning the Human Rights Act (e.g. on deportation and counter-terrorism issues).

Continuity and change

The UK has traditionally been viewed as a **unitary state** in which political power is concentrated at the centre and there is a high degree of centralisation and homogeneity. However, despite this centralisation, the UK was an unusual unitary state because it was a multinational state in which there were differences in the way that parts of the state were governed. For example, between 1922 and 1972, power was devolved to Northern Ireland but not to Scotland or Wales.

Devolution

In the late 1990s, policy-making powers were transferred from Westminster to the Scottish Parliament, Welsh Assembly and Northern Ireland Assembly. The UK now resembles a **quasi-federal state** with some of the features of a unitary state (e.g. supreme authority is located at the centre) and some of a federal state (e.g. subnational governments have extensive competences). Westminster makes domestic law for England and exercises its reserved powers on UK-wide issues. The Supreme Court resolves disputes over competences.

The Scottish Parliament, and the other devolved assemblies, now have primary legislative powers

Key term

Devolution The transfer of some policy-making powers from the centre to sub-national institutions, but which sees the state-wide legislature retain ultimate authority.

Devolution has been asymmetric — the Scottish Parliament is more powerful than the other devolved institutions — and a process rather than a one-off event, with additional powers transferred to the devolved institutions since 1999. The Scottish Parliament, Welsh Assembly and Northern Ireland Assembly all now have primary legislative powers (see Table 2.2). Westminster no longer makes law in these areas, but it retains sole responsibility for the reserved powers.

Table 2.2 Devolved and reserved powers

Devolved powers	Reserved powers
Health and social services	The constitution
Education	Economic and monetary systems
Economic development	UK common market
Environment	Defence and national security
Agriculture and fisheries	Foreign policy
Local government	Relations with the EU
Housing and planning	Nationality and immigration
Transport	Most areas of employment and social security policy
Culture, sport and tourism	Energy
Income tax rates and bands (Scotland) Control over 10p share of income tax (Wales)	
Law and order (Scotland) Justice and policing (Northern Ireland)	

In theory, Westminster has only delegated sovereignty to the devolved institutions and can override them if it wishes but, in practice, this could trigger a constitutional crisis. The status of the Scottish Parliament was safeguarded by the Scotland Act 2016 which states that it is 'a permanent part of the United Kingdom's constitutional arrangements' and cannot be abolished without the approval of the Scottish people in a referendum.

Devolution has changed the nature of politics in Scotland, Wales and Northern Ireland, and within the UK:

■ **Policy divergence.** Policies on care for the elderly, prescription charges, tuition fees and testing in schools differ across the UK.

■ **Political divergence.** In 2016, there were different parties in government in the UK (Conservatives) and in the devolved institutions in Scotland (SNP), Wales (Labour) and Northern Ireland (Democratic Unionist Party and Sinn Féin).

The endpoint of devolution is uncertain. The 2014 Scottish independence referendum rejected independence but the result was not decisive and did not endorse the status quo. Scotland's constitutional status is set to remain a salient issue, particularly since the 2016 EU referendum delivered a vote to leave the EU, despite a majority in Scotland voting to remain.

There are also questions about the status of England, the only nation of the UK not to have its own parliament. The West Lothian Question asks why MPs from Scottish constituencies are permitted to vote on legislation that only affects England, when MPs from England cannot vote on matters devolved to the Scottish Parliament. The Conservative government has introduced a system of 'English votes for English laws' (EVEL) to address this issue. MPs from England can block bills certified by the Speaker as 'England-only' in a new stage of the legislative process, but these bills still require majority support in the Commons. You can read more about EVEL in Chapter 4.

Multilevel governance

Devolution is part of a process in which power has been diffused and decisions are made within different tiers of government in a system of **multilevel governance**. Central government remains the predominant actor, but it does not have a monopoly over decision making. Instead, a range of institutions operating at different levels all have decision-making authority. These levels include:

■ Supranational level, such as the European Union (EU) which, until Brexit concludes, has exclusive competence in areas such as trade.

■ UK level, such as the UK government and Westminster parliament, which are the core decision-making bodies in areas such as taxation and defence.

■ Sub-national level, such as the devolved institutions in Scotland, Wales and Northern Ireland, which have primary legislative power in areas such as education and health.

■ Local level, such as elected local authorities and unelected agencies, which provide services such as local transport and housing.

The European Union

When the UK joined what was then the European Economic Community (EEC) in 1973, the organisation had nine member states and limited policy competences. National governments dominated decision making. By the time the UK voted to leave the European Union (EU) in 2016, the union had significantly expanded its membership (to 28 countries) and policy competences, creating the single market, economic and monetary union (EMU) and an area of freedom, security and justice. Supranational decision making had become more pronounced as member states lost their veto in many policy areas and the European Parliament played a greater role.

However, national governments working in the European Council set the agenda and shaped policy on major issues.

EU membership had important consequences for British policy and politics. In areas such as agriculture, business and the environment, much policy was made at EU level. EU law had primacy over national law, meaning that where the two were in conflict, national law had to be changed. This challenged parliamentary sovereignty, as well as its claims that parliament could make any law of its choosing and that this could not be overridden by any higher authority. Yet ultimate sovereignty remained located within the nation state: parliament could repeal the European Communities Act 1972. However, it is an expression of popular sovereignty — the in–out referendum — that will take the UK out of the EU. The reasons why Britain voted to leave the EU are discussed in Chapter 8.

Case study

Brexit and the UK political system

Leaving the EU (Brexit) will have a significant impact on the British political system. The referendum marked a shift towards popular sovereignty but many MPs sought to reassert parliamentary democracy. They demanded that parliament should decide whether to authorise the terms of withdrawal and of the UK's future relationship with the EU. This also reflected concerns that Brexit could further strengthen the executive in its relationship with the legislature. Brexit also has implications for UK territorial politics. The devolved institutions demanded a major role in Brexit negotiations, with the SNP government talking up the prospect of a second Scottish independence referendum and Northern Ireland ministers expressing concerns about what Brexit will mean for the border with the Republic of Ireland.

Questions
- How will Brexit change the UK political system?
- What are the most important consequences of Brexit for British politics?

Party and electoral systems

Party system

The UK was, with the USA, a leading example of a two-party system for much of the postwar period. The Conservatives and Labour together won an overwhelming majority of votes and parliamentary seats. The Conservatives have traditionally represented the interests and values of the middle class whereas Labour, which emerged from the trade union movement at the start of the twentieth century, represented the working class. The period 1945–70 is often regarded as one of ideological consensus in which both main parties supported state intervention in the economy (e.g. public ownership of key industries), full employment and the welfare state. Figure 2.1 shows party positions on a left–right scale at each general election from 1945 to 2015, where negative numbers are left-wing and positive numbers are right-wing. It confirms that Labour moved to the left and the Conservatives to the right in the 1970s and early 1980s, ending the period of consensus.

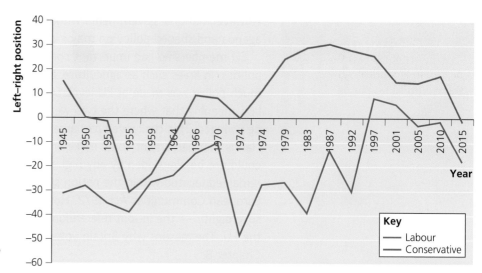

Figure 2.1 Left–right positions of Labour and the Conservatives, 1945–2015

Note: Negative numbers are left-wing; positive numbers are right-wing

Source: Comparative Manifesto Project (https://manifestoproject.wzb.eu)

Margaret Thatcher's governments (1979–90) overturned key parts of the postwar political settlement. They adopted free market policies such as privatisation, tax cuts, controlling inflation and greater competition in the welfare state. Tony Blair's New Labour governments (1997–2007) then combined free market policies with a commitment to social justice. David Cameron was more socially liberal than Thatcher (e.g. on same-sex marriage) but, in an era of austerity, followed Thatcherite policies on shrinking the state. Having narrowed under Blair and Cameron, ideological differences between the two main parties widened after Jeremy Corbyn became Labour leader.

The Conservatives, under Thatcher, and Labour, under Blair, were catch-all parties that appealed beyond their core vote. By the time Blair left office in 2007, the two-party system was coming under strain to the extent that the term 'multiparty system' seemed more appropriate.

Case study

Two-party or multiparty politics?

The 2010 and 2015 elections confirmed the rise of multiparty politics. The Liberal Democrats formed a coalition government with the Conservatives in 2010, an election that saw the two main parties secure just two-thirds of votes cast. The Conservatives secured a small parliamentary majority in 2015, but UKIP polled over 12% of the vote and the SNP won 56 of 59 seats in Scotland. At the 2017 election the Conservatives and Labour won 82% of the vote, the largest two-party share since 1970. This suggests a return to two-party politics, but other parties hold 70 seats in the House of Commons and the Conservative minority government depended on the Democratic Unionist Party for support. The SNP lost seats but remained the largest party in Scotland, illustrating that the UK has different party systems rather than a uniform party system.

Questions
- Does Britain now have a two-party system or a multiparty system?
- Was the 2017 general election a 'return to normal' in the way the electoral system operated?

Electoral systems

The **party system** is shaped, in part, by the electoral system. The single-member plurality (first-past-the-post) electoral system used for general elections has tended to reward the major parties and give a parliamentary majority to the party that secures most votes. This, its supporters claim, ensures strong and responsible government. Smaller parties (e.g. the Liberal Democrats and UKIP), whose support is thinly spread rather than concentrated in a region, are disadvantaged — there is no reward for coming second in a constituency. With the exception of the SNP, third and smaller parties have not won the number of seats that their share of the vote merited. First-past-the-post has thus acted as a life-support system for the two-party system.

However, the way the first-past-the-post system works is changing. With the number of marginal seats decreasing and smaller parties winning more votes and seats, the system is now less likely to produce single-party governments with comfortable parliamentary majorities. Beyond Westminster, proportional representation and mixed-member electoral systems have accelerated the trend towards multiparty politics. The mechanics of the different electoral systems used in the UK, plus their strengths and weaknesses, are explored in Chapter 10.

Voting behaviour and the media

The rise of multiparty politics also reflects changes in voting behaviour and the support bases of the main parties. In the early postwar period, most people voted for their natural class party — middle-class voters supported the Conservatives and working-class voters supported Labour — and had a strong identification with that party. Class voting has fallen sharply in the last 40 years as a result of changes in society and in the parties. Elections are now decided by valence politics: with little ideological difference between the main parties, voters make a judgement based on the party they think is most likely to deliver a strong economy and good public services, and the leader they prefer. Changes in voting behaviour are examined in detail in Chapter 11.

Print media

The media also plays an important role in election campaigns. Newspaper coverage is partisan rather than neutral. Most newspapers support a political party, and there are more Conservative-supporting newspapers than Labour-supporting ones (see Table 2.3). Newspapers owners can exercise significant influence as politicians seek their endorsement.

There are three broad perspectives on the political significance of the media:

- **Influence**. Newspapers have a direct influence over the voting behaviour of their readers. Research shows that, allowing for class and existing attitudes, readers of Labour-supporting newspapers are more likely to vote for Labour than are readers of pro-Conservative newspapers. The *Sun* claims to have influenced the outcome of recent elections, notably when running hostile campaigns against Labour in 1992 and 2015, or switching its support to Labour in 1997. Hostile press coverage did not prevent an increase in support for Labour in 2017, when the party used social media to target young voters.

The media play an important role in election campaigns

- **Reinforcement.** Newspapers reinforce views already held by their readers. Most people read a newspaper that reflects their political views but they often rely on television, rather than newspapers, for non-partisan coverage of politics.
- **Shaping the agenda.** Newspapers may not have a direct influence on voting but their coverage shapes the political agenda. Coverage of issues (such as immigration or crime) and party leaders helps to frame the way in which the issues and leaders are perceived by voters.

Table 2.3 Partisan support of daily newspapers at the 2017 general election

Newspaper	Party endorsement
Sun	Conservative
Mirror	Labour
Daily Star	None
Daily Mail	Conservative
Daily Express	Conservative
Telegraph	Conservative
The Times	Conservative
Guardian	Labour
Independent	None
Financial Times	Conservative

Television media

The introduction of televised leaders' debates in 2010 increased the importance of television coverage of elections and put the spotlight still more firmly on party leaders. Much television news coverage of elections focuses on the campaign (e.g. opinion polls, which were inaccurate during the 2015 and 2017 election campaigns) and party leaders, rather than policy issues.

Democracy in Britain

The Westminster model's vision of liberal democracy is a limited one. The UK is a representative democracy in which the government is held accountable through regular free elections. But, in the Westminster model, citizens have few opportunities for political participation beyond general elections. Representative democracy is valued for giving the political system legitimacy, rather than as a means of popular participation.

Opportunities for greater political participation

Despite the limitations of representative democracy, opportunities for political participation by citizens have been extended since the 1990s.

Elections beyond Westminster

Devolution has enhanced accountability and participation by decentralising decision-making power and creating new elected institutions. New positions in local government, such as elected mayors and police and crime commissioners (PCCs), are also directly elected. As a result of the Recall of MPs Act 2015, constituents can recall their MP if he or she is imprisoned or suspended from the House of Commons.

Increased use of referendums

Referendums have been held on UK-wide issues (electoral reform and EU membership), sub-national issues (devolution) and local issues (directly elected mayors). This has introduced an important element of direct democracy into the UK political system. Turnout has varied, from very high levels of participation in the Scottish independence referendum to very low turnout in referendums on elected mayors.

E-petitions

E-petitions that attract sufficient signatures (e.g. 100,000 signatures for Westminster petitions) are debated in the House of Commons or in the devolved institutions.

Party membership

Labour and Conservative party members play a greater role in electing the party leader, selecting candidates and proposing policy than was the case before the 1990s. New categories of membership (e.g. registered supporter) have also been created. Labour, the SNP and the Greens have seen the number of party members increase significantly in recent years.

Pressure groups and social movements

Together with direct action campaigns on issues such as climate change and austerity, these provide additional avenues for participation and protest. This fosters a pluralist democracy in which there is free and fair competition between competing interests. The role of pressure groups, and whether they enhance or diminish democracy, is explored in depth in Chapter 9.

Concern for the health of British democracy

The developments above suggest that democracy has been enhanced but other trends raise concern for the health of British democracy.

Turnout

Turnout in general elections held between 2001 and 2015 averaged 63%, and even the 69% in 2017 was far below the 81% average in the 1950s. Turnout varies significantly by social group, with turnout lowest among the working class, ethnic minorities and young (but this increased in 2017). Turnout in elections beyond Westminster, and in many referendums, is lower still.

Under-representation

Some social groups, including women, ethnic minorities and the working class, are under-represented in the decision-making process. They are less likely to vote and to become MPs. Some commentators argue that positive discrimination (e.g. all-women shortlists for candidate selection) is necessary to tackle under-representation in parliament. Pressure groups which represent established interests are more likely to have access to decision makers than those which represent minority views, thereby reinforcing inequalities.

Party membership

Despite recent increases in the membership of some parties, the proportion of citizens who are members of a party is lower than it was in the early postwar period.

Conduct of campaigns

The Electoral Commission oversees the conduct of elections and referendums by enforcing spending limits but it does not fact-check claims made by parties, campaign groups or the media.

Anti-politics

The negative trends and issues listed above reflect broader dissatisfaction and disengagement with traditional forms of politics and the political system. In general, satisfaction with the government and the prime minister over the last 10 years is lower than was the case in the early postwar period. Anti-establishment sentiment has also found voice in the rise of parties such as UKIP and in social movements. The 2016 EU referendum also revealed attitudinal and cultural fault lines within British politics. Leave voters were more likely to distrust politicians, be dissatisfied with the political system and be wary of cultural and social change. Remain voters tended to have greater faith in the political system and have socially liberal attitudes.

Forms of political participation have changed (see Table 2.4). Some traditional or conventional types of participation may have come under strain, but newer or non-traditional forms have also emerged.

Table 2.4 Traditional and non-traditional forms of political participation

Traditional	Non-traditional
Voting	Online activism
Attending a political meeting	E-democracy, e.g. signing an e-petition
Contacting an MP	Political consumerism, e.g. boycotting a product
Joining a political party	Joining a social movement
Joining a pressure group or trade union	Taking part in a demonstration or occupation

While the Hansard Society's annual Audit of Political Engagement reports consistently low satisfaction with the British political system, it does not find that this has fallen significantly in the last 15 years (see Figure 2.2).

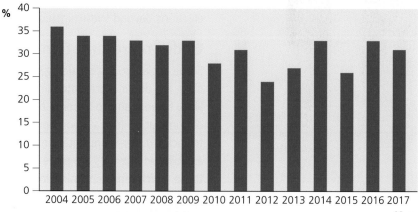

Figure 2.2 Satisfaction with the present system of governing Britain, 2004–17

Source: Audit of Political Engagement (www.auditofpoliticalengagement.org)

Case study

Rights and liberal democracy

The term 'liberal democracy' reflects the sometimes uneasy relationship between liberalism, with its emphasis on individual rights, and democracy, with its focus on participation and majority rule. Democratic participation has been strengthened by some recent developments but weakened by others. A similar pattern is apparent in terms of the rights of citizens that are essential to a healthy liberal democracy.

The Human Rights Act 1998 gave greater legal protection to civil liberties, and allowed citizens to take cases concerning human rights directly to the UK courts. However, the increased terrorist threat since the 9/11 attacks in the US has led to some restrictions on civil

liberties — not just for those suspected of involvement in terrorist activity, but also more generally in terms of greater surveillance.

The Freedom of Information Act 2000 gave citizens the right to access information held by public authorities. It also enabled media disclosure of issues such as MPs' abuse of the expenses system. But the government can deny freedom of information requests for details of how controversial decisions are made. Inquiries into the 2003 invasion of Iraq brought many documents into the public realm, but also revealed that ministers were not given full information before reaching a decision on military action.

Questions
- In what ways have the rights of citizens been enhanced in recent years?
- How have they come under strain?

10 Downing Street remains an enduring symbol of the British political system

Activity

Using the Audit of Political Engagement website (**www.tinyurl.com/z3vvxz2**), identify trends in attitudes to politics and the British political system.

The Westminster model under strain

To the casual observer, the enduring symbols of the British political system — the Houses of Parliament and 10 Downing Street — illustrate the high degree of continuity in British politics. Yet even an irregular follower of politics is likely to recognise that there have been some fundamental changes in British politics in recent years, including devolution and Brexit. These changes have put the traditional Westminster model of British politics under strain (see Table 2.5).

Table 2.5 Challenges to the Westminster model of politics

Feature of the Westminster model	Challenges to the Westminster model
Uncodified constitution	De facto 'higher law', e.g. Human Rights Act 1998 gives statutory basis for rights; Scotland Act 2016 states the permanence of the Scottish Parliament
Parliamentary sovereignty	EU membership Devolution Human Rights Act 1998 Use of referendums
Collective government	Presidentialisation Dilution of collective responsibility
Executive dominance over the legislature	Decline of party cohesion Reduced likelihood of single-party government with large parliamentary majority Government defeats in House of Lords
Limited role of the judiciary	Increase in judicial review Creation of Supreme Court
Unitary state	Legislative devolution Increased support for Scottish independence The 'English Question'
First-past-the-post (FPTP) electoral system	Changes to way FPTP operates (e.g. single-party government now less likely) New electoral systems beyond Westminster
Two-party system	Decline in support for Conservatives and Labour (until 2017) Rise of multiparty politics at Westminster and beyond
Representative democracy	Increased use of direct democracy (e.g. referendums) Fall in turnout at general elections Rise of anti-politics

What you should know

- The traditional UK political system is known as the Westminster model. Key features include an uncodified constitution, parliamentary sovereignty, the fusion of the executive and legislative system, the absence or weakness of sub-national and local government, a two-party system and a plurality electoral system. Some of these features have come under strain in the last few decades.
- The UK is a liberal democracy but the traditional Westminster model placed little emphasis on political participation. The increase in the number of elected institutions, greater use of referendums and the strengthening of citizens' rights have enhanced British democracy. But low turnout, under-representation of some social groups, restrictions on some civil liberties, plus the development of anti-politics sentiment have raised questions about the health of democracy in Britain.

Further reading

Democratic Audit (2017) The 2017 Audit of UK Democracy, www.democraticaudit.com/

Fairclough, P. (2014) 'UK democracy: how could it be improved?', *Politics Review*, Vol. 24, No. 2, pp. 30–34.

Hansard Society (2017) *Audit of Political Engagement* 14: www.tinyurl.com/gt3lz6a

The Constitution Unit: www.ucl.ac.uk/constitution-unit

LSE British Politics and Policy blog: www.tinyurl.com/7zealaz

SECTION
1

GOVERNMENT IN THE UK

Chapter 3

The constitution

> **Key questions answered**
> - What is a constitution?
> - What do we mean by uncodified and codified constitutions?
> - What are the sources of the UK constitution?
> - What key principles underpin the UK constitution?
> - What are the strengths and weaknesses of the UK constitution?
> - What constitutional reform has taken place since 1997 and how significant has it been?
> - Should the UK adopt a codified constitution?

On Sunday 2 October 2016, the Prime Minister, Theresa May, announced that the government would be presenting a 'Great Repeal Bill' to Parliament. The purpose of such a bill, she indicated, would be to overturn the European Communities Act 1972 and, in so doing, remove the supremacy of European Union law over UK law that has existed since that Act incorporated the provisions of the Treaty of Rome into our legal framework. Whereas in most other western democracies such a fundamental change in the political landscape would require a formal constitutional amendment, the doctrine of parliamentary sovereignty and the supremacy of statute law in the UK means that it is just as easy to remove the UK from the direct jurisdiction of the EU as it was to submit to it back in 1972.

Such apparent flexibility in the UK's constitutional arrangements stems in large part from the uncodified nature of our constitution. However, the ability to change even the most central elements of our system by means of a simple Act of Parliament is a double-edged sword: while it enables our institutions and systems to respond to immediate threats and challenges without the need for arcane, multi-stage procedures, it can leave the system wide open to ill-conceived changes that threaten individual freedoms and undermine the very principles upon which our system of government was founded.

A constitution is a body of laws, rules and practices that sets out the way in which a state or society is organised

What is a constitution?

Key terms

Bill of Rights An authoritative statement of the rights of citizens, often entrenched as part of a codified constitution.

Constitution The House of Lords Select Committee on the Constitution (2001) defined a constitution as 'the set of laws, rules and practices that create the basic institutions of the state and its component and related parts, and stipulate the powers of those institutions and the relationship between the different institutions and between those institutions and the individual' (www.tinyurl.com/grxnwu7).

Limited government A system in which the powers of government are subject to legal constraints as well as checks and balances within the political system.

A **constitution** is a body of laws, rules and practices that sets out the way in which a state or society is organised. A constitution establishes the relationship between the state and its citizens — and also between the various institutions that constitute the state. In this sense, the constitution provides a framework for the political system: establishing the main institutions of government, determining where decision-making authority resides and protecting the basic rights of citizens. This is often in a formal **Bill of Rights**.

In liberal democracies, the constitution provides an important defence against any abuse of power by the state, its institutions and its officials. It provides for a system of **limited government** under which a system of checks and balances serves to limit any danger of overmighty government and the rights of the citizen are protected from arbitrary state power. In many countries, the judiciary is empowered to use the constitution as a tool when deciding whether or not the state has acted in a manner which is lawful and legitimate (and therefore constitutional) and when it is has failed to do so (and therefore has acted unconstitutionally).

Constitutions should not be considered to be separate from normal political activity. Indeed, they are inherently political because of their impact upon day-to-day politics. Moreover, constitutions are not necessarily neutral because the framework that they provide (for example, the electoral system or the legislative process) may favour some actors at the expense of others.

In focus

Constitutionalism

This refers to the theory and practice of government according to the rules and principles of a constitution. A constitutional democracy is one which operates within the framework of a constitution that sets limits on the powers of government institutions and provides protection for the rights of citizens. A government or public authority acts in an unconstitutional manner when its actions are not in accordance with the principles and practices set out in the constitution.

Codified and uncodified constitutions

Key term

Codified constitution A single, authoritative document that sets out the laws, rules and principles by which a state is governed, and which protects the rights of citizens.

When comparing the constitutions of different nations, it is common to draw a distinction between those that are codified and those that remain uncodified. A **codified constitution** is one in which all of the fundamental rules that govern the operation of a given state and many, if not all, of the principles that underpin it, are set out in a single authoritative document. Codified constitutions, such as the US Constitution, can be described as constitutions with a capital 'C' because they assume an almost iconic position in the nation's psyche.

Key term

Uncodified constitution A constitution where the laws, rules and principles specifying how a state is to be governed are not gathered in a single document. Instead, they are found in a variety of sources — some written (e.g. statute law) and some unwritten (e.g. convention).

In contrast, an **uncodified constitution** has no single source for the rules and principles that govern the state — rather, they are found in a number of different places. The UK constitution is the prime example of this type of constitution. Although it is frequently described as 'unwritten', the term is misleading. For while it is true that the nation's constitutional practices and principles are not gathered in a single authoritative document, many are 'written' in common law (the decisions of the higher courts) and others can be found in statute law (Acts of Parliament) or other historical documents (see Table 3.1).

Table 3.1 Six key historical documents

Act or measure	Date	Significance
Magna Carta	1215	Guaranteed the right to a swift and fair trial
		Offered protection from arbitrary imprisonment
		Placed limitations on taxation
Bill of Rights	1689	Placed limitations on the power of the monarch
		Enhanced the status of parliament
		Prohibited cruel and unusual punishment
Act of Settlement	1701	Barred Roman Catholics, or those married to Roman Catholics, from taking the throne
		Resulted in the House of Hanover assuming the English throne
		Said to have paved the way for the Acts of Union (1707)
Acts of Union	1707	United the Kingdoms of England and Scotland to form Great Britain, governed from Westminster
Parliament Acts	1911/1949	Removed the power of the House of Lords to block money bills by imposing a maximum 2-year delay
		Reduced the power of the House of Lords to delay non-money bills by reducing the time limit to 1 year
European Communities Act	1972	The Act of Parliament that formally took the UK into the European Economic Community (EEC)
		Incorporated the Treaty of Rome into UK law, thus making European Law superior to domestic law

Although the difference between codified and uncodified constitutions is at the heart of many of the issues that we will be discussing in this chapter, the distinction is not as clear-cut as it might at first appear. In reality, no codified constitution could hope to spell out each and every practice, or cover every eventuality. In this sense, a codified constitution is not a detailed blueprint but a reference point for an evolving political system; a skeletal framework upon which other, lesser, rules can be neatly hung. Similarly, no constitution, however uncodified, could ever be entirely unwritten. In short, all constitutions must inevitably contain a mixture of written and unwritten elements.

Features of codified constitutions

Codified constitutions are generally produced at a critical juncture in a nation's history, most commonly in the wake of:
- newly found independence, e.g. the US Constitution of 1789
- a period of authoritarian rule, e.g. the Spanish Constitution of 1978
- war and/or occupation, e.g. West Germany's Basic Law of 1949

Activity

Undertake some research on the US Constitution and one other codified constitution of your choice. Look at the kind of provisions that they include. What features do they share in common? In what ways do they differ?

Key terms

Entrenched Difficult to change (literally 'dug in'); often requiring supermajorities — or approval by popular referendum.

Fundamental law Constitutional law that is deliberately set above regular statute in terms of status, and given a degree of protection against regular laws passed by the legislature.

In such situations, the political institutions established are explicitly granted their authority by the new constitution and a codified constitution is afforded the status of **fundamental law**, or higher law, placing it above ordinary law made by the legislature (or parliament). Under such a system, a constitutional court (or supreme court) is generally given the job of holding other key players, whether individuals or institutions, accountable to this supreme law.

Entrenchment and amendment

The provisions of codified constitutions are invariably **entrenched**, meaning that special procedures are needed for amendment. Whereas regular laws are generally enacted on the basis of a simple majority vote in the legislature, amending a codified constitution will generally require a supermajority far in excess of 50% in the legislature and/or approval by national referendum.

Their entrenched nature means that codified constitutions are often characterised as rigid, while uncodified constitutions are seen to be more flexible. However, degrees of flexibility are also evident in codified constitutions. For example, while the 1958 constitution of the French Fifth Republic has been amended 17 times in 50 years, there have been only 17 amendments to the US Constitution since the first ten amendments — known collectively as the Bill of Rights — were ratified in 1791.

The UK's uncodified constitution

The absence of any properly entrenched and superior fundamental law in the UK means that our constitution can be amended by a simple Act of Parliament. Moreover, the doctrine of parliamentary sovereignty holds that parliament has legislative supremacy, enabling it to pass laws on any matter of its choosing and to overturn any existing law. There are no constitutional no-go areas into which parliament cannot step. As the eighteenth-century constitutional lawyer William Blackstone once put it, 'Parliament can do everything that is not naturally impossible.'

Distinguish between

Codified and uncodified constitutions

Codified constitution
- The rules and principles governing the state are collected in a single authoritative document: the constitution.
- It has the status of fundamental law and is superior to all other law.
- It is entrenched, with special procedures for its amendment that make it difficult to change.
- The courts, particularly a constitutional court, use the constitution to determine whether the actions of other key players are constitutional.

Uncodified constitution
- There is no single authoritative document. Instead, the rules and principles governing the state are found in a number of sources, both written and unwritten.
- Constitutional laws have the same status as regular statute; there is no hierarchy of laws and no fundamental law.
- It is not entrenched so can be amended in the same way as ordinary law.
- Judicial review is limited because there is no single authoritative document that senior judges can use to determine whether or not an act or action is unconstitutional.

The sources of the UK constitution

As we have seen, uncodified constitutions tend to draw on a range of sources — some written and some unwritten. In the case of the UK constitution it is possible to identify five such sources:

■ statute law
■ common law
■ conventions
■ authoritative works (or 'works of authority')
■ European Union law and treaties

Statute law

Statute law is law created by parliament. Acts of Parliament have to be approved by the House of Commons, the House of Lords and the monarch before they are placed on the statute books, at which point they have the force of law. They are then implemented (or executed) by the executive and enforced by the courts. Not all Acts of Parliament are of constitutional significance because not all Acts have a bearing on the fundamental relationship between the state and the people or between the institutions that make up the state. The 1991 Dangerous Dogs Act, for example, can hardly be considered constitutional. That said, statute law is the supreme source of constitutional law in the UK because parliament is sovereign.

Examples of statute law that have been of historical importance in constitutional terms include:

■ Great Reform Act 1832, which extended the franchise
■ Parliament Acts 1911 and 1949, which established the House of Commons as the dominant chamber in our bicameral parliament
■ European Communities Act 1972, by which the UK joined the European Economic Community (EEC) and incorporated the Treaty of Rome (1958) into UK law

More recent examples include:

■ Scotland Act 1998, which created a Scottish Parliament
■ Human Rights Act 1998, which incorporated the rights set out in the European Convention on Human Rights (ECHR) into UK law
■ Fixed-term Parliaments Act 2011, which established fixed, 5-yearly elections to the Westminster Parliament

Common law

Common law includes legal principles that have been discovered, developed and applied by UK courts. Senior judges in the UK's higher courts use their power of **judicial review** to clarify or establish a legal position where statute law is absent or unclear. This case law forms a body of legal precedent that serves to guide both the lower courts and future lawmakers. However, one should remember that parliamentary sovereignty and the supremacy of statute law mean that the government of the day can always overturn such common law precedent by means of an Act of Parliament. It is for that reason, along with the absence of a superior fundamental law, that UK courts can never really be said to have declared the government's actions unconstitutional — only unlawful, or incompatible with the Human Rights Act.

Although the phrase 'common law' is normally taken to refer to the kind of judge-made law detailed above, it also includes customs and precedents that, unlike regular conventions, have become accepted as legally binding. A good example of this is the **royal prerogative** — the powers exercised in the name of the Crown. The Crown retains a number of formal powers that date back to the period before the UK began to morph into a constitutional monarchy in the late seventeenth century.

The royal prerogative

The Crown's prerogative powers traditionally included the right to:
- appoint ministers and choose the prime minister
- give royal assent to legislation
- declare war and negotiate treaties

Although held formally by the monarch, many of these powers came to be exercised by government ministers in the name of the Crown. Significantly, the first two decades of the twenty-first century saw a number of measures designed to limit the royal prerogative and enhance the role of parliament. For example, the prerogative power to dissolve parliament was ended by the Fixed-term Parliaments Act 2011 — just as the Constitutional Reform and Governance Act 2010 put the parliamentary scrutiny of treaties on a statutory basis. In spite of these changes, however, papers released in 2013 revealed that the monarch has been specifically asked to approve bills relating to prerogative powers and was advised by the government to withhold consent to a 1999 private members' bill which sought to transfer the power to declare war from the monarch to parliament. The royal prerogative is explored further when the powers of the prime minister are set out in Chapter 6.

Conventions

Conventions are rules or norms of behaviour that are considered to be binding. Although they are neither codified nor legally enforceable, the 2011 Cabinet Office Manual sought to bring together many of these conventions in a single document, adding yet another written source to the UK constitution.

It is their very usage over an extended period of time that gives conventions their authority. For example, the monarch, by convention, must give their assent to Acts of Parliament. No monarch has refused to give their assent since 1707, when Queen Anne refused to approve the Scottish Militias Bill. Thus if the monarch were to refuse a bill today, there would be a constitutional crisis.

While conventions may fall into disuse over time, new conventions can also be established. For example, during his short tenure as prime minister, Gordon Brown announced that the UK would not declare war without a parliamentary vote.

Authoritative works (or 'works of authority')

When commentators speak of 'works of authority' they are generally referring to a handful of long-established legal and political texts that have come to be accepted as the reference points for those wishing to know precisely 'who can do what' under the UK constitution. While these texts hold no formal legal status, they do have 'persuasive authority'. They can therefore be helpful in identifying, interpreting and understanding the core values that underpin the constitution — while also shedding light on the more obscure areas of constitutional practice.

Such works of authority include the following:

- Erskine May's *A treatise on the law, privileges, proceedings and usage of Parliament* (1844) is regarded as the bible of parliamentary practice, providing a detailed guide to its rules and practices.
- Walter Bagehot's *The English Constitution* (1867) sets out the role of the cabinet and the prime minister, describing the former as the 'efficient secret of the English constitution' and the latter as 'first among equals'.
- A. V. Dicey's *An Introduction to the Study of the Law of the Constitution* (1885) focused on parliamentary sovereignty and the rule of law (Dicey's 'twin pillars of the constitution'). It described a system of responsible cabinet government in a parliamentary democracy, with a constitutional monarchy.

European Union law

Following the European Communities Act 1972, the UK became a member of the European Economic Community (EEC) on 1 January 1973. The EEC was later renamed the European Community (EC) and then, after the Maastricht Treaty (1991) came into force in 1993, the European Union (EU). The treaties establishing the European Union, legislation emanating from the EU, and judgments of the European Court of Justice have all become a part of the British constitution. This is because under the 1958 Treaty of Rome, which was incorporated into UK law at the time of our joining the EEC, European law takes precedence over UK law.

Brexit and the status of EU law and treaties

Although UK referendums can only ever be advisory in nature due to parliamentary sovereignty, victory for the 'Leave' campaign in the 2016 EU referendum raised the possibility that the UK could leave the EU. Such an eventuality would naturally remove the UK from the control of EU law — thereby also removing this fifth source of the UK constitution. It should be noted, however, that Theresa May's proposed Great Repeal Bill would incorporate all existing EU law into UK statute law, at the same time as repealing the European Communities Act 1972. The status of EU law is dealt with more comprehensively in Chapter 8, when we consider the UK and the EU.

Key principles that underpin the UK constitution

Four key principles are said to underpin the UK constitution:

- parliamentary sovereignty
- the rule of law
- a **unitary state**
- parliamentary government under a constitutional monarchy

Devolution The process by which a central government delegates power to another, normally lower, tier of government, while retaining ultimate sovereignty.

Parliamentary sovereignty The doctrine that parliament has absolute legal authority within the state. It enjoys legislative supremacy: parliament may make law on any matter it chooses, its decisions may not be overturned by any higher authority and it may not bind its successors.

Sovereignty Legal supremacy; absolute law-making authority that is not subject to a higher authority.

Parliamentary sovereignty

Parliamentary sovereignty is the cornerstone of the UK constitution. **Sovereignty** means legal supremacy, so the doctrine of parliamentary sovereignty holds that the Westminster Parliament is the supreme law-making body. This legislative supremacy is constructed around three interconnected propositions:

- Parliament can legislate on any subject of its choosing.
- Legislation cannot be overturned by any higher authority.
- No parliament can bind its successors.

Parliamentary sovereignty holds that the Westminster Parliament is the supreme law-making body

Parliamentary sovereignty in practice

Parliamentary sovereignty is a legal theory which holds that the supreme law-making authority in the UK is held by the Westminster Parliament. However, EU membership, **devolution** and the use of referendums raise questions about how meaningful this doctrine is in practice.

- Under the European Communities Act 1972, parliament effectively agreed to make itself subservient to European law.
- New Labour's devolution programme saw the Scottish Parliament being granted tax-varying powers and primary legislative control over many areas of government operation.
- Although UK referendums are technically only advisory in nature, their increased use since 1997 could be said to have transferred a degree of legislative power from parliament back to the people.

There is also a gap between 'legal theory' and 'political reality', for no institution has absolute power to do as it wishes. Although William Blackstone's view that 'Parliament can do anything that is not naturally impossible' is regularly cited when explaining the doctrine of parliamentary sovereignty, the reality is that parliament is constrained in a number of other ways — not least the desire of MPs to be re-elected and the need for tax revenues to cover the costs of any policies implemented.

Questions

- How could recent developments be said to have undermined parliamentary sovereignty?
- What is the difference between 'legal theory' (i.e. *de jure*) and 'political reality' (i.e. *de facto*)?

We will revisit parliamentary sovereignty and the constraints acting on it in Chapter 5.

The rule of law

The **rule of law** defines the relationship between the state and its citizens, ensuring that state action is limited and responsible. According to A. V. Dicey (1885), the rule of law has three main strands:

- No one can be punished without trial.
- No one is above the law, and all are subject to the same justice.
- The general principles of the constitution, such as personal freedoms, result from judge-made common law, rather than from parliamentary statute or executive order.

What does all of this mean in practice?

- Everyone is equal under the law. Individuals charged under the law are entitled to a fair trial and should not be imprisoned without due regard for the legal process.
- The courts can hold government ministers, police officers and public officials accountable for their actions if they have acted outside the law or been negligent in their duties.
- Laws passed by parliament must be interpreted and applied by an independent judiciary, free from political interference. The rights of citizens are thus protected from arbitrary executive action.
- Citizens can take the government or a local authority to court if they feel they have been treated improperly.

The rule of law is an essential feature of a liberal democracy. Although parliamentary sovereignty theoretically enables parliament to abolish these rights, any sustained effort to overturn the key elements of the rule of law would be seen as illegitimate and anti-democratic, making it untenable. As we will see in Chapter 9, the Human Rights Act 1998 gives further protection to basic **civil liberties**.

A unitary state

Constitutions may be classified according to whether they concentrate political power at the centre or divide it between central and regional tiers of government. In this context, there is an important distinction to be made between unitary constitutions and federal constitutions. The traditional British constitution is a unitary constitution. Although the United Kingdom consists of four component nations — England, Scotland, Wales and Northern Ireland — it has been a highly centralised state in which legal sovereignty is retained by the Westminster Parliament.

In a unitary constitution:

- Subnational institutions do not have autonomous powers that are constitutionally safeguarded.
- Regional government may be weak or non-existent.
- Local government has little power.

In a federal constitution, such as in Germany or the USA, power is shared between national (federal) and regional (state) governments. Each tier of government is given specific powers and a significant degree of autonomy. Moreover, no single tier of government can abolish any other tier.

A 'nation of nations'?

Although the UK has traditionally been described as a unitary state, the label does not reflect fully its multinational character. An alternative is to see the UK as a union state or a 'nation of nations', as Professor Vernon Bogdanor has put it. A unitary state exhibits a high degree of both centralisation and standardisation: all parts of the state are governed in the same way and share a common political culture. In a union state, by contrast, important political and cultural differences remain.

These asymmetries reflect the different ways in which parts of the state were united. The component nations of the UK came together in different ways: Wales was invaded by England, Scotland joined the union through an international treaty, and Northern Ireland remained part of the UK after the establishment of the Irish Free State. Political and cultural differences survived. Scotland kept its own legal system, Wales retained its own language and Northern Ireland maintained its separate institutions and political parties. By the second half of the twentieth century, the interests of each nation were represented in London by a government department headed by a cabinet minister, but these departments were relatively weak and political power was concentrated at the centre. As we will see later in this chapter, it could be claimed that the devolution programme launched by the Labour government in the wake of the 1997 general election has raised further questions about the UK's status as a unitary state.

Distinguish between

Unitary, union and federal states

Unitary state
- A highly centralised state in which political power is concentrated at the centre.
- Central government has ultimate authority over subnational institutions.
- The centre dominates the political, economic and cultural life of the state.
- All areas of the state are governed in the same way and there is a very high degree of administrative standardisation.

Union state
- A state whose component parts have come together through a union of crowns or by treaty.
- There is a high degree of administrative standardisation but the component nations retain some of their pre-union features (e.g. separate churches or legal systems).
- Political power is concentrated at the centre but the component nations have some degree of autonomy (e.g. through devolution).

Federal state
- A state in which the constitution divides decision-making authority between national (federal) and regional (state) tiers of government.
- The different tiers of government are protected by the constitution: one tier cannot abolish the other.
- The regions within the state have a distinctive political, and often cultural, identity.

Activity

Using the UK material provided in the section above and examples of other countries from your own research, explain why one could argue that the UK is no longer a unitary state. Then explain why one should not see the UK as a truly federal state.

Under the UK constitution the monarch is still the formal head of state

Parliamentary government under a constitutional monarchy

Under the UK constitution, government takes place through parliament under a **constitutional monarchy**. Government ministers are politically accountable to parliament and legally accountable to the Crown, and must face the verdict of the electorate every 5 years. Between general elections, a government relies on its majority in the House of Commons to survive and enact its legislative programme.

The balance of power between the different institutions of the state has, of course, altered over time. The Glorious Revolution of 1689 established the supremacy of parliament over the monarchy. The key conventions of the constitutional monarchy gradually fell into place: the monarch retained formal powers (e.g. to assent to legislation) but their usage was constrained. The extension of the franchise enhanced the position of the House of Commons; it had overtaken the House of Lords as the predominant legislative chamber by the early twentieth century. Political parties emerged as key actors in the conduct of government. The first-past-the-post (FPTP) electoral system and two-party system tended to produce single-party governments. The majority party thus controlled the cabinet and exercised considerable discipline over its members in the House of Commons.

By the mid-nineteenth century, the UK political system was, according to A. V. Dicey, one of **cabinet government**. Cabinet was then the key policy-making body, the 'efficient secret' of the English constitution. Yet a century later, considerable power was vested in the office of prime minister, leading some commentators to argue that **prime-ministerial government** had replaced cabinet government (see Chapter 6).

> ### Key terms
>
> **Cabinet government** A system of government in which executive power is vested not in a single individual but in a cabinet whose members operate under the doctrine of collective responsibility.
>
> **Constitutional monarchy** A political system in which the monarch is the formal head of state but the monarch's legal powers are exercised by government ministers.
>
> **Parliamentary government** A political system in which government takes place through parliament and in which the executive and legislative branches are fused.
>
> **Prime-ministerial government** A system of government in which the prime minister is the dominant actor and is able to bypass the cabinet.
>
> **Westminster model** A form of government exemplified by the British political system in which parliament is sovereign, the executive and legislature are fused and political power is centralised.

Strengths and weaknesses of the UK's constitution

The Westminster model

The UK's traditional constitution is known as the **Westminster model**. This describes the workings of the British political system and claims (or assumes) that this is how a political system ought to operate.

Supporters of the traditional constitutional settlement argue that it has a number of enduring strengths. While they recognise that improvements are required, they believe that reform should be limited and pragmatic. Changes should work with the grain of the existing constitution rather than overhaul it. Critics of the traditional constitution argue that it has a number of serious weaknesses that can only be rectified by a significant reform programme (see Table 3.2).

Table 3.2 Strengths and weaknesses of the UK constitution

Strengths	Weaknesses
Adaptability The UK constitution has evolved gradually in the face of changed circumstances. Pragmatic reforms, introduced where there is a clear case for change, have enabled the constitution to adapt without the need for parliamentary supermajorities or approval by means of a referendum. This is why Conservatives tend to view the constitution as an 'organic', living body of rules, rather than an artificial creation.	**Outdated and undemocratic** Critics of the traditional constitution portray it as outdated, inefficient and undemocratic. Key elements of common law, notably the royal prerogative, date back to medieval times — just as the House of Lords is a throwback to a pre-democratic era. It is hard to justify the hereditary principle in a liberal democratic state.
Strong government The traditional constitution provides for strong and effective government. Although the doctrine of parliamentary sovereignty dictates that the legislature holds supreme authority within the political system, the executive is where day-to-day power resides *de facto*. This is because the process of government is conducted by political parties — the cabinet is party-based and the governing party generally exercises significant control over the legislative process in the House of Commons through its majority. The government is therefore able to implement most of its political objectives.	**Concentration of power** Power is concentrated dangerously at the centre and there are few safeguards against the arbitrary exercise of state power. Parliamentary sovereignty and the absence of a codified constitution mean that even the key tenets of the rule of law are not fully protected. A government with a strong majority can force through legislation, undermining civil liberties and weakening other institutions — what Lord Hailsham referred to as an 'elective dictatorship'. Neither local nor subnational government has constitutionally protected status.
Accountability Although it holds considerable power by virtue of its control of the legislature, the government is accountable to both parliament, which scrutinises its activities, and the wider electorate. In a general election operating under a two-party system, voters effectively choose between alternative governments. An unpopular government will pay the price at the polls.	**Lack of clarity** The uncodified nature of the constitution creates problems of clarity and interpretation. It is not always immediately clear where a government has acted unconstitutionally. Parliament, controlled by the government of the day, is the final arbiter of the constitution. The government can even use its control of the legislature to pass new Acts that overturn unfavourable rulings in the courts. The rights and responsibilities of citizens are poorly defined and entrenched, making it difficult for citizens to engage with the system.

Constitutional reform since 1997 and its significance

Context

For much of the early part of the twentieth century, there was a broad political consensus in support of the constitution and the key institutions of the UK state. The Westminster model was held up as a paragon of constitutional theory and practice. The constitution evolved in a largely peaceful and pragmatic fashion. Governments of different political persuasions were happy to work within the existing constitutional framework. Political elites and the electorate regarded the constitution as legitimate and effective.

However, in the final two decades of the century, broader changes in society and in political culture led groups such as Charter 88 (more recently renamed Unlock Democracy) to put forward the case for wholesale constitutional change. Although the Labour Party had traditionally viewed constitutional reform as an unwelcome distraction from its main goal of improving conditions for the working class, the party came to embrace the need for wholesale constitutional change during an 18-year spell in opposition (1979–97).

Members of Charter 88 show their support for reforming the House of Lords

New Labour and constitutional reform, 1997–2010

The constitutional reforms introduced by the Labour governments (1997–2010) are discussed in their proper context in other chapters. Here, the main reforms are outlined (see Table 3.3) and their significance is assessed.

Labour emerged victorious from the 1997 general election after promising a programme of constitutional reform that was driven by four interlocking themes:

- **Modernisation.** Institutions such as parliament, the executive and the civil service were using outdated and inefficient procedures that demanded reform.
- **Democratisation.** Participation in the political process would be encouraged through electoral reform and greater use of referendums.
- **Decentralisation.** Decision-making powers would be devolved to new institutions in Scotland and Wales, with the role of local government also being enhanced.
- **Rights.** The rights of citizens would be strengthened and safeguarded.

Most of the key reforms that followed were introduced by Tony Blair's first administration (1997–01), although the Constitutional Reform Act 2005 that followed later also brought significant changes to the UK judiciary. While constitutional reform appeared to be an early priority for Gordon Brown's government (2007–10), the impact of the global economic crisis that coincided with Brown's short tenure in office meant that little of note was achieved in the field of constitutional affairs during that period.

Table 3.3 New Labour's constitutional reforms, 1997–2010

Area	Reforms
Rights	The Human Rights Act 1998 incorporates the European Convention on Human Rights into UK law The Freedom of Information Act 2000 gives greater access to information held by public bodies
Devolution	A Scottish Parliament with primary legislative and tax-raising powers A Northern Ireland Assembly with primary legislative powers A Welsh Assembly with secondary legislative powers A directly elected mayor of London and a London Assembly Elected mayors in some English authorities
Electoral reform	New electoral systems for devolved assemblies, for the European Parliament and for elected mayors
Parliamentary reform	All but 92 hereditary peers are removed from the House of Lords Limited reforms to the workings of the House of Commons
Judiciary	The Constitutional Reform Act 2005 Supreme Court started work in October 2009 New judicial appointments system Changes to role of lord chancellor

Rights

The Human Rights Act (HRA, 1998) enshrined most of the provisions of the European Convention on Human Rights (ECHR) in UK law. The rights protected by the convention include:

- the right to life
- the right to liberty and personal security
- the right to a fair trial
- respect for private and family life
- freedom of thought and expression
- freedom of peaceful assembly and association
- the right to marry and start a family
- freedom from torture and degrading treatment
- freedom from discrimination

The HRA requires the British government to ensure that legislation is compatible with the ECHR. All bills introduced at Westminster or in the devolved assemblies are reviewed by lawyers with a view to ensuring that they are 'HRA-compliant'. Before the HRA came into force, cases were heard by the European Court of Human Rights (ECtHR) in Strasbourg. Although UK courts can now hear cases under the ECHR, they cannot automatically overturn legislation that they deem to be incompatible with its provisions: it is up to ministers to decide whether or not to amend or repeal the offending statute.

It is important to remember that signatories to the ECHR have the right to request a derogation (a temporary exemption) from its provisions where they are facing a crisis that threatens the security of the nation. Thus it was that in the wake of 9/11, the UK government forced a derogation from Article 5 of the ECHR (the right to liberty and security) in order to allow for the detention of foreign nationals suspected of terrorist activity.

Devolution

Devolution involves the transfer of certain executive and legislative powers from central government to subnational institutions. In 1999, power was devolved to new institutions in Scotland, Wales and Northern

Key terms

Asymmetric devolution A form of devolution in which the political arrangements are not uniform, but differ from region to region.

Quasi-federalism Where the central government of a unitary state devolves some of its powers to subnational governments. It exhibits some of the features of a unitary state and some of a federal state. In legal theory there is one supreme legal authority located at the centre, as in a unitary state. But in practice the centre no longer makes domestic policy for some parts of the state and it would be difficult politically for the centre to abolish the subnational tier of government. Different policy frameworks operate within the state. Senior judges rule on questions concerning the division of competences.

West Lothian Question Originally posed by Labour MP Tam Dalyell in a Commons debate back in 1977, the West Lothian Questions asks 'Why should Scottish MPs be able to vote on English matters at Westminster, when English MPs cannot vote on matters devolved to the Scottish Parliament?'

Ireland, following 'yes' votes in referendums in each nation. The new system was one of **asymmetric devolution**, rather than following a standardised blueprint; the devolved bodies have different powers and distinctive features. Devolution has been a process rather than an event, with further powers devolved since 1999.

The Scottish Parliament was given primary legislative powers across a range of policy areas at the time of its creation, along with tax-varying powers. Subsequent reforms have seen the parliament's legislative primacy extended into a wider range of policy areas, and the Scotland Act 2012 granted the parliament tax-raising powers. Together with the Scottish government, it now has sole responsibility for policy on issues such as education, health and local government. Granting such wide-ranging powers to the Scottish government while still allowing Scottish MPs at Westminster to vote on laws that no longer directly affected their constituents, brought the so-called '**West Lothian Question**' into sharp focus.

The National Assembly for Wales, commonly referred to as the Welsh Assembly, was initially weaker than the Scottish Parliament. It had secondary legislative and executive powers but no primary legislative authority. This meant that it could only fill in the details of, and implement, legislation passed by Westminster in policy areas such as education and health.

The Northern Ireland Assembly was granted legislative powers over a similar range of policy areas to the Scottish Parliament but does not have tax-raising powers. Special procedures were established in the assembly to ensure cross-community support.

These changes clearly did not turn the UK into a federal system but, for the reasons identified earlier in this chapter, some used the term '**quasi-federalism**' when seeking to attach a label to the state of affairs that resulted from New Labour's devolution programme.

Regional and local government

Tony Blair's governments also made changes to local government in England, most notably in the capital where a new directly elected mayor of London was granted significant power in areas such as environment and transport. The latter resulted in the introduction of a congestion charge for motorists entering central London. These changes also saw the creation of a London Assembly, a body tasked to scrutinise the mayor's actions.

Outside of London, all local authorities were obliged to reform their political management, with the government keen to extend the elected mayor model beyond London. However, by 2016 there were only 17 such mayors nationwide.

Electoral reform

Labour's record on electoral reform between 1997 and 2010 was a mixed one. The 1998 Jenkins Report, the product of the Independent Commission on the Voting System established by the Labour government a year earlier, had recommended replacing the first-past-the-post (FPTP) system used in elections to the Westminster Parliament, with a hybrid system known as alternative vote plus (AV+). This system would have combined the majoritarian AV system with a proportional list-based 'top-up'. Despite establishing the commission, Labour singularly failed to act on its central recommendation.

Although no change was made to the system used in elections to the Westminster Parliament, other systems were adopted for the new devolved institutions and for some other elections (see Table 3.4).

UK electoral systems and the debate over electoral reform are dealt with more comprehensively in Chapter 10.

Table 3.4 The main electoral systems in use in the UK, 2016

Institution	Electoral system	System type
Westminster Parliament	First-past-the-post (FPTP)	Simple plurality
English and Welsh local elections	First-past-the-post (FPTP)	Simple plurality
Directly elected mayors	Supplementary vote (SV)	Majoritarian
London Assembly	Additional member system (AMS)	Hybrid/mixed
Scottish Parliament	Additional member system (AMS)	Hybrid/mixed
Scottish local government	Single transferable vote (STV)	Proportional
Welsh Assembly	Additional member system (AMS)	Hybrid/mixed
Northern Ireland Assembly	Single transferable vote (STV)	Proportional
European Parliament	Regional party list	Proportional

Parliamentary reform

The House of Lords Act 1999 abolished the right of all but 92 hereditary peers (those who inherited their titles) to sit and vote in the upper house. This was intended as the first stage of the reform process. The Lords now comprised mainly life peers and no political party had an overall majority. But the Labour governments made little progress with the second stage of the reforms, which would have settled the final composition and powers of the reformed House of Lords. Although various papers and a number of bills were brought forward for debate, there was a fundamental division between the Commons and the Lords on how reform should progress, with the Commons generally favouring a partially or entirely elected second chamber and the Lords favouring an appointed model.

Labour's initiatives to reform the House of Commons were similarly unconvincing. Changes to Prime Minister's Question Time and the working hours of the Commons, for example, were significant if unspectacular. Gordon Brown's 2010 'Governance of Britain' Green Paper aimed to limit the powers of the executive and make it more accountable to parliament but tangible progress stalled in the face of the global financial crisis.

The recommendations of the 2009 Reform of the House of Commons Committee, chaired by Tony Wright, came into force in the wake of the 2010 general election but once again the changes made could hardly be considered of great constitutional significance:

- chairs of select committees to be elected by backbenchers
- a backbench business committee to determine the business of the House of Commons for 1 day each week
- a petitions committee to select issues for debate that have been suggested by the public via e-petitions

Activity

Using the information provided above (including Table 3.3) and your own research, produce a table summarising the main elements of New Labour's constitutional reform programme. Include an assessment of success or failure against each reform.

Judiciary

The Constitutional Reform Act 2005 focused on judicial reform. A Supreme Court, which started work in October 2009, became the UK's highest court and removed the judicial role of the House of Lords. This enhanced the separation of powers but the Supreme Court does not have the authority to strike down legislation.

The Act also greatly reduced the role of lord chancellor — crucially, removing the incumbent's roles as head of the judiciary and speaker of the House of Lords. This further served to enhance the separation of powers, with the lord chancellor (now 'Justice Secretary') no longer taking a lead in all three branches of government (see Chapter 7).

The Conservatives and constitutional reform, 2010–16 (alone and in coalition with the Liberal Democrats)

The coalition and constitutional reform, 2010–15

Coalition governments inevitably involve a degree of compromise and the Conservative–Liberal Democrat administration in power between 2010 and 2015 was no exception to that rule. Although some significant changes were made to the UK's constitutional arrangements, most of the other significant changes proposed in the 2010 coalition agreement (see Table 3.5) stalled (such as reform of the House of Lords) or were approved only in a watered-down form (such as the Recall of MPs Act 2015).

Table 3.5 An overview of the Conservative–Liberal Democrat coalition agreement and constitutional reform

Coalition agreement	Delivery	Success or failure?
Freedom Bill	Protection of Freedoms Act 2012	✓
Establish a commission on a British Bill of Rights	Reported, inconclusively, in December 2012	✓
Hold a referendum on whether to move to the alternative vote system for UK general elections	Referendum in April 2011 brought a decisive 'No' vote	✓
Recall of MPs	Recall of MPs Act 2015 — though more limited in scope than originally envisaged	✓
Create a statutory register of lobbyists	Transparency of Lobbying, Non-Party Campaigning and Trade Union Administration Act 2014 required registration of 'consultant lobbyists'	✓
Reduce the number of MPs	Rejected in the wake of Lords reform reversal	✗
Equalise the size of constituency electorates	Rejected in the wake of Lords reform reversal	✗
Establish a committee to bring forward proposals for a wholly or mainly elected upper chamber elected under proportional representation	House of Lords Reform Bill introduced in June 2012, but abandoned in August of that year House of Lords Reform Act 2014 allowed peers to retire or resign	✓
Establish greater power for local government	Little progress — although under the Local Democracy, Economic Development and Construction Act 2009, five 'Combined Authorities' were created in England between 2010 and 2015	✗
Set 5-year fixed-term parliaments	Fixed-term Parliaments Act 2011	✓

Of the changes that were made under the coalition, only five can be seen as worthy of more detailed consideration.

- **Fixed-term Parliaments Act 2011.** The Act established a pattern of fixed general elections every 5 years, starting in 2015. It thereby removed the ability of the prime minister to call an election at a politically advantageous time although its limitations were made clear by the calling of an early election in 2017.
- **The Scotland Act 2012.** The Act gave the Scottish government the power to vary income tax up or down by 10 pence in the pound and devolved further powers to the Scottish government, including in the area of the regulation of controlled drugs. It also allowed the Scottish government to borrow up to £2.2bn per annum.
- **The Protection of Freedoms Act 2012.** Coming in the wake of an avalanche of control measures designed to meet the threat posed by terrorists in the wake of 9/11, the Act offered citizens greater protection from the state by putting in place proper scrutiny of the security services and oversight of surveillance and data collection.
- **House of Lords Reform Act 2014.** The Act was aimed at halting the inexorable increase in the number of those eligible to sit and vote in the House of Lords, by giving existing peers the right to retire or resign their seats in the chamber. It also allowed peers to be removed as a result of serious criminal offences or non-attendance. Fifty-four peers had resigned under the terms of the Act by 2016, with a further four removed as a result of non-attendance.
- **The Wales Act 2014.** The Wales Act was the UK government's response to the Silk Commission's recommendations on further devolution to Wales. Although it was fairly modest in scope, the Act transferred control of some smaller taxes to devolved institutions in Wales. It also put in place a mechanism by which devolution of other lower-level taxes could be developed, with the approval of the Westminster Parliament, and provided the legal framework required for a Welsh referendum on the partial devolution of income tax. Symbolically, the Act also changed the name of the Welsh executive from the Welsh Assembly government to the Welsh government.

The Conservatives and constitutional reform, 2015 onwards

The Conservatives' 2015 general election manifesto made few promises regarding constitutional reform — quite the reverse, in fact. On Lords reform, for example, the manifesto stated that 'While we still see a strong case for introducing an elected element into our second chamber, this is not a priority in the next Parliament.' That said, it should be noted that the new Conservative government had delivered on most of the election promises it had made in the field of constitutional reform within 2 years of taking office in a single-party government. The Scottish government was given greater fiscal (financial) autonomy under the Scotland Act 2016 — see the case study below — and the Wales Act 2017 gave the Welsh Assembly tax-raising powers, further cementing the primary legislative authority that devolved institutions in Wales had been granted in the wake of the 2011 Welsh referendum.

Moreover, although the controversial **Barnett formula** has been left in place in the wake of these and earlier reforms, English MPs have now been given special privileges in respect of those matters affecting England alone (a form of 'English votes for English laws'), as promised in the Conservative manifesto.

'English votes for English laws'

The 2013 report of the Commission on the Consequences of Devolution for the House of Commons (aka the McKay Commission) recommended that only English MPs should be allowed to vote on measures which were identified as affecting only England. Changes to House of Commons standing orders made in the wake of the 2015 general election mean that this form of 'English votes for English laws' is now in place. The new system was used for the first time in January 2016, when only those MPs representing English constituencies were permitted to vote on some elements of a Housing and Planning Bill.

Case study

The implications of the Scotland Act 2016

The Scotland Act 2016 put into place many of the recommendations of the Smith Commission, the latter having been established in the immediate aftermath of the clear 'No' vote in the 2014 Scottish independence referendum. The Act made a number of significant changes (see Figure 3.1):

■ Devolved institutions were granted new powers over taxation, being allowed to set the rates and thresholds for income tax as well gaining control of 50% of VAT levies.

■ These changes meant that, for the first time, the Scottish government was responsible for raising more than 50% of the money that it spends.

■ The Scottish Parliament was given legislative power over a range of new areas — including road signs, speed limits and some welfare benefits.

■ The Scottish government was given control over its electoral system, although a two-thirds supermajority in the Scottish Parliament was required for any changes to be made.

Crucially, the Act also recognised the permanence of devolved institutions in Scotland and determined that a referendum would be required before either the

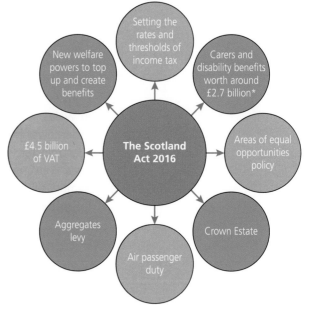

*Based on 2014/15 spend in Scotland
Source: www.gov.uk/scotland-office

Figure 3.1 The Scotland Act 2016 in overview

Scottish Parliament or the Scottish government could be abolished.

Questions

■ To what extent could the Scotland Act 2016 be seen to address the concerns of those who had voted in favour of Scottish independence in the 2014 referendum?

■ How could the Act be said to have strengthened the case in favour of 'English votes for English laws' at Westminster?

Brexit

It is worth remembering that as well as delivering on its manifesto promises with regards to subnational government, the Conservative government has also delivered on an earlier promise to hold an 'in/out' referendum on the UK's membership of the EU. As we have already noted, the result of the referendum vote could have significant implications for the UK's constitutional arrangements.

Should the UK adopt a codified constitution?

The Labour governments' reforms between 1997 and 2010 resulted in a greater codification of the British constitution. The Human Rights Act 1998 and the Scotland Act 1998, for example, saw important constitutional principles written into statute law. Some scholars and judges even claim that such acts have *de facto* status as fundamental law or 'constitutional statutes'. But the Labour governments did not take their constitutional reforms to their logical conclusion — a codified constitution.

Although Labour and the Liberal Democrats proposed moves towards a codified constitution in their 2010 election manifestos, the Conservative–Liberal Democrat coalition agreement made no such commitment. Since 2015, the Conservatives, now in government alone, have given no indication that this is a route they wish to take.

Arguments in favour of a codified constitution

Supporters of a codified constitution claim that it would provide greater clarity on what is, and what is not, constitutional. The rules governing the British political system would be set out in an authoritative document, reducing the ambiguities that exist in the current uncodified constitution and its myriad of conventions. The rights of citizens would also be given further constitutional protection. A codified constitution would tackle the centralisation of power (and the potential for 'elective dictatorship') by setting limits on the power of the executive and introducing more effective institutional checks and balances. Local and subnational governments would enjoy constitutional protection.

In drawing up a codified constitution, politicians and the public would have to give greater thought to the core principles of the British constitution than was evident during Labour's reform programme. The process of drawing up the new constitution would also educate citizens and, proponents hope, provide the people with a greater sense of shared values and citizenship, while bestowing additional legitimacy on the political system.

Arguments against a codified constitution

Opponents argue that codification would remove the flexibility and adaptability that is often seen as a key strength of the existing uncodified constitution. The British constitution has endured because it has developed organically and been adapted when the case for change has been proven. A codified constitution may reflect the mood of the time when it was produced — although this may also be doubtful, given the difficulty of forging consensus — but values change and constitutional legislation often requires amendment within a few years because of unintended consequences or the emergence of new issues. Codified constitutions are rigid and not easy to change. Codification, critics argue, would place too much power in the hands of judges because they would be called upon to determine whether laws and political processes are constitutional. A government acting on a popular mandate to introduce, say, stricter measures on law and order could find its legislation overturned by the courts. Judges would become more overtly political and this might reduce faith in the legal system.

A move to a codified constitution would bring about a fundamental change in the British political system and in the country's political culture. The traditional view is that a codified constitution would be incompatible with parliamentary sovereignty. Whereas codified constitutions set limits on the powers of the legislature and executive, the doctrine of parliamentary sovereignty gives Westminster supreme authority. A codified constitution could not be entrenched or have the status of fundamental law for so long as parliament retains the power to alter it at will.

An extensive national debate that produces elite and popular consensus on the guiding principles of the political system and authorising their codification might offer a way out of this conundrum. In such circumstances, parliament would be reluctant to counter the express will of the people. But disputes over the treatment of England in the post-devolution UK, reform of the House of Lords and the future of the Human Rights Act suggest that elite (and popular) consensus on the constitution is some way off.

Debate

Should the UK have a codified constitution?

Yes
- It is the logical conclusion of recent constitutional reforms.
- It would provide greater clarity on what is constitutional.
- It would be an authoritative reference point for the courts.
- It would set limits on the powers of the state and its institutions.
- It would provide greater protection for the rights of citizens.
- It would better inform citizens about the values and workings of the political system.

No
- Pragmatic adaptation has worked well and is preferable.
- There is no agreed process for establishing a codified constitution.
- There is no elite consensus on what a codified constitution should include.
- It would be rigid and difficult to amend.
- It would give judges, who are unaccountable, greater political power.
- There is no great popular demand and other issues are more important.

'Where next' for constitutional reform?

There is a remarkable degree of consensus regarding what needs to be done. The problem lies more in the areas of strategy and delivery. In common with so many 'new dawns', New Labour's constitutional reform programme ran aground long before the end of the party's first term in office. What followed between 2001 and 2016, under administrations of various political hues, was essentially piecemeal; a tinkering series of halfway houses and dead ends.

Aims of further constitutional reform

In 2013, the Electoral Reform Society published *Reviving the Health of Our Democracy*, in which they argued that the UK's constitutional arrangements should be remodelled with a view to delivering three clear outcomes:

Activist campaigning for voting reform, July 2015

- **active participation and engagement,** giving everyone the opportunity to shape the decisions that affect their lives
- **fair representation,** ensuring our institutions reflect the people they serve, their choices and identities
- **good governance** in the form, function and culture of democratic decision making

What might these headline goals mean in terms of making concrete changes to our constitutional arrangements — and how far down this road have we travelled since 2013?

Encouraging active participation and engagement

Many of the obvious changes that were suggested at the time of the 2013 paper have now been piloted in one form or another.

- **Simplifying voter registration.** The system was indeed changed from a household-based system of registration to individual voter registration. However, far from improving electoral participation, the result of this change was a fall in voter registration.
- **Lowering the voting age to 16.** Sixteen-year-olds were allowed to vote in the 2014 Scottish referendum but were not given a voice in the 2015 general election or in the 2016 UK-wide EU referendum.
- **Making wider use of e-democracy.** Online petitions, citizens' assemblies and citizens' juries have all been trialled.
- **Opening up candidate selection.** Although the major parties' dalliance with primaries, public hustings and one-member-one-vote offered the prospect of wider access to elected office, the reality is that in spite of a larger number of female MPs being elected, the socioeconomic profile of those elected to the Commons has not been radically altered.

Delivering fair representation

- **Electoral reform.** Although there is general agreement that the first-past-the-post (FPTP) system used in elections to the Westminster Parliament is, at best, inequitable, there has been no tangible progress towards reform since the 2011 alternative vote (AV) referendum.
- **Redrawing electoral districts.** The Boundary Commissions have made proposals that would see a move towards more equal parliamentary constituencies ahead of the 2020 general election, with consultation on those proposals under way in 2016.

Providing for good governance and restoring trust

- **Completing Lords reform.** The second stage of Lords reform that was promised back in 1997, whereby the second chamber would become at least partly elected, is no closer to completion now than it was in the wake of the House of Lords Act 1999. As we have seen, the House of Lords Reform Act 2014 is barely worthy of such an impressive title.
- **Modernising the Commons.** Although there have been some efforts to regulate lobbying and reform party funding since 2013, there has likely been too little movement on this front to restore confidence in politics. The Recall of MPs Act 2015, which established a mechanism considerably weaker than that operating in many states in the USA, also fell short of expectations.

- **Enhancing local democracy.** Devolved institutions in Scotland and Wales have seen their powers extended, in both scope and depth, but local government has not enjoyed the kind of renaissance envisaged either by the Electoral Commission or by the main UK parties in their 2015 general election manifestos.

Ultimate destination uncertain; route unclear

Given that there is still some considerable debate over precisely where constitutional reform should be headed, it is perhaps no surprise that the route towards that final destination remains similarly unclear. Writers such as Vernon Bogdanor have suggested that one way out of this impasse might be to establish a US-style constitutional convention:

> It is becoming increasingly clear that our constitutional forms are relics of a previous era, and that we need to bring them into alignment with the social forces of the modern age. The task now is to channel the democratic spirit into constructive channels. That is the fundamental case for a constitutional convention, with popular participation, to consider the constitution as a whole. But, before such a convention sits, it needs to be preceded by a learning process. The best way of achieving this would be through a Royal Commission, or equivalent body, which would hold hearings in public in different parts of the country; hearings which would be highlighted in the media. The Commission would take on the task of collecting the thoughts of the interested public and providing options for the constitutional convention to consider.
>
> Vernon Bogdanor (2015) *The Crisis of the Constitution: The General Election and the Future of the United Kingdom*

What you should know

- The British constitution is uncodified. The most important provisions are not gathered in one document, but are found in a variety of sources: Acts of Parliament, the common law, conventions, works of authority, and the treaties and law of the European Union. The uncodified nature of the British constitution means that it can be adapted to meet new political realities, but also that there is no definitive view of what is unconstitutional and that protection of individual rights is limited.
- Parliamentary sovereignty is the core principle of the British constitution. It establishes parliament as the supreme law-making body. But this legal theory has come under pressure given EU membership, the Human Rights Act 1998, devolution and the use of referendums. Political practice also differs significantly from legal theory. No institution has absolute power; all are subject to significant internal and external constraints. The UK, however, has been a highly centralised state.
- The constitution was changed significantly by the Labour governments between 1997 and 2010. Devolution, the Human Rights Act, new electoral systems and reform of the House of Lords changed the constitutional landscape. They provided greater protection for the rights of citizens and introduced more effective checks and balances and more democratic elements into the political system. The reforms have important implications for parliamentary sovereignty. Critics claim that the reform programme was incomplete and lacked a unifying vision.
- The new constitutional settlement continues to evolve. The Scottish Parliament and Welsh Assembly have gained more powers, and a form of 'English votes for English laws' came into play in 2015. Although the 2011 alternative vote (AV) referendum ended the immediate prospect of electoral reform, the coalition government was able to introduce fixed-term parliaments.
- Debates continue on reform of the House of Lords, the government of England, the Human Rights Act and codification of the constitution. The constitution is not above politics, but is an important political issue in its own right.

UK/US comparison

The UK and US constitutions

- Unlike the uncodified constitution under which the UK is governed, the US Constitution is codified. It was drafted by the Founding Fathers in 1787, 4 years after the former colonies had secured their independence from Britain.
- The US Constitution has seven articles, the first three of which set out the role and powers of (respectively) the legislature, the executive and the judiciary.
- In common with the UK, some important features of the US political system are not described in the constitution, but have emerged through case law or as conventions. These include, for example, the Supreme Court's power of judicial review.
- The US Constitution is entrenched. The constitution establishes special procedures for its amendment. Amendments must be approved by two-thirds of members in both houses of Congress and ratified by three-quarters of state legislatures in the 50 states. Since the first ten amendments were ratified as the Bill of Rights in 1791, 17 other amendments have been added, two of which (the 18th and 21st) cancel each other out. The UK constitution is not entrenched: there are no special procedures for its amendment.
- The Bill of Rights sets out the rights of individual US citizens and protects them from state encroachment. The Human Rights Act 1998 incorporated ECHR rights into UK statute law.
- The US Constitution is subject to extensive judicial review. The Supreme Court can declare Acts of Congress and the actions of the executive, as well as the actions of state legislatures and executives, to be unconstitutional and strike them down. Parliamentary sovereignty and the uncodified constitution mean that judicial review is far more limited in the UK.
- The US Constitution is a federal constitution. The 10th Amendment states that all powers not delegated to the federal government by the constitution, or prohibited by it to the states, are reserved to the states or the people. The UK has traditionally been seen as a unitary state, but has developed quasi-federal features since 1997.
- The US Constitution establishes a strict separation of powers. The executive, legislature and judiciary have different powers and personnel. Checks and balances prevent one branch of government becoming pre-eminent. The UK has a partial fusion of powers where the executive dominates the legislature.
- The US Constitution establishes a presidential system of government in which the head of the executive branch is directly elected, the executive and legislative branches have distinct membership and functions, and neither branch can dismiss the other. The UK has a parliamentary system in which the prime minister is the leader of the largest party in the House of Commons, the executive and legislative branches are fused, and the House of Commons can dismiss the government.

Further reading

Bogdanor, V. (2016) 'The UK Constitution: do we need a constitutional convention and a codified constitution?', *Politics Review*, Vol. 26, No. 1, pp. 23–25.

Campbell, R. (2015) 'How strong is UK representative democracy?', *Politics Review*, Vol. 25, No. 2, pp. 28–31.

Fairclough, P. (2014) 'UK democracy: how could it be improved?', *Politics Review*, Vol. 24, No. 2, pp. 30–33.

Norton, P. (2015) 'UK Constitution: is it a sufficient check on executive power?', *Politics Review*, Vol. 24, No. 3, pp. 12–15.

Exam-style questions

Short-answer questions

1 Explain, with examples, the principle of parliamentary sovereignty.

2 Explain, with examples, the role of constitutional conventions.

3 Explain and analyse three sources of the UK constitution.

4 Explain and analyse three constitutional reforms introduced since 2010.

Mid-length questions

1 Describe the main features of the UK constitution.

2 Describe the main functions of a constitution.

3 Analyse and evaluate the arguments in favour of the UK adopting a codified constitution.

4 Analyse and evaluate the arguments in favour of further constitutional reform.

Essay questions

1 Evaluate how far an uncodified constitution remains appropriate in the modern British political process.

2 Evaluate how far constitutional reforms since the general election of 1997 have improved the British political system.

3 Analyse and evaluate the arguments for retaining an uncodified constitution for the UK political system.

4 'Constitutional reform in the UK has not gone far enough.' How far do you agree with this statement?

In your answer you must:

- Refer to at least one pre-2010 reform and one post-2010 reform.

- Draw on relevant knowledge and understanding of UK politics.

Chapter 4

Devolution

> **Key questions answered**
> - What is devolution?
> - What are the powers of the Scottish Parliament, Welsh Assembly and Northern Ireland Assembly?
> - What is the 'English Question', and how might it be answered?
> - What have been the implications of devolution for UK politics?

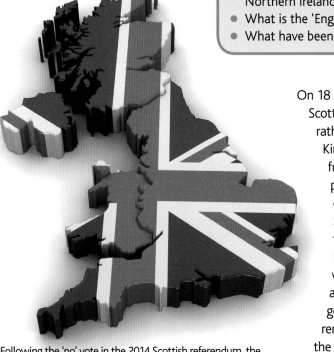

Following the 'no' vote in the 2014 Scottish referendum, the UK remains a multinational state made up of four nations

On 18 September 2014, 55% of voters in the referendum on Scottish independence voted against independence. But rather than strengthening Scotland's place in the United Kingdom, the vote created further uncertainty about the future of the Union and devolution. Government and politics in Scotland is diverging from the other nations of the UK. Following the Scotland Act 2016, the Scottish Parliament will be able to set different income tax rates and alter some welfare benefits. The Scottish National Party (SNP) is the dominant party in Scotland, winning the last three Scottish Parliament elections and most Scottish constituencies at the 2015 and 2017 general elections. The constitutional status of Scotland remains a salient issue, particularly in light of Brexit, but the rise of the unionist parties in 2017 dampened calls for a second independence referendum.

What is devolution?

Key terms

Devolution The transfer of political power, but not sovereignty, from central government to subnational government.

Primary legislative power Authority to make laws on devolved policy areas.

Devolution is the transfer of policy-making powers from the centre to subordinate subnational institutions. However, the state-wide legislature retains ultimate authority. Devolution in the UK has been asymmetric: each of the devolved institutions has different powers and distinctive features. It has also been a process rather than a one-off event.

The Scottish Parliament is the most powerful of the devolved institutions. It has **primary legislative powers** — that is, it is responsible for law-making in devolved matters — and tax-raising powers. The Welsh Assembly initially had only executive powers, determining how Westminster legislation was implemented in Wales. After the 2011 referendum, it gained primary legislative authority in devolved matters and is set to gain tax-raising powers under the Wales Act 2017. The Northern Ireland Assembly has primary legislative powers but only limited powers over tax.

Origins of devolution

Devolved institutions were not established in Scotland and Wales until 1999 but pressure for devolution had been building since the 1970s when discontent with the UK political system and a revival of national cultures prompted a growth of Scottish and Welsh **nationalism**. The Scottish National Party (SNP) and Plaid Cymru made electoral breakthroughs at Westminster. The Labour government of James Callaghan (1976–79) responded by holding referendums on the creation of legislative assemblies in Scotland and Wales. The 1979 Welsh referendum produced a decisive 'no' as only 20% backed an assembly. In Scotland, 52% of those who voted supported devolution. But Westminster had stipulated that a Scottish assembly would not be created unless it was supported by 40% of the Scottish electorate — and only 33% of the electorate turned out to vote 'yes'.

Demands for devolution in Scotland re-emerged during the long period of Conservative government (1979–97). Labour and the Liberal Democrats supported devolution, as did key groups in Scottish civil society. Soon after the 1997 general election, the Blair government held referendums in Scotland and Wales to approve its policy on devolution. In Scotland, voters were asked whether they supported (1) a Scottish Parliament and (2) tax-varying powers for the parliament — 74.3% supported a Scottish Parliament and 63.5% supported tax-varying powers. In Wales, 50.3% voted 'yes' to a Welsh Assembly on a turnout of 50.1%. Much of western Wales, which has a higher proportion of Welsh speakers, supported devolution but eastern Wales did not.

The Scottish Parliament and government

The Scottish Parliament has 129 members (MSPs) elected by the additional member system (AMS):

- 73 MSPs (57% of the total) are elected in single-member constituencies using the first-past-the-post (FPTP) system.
- 56 MSPs (43% of the total) are 'additional members' chosen from party lists. They are elected in eight multi-member regions, each of which elects seven members using the regional list system of proportional representation (PR). These seats are allocated to parties on a corrective basis so that the distribution of seats reflects more accurately the share of the vote won by the parties.

The Scottish Parliament buildings in Edinburgh

Elections were initially held every 4 years but this was extended to every 5 years after the 2011 election.

Electoral systems

Whereas the House of Commons is elected by the first-past-the-post (FPTP) system, the Scottish Parliament and Welsh Assembly are elected by the additional member system (AMS) and the single transferable vote (STV) is used to elect the Northern Ireland Assembly. The mechanics of these electoral systems, and their strengths and weaknesses, are examined in Chapter 10.

The Scottish government, known as the Scottish executive until 2007, draws up policy proposals and implements legislation. The first minister, usually the leader of the largest party, heads the government and appoints the cabinet. Labour was in coalition with the Liberal Democrats from 1999 until 2007. Since then, the SNP has been the governing party. Nicola Sturgeon replaced Alex Salmond as SNP leader and first minister in 2014.

Devolved powers

The Scotland Act 1998 gave the Scottish Parliament primary legislative powers in a range of policy areas, including law and order, health, education, transport, the environment and economic development. Westminster no longer makes law for Scotland on these matters. Additional policy areas have since been devolved (see Table 4.1).

Table 4.1 Major powers of the devolved institutions, 2017

Policy area	Scottish Parliament	Welsh Assembly	Northern Ireland Assembly
Tax	Income tax rates and bands Other specified taxes and duties (e.g. air passenger duty, landfill tax, stamp duty)	Welsh rate of income tax, i.e. control over 10p share of income tax Other specified taxes and duties (e.g. landfill tax, stamp duty)	Corporation tax
Health and social policy	Health service Social services Some welfare benefits Abortion law	Health service Social services	Health service Social services Some welfare benefits
Environment etc.	Agriculture and fisheries Economic development Environment Housing Local government Planning Transport (including speed limits, road signs and rail franchises) Onshore gas and oil extraction	Agriculture and fisheries Economic development Environment Housing Local government Planning Transport (including speed limits, road signs and rail franchises) Onshore gas and oil extraction	Agriculture and fisheries Economic development Environment Housing Local government Planning Transport
Education and culture	Primary and secondary education University education Culture and language Sport Tourism	Primary and secondary education University education Culture and language Sport Tourism	Primary and secondary education University education Culture and language Sport Tourism
Law and home affairs	Justice Police Prisons Elections	Elections	Justice Police Prisons Elections

The Scotland Act 1998 also gave the Scottish Parliament tax-varying powers: it could raise or lower the rate of income tax in Scotland by up to 3% (i.e. 3 pence in the pound). To date, these powers have not been used but the Scotland Act 2012 then gave the Scottish Parliament the power to set a Scottish rate of income tax higher or lower than that in the rest of the UK, from 2016 onwards. Finally, the Scotland Act 2016 devolved control of income tax rates and bands, and gave the Scottish Parliament 50% of the VAT revenue raised in Scotland. This gives the Scottish Parliament control of around £15 billion. The block grant from the UK Treasury will be reduced as Scotland raises more of its own revenue.

Reserved powers

Limits on the Scottish Parliament's legislative powers were established by the Scotland Act 1998. The following 'reserved powers' remain the sole responsibility of Westminster:

- UK constitution
- defence and national security
- foreign policy, including relations with the EU
- fiscal, economic and monetary systems
- common market for British goods and services
- employment legislation
- social security (but with some areas devolved to Scotland and Northern Ireland)
- broadcasting
- nationality and immigration
- nuclear energy

The Scotland Act 1998 stated that Westminster remains sovereign in all matters but had chosen to exercise its sovereignty by devolving legislative responsibility without diminishing its own powers. Westminster retained the right to override the Scottish Parliament in areas where legislative powers had been devolved. It could, in theory, also abolish the devolved institutions. But the Scotland Act 2016 states that:

- Westminster will not legislate on devolved matters without consent.
- The Scottish Parliament and government are 'a permanent part of the United Kingdom's constitutional arrangements'.
- The Scottish Parliament and government cannot be abolished unless approved in a referendum in Scotland.

Further devolution or independence?

After the SNP entered office in 2007, the UK Labour government set up the Calman Commission to consider further devolution of powers. Its 2009 recommendation to give the Scottish Parliament the power to set a Scottish rate of income tax was enacted in the Scotland Act 2012. But the SNP's landslide victory in the 2011 Scottish Parliament election put an independence referendum firmly on the agenda. Although the constitution is a reserved power, Westminster granted the Scottish Parliament temporary powers to hold a referendum.

The 2014 independence referendum

In the 2014 independence referendum, the Yes Scotland campaign, fronted by the SNP, argued that the people of Scotland were best placed to make decisions that affect Scotland, and highlighted economic and social policies that an SNP government would pursue. The SNP's vision was of an independent Scotland that was part of a 'personal union' with the UK. It would retain the queen as head of state and keep the pound in a currency union with the UK. But Scotland would have its own written constitution and full responsibility for welfare, foreign and defence policy.

The pro-Union campaign, Better Together, was supported by Labour, the Conservatives and the Liberal Democrats. It argued that Scotland enjoyed the best of both worlds in the UK — extensive devolution as well as the economic, political and cultural benefits of the Union. Better Together argued that independence would damage Scotland's economy and the UK Treasury insisted that there would be no currency union with an independent Scotland. The European Commission also warned that an independent Scotland would not automatically become a member of the EU.

The referendum on 18 September 2014 asked: 'Should Scotland be an independent country?' The result was a 55.3% 'no' vote. But 1.6 million voters (44.7%) supported independence (see the case study). Four local authority areas — Glasgow, Dundee, West Dunbartonshire and North Lanarkshire — returned a majority 'yes' vote. Turnout, at 84.5%, was very high.

Case study

Who voted for Scottish independence?

There were some significant demographic differences between 'yes' and 'no' voters in the Scottish independence referendum. Men were more likely than women to vote for independence, as were working-class voters and those aged under 55. The most deprived areas of Scotland produced the largest 'yes' votes.

There were also attitudinal differences. People who believed that independence would have negative consequences for the Scottish economy were more likely to vote 'no'. National identity was also important to how people voted. The majority of people who identify themselves as 'Scottish not British' and 'more Scottish than British' voted for independence. But only a small proportion of people identifying themselves as 'more British than Scottish' or 'equally Scottish and British' did so.

Scottish independence referendum campaigners

SNP voters were, unsurprisingly, much more likely to vote for independence than supporters of other parties. The Yes Scotland campaign also attracted significant support from Labour voters.

Questions
- What were the main issues in the referendum campaign?
- Why did the referendum not resolve the issue of Scottish independence?

The Scotland Act 2016

In the final stages of the referendum campaign, the leaders of the three main UK parties issued a vow to deliver further devolution in the event of a 'no' vote. The result was the Scotland Act 2016. The new powers devolved by the Act include:

- the power to set income tax rates and bands
- some additional taxes and duties, including air passenger duty and aggregates levy
- the right to receive 50% of the value-added tax (VAT) raised in Scotland
- control over certain welfare benefits, including the Disability Living Allowance, Personal Independence Payment, the housing element of Universal Credit, and the 'bedroom tax'
- road signs and speed limits, rail franchises, and onshore gas and oil extraction (e.g. fracking)
- the franchise (i.e. who has the right to vote) for Scottish Parliament elections (subject to two-thirds majority support in the parliament)

The new powers did not go far enough for the SNP and the changes fall short of 'devomax', in which the Scottish Parliament would have full responsibility for all taxes, duties and spending (i.e. full fiscal autonomy). But the Act marks a major extension of devolution by creating Scottish tax and welfare systems that differ from those in the rest of the UK. The Scottish Parliament now has greater powers than subnational governments in many other European states.

Activity

Using the websites of the Scottish Parliament and Scottish government, as well as news sites, find examples of legislation currently being proposed in Scotland. To what extent is the Scottish government making use of the new powers devolved to Holyrood?

The Welsh Assembly and government

The debating chamber inside the Senedd, National Assembly for Wales building in Cardiff

The National Assembly for Wales, commonly known as the Welsh Assembly, has 60 members elected by the additional member system (AMS):

- 40 members are elected in single-member constituencies using the first-past-the-post (FPTP) system
- 20 members are elected in five multi-member regions using the regional list system of proportional representation

Elections were initially held every 4 years but this was extended to every 5 years by the Wales Act 2014.

The Welsh government, known as the Welsh Assembly government before 2011, formulates and implements policy. The first minister (originally first secretary), who is normally the leader of the largest party in the assembly, heads the government and appoints the cabinet.

Labour has been in power, either alone or in coalition, since the first election to the assembly in 1999:

- Labour–Liberal Democrat coalition 1999–2003
- Labour government 2003–07 (no majority)
- Labour–Plaid Cymru coalition 2007–11
- Labour–Liberal Democrat coalition 2016–

Carwyn Jones became first minister in 2009.

The powers of the Welsh Assembly have expanded since its creation but are not as extensive as those of the Scottish Parliament. It now enjoys primary legislative powers and, under the Wales Act 2017 moved to a system of reserved powers similar to that in Scotland. Initially the assembly had only executive and secondary legislative powers, which meant that it determined how to implement legislation on a range of Welsh issues that had been passed by Westminster.

The Government of Wales Act 2006 enabled the assembly to ask for further powers to be transferred from Westminster, and allowed it to gain primary legislative powers if approved in a referendum. The 2011 referendum resulted in a 64% 'yes' vote. This confirmed that devolution is the preferred constitutional option for Welsh voters but support for independence is much lower than in Scotland, at around 10%.

Following the 2011 referendum, the assembly duly gained the power to make primary legislation in the existing 20 devolved areas. These had been specified in the Government of Wales Act 1998 and included education, health, transport, the environment and economic development (see Table 4.1). Additional policy areas have since been devolved. With the Scottish Parliament gaining new powers, the Conservative–Liberal Democrat UK coalition government established the Silk Commission to consider the case for the transfer of further powers to the Welsh Assembly. The Wales Act 2014 put into place the first tranche of Silk's proposals by devolving control of landfill tax and stamp duty.

The Wales Act 2017 featured proposals made in a second Silk Report. It specified a list of matters that are reserved to Westminster: all other areas are devolved to the assembly. The Act will create a Welsh rate of income tax by giving the assembly control over a portion (10 pence in the pound) of income tax and at the same time remove the need for a referendum in order to do this, as was specified in the Wales Act 2014. Newly devolved matters will include assembly and local government elections, fracking, rail franchising and road speed limits. The Welsh government wanted policing and justice to be devolved (as Silk recommended), but the UK government did not agree to it.

The Wales Act 2017 established the assembly and Welsh government as a permanent feature of the UK constitution. Subject to the support of two-thirds of its members, the assembly will be able to rename itself the 'Welsh Parliament'.

The Northern Ireland Assembly and executive

Stormont Castle, Belfast, was the home of the Stormont Parliament from 1922 to 1972. Now the Northern Ireland Assembly sits here

Key terms

Nationalist An adherent of a political position in Northern Ireland who supports constitutional means of achieving improved rights for Catholics and the eventual incorporation of the six counties of Northern Ireland into the Republic of Ireland.

Unionist An adherent of a political position in Northern Ireland who supports the continued union between Great Britain and Northern Ireland.

Politics and government in Northern Ireland differs from elsewhere in the UK. Differences include:

- **Communal conflict.** The main political divide in Northern Ireland is that between **unionists** and **nationalists**. Unionists want Northern Ireland to remain part of the UK. Nationalists favour a united Ireland or a greater role for the Republic of Ireland in the affairs of Northern Ireland. Unionists identify with the British state and tend to be Protestant, whereas nationalists identify themselves as Irish and tend to be Catholic. Catholics made up 45% of the Northern Ireland population in 2011.
- **Distinctive party system.** Elections are contested between unionist and nationalist parties and the main electoral issue is the constitutional status of Northern Ireland. The main UK parties tend not to field candidates in Northern Irish elections.
- **Security.** Terrorist campaigns by republican and loyalist paramilitary organisations killed more than 3,600 people during the Troubles (see Figure 4.1) and British soldiers patrolled the streets for several decades. The IRA has adhered to a ceasefire since 1995 but breakaway republican groups remain active.

Figure 4.1 Deaths due to the security situation in Northern Ireland, 1969–2003

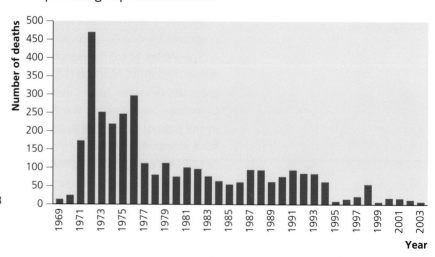

Source: data from CAIN web service (http://cain.ulst.ac.uk)

Note: Data include civilians, police, army personnel and members of paramilitary groups.

■ **Separate system of government.** Northern Ireland has been governed differently from the rest of the UK. Between 1922 and 1972, it was the only part of the UK to have its own parliament. Then, under direct rule, the secretary of state for Northern Ireland had significant policy-making powers. Devolution in Northern Ireland is also distinctive as it is designed so that unionist and nationalist parties share power.

The Good Friday Agreement

Years of negotiations between the UK and Irish governments, and some of the Northern Irish political parties, with the aim of achieving peace resulted in the 1998 Good Friday Agreement (the Belfast Agreement). It established **power-sharing devolution** and required the UK and Irish governments to amend their constitutions to clarify the status of Northern Ireland.

The Northern Ireland Assembly consists of 108 members, elected by the single transferable vote (STV) system of proportional representation. The number of assembly members is expected to be cut to 90 ahead of the 2021 election. Elections were initially held every 4 years but this was extended to 5 years after the 2011 election although this depends on the maintenance of the power-sharing agreement, as shown in 2017.

The assembly has primary legislative powers in a range of policy areas (see Table 4.1). It does not have major tax-raising powers, although corporation tax was devolved in 2015. Some legislative measures require cross-community support from both unionist and nationalist parties.

The Northern Ireland Executive is led by a first minister and deputy first minister. The first minister is the leader of the largest party in the assembly, and the deputy first minister is from the second largest party. Ministerial posts are allocated on a proportional basis according to party strength. The agreement thus ensures power sharing, with both unionists and nationalists represented in government. In 2016, the Ulster Unionist Party (UUP) and Social Democratic and Labour Party (SDLP) declined to nominate ministers and formed an official opposition. The DUP (Democratic Unionist Party, the largest unionist party which originally opposed the Good Friday Agreement) and Sinn Féin (a republican party with close links to the IRA) have shared power since 2007. Arlene Foster of the DUP became first minister in 2016; Sinn Féin's Martin McGuinness was deputy first minister from 2007 until 2017.

Devolution remains the preferred constitutional choice of a majority of voters in Northern Ireland (see Figure 4.2). However, the Assembly collapsed in 2017 when disputes between the DUP and Sinn Féin saw the latter refuse to nominate a new deputy first minister. Fresh elections to the Assembly were held, but agreement on a power-sharing executive had not been reached ahead of the UK general election.

Key term

Power-sharing devolution A form of devolution in which special arrangements ensure that both communities in a divided society are represented in the executive and assent to legislation on sensitive issues.

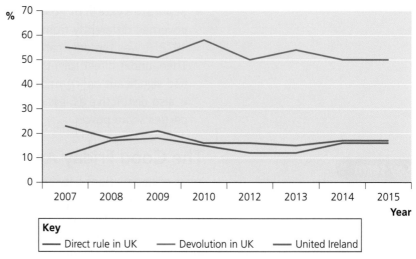

Source: Northern Ireland Life and Times Survey (NB No data available for 2011)

Figure 4.2 Constitutional preference of Northern Ireland voters, in answer to the question: 'What do you think the long-term policy for Northern Ireland should be?'

How should England be governed?

Devolution in Scotland, Wales and Northern Ireland has raised the 'English Question': how should England be governed? Underpinning the question is a sense that the interests and identity of England have not been recognised fully within the post-devolution UK. Some of the proposed solutions address England's place within the Union; others are concerned with the internal governance of England:

- an English Parliament
- 'English votes for English laws' at Westminster
- elected regional assemblies

Answering the English Question has proved difficult because the proposed solutions raise further problems, and none enjoy cross-party support in parliament or widespread support among voters.

An English parliament

England is the only part of the UK not to have its own devolved parliament. An English parliament would have legislative powers over domestic English issues. Powers that could be devolved to an English parliament could be equivalent to those already devolved to the Scottish Parliament. It could sit at Westminster or outside London. An English executive or government could also be created to implement policy.

There is little support for an English parliament within the major political parties, although it is favoured by UKIP and some Conservative MPs.

Arguments made in favour of an English parliament include:

- It would complete devolution within the UK, and resolve the English Question, by giving England its own parliament.
- It would create a more coherent system of devolution, with a federal UK Parliament and government responsible for UK-wide issues — rather than, at present, these combined with English issues.
- It would give political and institutional expression to English identity and interests.

Arguments against the creation of an English parliament include:

■ It would create an additional layer of government and create tensions between the UK government and an English parliament and government.

■ 'Devolution all round' would not create a coherent and equitable system because England is much bigger than the other nations of the Union.

■ There is only limited support in England for an English parliament (see Figure 4.3).

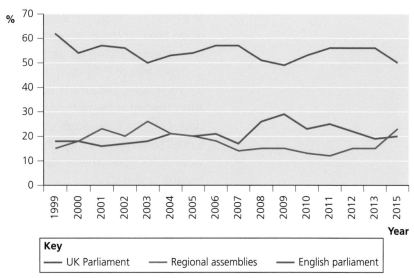

Source: British Social Attitudes surveys

Figure 4.3 Attitudes in England towards how England should be governed, 1999–2015

'English votes for English laws' at Westminster

MPs no longer make law on matters that have been devolved to the Scottish Parliament, Welsh Assembly and Northern Ireland Assembly. This raises questions about the role of MPs from the different parts of the UK. The **West Lothian Question** asks why MPs representing Scottish constituencies at Westminster should be permitted to vote on purely English matters (e.g. local government in England) when English MPs have no say over matters devolved to the Scottish Parliament. The question is named after Tam Dalyell, then Labour MP for West Lothian, who raised it during debates on devolution in the 1970s.

There have been relatively few cases in which legislation on English issues would not have come into force without the support of MPs representing Scottish constituencies. Two of these arose in 2003–04, when legislation on foundation hospitals and university tuition fees in England would not have passed without the votes of Labour MPs from Scotland. These MPs argued that the bills included clauses relating to Scotland and that changes to public spending in England would affect spending in Scotland.

The Conservatives, whose MPs predominantly represent English constituencies, have argued for 'English votes for English laws' (EVEL) since devolution. This would introduce special procedures in the House of Commons for dealing with legislation that affects only England. The Conservative–Liberal Democrat coalition established the McKay Commission to examine the issue. In 2013, it recommended that

Key term

West Lothian Question Why should Scottish MPs be able to vote on English matters at Westminster when English MPs cannot vote on matters devolved to the Scottish Parliament?

parliamentary procedures be adapted so that a majority of English MPs is needed to pass legislation which affects only England. After the Scottish independence referendum, David Cameron stated that further devolution in Scotland must be accompanied by EVEL.

In October 2015, MPs voted to amend the Standing Orders of the House of Commons to introduce EVEL. The new procedures provide a 'double veto'. Bills certified by the speaker as England-only are considered in a Legislative Grand Committee — an additional stage of the legislative process — where MPs representing English constituencies can veto them, or parts of them. But these bills still require majority support in the House of Commons, and MPs from Scotland, Wales and Northern Ireland can vote on (and thus block) them at the third reading. The new procedures were used for the first time in January 2016 for parts of the Housing and Planning Bill.

Opponents of EVEL claim that determining the territorial extent of bills will be problematic, particularly as decisions on public spending in England may affect funding in the rest of the UK. They also argue that it creates different classes of MPs. EVEL would also make it more difficult for a government with a small parliamentary majority to deliver its manifesto commitments. Only six of 19 UK governments elected since 1945 have had enough MPs from England to give them an overall parliamentary majority.

Elected regional assemblies

The Blair governments planned to create directly elected regional assemblies with limited executive functions in the eight English regions outside London. But these plans were dropped when 78% of voters voted 'no' in a 2004 referendum on whether there should be an assembly in northeast England. Arguments in favour of devolution to the English regions include:

- It would bring decision making closer to the people and address the differing interests of the English regions.
- It would create a more balanced devolution settlement within the UK because England is too large to have its own parliament.
- It would enhance democracy as regional assemblies would take over the functions of unelected **quangos**.
- Areas such as Cornwall, Yorkshire and the northeast have a strong sense of regional identity.
- Regional assemblies could act as a catalyst for economic and cultural regeneration.

Arguments against the creation of regional assemblies include:

- Few areas of England have a strong sense of regional identity.
- It would break up England and fail to provide expression for English interests and identity.
- There would be tensions between regional and local government.
- Regional assemblies would be dominated by urban rather than rural interests.
- There is little public support for creating a regional layer of government in England.

Labour and the Conservatives now support executive devolution, in which some functions (e.g. control of funding and limited rights of policy initiative) are transferred to city regions or combined authorities. But these bodies do not have law-making powers and, while there may be directly elected mayors, there are no elected assemblies.

Key term

Quango A quasi-autonomous non-governmental organisation; an unelected public body responsible for the funding or regulation of an area of public policy.

Local government in England

Local authorities are the lowest level of government in the UK and in England are the only elected branch of government below central government. In 2017, the structure of local government in England was:

- 55 unitary authorities, responsible for a full range of local services
- 27 county councils, responsible for some local services (e.g. education, social services, policing and transport) in the shires
- 201 district councils, responsible for some local services (e.g. housing, leisure and refuse collection) in the shires
- 36 metropolitan borough councils, responsible for a full range of local services in urban areas

In London, the Greater London Authority has strategic responsibility for economic development, transport, planning and policing. It consists of a directly elected mayor and a 25-member London Assembly. The mayor sets the budget and determines policy for the authority. The main mayoral initiative was the congestion charge, introduced in 2003.

Sadiq Khan attends his first mayor's question time at City Hall, the headquarters of the Greater London Authority, on 25 May 2016 in London

Despite encouragement by central government, only 16 local authorities outside London had directly elected mayors in 2016. Six more took office in the combined authorities in 2017.

Local authorities are responsible for many services used by citizens on a day-to-day basis, including:

- education (e.g. some schools)
- social services (e.g. residential care and care in the community)
- housing (e.g. public housing)
- roads (e.g. maintenance and regulation of smaller roads) and public transport (e.g. bus services)
- planning (e.g. decisions on planning applications)
- environmental health (e.g. refuse collection and recycling)
- leisure services (e.g. libraries and leisure centres)

Rather than providing these services directly, local authorities now organise, regulate and fund their provision by bodies such as housing associations, health trusts, academy schools and private companies.

Combined authorities, which consist of adjoining local councils, have been granted additional funding and policy-making powers on issues such as transport, health, economic development and policing. But they do not have law-making powers. The Greater Manchester combined authority was created in 2011 and a further eight authorities were in place by 2017.

Local authorities receive most of their funding in the form of grants from central government. The council tax, a local tax on domestic properties, is the main way in which local authorities can themselves raise revenue.

The impact of devolution on UK politics

Synoptic links

The constitution

Devolution has been one of the most significant of the reforms to the UK constitution over the last two decades. However, critics argue that both devolution and constitutional reform have been pursued in an ad hoc fashion without due regard for the bigger picture. Chapter 3 examines these issues in more detail.

Key terms

Federal state A federal state (normally) sees sovereignty divided between two tiers of government. Power is shared between national government (the federal government) and regional government (the states). Regional government is protected by the constitution — it cannot be abolished or reformed significantly against its will.

Quasi-federal A quasi-federal state is one in which the central government of a unitary state devolves some of its powers to subnational governments. It has some of the features of a unitary state and some of a federal state. Legally, there is a supreme legal authority located at the centre, as in a unitary state. But in practice, the centre no longer makes domestic policy for some parts of the state and it would find it difficult politically to abolish the subnational tier of government.

Devolution has had a significant impact on the UK political system. It has created a new relationship between the nations of the UK, providing institutional recognition of the distinctiveness of these nations while also reflecting their membership of the Union. The post-devolution UK no longer fits the criteria of a highly centralised unitary state, but nor is it a **federal state** with power constitutionally divided between autonomous institutions. Some commentators argue that creating a federal state would address the anomalies created by devolution (see the debate).

A quasi-federal UK

Professor Vernon Bogdanor characterises the UK as a **quasi-federal** state that has some federal characteristics but retains some of the features of a unitary state. When William Gladstone tried (and failed) to recognise the multinational character of the UK by devolving power to a legislative assembly in Ireland in the late nineteenth century, constitutional theorist A. V. Dicey argued that there could be no halfway house between parliamentary sovereignty and separatism. A century later, Labour's devolution settlement took the UK into this middle ground. The main features of quasi-federalism are:

- **Limited parliamentary sovereignty.** In legal terms, Westminster remains sovereign because it can overrule or abolish the devolved bodies. In practice, however, Westminster is no longer sovereign over domestic matters in Scotland, Wales and Northern Ireland — it does not have unlimited power. Westminster has accepted that it will not impose legislation in devolved areas. The Scotland Act 2016 established in statute that Westminster cannot legislate in devolved areas without consent, and recognised that the devolved institutions are permanent features of the UK's constitutional landscape. It further constrains parliamentary sovereignty by stating that devolution can only be overturned by a referendum (i.e. through popular sovereignty).
- **Quasi-federal parliament.** Westminster operates as an English parliament in the sense that it makes domestic law in England but is a federal parliament for Scotland, Wales and Northern Ireland because it retains reserved powers on major UK-wide matters. MPs from Scotland, Wales and Northern Ireland have few constituency responsibilities and deal mainly with economic and foreign affairs issues in the House of Commons.

- **Joint Ministerial Committee.** UK ministers and their counterparts from the devolved administrations meet here to consider non-devolved matters which impinge on devolved issues (e.g. Brexit) and resolve disputes. The UK government is the lead player.
- **Supreme Court.** The UK Supreme Court resolves disputes over competences by determining if the devolved bodies have acted within their powers.

Debate

Should the UK become a federal state?

Yes

- The creation of a federal state would provide a coherent constitutional settlement for the UK and its nations, establishing a clearer relationship between the UK government and the governments of England, Scotland, Wales and Northern Ireland.
- Establishing a federal state would resolve some of the anomalies (e.g. the West Lothian Question) that have arisen under the current ad hoc approach to devolution.
- Creating an English parliament and government as part of a federal UK would answer the English Question.
- The status of the Westminster Parliament would be clarified: it would be a federal parliament dealing with issues such as border control, defence and foreign affairs.
- The House of Lords could be reformed, to become a chamber representing the component nations of the UK, or abolished.

No

- Federalism works best in states in which there is not a dominant nation or region (e.g. the USA or Germany) — it is unsuitable for the UK where England makes up four-fifths of the population.
- An English parliament would rival the Westminster Parliament, particularly if different parties were in government in England and the UK, and English MPs could still be a majority at Westminster.
- Measures to reduce the dominance of England, such as the creation of elected assemblies in the English regions, would be problematic and unpopular.
- Disputes over funding occur in federal states: creating a federal UK would not automatically resolve difficult issues such as equity of funding and welfare provision.
- There is little public appetite for a federal UK, with devolution being the preferred constitutional position for voters in Scotland, Wales and Northern Ireland.

Policy divergence

The devolved institutions of Scotland, Wales and Northern Ireland have introduced policies which differ from those pursued by the UK government for England. Policy divergence was evident in health and education before devolution and has become more pronounced since (see Table 4.2). The Scottish Parliament's new powers on tax and spending raise the prospect of further divergence within the UK welfare state.

Policy differences may be regarded as positive because the devolved institutions have responded to the concerns of their electorate. Policies such as the ban on smoking in public places in Scotland and charges for using plastic shopping bags in Wales were taken up subsequently by other governments. However, divergence may also undermine the principle of equal rights for UK citizens. Northern Ireland is the only part of the UK where same-sex marriage remains illegal.

Activity

Using news sites and the websites of the devolved institutions, find examples of debates over policy divergence in health and education. Is divergence generally regarded as a good or a bad thing?

Table 4.2 Examples of policy divergence in health and education, 2016

England	Scotland	Wales	Northern Ireland
Prescription charges (£8.40 in 2016)	Prescription charges abolished (2011)	Prescription charges abolished (2007)	Prescription charges abolished (2010)
NHS internal market; major restructuring in 2013 applies only to NHS England	Restructuring of NHS; NHS internal market abolished	Restructuring of NHS; NHS internal market abolished	Restructuring of NHS; limited NHS internal market
Plan to cap costs of personal care for the elderly	Free long-term personal care for the elderly	Costs of personal care for the elderly are capped	Most care in the home is free for those aged over 75
Tuition fees	No tuition fees for Scottish students at Scottish universities	Tuition fees grant for students from Wales studying in Wales or the rest of the UK	Lower tuition fees for Northern Irish universities
School league tables	School league tables abolished (2003)	School league tables abolished (2001)	School league tables abolished (2001)
National curriculum tests (SATs) for primary school pupils	National school tests abolished (2003); new primary school tests from 2017	SATs replaced by new national tests for children aged 7 to 14	No national tests

Funding

The devolved administrations are funded by block grants from the UK Treasury, the size of which is settled by the Barnett formula. Agreed in 1978, the formula translates changes in public spending in England into equivalent changes in the block grants for Scotland, Wales and Northern Ireland, calculated on the basis of relative population. As a result, Scotland, Wales and Northern Ireland receive more public spending per head of population than England. For 2012/13, if the UK level was taken as 100, then government funding for England was 97, for Wales 111, for Scotland 116, and for Northern Ireland 124. In 2016, the block grant for Scotland was £28 million, for Wales £14 million and for Northern Ireland £10 million.

Critics claim that this amounts to an English subsidy of the rest of the UK. However, Scotland and Wales have seen their share of public spending squeezed. The Barnett formula does not take account of relative needs (e.g. the health, living standards and age of the population in each nation). The formula is not set out in statute law but the UK government remains committed to it and has been reluctant to undertake major revisions in how the block grants are calculated.

Britishness

Britishness is an umbrella identity that provides a common bond between the peoples of the UK while maintaining their distinctive national (i.e. English, Welsh, Scottish and Northern Irish) identities. British identity has been built around symbols of the British state, such as the monarchy, parliament and the National Health Service.

The number of people describing themselves as primarily Scottish, Welsh or English increased during the first decade of devolution and then tended to stabilise (see Table 4.3). Those with strong English identities are more likely to support an English parliament and EVEL, and those with strong Scottish identities are more likely to favour independence.

Table 4.3 National identity in England, Scotland and Wales

Identity	1997	2003	2012
England			
English not British	7	17	17
More English than British	17	19	12
Equally English and British	45	31	44
More British than English	14	13	8
British not English	9	10	10
Scotland			
Scottish not British	23	31	23
More Scottish than British	38	34	30
Equally Scottish and British	27	22	30
More British than Scottish	4	4	5
British not Scottish	4	4	6
Wales			
Welsh not British	17	21	21
More Welsh than British	26	27	17
Equally Welsh and British	34	29	35
More British than Welsh	10	8	8
British not Welsh	12	9	17

Sources: England and Scotland: British Social Attitudes surveys; Wales: Curtice, J. (2013) 'Future identities: Changing identities in the UK — the next 10 years', Government Office for Science

What next?

Two decades on from the creation of the devolved institutions, the end point of the devolution process is uncertain. Devolution was designed to safeguard the Union and weaken Scottish nationalism. But the Union looks more fragile than it did 20 years ago (see the debate). The Scottish independence referendum showed that supporters of the Union have not developed a renewed vision for political, economic, social and cultural Union.

Debate

Has devolution undermined the Union?

Yes

- The piecemeal approach to devolution has meant that problems (e.g. the West Lothian Question) have not been addressed effectively.
- Insufficient attention has been paid to the purpose and benefits of the Union and Britishness in the post-devolution UK.
- The rules of the game on policy coordination and dispute resolution are not clear enough.
- Policy divergence has undermined the idea of common welfare rights in the UK.
- The SNP has become the dominant political party in Scotland and support for Scottish independence has increased.
- There is some unease in England about the perceived unfairness of the devolution settlement.

No

- Devolution has answered Scottish, Welsh and Northern Irish demands for greater autonomy, bringing decision making closer to the people.
- Devolution has proceeded relatively smoothly, without major disputes between the UK government and the devolved bodies.
- Policy divergence reflects the different interests of the nations of the UK and has allowed initiatives that have been successful in one nation to be copied.
- Most people in the UK still feel British to some degree, and devolution is the preferred constitutional position for voters in Scotland, Wales and Northern Ireland.
- Devolution has delivered peace and power sharing in Northern Ireland after 30 years of violence and instability.

Synoptic links

The European Union

Relations with the EU are a reserved matter but many policy areas in which the EU, has competence (e.g. agriculture and the environment) are devolved. The devolved institutions are consulted on UK policy in the EU, but once the UK's negotiating position has been settled, the devolved institutions are bound by it. The EU is examined in more detail in Chapter 8.

Pragmatic adaptation has characterised the development of the post-devolution UK. But this has seen devolution develop in piecemeal rather than coherent fashion and left important problems unresolved. EVEL is the latest attempt to address the status of England but lacks cross-party support. The Barnett formula survives uneasily in the absence of agreed alternatives.

The 2016 referendum vote to leave the EU creates new issues. A majority of voters in Scotland and Northern Ireland voted to remain in the EU, while England and Wales supported Brexit. Nicola Sturgeon, the leader of the SNP, argues that Scotland should not be forced out of the EU against its will, and has called for a second referendum on Scottish independence. The devolved institutions claim that the UK government requires their consent and they will seek to influence its decisions on Brexit.

What you should know

- The UK was a highly centralised state for most of the twentieth century. Territorial ministries provided some recognition at the centre for the distinctive interests of Scotland and Wales, but between 1922 and 1972 Northern Ireland was the only part of the UK to have its own assembly.
- Powers were transferred from Westminster to the Scottish Parliament, Welsh Assembly and Northern Ireland Assembly in 1999. Devolution is asymmetric: the devolved institutions have different powers and institutional arrangements.
- Devolution is also an ongoing process, with additional powers transferred to the devolved bodies since 1999. The 2014 referendum rejected Scottish independence but did not resolve the issue of Scotland's constitutional status.
- Devolution has raised questions about the government of England which have yet to be answered fully. Each of the proposed solutions — an English parliament, EVEL and English regional assemblies — is problematic.

UK/US comparison

Federalism in the USA

- The USA is a federal state in which law-making power is divided between two tiers of government: the federal government (located in Washington, DC) and the governments of the 50 states of the USA. The UK is a unitary state, but since devolution it has taken on quasi-federal features.
- The two tiers of government in the USA are protected by the constitution. Their powers are inalienable. One tier of government cannot abolish the other. The division of powers can only be altered by amendment to the constitution, which requires special procedures. In the UK, Westminster retains parliamentary sovereignty. In practice, parliament has recognised that it no longer has authority over devolved policies.
- Powers reserved to the US federal government include defence, foreign policy, the US currency and the US single market. Relatively few powers are reserved exclusively to the states (e.g. local taxes), but power is shared between the federal and state governments in many areas (e.g. criminal and civil law, health and education). Westminster has reserved powers over issues such as defence, foreign policy, the constitution and the UK currency.
- There is significant policy divergence between the 50 states of the USA (e.g. on the death penalty and drug laws). Devolution has produced limited policy divergence between the nations of the UK.
- The US Supreme Court makes binding judgments where disputes arise about the distribution of powers between federal and state governments. The UK Supreme Court pronounces on whether the devolved bodies have acted within their powers, but it cannot strike down legislation.

Further reading

Bogdanor, V. (2010) 'Sovereignty and devolution: quasi-federalism?', *Politics Review*, Vol. 19, No. 3, pp. 12–15.

Bradbury, J. (2017) 'Devolution in the UK: has it been a success?, *Politics Review*, Vol. 26, No. 4, pp. 8–11.

Curtice, J. (2014) 'The Scottish independence referendum: the result analysed', *Politics Review*, Vol. 24, No. 2, pp. 2–5.

Mitchell, J. (2016) 'The 2016 Holyrood elections: governing competence and the constitution', *Politics Review*, Vol. 26, No. 1, pp. 18–20.

Centre on Constitutional Change: www.centreonconstitutionalchange.ac.uk

The Constitution Unit: www.ucl.ac.uk/constitution-unit

Devolution Matters: https://devolutionmatters.wordpress.com

What Scotland Thinks: http://whatscotlandthinks.org

Exam-style questions

Short-answer questions

1 Explain, with examples, the West Lothian Question.

2 Explain, with examples, the powers of the Scottish Parliament.

3 Explain and analyse three limitations on the powers of the Scottish Parliament.

4 Explain and analyse three consequences of devolution since 1997.

Mid-length questions

1 Describe the main features of English Votes for English Laws.

2 Describe the main features of the Good Friday Agreement.

3 Analyse and evaluate the arguments in favour of an English parliament.

4 Analyse and evaluate the consequences of devolution for the UK political system.

Essay questions

1 Evaluate the view that greater devolution is required across the UK political system.

2 Evaluate the extent to which devolution has improved representative democracy in the UK.

3 'Devolution will inevitably lead to the breakup of the United Kingdom.' Analyse and evaluate this statement.

4 'Devolution has greatly improved democracy and representation across the UK.' How far do you agree with this statement?

In your answer you must:

- Refer to regional devolution and city-based devolution.

- Draw on relevant knowledge and understanding of UK politics.

Chapter 5

Parliament

> ## Key questions answered
> - How are the House of Commons and the House of Lords structured and what roles do they play in parliament?
> - What are the comparative powers of the Commons and the Lords?
> - What are the main functions of parliament?
> - How effective is parliament in performing these functions?
> - How does parliament interact with the executive?

The UK has a system of parliamentary government in which government takes place through Parliament. The House of Commons debate on air strikes on Syria on 2 December 2015 illustrated the centrality of parliament to British politics. Parliament was the arena for debate on an issue that stirred opinion across the nation, and it took the crucial decision to launch air strikes against Islamic State (IS) in Syria. During a 10-hour debate, the prime minister, leader of the opposition and MPs from across the political spectrum made eloquent and impassioned speeches setting out the case both for and against extending the RAF campaign. In 2013, the Commons had voted against air strikes in Syria. Given the emerging convention that the prime minister should not commit troops overseas without the approval of parliament, David Cameron accepted the verdict of the House. But in 2015, with civil war in Syria escalating and IS staging terrorist attacks in Europe, MPs voted by 397 to 223 in favour of military action. Within hours, the RAF bombed IS positions in Syria — and opponents of the bombing demonstrated against the decision of the Commons.

Protestors gather in Parliament Square during the House of Commons debate on air strikes on Syria, 2 December 2015

The UK has a bicameral **legislature** — that is, a **parliament** with two chambers:

- the **House of Commons**, which is the lower chamber
- the **House of Lords**, which is the upper chamber

In addition, the monarch retains a formal and ceremonial role in parliament (see the case study).

In focus

Bicameralism

This term describes a political system in which there are two chambers in the legislature. The lower house is usually elected in a general election and tends to be the dominant chamber. The composition of the upper house varies: it may be directly elected or indirectly elected (e.g. appointed by ministers), or be a hybrid of both.

Bicameralism has a number of benefits: the upper house provides checks and balances, provides for greater scrutiny and revision of legislation, and may represent different interests (e.g. states in a federal system). Problems may also arise: there may be institutional conflict between the two houses which produces legislative gridlock, and an indirectly elected upper house may frustrate the will of the democratically elected lower house.

The House of Commons: structure and members

The House of Commons is a democratically elected chamber of 650 Members of Parliament (MPs). Each MP is elected in a single-member constituency by the first-past-the-post (FPTP) electoral system. The number of MPs is not fixed and can change following reviews of parliamentary constituencies. In 2016, the Conservative government confirmed its commitment to cut the number of MPs to 600 and equalise constituency size by 2020.

In the Commons chamber, the governing party (or parties) sits on the benches to the right of the speaker's chair and members of opposition parties sit on the benches to its left. More than 100 MPs hold ministerial positions in the government. The main opposition party appoints 'shadow ministers'. Ministers and shadow ministers are known as **frontbenchers** because they occupy the benches closest to the floor of the chamber. Most MPs have no ministerial or shadow ministerial posts and are known as **backbenchers**.

Almost all MPs represent a political party but there are exceptions. Sylvia Hermon, once an Ulster Unionist MP, was re-elected as an independent in North Down in 2010 and 2015. Richard Taylor, a campaigner against the closure of a local hospital, was elected in Wyre Forest in 2001 and 2005. Former BBC journalist Martin Bell defeated Neil Hamilton, who had been accused of accepting 'cash for questions', in Tatton in 1997.

MPs gather in the House of Commons

Activity

Identify the MP for your constituency and find key biographical details. Were they born or did they grow up in the area? What was their occupation before they entered parliament? When were they first elected? Have they held ministerial office?

Pay and privilege

MPs are paid a salary. This was almost £75,000 in 2016. Increases are set by the Independent Parliamentary Salaries Authority which also regulates and pays MPs' parliamentary expenses. These cover the costs of running an office and employing staff, plus accommodation in and travel to London. The system was overhauled after the 2009 MPs' expenses scandal which resulted in hundreds of MPs having to pay back expenses they had claimed, and four of them being jailed.

MPs who faced criminal charges over their expenses unsuccessfully claimed that they should not face prosecution because of **parliamentary privilege**. This is the legal immunity enjoyed by members of the House of Commons and House of Lords. It ensures that they can carry out their parliamentary duties without interference. The two most important elements of parliamentary privilege are:

- **Freedom of speech.** Members of both houses are free to raise any issue in parliament without fear of prosecution. MPs have, for example, revealed information subject to court injunctions (e.g. the identity of celebrities who have been granted an injunction to remain anonymous).

Key term

Parliamentary privilege The legal immunity enjoyed by members of parliament, particularly their right to free speech in parliament.

■ **Exclusive cognisance.** This is the right of each house to regulate its own internal affairs without interference from outside bodies (e.g. the courts).

As the expenses scandal showed, parliamentary privilege does not mean that MPs are above the law. MPs who are imprisoned, or suspended from the House for at least 21 sitting days, may be dismissed by voters under the Recall of MPs Act 2015. If, after 8 weeks, 10% of eligible electors have signed the recall petition, their seat is declared vacant and a by-election scheduled. The MP subject to recall can stand in this by-election. There is no right of recall in cases where an MP defects to another party or where constituents disapprove of their voting record.

Key office holders

Whips

The party system in the House of Commons has traditionally been strong. Parties appoint a number of MPs to act as **whips**. They have three main roles:

■ Ensuring that MPs attend parliamentary **divisions** (votes), and approving the absence of MPs when their vote will not be required.
■ Issuing instructions on how MPs should vote. Each week, MPs receive instructions on their attendance — also known as a **whip**. Debates where there will be a vote are underlined. A 'three-line whip' is a strict instruction to attend and vote according to the party line, or face disciplinary action. It is issued on the most important divisions.
■ Enforcing discipline within the parliamentary party. The whips seek to persuade wavering MPs to vote with their party by providing assurances, making offers and issuing threats. Rebellious MPs may be expelled from the parliamentary party by having the whip withdrawn (but may retain their parliamentary seat as an independent MP).

The speaker

The speaker of the House of Commons presides over debates in the chamber, selecting MPs to speak and maintaining order. He or she may temporarily suspend MPs who break parliamentary rules. The speaker is elected by MPs in a secret ballot. He or she must stand down from the post at a general election but is normally re-elected at the start of the next parliament. Once chosen, the speaker gives up their party affiliation and is non-partisan. The speaker does not vote unless there is a tie, in which case he or she has the casting vote — but uses it to provide further debate rather than a final decision.

The speaker has occasionally been embroiled in controversy. Michael Martin became the first speaker to be forced from office in 174 years when he resigned in 2009. Martin was criticised for his handling of the MPs' expenses scandal and was viewed as an obstacle to reform. He stepped down before a motion of no confidence could be heard. John Bercow has been a reforming speaker (see the case study) but his approach has irritated some MPs.

> **Key term**
>
> **Division** A vote in parliament.
> **Whip** (a) A party official responsible for ensuring that MPs turn up to parliamentary votes and follow party instructions on how to vote. (b) An instruction to vote that is issued to MPs by political parties.

Case study

Speaker John Bercow

John Bercow was elected as speaker in 2009 following Michael Martin's resignation. He won despite having limited support among his fellow Conservative MPs. Bercow has been a reforming speaker who has sought to enhance parliamentary scrutiny of the executive and champion backbench MPs. Concerned that ministers were making fewer statements to the Commons, Bercow has granted more 'urgent questions'. If a request from a frontbench or backbench MP for an urgent question is granted, a minister must make a statement to the Commons and answer questions that day.

In 2015–16, the speaker granted 77 requests for urgent questions. Bercow has also called more backbench MPs to speak in debates, and supported measures to increase the number of women MPs.

On the final day of the 2010–15 parliament, the government tabled a motion requiring the speaker to be subject to a secret ballot at the start of the next parliament. Although many Conservatives were unhappy with Bercow's manner, the motion was defeated. Bercow was then re-elected unopposed after the 2015 general election.

Questions

- How successful has Bercow been in enhancing parliamentary scrutiny of the executive?
- How important is the speaker to the functioning of the Commons?

The House of Lords: structure and members

The House of Lords is an unelected chamber and is subordinate to the House of Commons. Members, known as **peers**, do not receive a salary but can claim a daily attendance allowance. The house is chaired by the Lord Speaker, who is elected by peers and is politically neutral. Lord Fowler, a former Conservative cabinet minister, became Lord Speaker in 2016.

The House of Lords has different categories of members:

- **hereditary peers**
- **life peers**
- Lords Spiritual — two archbishops and 24 senior bishops of the Church of England

The first two categories will be examined in more detail.

Hereditary peers

The House of Lords Act 1999 ended the right of all but 92 hereditary peers to sit and vote in the Lords. Before it came into force, the House of Lords had more than 750 hereditary peers who had inherited their title and a place in the upper house. The Peerages Act 1963 allowed hereditary peers to renounce their titles and membership of the Lords. It enabled Alec Douglas-Home, the 14th Earl of Home, to leave the Lords and win a by-election to the House of Commons when he became Conservative Party leader and prime minister in 1963. The Act also allowed women hereditary peers to sit in the Lords.

The House of Lords Act 1999 transformed the hereditary element of the Lords into a new category of 'elected hereditary peers'. The 15 hereditary peers who became deputy speakers were chosen in a ballot of the whole house. Two others hold royal appointments. The remaining 75 were elected by ballots of hereditary peers from their party and crossbench groups. When an elected hereditary peer dies or resigns, a

The House of Lords in session

by-election is held in which peers from the same group as the former member choose a replacement from the register of hereditary peers. Thirty by-elections had been held by August 2016.

Life peers

The Life Peerages Act 1958 gave the prime minister the right to appoint members to the upper house for life. Their title and right to sit in the Lords cannot be inherited. Since the removal of most hereditary peers, life peers are the largest category of members of the upper house, numbering 695 in November 2016 (see Table 5.1). The independent House of Lords Appointments Commission recommends individuals for appointment as non-party peers, and vets those nominated by political parties.

Table 5.1 The House of Lords by party, 1999 and 2017

Party	October 1999			May 2017		
	Life peers	Hereditary	Total	Life peers	Hereditary	Total
Conservative	172	299	471	204	49	253
Labour	160	19	179	197	4	201
Liberal Democrats	49	23	72	98	4	102
Crossbench	128	225	353	143	32	175
Bishops	0	0	26	0	0	26
Other	32	80	112	37	1	39
Total	**581***	**759***	**1366***	**679**	**90**	**796**

* 'Total' for October 1999 includes 113 hereditary peers and 40 life peers on leave of absence.

Source: www.parliament.uk

Contains public sector information licensed under the Open Government Licence v3.0.

The Life Peerages Act 1958 and the House of Lords Act 1999 brought about significant changes to the composition and working of the House of Lords. The creation of life peers increased the diversity and professionalism. Life peers include former MPs (some 20% of members of the Lords), and leading figures from business, education and the arts. Life peers also play a more active role in the Lords.

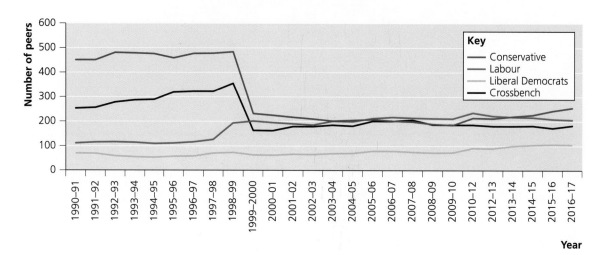

Source: www.parliament.uk

Contains public sector information licensed under the Open Government Licence v3.0.

Figure 5.1 Party strength in the House of Lords, 1990–2017

Prior to 1999, many hereditary peers took the Conservative whip. Their removal ended the Conservative Party's historical predominance in the upper house (see Figure 5.1). No party now has a majority in the Lords (see Table 5.1). Crossbench members of the upper house have no formal party allegiance. Prime ministers use their power to nominate life peers to alter the party balance within the Lords. The removal of hereditary peers also increased the proportion of women in the Lords. In May 2017, there were 207 women peers — making up 26% of the house compared to 9% before 1999.

The House of Lords Reform Act 2014 allowed peers to resign voluntarily and further legislation in 2015 allowed members convicted of serious criminal offences to be expelled or suspended. Nonetheless, the size of the Lords has grown with more than 650 life peerages created between 1997 and 2016. The Lords is the world's second largest legislative chamber (after the Chinese National People's Congress) and its size risks damaging its reputation and ability to function.

The removal of most hereditary peers was intended to be the first step towards wider reform of the Lords but reform has stalled as MPs and peers have been unable to agree on whether a reformed upper chamber should be wholly appointed, partially elected or wholly elected (see the case study). There have been disagreements about the impact of an elected House of Lords on the primacy of the House of Commons (see below), and on details such as when and how elections would be held, and the future of the Lords Spiritual (bishops).

Reform of the House of Lords

A number of proposals for major reform of House of Lords have been introduced since 1999. All have failed. They include:

- **Free vote, 2003.** MPs had a free vote on seven options proposed by a parliamentary joint committee. None secured majority support. Peers voted for a wholly appointed House.
- **White Paper, 2007.** This proposed a hybrid House: 50% appointed and 50% elected. A series of votes on reform options were held. A wholly elected House was approved by MPs, as was the 80% elected option. But some who backed the former were trying to wreck the process. The Lords supported a wholly appointed House.
- **House of Lords Bill, 2012.** This proposed a chamber of 360 elected members, 90 appointed members, 12 bishops and 8 'ministerial members'. MPs approved the second reading of the bill but 91 Conservative MPs rebelled and Labour indicated that it would vote against a 'programme motion' and thus prevent timely passage of the bill. The government abandoned the bill.

Questions
- Why did these reform proposals fail?
- What reforms to the House of Lords are the main political parties now proposing?

Comparative powers of the Commons and the Lords

The House of Commons has been the dominant chamber for over a century. It has a number of exclusive powers:

- **The right to insist on legislation.** In cases of conflict over legislation, the Lords should ultimately give way to the Commons.
- **Financial privilege.** The Lords cannot delay or amend money bills.
- **The power to dismiss the executive.** If the government is defeated on a motion of no confidence, it must resign.

The primacy of the Commons is underpinned in legislation, notably the Parliament Acts of 1911 and 1949, and in constitutional conventions. The main conventions covering the relationship between the two chambers are:

- **The Salisbury Doctrine.** Bills implementing manifesto commitments are not opposed by the Lords.
- **Reasonable time.** The Lords should consider government business within a reasonable time.
- **Secondary legislation.** The Lords does not usually object to secondary legislation.

Conventions do not have the force of law and, in order to operate smoothly, a shared understanding of their application is required. A parliamentary Joint Committee on Conventions (2006) supported the primacy of the Commons and the principles underpinning these conventions.

The Parliament Act

The House of Lords does not have a veto over legislation approved by the House of Commons. It can only delay most bills passed by the House of Commons for up to 1 year. Prior to 1911, it could block bills passed by the Commons indefinitely. The Parliament Act 1911 restricted this veto power to two parliamentary sessions (i.e. 2 years), which was subsequently reduced to 1 year by the Parliament Act 1949.

These measures transformed the Lords from a vetoing chamber into a revising chamber. The Lords can propose amendments to bills passed by the Commons. The Commons can then accept these amendments, reject them or introduce new amendments of its own. But the Lords cannot force the Commons to accept its amendments. If the Commons refuses to accept the wishes of the Lords, the upper house is faced with the choice of backing down or blocking the bill from becoming law for 1 year. If it chooses the latter, the bill can still be passed unchanged in the following session of parliament without the consent of the Lords, under the terms of the Parliament Act. This has happened with only four pieces of legislation:

- War Crimes Act 1991
- European Parliamentary Elections Act 1999
- Sexual Offences (Amendment) Act 2000
- Hunting Act 2004

Financial privilege

The House of Lords cannot delay or amend money bills (also known as 'supply bills'): that is, bills solely concerned with national taxation, loans or public money. The Parliament Act 1911 states that any bill certified by the speaker as a money bill which is not passed by the Lords unamended within 1 month can receive royal assent without the agreement of the Lords. Each year, an Appropriation Bill authorising government spending is passed by the Commons — for this bill the Lords stage is a purely formal one. Sections of the Finance Bill, which follows the chancellor of the exchequer's budget announcement, are not normally challenged in the Lords even though the bill is not usually designated as a money bill.

The Commons can also claim financial privilege when the Lords passes an amendment to legislation that has financial implications, such as creating new spending. The Conservative–Liberal Democrat coalition government invoked financial privilege during the final stages of the Welfare Reform Bill in 2012. The Lords backed down but some peers complained that ministers were abusing their powers. The Commons has also claimed financial privilege on issues ranging from counter-terrorism (2008) to identity cards (2010) and support for child refugees (2016).

Confidence and supply

The government requires the **confidence and supply** of the House of Commons to remain in office. Supply refers to the authorisation of government spending by the Commons. Traditionally, a government defeated on a key supply bill is expected to resign.

The Commons can remove the government by defeating it in a **motion of no confidence** (also known as a vote of confidence) or a **confidence motion**. The Lords does not vote on confidence motions. Before 2011, defeat in the Commons on such a motion or on the Queen's Speech would trigger the resignation of the government. There have been 23 votes of no confidence and 3 votes of confidence since 1945. The only government defeat on a motion of no confidence since 1924 occurred in March 1979, when James Callaghan's Labour government lost by one vote.

The Fixed-term Parliaments Act 2011 clarified and limited what is treated as a confidence motion. Only a Commons motion stating 'That this House has no confidence in Her Majesty's Government' is now treated as a motion of no confidence. If passed, and no alternative government is approved by the Commons within 14 days, parliament is dissolved and a general election called.

The Salisbury Convention

The **Salisbury convention** (sometimes known as the Salisbury-Addison convention) states that the House of Lords should not vote against a bill that seeks to enact a manifesto commitment of the governing party on second or third reading, nor should it agree 'wrecking amendments'. Its origins lie in the idea of the mandate developed by Conservative prime minister, Lord Salisbury, in the late nineteenth century — that general election victory gives the governing party the authority to implement the programme it presented to the electorate. The convention developed in the 1940s as an acceptance that the unelected Lords should not frustrate the will of the elected Commons.

A convention is not a law but relies on a prevailing political understanding that may change. The Salisbury convention has come under strain. In 2006, peers voted against an identity cards bill, despite it featuring in Labour's 2005 manifesto. They argued that Labour had not won sufficient support at the election to claim a democratic mandate, and that the convention was outdated as it related to a time when the upper house had an inbuilt Conservative majority. Application of the doctrine under the Conservative–Liberal Democrat coalition was questionable because the coalition agreement had not been put before voters. The Conservative minority government that took office in 2017 will struggle to claim that it has a democratic mandate to enact its manifesto commitments.

'Reasonable time' convention

The government needs to get its legislative proposals through parliament in a reasonable time. Whereas the government has significant control of the parliamentary timetable in the Commons, it does not have this in the Lords. The convention thus emerged that the Lords should consider all government business within a reasonable time. It should not deliberately overlook or delay consideration of government bills and should ensure that they are passed by the end of the session. Reform proposals have included a 60-day limit for consideration of government business by the Lords, although critics claim this would weaken parliamentary scrutiny.

Secondary legislation and the Lords

Parliament delegates to ministers the authority to issue secondary legislation which brings into force or amends part of an Act (see below). The Parliament Acts do not cover secondary legislation but it is a convention that the Lords does not usually reject it. The term 'usually' suggests that this is neither rigid nor universally accepted. In 2015, the Lords amended two regulations on tax credits. The government responded by establishing the Strathclyde review of the primacy of the Commons in this area. The review recommended that the Commons should be able to override any Lords vote to reject secondary legislation. But the May government announced that it had no plans to curb the power of the Lords.

A more assertive House of Lords

The House of Lords has become more assertive in the legislative process since the removal of most hereditary peers in 1999. It blocked the Sexual Offences (Amendment) Act 2000 and the Hunting Act 2004, forcing the government to employ the Parliament Act in the following session.

Government defeats in the Lords have also become more frequent (see Figure 5.2). The Blair and Brown governments were defeated only seven times in the House of Commons but more than 400 times in the House of Lords. Many of these defeats occurred on judicial and constitutional matters (including counter-terrorism and restrictions on the right to trial by jury), which are of particular interest to peers. The 2010–15 coalition government suffered 99 defeats in the Lords, notably on judicial matters and welfare reform. In 2015–16 alone, the Conservative government was defeated on 60 votes.

Four out of every ten defeats in the Lords (including legislation on religious hatred and time limits on anti-terrorism) were substantially accepted by the Blair and Brown governments. The coalition government dropped key provisions from the Public Bodies Bill 2010–12, including plans to privatise the Forestry Commission, after it ran into trouble in the Lords, and agreed to 1,257 of the 3,449 amendments made by the Lords in the 2014–15 session.

> ### Activity
>
> Find recent examples of government defeats in the House of Lords by consulting the Constitution Unit's running tally: www.tinyurl.com/7p9kgjk

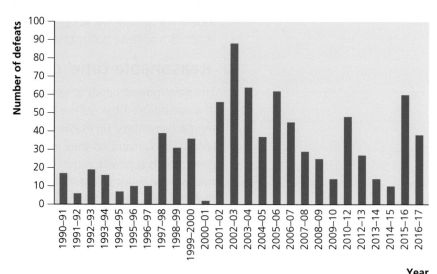

Figure 5.2 Government defeats in the House of Lords, 1990–2017

Source: www.parliament.uk

Contains public sector information licensed under the Open Government Licence v3.0.

The increased effectiveness of the House of Lords in checking the powers of the executive and forcing changes to legislative proposals has resulted from a number of factors:

- **Party balance.** No party has a majority in the House of Lords, so governments must win cross-party support for their legislation. The votes of Liberal Democrat peers often proved crucial under Labour (1999–2010) and the Conservatives (2015–): if they vote with the opposition, the government faces defeat. Crossbenchers were influential under the Conservative–Liberal Democrat coalition but are not a cohesive block. The government is most likely to give ground when its own peers rebel or abstain.

■ **Enhanced legitimacy.** The reformed Lords is more confident of its legitimacy and more willing to flex its muscles on legal and constitutional issues.

■ **Government mandate.** Peers have questioned whether the Salisbury Doctrine should apply in periods of coalition or when the governing party wins the support of less than a third of the electorate.

■ **Support from MPs.** The Lords has been most effective in forcing the government to amend its proposals when MPs, particularly backbenchers from the governing party, support their amendments.

Debates about relative powers

The relative powers of the two chambers reflect their different functions (such as the Commons' role in confidence and supply) and legitimacy. The Commons has primacy because it has the democratic legitimacy which the Lords lacks. However, it is helpful to consider two aspects of legitimacy:

■ Input legitimacy concerns the composition of an institution and its responsiveness to citizens' concerns as a result of participation by, and representation of, the people.

■ Output legitimacy concerns the quality and effectiveness of an institution's performance and outcomes for the people.

The Commons has input legitimacy because of its composition (it is directly elected and accountable to voters), whereas the Lords has output legitimacy because of what it delivers (its scrutiny and revision produce better quality legislation).

Reform of the House of Lords

The House of Lords Act 1999, and subsequent reform proposals, focused primarily on the composition of the Lords rather than its relationship with the Commons, but changes to its membership affect the legitimacy and powers of the Lords.

Supporters of a wholly or mainly elected upper house claim that only elections bring legitimacy and that an elected house would be better able to challenge executive power. If proportional representation were used, no single party would dominate and long, non-renewable terms in office would encourage members to be independent.

Those favouring an appointed house note that the Lords has a different role to the Commons. It is a revising chamber which has more time to scrutinise legislative proposals, while its members possess particular expertise and are not constrained by concerns about re-election. An elected upper house, critics argue, would produce competing claims of legitimacy, creating a rival to the Commons and bringing legislative gridlock. They say a wholly elected chamber would lose the independence of crossbenchers, and strengthen the role of parties.

Should the House of Lords be wholly elected?

Yes

- A fully elected House of Lords would have the legitimacy that can only be derived from democratic elections.
- It would be more confident in its work of scrutinising and amending government bills, thus improving the quality of legislation.
- If no party has a majority, as would be likely under proportional representation, it would challenge the dominance of the executive.
- If elected by proportional representation, it would be more representative of the electorate.

No

- It would come into conflict with the House of Commons, as both Houses would claim democratic legitimacy.
- Institutional conflict between two elected chambers with similar powers would produce legislative gridlock.
- An appointed house would retain the expertise and independence of crossbench peers.
- The problems associated with party control in the House of Commons would be duplicated in an elected upper house.

Activity

What should a reformed House of Lords look like? In answering this question, you should think about both its composition and its functions. How should the House of Lords be composed? Some options include:

- direct election of all members (How should they be elected?)
- direct election of a majority of members (What proportion?)
- members without party allegiance appointed by an independent body
- nominees of political parties that are represented in the House of Commons
- members appointed by virtue of the positions they hold (e.g. government ministers, representatives of the Church of England and other faiths)

Should the following functions of the upper house be reduced, maintained or developed?

- scrutiny of government legislation
- specialist investigation
- initiating legislation
- debating major issues
- holding the executive to account
- representation

Functions of parliament

Synoptic links

The Supreme Court

The House of Lords used to have a judicial role. The Law Lords — senior judges who sat in the Lords — acted as the UK's highest court of appeal. The Supreme Court took over this role in 2009. Its role and relationship with parliament are examined in Chapter 7.

Parliament performs a number of functions, the most significant being:

- legislation
- scrutiny and accountability
- debate
- recruitment of ministers
- representation

This section outlines the main parliamentary procedures for dealing with these functions, with a particular focus on the House of Commons given its status as the dominant chamber. It also assesses how effective parliament is in performing these roles.

Legislation

Parliament is the legislative branch, or legislature, of a political system. This indicates that parliament's main function is making law.

Synoptic links

Parliamentary sovereignty

The doctrine of parliamentary sovereignty is a core principle of the UK constitution. It states that no higher authority can overturn laws made by parliament. But it has come under pressure from a range of constitutional reforms, including devolution, referendums, the Human Rights Act (see Chapter 3), and the European Union (see Chapter 8).

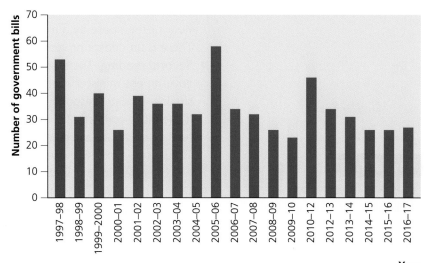

Source: www.parliament.uk

Contains public sector information licensed under the Open Government Licence v3.0.

Figure 5.3 Number of government bills introduced per session, 1997–2017

Key terms

Act of Parliament A law passed by parliament.

Bill A proposal for a new law, or change to a current law, that has yet to complete the parliamentary legislative process.

Green Paper A government document setting out various options for legislation and inviting comment.

Public bill A bill concerning a general issue of public policy, introduced by a government minister.

White Paper A government document setting out a detailed proposal for legislation.

The legislative process

A **bill** is a draft legislative proposal that is debated in parliament. When a bill has completed the legislative process and enters into law, it is known as an **Act of Parliament**. The most significant bills are **public bills**. These concern general issues of public policy. The government generally introduces between 25 and 35 public bills each session (see Figure 5.3).

The government sets out its legislative programme in the Queen's Speech at the beginning of a parliamentary session. For a minority government, the votes at the end of this debate may determine its chances of survival.

Pre-legislative scrutiny has increased in recent years. The government may produce a consultative **Green Paper** setting out options for legislation, and/or a **White Paper** explaining the objectives of government policy. Draft bills are also published and scrutinised by a select committee or joint committee. Seventy-five draft bills were published between 1997 and 2010, and 35 during the 2010–15 parliament. Committee recommendations may lead to redrafting of parts of a bill (as happened with the coalition government's bills on the recall of MPs) or influence debate. However, committees have limited time to consider the draft bill and the government can ignore their objections. The coalition government piloted a 'public reading stage' for three bills where members of the public could comment on proposed legislation online. The comments were collated for consideration by a public bill committee.

Legislation follows an established process of debate, scrutiny and amendment (see Figure 5.4). Most legislation originates in the House of Commons but some bills on non-controversial or complex matters of law are introduced in the House of Lords. The main stages in the legislative process for a bill introduced in the House of Commons (except a money bill) are as follows:

- **First reading.** The formal presentation of the title of the bill on the floor of the house by a minister from the responsible department. There is no debate or vote at this stage.
- **Second reading.** The main debate on the principle of the bill. The government minister explains and justifies the objectives of the bill, the shadow minister responds and backbenchers contribute to the debate. If the bill is contested, a vote is taken. Government defeats at second reading stage are extremely rare, occurring only twice since 1945. The last was in 1986 when the Sunday Trading Bill was defeated by 14 votes, despite a government majority of 140.
- **Committee stage.** Bills are sent to a **public bill committee** — known as a standing committee until 2006 — where detailed scrutiny of each clause takes place and amendments can be made. Amendments are often tabled by the government as it seeks to clarify or improve the bill. A new public bill committee is established for each bill and is named after it. Once the bill has completed this stage, the committee is dissolved. In the 2015–16 session, there were 22 public bill committees. Membership, which ranges from 16 to 50, reflects party strength in the Commons and the whips instruct MPs how to vote. Public bill committees may take evidence from outside experts. Finance bills and bills of constitutional significance (e.g. on the EU referendum) are scrutinised on the floor of the Commons, in a **Committee of the Whole House**.
- **Report stage.** Amendments made in committee are considered by the full House of Commons. It may accept, reject or alter them. MPs not on the public bill committee now have an opportunity to table amendments. John Major's Conservative government lost a report stage vote on the Maastricht Treaty in 1993, but made the issue a matter of confidence and won by 40 votes. In 2015, new procedures were introduced for bills concerned solely with English matters (see the case study).

Key terms

Committee of the Whole House A meeting held in the chamber in which the full House of Commons considers the committee stage of a public bill.

Public bill committee A committee responsible for the detailed consideration of a bill.

Case study

'English votes for English laws'

In 2015, additional legislative stages were added for bills certified as covering solely English matters. This is known as 'English votes for English laws' (EVEL). After report stage, these bills are sent to a Legislative Grand Committee in which all MPs can take part in debates, but only those representing English constituencies can vote or propose amendments. The committee can veto the bill or parts of it. If this happens, the bill is reconsidered by the whole house. Should the Legislative Grand Committee again withhold consent, the bill cannot progress any further. If it refuses to support parts of the bill, they are removed.

The new procedures provide a 'double veto'. MPs from English constituencies can veto bills or parts of bills by refusing to give their consent. But bills on English matters still require majority support in the Commons, and all MPs can vote in the other stages of the legislative process.

In the first year of the new procedure, nine bills were certified as requiring the EVEL. 14 votes were held but the results would not have differed had EVEL not applied. The government was defeated in 2016 on plans in the Enterprise Bill to relax Sunday trading laws in England and Wales. If SNP MPs had not voted against them, they would have been approved. But the clause had not been certified as requiring EVEL.

Questions
- What problems are 'English votes for English laws' intended to address?
- What additional problems might it create?

- **Third reading.** A debate on the amended bill on the floor of the House. No further amendments are permitted.
- **House of Lords stages.** The bill is sent to the House of Lords, where these stages are repeated. If amendments to the bill are made in the Lords, the Commons may agree to them, reject them or amend them further. A bill may go back and forth between the two houses in a process known as 'parliamentary ping-pong'. This happened between 2010 and 2012, when the Commons overturned a series of Lords' amendments on legal aid and welfare reform. If agreement cannot be reached, the government must decide whether to accept changes made by the Lords, drop the bill or invoke the Parliament Act.

Most public bills must pass all of these stages in one session of parliament, but the Commons may vote to carry over a bill and complete its progress in the next session.

In post-legislative scrutiny, government departments can submit memorandums on legislation to select committees between 3 and 5 years after a law came into force. The committee may conduct an inquiry into the Act.

Synoptic links

Parliament and devolution

The devolution of powers to the Scottish Parliament, Welsh Assembly and Northern Ireland Assembly brought about significant procedural changes in the Westminster Parliament. It no longer legislates on or debates devolved matters, and MPs cannot ask questions on them. 'English votes for English laws' is one answer to the West Lothian Question, which asks why MPs representing Scottish constituencies at Westminster should be permitted to vote on purely English matters (such as local government in England) when English MPs have no say over matters devolved to the Scottish Parliament. Devolution is examined in depth in Chapter 4.

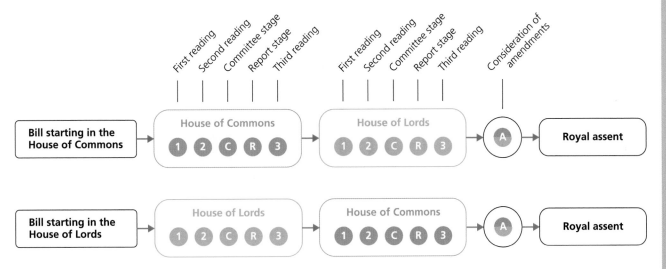

Source: www.parliament.uk

Contains public sector information licensed under the Open Government Licence v3.0.

Figure 5.4 The passage of a bill into law

Key term

Private members' bill A bill sponsored by a backbench MP.

Other bills

Legislative proposals initiated by backbench MPs rather than by government ministers are known as **private members' bills**. They can take one of three routes:

- **Ballot.** Early in each parliamentary session, 20 names of MPs who wish to introduce a bill are drawn in a ballot. These ballot bills are allocated time on 13 Fridays in the session but some fall victim to filibustering, where MPs talk until the bill runs out of time. Some MPs seek help from lobbyists when drawing up a bill. Others take a bill handed out by the government — these are legislative proposals which the government supports but does not wish to pursue in its parliamentary time.
- **Ten Minute Rule Bill.** MPs have 10 minutes to make a speech to introduce a bill, or to talk about an aspect of an existing piece of legislation. Few new bills get beyond this first hurdle, so many MPs use this route as a means of drawing attention to a particular issue.
- **Presentation.** An MP presents a bill on the floor of the house by introducing the name of the bill. There is no debate at this point.

A number of private members' bills become law in each session (see Figure 5.5). These tend to enjoy the support, or benevolent neutrality, of the government. Time constraints and the difficulty of persuading other MPs to back a proposal mean that most fall at an early stage. Two landmark laws to originate as private members' bills were the Murder (Abolition of Death Penalty) Act 1965 and the Abortion Act 1967. Both had government support. More recent examples include the Gangmasters (Licensing) Act 2004, which had government support following the deaths of 21 immigrant labourers at Morecambe Bay, and the House of Lords Reform Act 2014, which had cross-party support in both chambers.

Figure 5.5 Successful private members' bills, 1990–2017

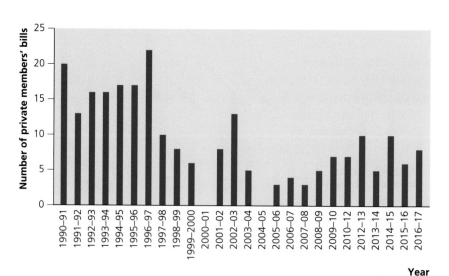

Year

Source: www.parliament.uk

Key term

Secondary legislation A law made by ministers, who have been granted this authority by an Act of Parliament, rather than made by parliament.

Secondary legislation

Acts of Parliament are primary legislation. The authority to issue **secondary legislation**, also known as delegated legislation, in specific policy areas is delegated by parliament to government ministers. Some 3,500 pieces of secondary legislation, known as statutory instruments, are issued each year on matters such as immigration, taxation and education. They are scrutinised by the statutory instruments committee.

Effectiveness of legislatures

In theory, the UK Parliament can make, amend or repeal any law it chooses but the situation is very different in practice. The government is responsible for most laws passed by parliament. Philip Norton, an academic expert on parliament and member of the House of Lords, developed a threefold classification of legislatures:

- **Policy-making legislatures.** These amend or reject legislative proposals made by the executive, and can put forward alternative bills.
- **Policy-influencing legislatures.** These can modify or reject legislative proposals from the executive but are unable to develop extensive legislative proposals of their own.
- **Legislatures with little or no policy influence.** These are unable to modify or veto legislative proposals from the executive, and cannot formulate meaningful alternative policy proposals of their own.

The UK Parliament is a policy-influencing legislature. Law making occurs through, not by, parliament. It has only modest influence over policy and reacts to government proposals rather than taking the lead in formulating policy. Parliament can vote against government bills and pass amendments. But parliament's effectiveness in making and scrutinising law is limited by the dominance of the executive. This is evidenced by:

- **Government bills.** Most bills originate from the government. Private members' bills have little chance of success without government backing.
- **Parliamentary timetable.** The executive controls much of the legislative timetable and can use 'guillotine motions' to curtail the time available for debate and scrutiny.
- **The 'payroll vote'.** Ministers and parliamentary private secretaries are required to support the government or resign. Over 40% of MPs from the governing party are on this 'payroll vote'.
- **Party discipline.** The whip system ensures that government proposals are rarely defeated and that amendments to them are acceptable.

Scrutiny and accountability

Parliamentary scrutiny is an essential function of a legislature. In addition to scrutinising a government's legislative proposals, parliament also exercises a general scrutiny and oversight role. It scrutinises the actions of the executive and ensures government **accountability** by requiring ministers to explain and justify their actions. The convention of individual ministerial responsibility states that ministers are accountable to parliament; they must explain and justify their policies and actions — and those of their department — in parliament.

Key terms

Accountability The principle that an office holder or institution must account for their actions. In a system of parliamentary government, ministers are accountable to parliament and to the electorate. They have a duty to explain their policies and actions to parliament. Ministers may also be held responsible for policy failures. MPs face the electorate at a general election, where their constituents may take into account their record in office when deciding whether to vote for them.

Parliamentary scrutiny The role of parliament in examining the policies and work of the executive, and holding it to account.

Parliamentary questions

Government ministers face questions from MPs on the floor of the house. The parliamentary timetable includes **question time** sessions for ministers from each government department. In addition to questions tabled in advance, ministers answer topical questions on issues relating to their department. Speaker Bercow has required ministers to answer urgent questions more frequently.

The most high-profile event is Prime Minister's Question Time (also referred to as PMQs), which takes place each Wednesday at noon for half an hour. This provides an opportunity for the leader of the opposition, the leader of the third largest party and backbenchers to question the prime minister. A backbencher might raise a constituency matter, but many government backbenchers ask questions drafted by the whips which are intended to flatter, rather than probe. The leader of the opposition may try to shape the agenda or highlight policy failure. As leader of the opposition in the 2015–16 parliamentary session, Jeremy Corbyn tried to change the gladiatorial style by asking questions sent in by members of the public. Speaker Bercow has called more backbenchers during PMQs and sought, with limited success, to reduce noise levels in the chamber. Overall, Prime Minister's Question Time provides parliamentary theatre, rather than effective scrutiny.

> ### Key term
>
> **Question time** Parliamentary time, including Prime Minister's Question Time, in which backbenchers and opposition frontbenchers ask oral questions to government ministers.

Theresa May's first PMQs as prime minister, July 2016

> ### Activity
>
> Watch a session of Prime Minister's Question Time. How effective was it in scrutinising the policies and actions of the government? How might it have been improved?

Oral questions make up an important part of the business of the house (see Figure 5.6) but most parliamentary questions take the form of written questions to ministers requesting information on issues of public policy. There were 35,000 written questions in the 2015–16 session compared to 3,600 oral questions answered in the Commons.

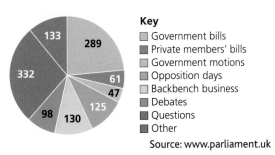

Key
- Government bills
- Private members' bills
- Government motions
- Opposition days
- Backbench business
- Debates
- Questions
- Other

Source: www.parliament.uk

Contains public sector information licensed under the Open Government Licence v3.0.

Figure 5.6 Time spent on business on the floor of the House of Commons, 2015–16 (total hours)

The role and significance of the opposition

The largest party not included in the government forms the official **opposition**. The leader of the opposition has special privileges, including an additional salary, the right to respond first to the prime minister on major statements, and the right to ask six questions at Prime Minister's Question Time — the only MP permitted to respond to the prime minister with further questions. He or she appoints a shadow cabinet to follow the work of government departments.

The House of Commons architecture is confrontational, with the government and opposition facing each other across the chamber. The opposition is expected to perform two major tasks that do not always sit easily together. First, it should oppose many of the government's legislative proposals and harry the government by tabling amendments and forcing votes. But the opposition should also try to appear as an alternative government-in-waiting. It will need to develop its own policies and may support government measures that it agrees with. When the government has a small majority, the opposition may be able to force policy retreats.

The government enjoys significant institutional advantages in parliament. It can draw upon the expertise of the civil service, while the opposition relies on limited state funding known as 'Short money'. Introduced in 1975, this is available to **opposition** parties that secured either two seats or one seat and more than 150,000 votes at the last general election. The funding is used to assist parties in carrying out their parliamentary business and cover travel expenses. A budget for the office of the leader of the opposition is also provided. In 2015–16, Labour received £6.8 million in Short money, but the Conservative government proposed reductions in the funding.

The opposition has limited opportunities to set the agenda in parliament. Opposition parties are permitted to choose the topic for debate on 20 days in the parliamentary year ('opposition days'), 17 of which are allocated to the official opposition. This gives them an opportunity to advance their agenda or expose government failings. A 2009 Liberal Democrat motion on British citizenship for Gurkha veterans produced a rare government defeat on an opposition motion.

The effectiveness of the opposition is also shaped by its own circumstances. A party that has just lost a general election cannot convincingly claim a mandate for its policies. It may also be divided. Internal divisions saw Jeremy Corbyn allow Labour MPs free votes on crucial issues such as air strikes on Syria and the renewal of Trident in 2015–16.

The work of select committees

Select committees have extended and enhanced parliamentary scrutiny of the executive. The overall aim of select committees is to hold government accountable for policy and decision making, and support parliament in scrutinising legislation and government spending (see the case study). They highlight important issues, bring expert contributions to debates, hold the government accountable for policy problems and issue evidence-based recommendations.

Key term

Select committee A committee responsible for scrutinising the work of a government, notably of a particular government department.

Case study

Core tasks of select committees

In 2012, the Liaison Committee set out ten core tasks for departmental select committees:

- **strategy** — to examine the strategy of the government department, including its key objectives and priorities
- **policy** — to examine policy and make proposals
- **expenditure and performance** — to examine departmental spending and delivery
- **draft bills** — to scrutinise draft bills
- **bills and delegated legislation**— to help the Commons to consider bills and legislation
- **post-legislative scrutiny** — to examine the implementation of legislation

- **European scrutiny** — to scrutinise EU policy developments and legislative proposals
- **appointments** — to consider departmental appointments and hold pre-appointment hearings, if necessary
- **support for the House** — to produce reports for debate in the Commons
- **public engagement** — to help the Commons to make their work accessible to the public

Questions
- Which of these tasks are most important?
- How well do select committees perform these functions?

Activity

Using the parliament website, **www.parliament.uk/business/committees**, identify the chairs of the departmental select committees. What is their background and political experience?

Departmental select committees were created in 1979 to scrutinise the policy, administration and expenditure of government departments. There were 21 departmental select committees in 2016. Some, like the Treasury Select Committee and Foreign Affairs Select Committees, have sub-committees.

Most select committees have 11 members. The largest is the select committee on exiting the European Union which has 21 members. Membership reflects the party balance in the Commons. Chairs of committees are allocated to parties according to their relative strength. Since 2010, select committee chairs are elected by all MPs in a secret ballot using the alternative vote system. Successful candidates often have a reputation for independence or particular expertise. The Health Select Committee has, for example, been chaired by former secretary of state for health Stephen Dorrell and former GP Sarah Wollaston. Prior to 2010, members of select committees were appointed by party whips but they are now elected by secret ballot within party groups. The new system of elections has enhanced the autonomy and profile of select committees.

Since a unanimous select committee report is likely to carry maximum weight, members aim to strike compromises across party lines. Over time, committee members can become more expert in their chosen field than relevant ministers, who usually have short tenures in office.

Select committees decide which issues they are going to examine. They have wide powers to summon witnesses and to examine restricted documents. Committees spend much of their time questioning ministers, officials and outside experts. Some witnesses are reluctant to provide full and frank evidence. Confrontations with high-profile figures such as media mogul Rupert Murdoch, entrepreneur Mike Ashley and businessman Sir Philip Green made media headlines. However, MPs have been accused of being overly aggressive in their interrogations. Some select committee investigations have been highly influential, notably the Culture, Media and Sport Committee inquiry into phone hacking (see the case study). In 2015–16, departmental select committees held some 700 meetings and produced almost 100 reports.

Case study

Recent high-profile select committee inquiries

- Culture, Media and Sport Select Committee inquiry (2009–10) into press standards, privacy and libel was critical of the conduct of the press. It heard evidence of illegal phone-hacking by journalists at the now defunct *News of the World* newspaper, leading to police investigations and the Leveson Inquiry into press conduct.
- Culture, Media and Sport Select Committee inquiry (2011–12) into phone-hacking at News International heard evidence from Rupert Murdoch and James Murdoch.
- Health Select Committee inquiry (2011) into public health identified problems with the coalition government's proposals for NHS reform. It helped persuade the government to make significant changes to the Health and Social Care Bill.
- Treasury Committee inquiry (2012) into the banking crisis identified issues with the rigging of the LIBOR lending rate and helped shape policy on regulation of the banking sector.
- Justice Committee inquiry (2012) into the presumption of death of missing persons proposed a new statutory process in which a certificate of presumed death is issued. This subsequently became law through a private members' bill, supported by the government, based on the committee's recommendations.
- Business, Energy and Industrial Strategy Committee inquiry (2016) into the sale and acquisition of the high-street department store chain BHS was highly critical of Sir Philip Green and concluded that he had a 'moral duty' to resolve problems with the BHS pension scheme.
- Business, Energy and Industrial Strategy Committee inquiry (2016) into working practices at retailer Sports Direct concluded that Mike Ashley must be held accountable for 'extremely disturbing' working practices at the company.
- Foreign Affairs Committee inquiry (2016) into UK intervention in Libya concluded that the UK's 2011 actions in Libya were ill-conceived and that other political options should have been attempted. It stated that David Cameron was ultimately responsible for the failure to develop a coherent strategy.

Questions
- How did the government respond to these inquiries?
- How, and why, were select committees able to influence the agenda in these cases?

The government must respond to select committee reports but is not required to accept their recommendations. A study by the Constitution Unit (2011) found that governments accept around 40% of select committee recommendations. Many of these recommendations proposed limited policy change.

Select committees cannot introduce their own legislative proposals but they are now involved in pre-legislative scrutiny, where they make suggestions to improve draft bills, and post-legislative scrutiny, where they examine whether legislation has been effective.

Since 2008, select committees have also held pre-appointment hearings for public appointments to some 60 positions (including the chair of Ofcom and the Governor of the Bank of England). They do not have the power to veto appointments. Select committees have either rejected or been divided on the suitability of more than a dozen candidates. In practice, many public appointments are now subject to a 'double lock' of government and parliamentary approval. Yet in 2016, Amanda Spielman became head of Ofsted despite the Education Select Committee expressing concerns about her expertise.

Debate

Are select committees effective in scrutinising the executive?

Yes

- Select committees scrutinise the policies and actions of government, conducting detailed examinations of controversial issues.
- They question ministers, civil servants and outside experts, and can request access to government papers.
- Many select committee recommendations are accepted by the government.
- The election of chairs and members by MPs has enhanced the independence of select committees.

No

- A government with a majority in the Commons will also have a majority in committees.
- Ministers and civil servants may not provide much information when questioned, and access to documents may be denied.
- They have no power to propose policy — governments can ignore recommendations made by select committees.
- Some members do not attend regularly; some may be overly abrasive when questioning witnesses.

Other committees

Other important (non-departmental) select committees in the Commons include:

- **Liaison Committee.** This consists of the chairs of all select committees. Its most significant meetings are the twice-yearly sessions in which the prime minister is questioned on public policy.
- **Public Accounts Committee.** This examines government expenditure to check that value for money is being achieved. It does not consider the merits of government policy. It is chaired by a senior opposition MP.
- **Public Administration and Constitutional Affairs Committee.** This examines constitutional issues and the role of the civil service.

There are also six main select committees in the House of Lords which conduct inquiries on topical issues.

Debate

Parliament is the crucial national arena for the discussion of major (and minor) political issues. MPs express their views and try to influence policy in a range of debates on current events and government actions. Half-hour adjournment debates held at the end of each day give MPs a chance to raise a particular issue. An MP can request that an emergency debate is held on a specific matter requiring 'urgent consideration'. The speaker and MPs must approve the request. Only four emergency debates were held in the 2010–15 Parliament, but four were then held in the 2015–16 session including one on the Europe refugee crisis and one on the UK steel industry.

Many debates are poorly attended, but those at times of crisis can provide moments of high drama. In 1940, prime minister Neville Chamberlain resigned after losing the support of his party following a debate on the German invasion of Norway. The debates that preceded the 2003 invasion of Iraq and 2015 bombing of Syria saw high-quality contributions that reflected the difference of opinion across the nation.

The number and range of issues debated in the Commons has increased since the introduction of sessions in the Grand Committee Room just off Westminster Hall. These deal with non-controversial issues, select committee reports and motions chosen by the Backbench Business Committee (BBBC) and Petitions Committee. Amendments cannot be tabled or votes held on these debates. In the 2015–16 session, there were 113 days of these debates.

The Backbench Business Committee, created in 2010, has given MPs greater opportunity to shape the parliamentary agenda. It decides the topic for debate on the floor of the Commons and in Westminster Hall for roughly 1 day per week. MPs pitch ideas for debate to the committee, which takes account of backbench opinion and select committee reports (plus, until 2015, e-petitions) when determining subjects for debate. Topics selected for debates that subsequently shaped the parliamentary agenda include a referendum on the European Union and the release of documents on the 1989 Hillsborough disaster (both debated in 2011). But the government can ignore motions passed in such debates, as they did with the motion to lower the voting age to 16. In 2012, the government unilaterally changed the way BBBC members are elected, so that they are now elected within party groups rather than by the whole house. This makes it more difficult for MPs with a record of independence to get on the committee.

Responsibility for considering public e-petitions for debate in parliament passed to a new Petitions Committee in 2015. E-petitions that attract more than 100,000 signatures are normally debated. Thirty-two such petitions were debated between 2011 and 2015, including ones on fuel duty and an EU referendum — with a petition on a second EU referendum then debated in 2016.

Debate

Has the Backbench Business Committee (BBBC) been a success?

Yes

- It has given backbench MPs greater say over the parliamentary timetable.
- It has enabled debate on, and raised the profile of, issues that would otherwise not have been discussed in depth in parliament, including an EU referendum.
- Debates initiated by the BBBC have influenced government policy, including those on reducing fuel and beer duty.
- It was a successful vehicle for public engagement with parliament, allocating time for debate for topics receiving 100,000 signatures in an e-petition — an innovation that led to the creation of the Petitions Committee.

No

- The government does not have to respond to, or accept, motions passed after debates scheduled by the BBBC.
- The government allocates time for BBBC debates at short notice and in an ad hoc way.
- The government ignored criticism from the BBBC and forced through changes which give party groups greater say in the election of BBBC members.
- Smaller parties are under-represented: 7 BBBC members are Conservative or Labour MPs, the other being from the SNP.

Recruitment of ministers

Government ministers must be members of either the House of Commons or the House of Lords. Parliament is, therefore, a recruiting ground for government and, traditionally, future ministers have forged their reputations in the House of Commons. However, parliament's effectiveness in the recruitment and development of future government ministers has become questionable for the following reasons:

- **Communications skills.** Being an effective communicator is important for the career prospects of an MP. But television, rather than parliament, is now the key arena in which MPs display their communications skills.
- **Experience.** There has been a high turnover of MPs recently: 227 new MPs entered the Commons in 2010, a further 182 in 2015 and 98 in 2017. Government needs people with managerial, leadership and organisational skills. Around one in five MPs worked in politics (in roles such as researchers or advisers) before entering parliament. The proliferation of career politicians, with little experience of life beyond politics, widens the gap between the political class and ordinary voters.
- **Conformity.** Loyal MPs have better prospects of ministerial office than rebels. However, some MPs may not aspire to ministerial office and the strengthening of select committees offers an alternative career route.

Representation

There are competing perspectives on **representation**:
- delegate model
- trustee model
- constituency representation
- party representation
- descriptive or functional representation

Delegate model

A **delegate** is an individual selected to act on behalf of others on the basis of clear instructions. They should not depart from these instructions in order to follow their own judgement or preferences. However, MPs are not expected to act as delegates, slavishly bound by the instructions of voters. There is unlikely to be a consensus among voters in a constituency on complex issues and ascertaining the views of the majority on every issue would be difficult. Instead MPs are **representatives** who are free to exercise their own judgement on issues.

Trustee model

Edmund Burke (1729–97) proposed the **trustee** model of representation. MPs are responsible for representing the interests of their constituents in parliament. Once elected, they are free to decide how to vote based on their own independent judgement of the merits of an issue. Burke's perspective had a strong elitist undercurrent: it assumed that MPs knew best because they had a greater understanding of affairs of state.

Key terms

Delegate An individual authorised to act on behalf of others but who is bound by clear instructions.

Representation The process by which an individual or individuals act on behalf of a larger group.

Representative (a) *noun:* an individual who acts on behalf of a larger group but is free to exercise their own judgement; (b) *adjective:* exhibiting a likeness or being typical.

Trustee An individual who has formal responsibility for the interests of another (in law, this will often be property).

Distinguish between

Delegates and trustees

Delegates
- Delegates are given clear instructions on how they are to act on behalf of the people they represent.
- They must follow these instructions in full and must not adapt them based on their own judgement of the issues.
- They must not vote on the basis of their personal views.

Trustees
- Trustees should take account of the interests and values of the group they represent but are not bound by strict instructions from them.
- They are free to exercise their own judgement on issues and to vote accordingly.
- They may vote according to their conscience.

Key term

Constituency A geographical territory for which one or more representatives are chosen in an election.

Constituency representation

MPs are expected to protect and advance the collective interests of the **constituency** they represent, and to represent the interests of individual constituents. Constituency work takes up around half of an MP's time. MPs hold regular surgeries in which constituents can discuss problems or concerns. They may then take up grievances that individual constituents have against a public authority: for example, by contacting the relevant body, writing to a minister or raising the issue in the Commons. MPs also champion the interests of their constituency as a whole — for example, by seeking investment and defending public services or key employers.

Some MPs win favourable local reputations and reap a sizeable personal vote in a general election. The Hansard Society's 2016 *Audit of Political Engagement* showed that 35% of people were satisfied with the way their local MP was doing his or her job, compared to 29% who were satisfied with MPs in general.

Party representation

Political parties dominate elections. Almost all successful general election candidates are elected not for their personal beliefs and qualities, but because they represent a political party. Striking the right balance between representing the views of the local party members who selected them and of the voters who elected them can be tricky for MPs.

Descriptive representation

Descriptive representation occurs when a legislature mirrors the society it represents. In this perspective, parliament should be a microcosm of society with all major social groups included in numbers proportional to their size in the electorate. In the UK, attention has focused on the under-representation of women in the House of Commons. The number of women MPs has risen in recent decades, reaching 208 in 2017, but women make up only 32% of the Commons compared to 51% of the UK population.

Labour tends to have a higher proportion of women candidates and MPs than the Conservatives or Liberal Democrats (see Table 5.2). This reflects Labour's use of all-women shortlists (see the case study). Twelve of the 35 SNP MPs elected in 2017 were women.

Twelve of the 35 SNP MPs elected in 2017 were women, including Mhairi Black, the youngest MP to be elected since 1832

Table 5.2 Women candidates and MPs, 1983–2017

Year	Conservative		Labour		Liberal Democrat		Total women MPs (including MPs from other parties)
	Candidates	MPs	Candidates	MPs	Candidates	MPs	
1983	40	13	78	10	75	0	23
1987	46	17	92	21	106	2	41
1992	63	20	138	37	143	2	60
1997	69	13	157	101	140	3	120
2001	92	14	146	95	135	5	118
2005	118	17	166	98	142	10	128
2010	151	49	189	81	137	7	143
2015	169	68	214	99	166	0	191
2017	183	67	256	119	185	4	208

Case study

Increasing the number of women candidates

Parties have used a number of methods to increase the number of women candidates at general elections. These include:

■ **All-women shortlists.** Used by Labour in every general election since 1997 (except 2001), these gender quotas require some constituency parties to select their parliamentary candidate from a list consisting only of women. This boosted significantly the number of female Labour MPs elected in 1997. The Sex Discrimination (Election Candidates) Act 2002 permits political parties to use positive measures to reduce inequality in the number of women elected to parliament. All-women shortlists are 'equality guarantees': they ensure that a woman candidate will be selected in a constituency. Critics argue that candidates should be selected on the basis of merit alone.

■ **Priority lists.** David Cameron introduced a priority list (the 'A list') in 2005 for the top 100 Conservative target seats. Constituency associations were required to draw up shortlists on which at least half the aspirant candidates were women. This was an 'equality promotion' initiative that set a general target of more women MPs, but did not guarantee that women would be selected in winnable seats. Only 19 of the 49 women Conservative MPs elected in 2010 had been on the 'A list'. This approach was dropped but the culture in the party was changing and more women were selected in winnable seats in 2015.

These 'demand-side' initiatives have helped to increase the number of women MPs, but 'supply-side' obstacles remain. Career choices, family, money and a lack of political connections may prevent women from putting themselves forward as candidates.

Questions
■ What measures should parties employ to increase the number of women MPs?
■ Should these measures be extended to other groups that are under-represented in parliament?

Other areas of under-representation in the House of Commons include:
■ **Ethnic diversity.** The number of black and minority ethnic (BAME) MPs rose from 41 to 52 at the 2017 general election, but this is only 8% of the house, compared to 14% of the population.
■ **Age.** Young and older people are under-represented in the Commons, with most MPs being in the 35 to 55 age range. The SNP's Mhairi Black was only 20 when first elected in 2015 – the youngest MP to be elected since 1832.

- **Sexual orientation.** 45 MPs elected in 2017 define themselves as lesbian, gay or bisexual, the highest number in the world.
- **Education.** 29% of MPs elected in 2017 attended a fee-paying school, compared to 7% of voters, but the number is in long-term decline. Nine out of ten MPs are university graduates.
- **Social class.** The number of MPs who previously had manual occupations has been falling. MPs who worked in business are more likely to be Conservatives, and those who worked in the public sector (e.g. teachers) Labour.

The relationship between parliament and the executive

The relationship between parliament and government is an unequal one, with the executive the dominant actor. The government has significant control over the legislative process. There is a good reason for this: if the government did not have this power, it could not fulfil its mandate or govern effectively. But executive dominance does not mean that parliament is impotent.

Legislative–executive relations are shaped not only by the institutional resources they possess, but also by the political context. Key factors include:

- the government's parliamentary majority
- the extent of party unity

How important is the size of the government's majority?

The size, or absence, of a majority for the governing party in the House of Commons is an important factor in the relationship between the legislature and executive. The first-past-the-post (FPTP) electoral system often, but not always, delivers a working majority for the party that wins most votes in a general election. A government with a large majority is in a commanding position, able to push its legislation through parliament by utilising the whip system and controlling the parliamentary timetable.

The larger a government's majority, the less likely it is that the other parties in the Commons will be able to defeat or amend government bills. The ability of backbenchers to influence policy is also limited because a government with a substantial majority can absorb dissent within its own ranks. With a majority of 167 at the 2001 election, the Blair government survived large rebellions from Labour backbenchers on Iraq, tuition fees and foundation hospitals. The government suffered its first Commons defeat within months of its majority being cut to 65 at the 2005 election.

A governing party that has a slender majority, or none at all, can find itself in a precarious position. A hung parliament occurs when no single party commands an absolute majority of seats in the House of Commons. Then, a minority government or coalition government is likely.

Minority government

In a minority government, the party with the largest number of seats governs alone. It may be able to persuade a smaller party to support it on the budget and Queen's Speech. This is known as a 'confidence and supply' deal. It must still find parliamentary majorities on a bill-by-bill basis. A minority government may be relatively stable in the short term, particularly if other parties do not want another general election. It is difficult to sustain a minority government for long, although the Fixed-term Parliaments Act 2011 limits what counts as a confidence motion.

There have been four postwar minority governments:

- **Wilson government (1974).** Harold Wilson's Labour government had no majority after the February 1974 election. Wilson called another election in October and won a majority of 3 seats.
- **Callaghan government (1976–79).** Labour's majority disappeared after by-election defeats. Under the 1977–78 'Lib–Lab pact', the Liberals supported the government on key votes in the Commons.
- **Conservative government (1996–97).** John Major's government lost its majority in 1996 following by-election defeats and defections. It was supported by Ulster Unionists on some divisions but there was no formal deal.
- **Conservative government (2017–).** Theresa May agreed a confidence and supply deal with the Democratic Unionist Party after losing her parliamentary majority in the 2017 general election.

Coalition government

In a coalition government, two or more parties form the government, having reached a formal agreement on a legislative programme and cabinet posts. When the 2010 election failed to deliver an outright majority for the Conservatives, they formed a coalition with the Liberal Democrats. This was the first coalition since that led by Winston Churchill (1940–45) during the Second World War, and the first in peacetime since the National Government of the 1930s.

The Conservative–Liberal Democrat coalition had a healthy working majority of 79. This proved sufficient for the government to get much of its legislation through the Commons. The coalition agreement permitted the Liberal Democrats to abstain on parliamentary votes on tuition fees and nuclear power. But disputes between the coalition partners saw two key bills fall when rebel Conservative MPs blocked House of Lords reform and Liberal Democrats blocked the revision of constituency boundaries.

How effective are backbench MPs?

The strengthening of select committees, creation of the Backbench Business Committee (BBBC) and greater use of urgent questions have given backbench MPs more opportunity to scrutinise government. However, the high failure rate for private members' bills suggests that backbench MPs have little impact on legislation.

It is a common perception that MPs slavishly follow the party whip and MPs do indeed vote with their party on the overwhelming majority of divisions in the Commons. When a **parliamentary rebellion** occurs, it is usually small and can easily be absorbed by a government with a working majority. But

Key term

Parliamentary rebellion A division in which MPs vote against their party whip.

rebellions have become more frequent in recent decades and, along with the threat of rebellion, may force concessions from the government.

In the 1950s and 1960s, the Conservative governments of Eden, Macmillan and Douglas-Home suffered no defeats in the Commons. Things changed in the 1970s when ideological divisions within the Labour and Conservative parties became more pronounced. The rate of rebellion has increased since the 1990s:

- **Major government (1992–97).** Conservative rebellions on the Maastricht Treaty (1992–93) saw Major call a confidence motion to force the treaty through the Commons. Further rebellions followed on gun control and VAT on domestic fuel.
- **Blair (1997–2007) and Brown (2007–10) governments.** The rebellion by 139 Labour MPs on the 2003 vote on the invasion of Iraq was the largest in a governing party in modern British politics. There were also significant rebellions on foundation hospitals (2003) and university tuition fees (2005). In the 2005–10 parliament, the government was defeated on 90-day detention of terrorist suspects (2005), the Racial and Religious Hatred Bill 2006 and the right of Gurkhas to live in the UK (2009).
- **Conservative–Liberal Democrat coalition government (2010–15).** According to research by Professor Philip Cowley, coalition MPs rebelled in 35% of votes in the Commons between 2010 and 2015. This was the most rebellious parliament of the postwar era. However, the government experienced relatively few defeats because Conservative and Liberal Democrat MPs tended to rebel on different issues. Conservatives rebelled on constitutional and European Union votes. Ninety-one Conservatives opposed the House of Lords Bill in 2012, a postwar record for a second reading rebellion, forcing it to be abandoned. A year earlier, 81 Conservatives voted for a referendum on EU membership, with eurosceptic dissent eventually forcing David Cameron to promise an in/out referendum. Liberal Democrats rebelled most frequently on welfare and social policy. The government's most significant defeat was on a 2013 motion on military action in Syria: 30 Conservatives and 9 Liberal Democrat MPs voted with the opposition to oppose air strikes.
- **Conservative government (2015–17).** It lost votes on EVEL, the conduct of the EU referendum and changes to Sunday trading laws.

MPs also exert influence through more subtle methods than rebellion. If the whips expect significant opposition to a measure, the government may withdraw or revise it rather than risk defeat or provoke ill-will. Labour made concessions on its 2008 plans to abolish the 10% income tax band and the Conservatives dropped tax changes in 2012 and 2015 because of fears of rebellion.

Has parliament become more effective?

Parliamentary scrutiny of the executive has been enhanced in recent years by the increased assertiveness of backbench MPs and the House of Lords. In 2009, a select committee on reform of the House of Commons, chaired by Labour MP Tom Wright, recommended changes to parliamentary procedures that enhanced parliamentary scrutiny and its agenda-setting ability:

- the election of select committee chairs and members
- the creation of the Backbench Business Committee (BBBC)
- new mechanisms for citizens to petition parliament

Activity

Consult Philip Cowley and Mark Stuart's 'Revolts' website for analysis of recent backbench rebellions:
http://revolts.co.uk

The prime minister is now obliged to get parliamentary consent before calling an early election. In short, parliament now exercises significant constraint on executive power.

Parliament and Brexit

Brexit poses significant challenges for parliament. The 2016 EU referendum was a move away from parliamentary sovereignty towards popular sovereignty. It provoked competing claims of legitimacy. The government claimed that parliament should not frustrate Brexit but many MPs sought to reassert parliamentary democracy. Some noted that referendums are advisory rather than binding; others accepted the result but argued that the terms of withdrawal should be subject to parliamentary consent.

Debates about the role of parliament also reflected concerns that Brexit could further strengthen the executive in its relationship with the legislature. The Supreme Court ruled that the government did not have the prerogative power to trigger Article 50 without the involvement of parliament. On its third reading in the Commons, 494 MPs voted in favour of the European Union (Notification of Withdrawal) Bill and 122 against. But a minority Conservative government will find it difficult to get its Brexit legislation through parliament.

The government plans to introduce a 'Great Repeal Bill' to repeal the European Communities Act 1972 and translate EU law into domestic law. The domestic law could then be amended, replaced or repealed when the UK leaves the EU. This would pose challenges for parliament by creating a complex and significant workload. Secondary legislation is, therefore, likely to be used extensively but this would strengthen the executive and weaken parliament. Finally, it is important to remember that Brexit may also provoke differences between the Commons and the Lords.

Debate

Is parliament an effective check on the power of the executive?

Yes

- The executive's control over the parliamentary timetable has been weakened by the creation of the Backbench Business Committee (BBBC) and the greater use of urgent questions.
- Backbench MPs provide greater checks on government policy than in the past, with increased incidents of rebellion a constraint on government action.
- The reformed House of Lords, in which no party has a majority, is a more effective revising chamber — amendments made in the Lords often force the government to rethink legislation.
- Select committees have become more influential, with governments accepting around 40% of their recommendations. The election of select committee chairs and members has enhanced their independence.

No

- The executive exercises significant control over the legislative timetable and MPs hoping to steer legislation through parliament face significant obstacles.
- Government defeats are rare — most backbench MPs from the governing party obey the whip on a majority of votes.
- The government is usually able to overturn hostile amendments made in the House of Lords, and can resort to the Parliament Act to bypass opposition in the Lords.
- Select committees have little power. The government is not required to accept their recommendations and often ignores proposals that run counter to its preferred policy.

Has parliament's reputation improved?

Parliament's reputation was damaged by the 2009 MPs' expenses scandal. The Hansard Society's annual Audit of Political Engagement has traced public attitudes towards parliament. The 2017 report found that only 30% of people were satisfied with how parliament works — a partial recovery from the lows seen during the expenses scandal (see Figure 5.7). More people agreed than disagreed in 2017 that parliament 'debates and makes decisions about issues that matter to me' and 'holds the government to account'. However 73% agreed that 'parliament is essential to our democracy'.

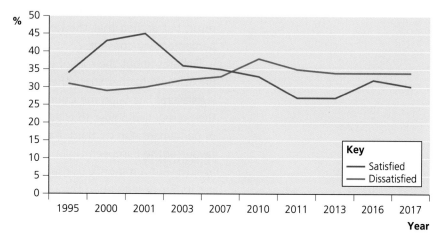

Source: www.auditofpoliticalengagement.org/reports

Figure 5.7 Public satisfaction with the way parliament works, 1995–2017

What you should know

- The UK has a system of parliamentary government in which government takes place through parliament. There is a fusion, rather than separation, of powers. The executive is the dominant actor but its ability to control proceedings in parliament is affected by the size of its majority, the extent of party unity and the assertiveness of the House of Lords.

- Parliament comprises the monarchy, the House of Lords and the House of Commons. The House of Commons is the dominant chamber. It consists of 650 MPs who are directly elected. Almost all are members of a political party. The House of Lords is a revising chamber and can delay legislation for a year. It is unelected. Since the 1999 reform that removed all but 92 hereditary peers, life peers make up the largest category of members. The judicial role of the House of Lords ended in 2009.

- Parliament is the supreme legislative body in the UK but it is a policy-influencing rather than policy-making institution. Most successful bills originate from the government. Party discipline and government control of the parliamentary timetable ensure that most government proposals are accepted by the Commons.

- Parliament debates important issues, scrutinises government actions and holds it to account. Select committees carry out detailed examinations of the activities of government departments but the government is not required to accept their recommendations.

- Reforms introduced by the Conservative–Liberal Democrat coalition (2010–15) enhanced the status of select committees and gave backbench MPs greater say over the parliamentary timetable. But the MPs' expenses scandal (2009) weakened public trust in parliament. The under-representation of women and the rise of career politicians also damage the image of parliament.

- Reform of the House of Lords stalled after the completion of the first stage in 1999. Support has grown for a wholly elected or mainly elected upper house. This would enhance the legitimacy of the second chamber but might create tensions between the Lords and Commons.

UK/US comparison

UK Parliament and US Congress

- The US Congress is a bicameral legislature. The lower chamber is the House of Representatives, which consists of 435 elected members. The Senate, which consists of 100 elected members, is the upper chamber. The two chambers have broadly equal powers. In the UK, only the House of Commons is elected. The unelected House of Lords is politically and legally subordinate.

- Congress is a policy-making legislature. It can reject or amend proposals from the president, and puts forward legislative proposals of its own. Most proposals come from the president, who has the power of veto — although this can be overridden by Congress. The UK Parliament is a policy-influencing legislature that modifies government proposals but does not propose extensive bills of its own.

- There is a strict separation of powers in the USA. Members of the executive branch cannot be members of the legislature. The president cannot dismiss Congress, but Congress can impeach the president. The US Constitution also gives Congress the power to declare war, and Senate the power to veto appointments made by the president.

- Party discipline has grown stronger in the USA but it is still weaker than in the UK. A president cannot rely on the support of members of his own party in Congress. Members of Congress are more independent-minded and more likely than MPs to place the interests of their constituents above those of party.

- Standing committees in Congress have significant influence over US government departments. Committee chairs are powerful figures in Congress. Departmental select committees in the UK are much less powerful.

Further reading

Kelso, A. (2013) 'Parliament: what does it do and how effectively does it do it?', *Politics Review*, Vol. 22, No. 2, pp. 18–21.

Kelso, A. (2015) 'The House of Lords: why has it not been reformed yet?', *Politics Review*, Vol. 25, No. 2, pp. 12–15.

Kelso, A. (2016) 'Parliament: how effective are backbench MPs?', *Politics Review*, Vol. 26, No. 2, pp. 28–31.

Norton, P. (2013) *Parliament in British Politics* (2nd edn), Palgrave.

Russell, M. (2011) 'Why does the House of Lords matter?', *Politics Review*, Vol. 20, No. 4, pp. 18–20.

Hansard Society: www.hansardsociety.org.uk

Parliament: www.parliament.uk

Parliaments and legislatures: www.tinyurl.com/zhnx472

TheyWorkForYou: www.theyworkforyou.com

Exam-style questions

Short-answer questions

1 Explain, with examples, the ways in which MPs serve their electorate.

2 Explain, with examples, the role of the speaker of the House of Commons.

3 Explain and analyse three limitations on the powers of the House of Lords.

4 Explain and analyse the importance of three types of parliamentary committee.

Mid-length questions

1 Describe the main functions of parliament.

2 Describe the main features involved in the process of passing legislation in the UK Parliament.

3 Analyse and evaluate the powers of the House of Lords.

4 Analyse and evaluate the representativeness of the House of Commons.

Essay questions

1 Evaluate the extent to which the House of Lords can act as a check on the House of Commons.

2 Evaluate the extent to which parliament is effective in carrying out its various functions.

3 Evaluate the extent to which parliament fulfils its representative role in UK politics.

4 'The only purpose of backbench MPs is to support their party leadership.' Analyse and evaluate this statement.

5 'Parliamentary reforms since 1997 have gone too far.' How far do you agree with this statement?

In your answer you must:

- Refer to reforms of the House of Commons and the House of Lords.

- Draw on relevant knowledge and understanding of UK politics.

Chapter 6

The prime minister and executive

Key questions answered

- How is the executive structured, what role does it play and what powers does it hold?
- What are the different functions and powers of the prime minister and cabinet?
- What are collective ministerial responsibility and individual ministerial responsibility, and how are they significant?
- What are the relative powers of the prime minister and cabinet, and where does power lie within the executive?
- What power do the prime minister and cabinet have to dictate events and determine policy?

Theresa May speaking outside No. 10 Downing Street in July 2016, having accepted Her Majesty's invitation to form a government

On 13 July 2016, David Cameron tendered his resignation as prime minister at a private audience with the queen. Within an hour, Theresa May had accepted Her Majesty's invitation to form a government. Cameron had announced his intention to resign on 24 June 2016, shortly after the announcement that the UK had voted to leave the European Union (EU). He had called the referendum and led the campaign to remain in the EU but the vote for Brexit made it apparent that he no longer had the support of many Conservative MPs and that his popularity with voters had been fatally undermined. In order to secure a clear mandate for her vision of Brexit, May called a general election for 8 June 2017.

Initially, Cameron expected to stay in Downing Street until late summer as the Conservative Party chose his successor. But events moved rapidly when Andrea Leadsom withdrew from the leadership contest on Monday, 11 July. Cameron held his final cabinet meeting the following day, then attended his final Prime Minister's Question Time on the Wednesday before being driven to Buckingham Palace. For the seventh time since 1945, a prime minister had resigned part way through their term of office — and, again, at a time that was not of their choosing.

The executive

The **executive** is the branch of government concerned with the formulation and implementation of policy (see Figure 6.1). It is the heart of government, providing both the 'high politics' of national leadership and the mundane day-to-day administration of government.

The main institutions of the executive are:

- **prime minister** — the head of government and chair of the cabinet
- **cabinet** — the committee of senior ministers which is the ultimate decision-making body of government
- **ministers** — appointed by the prime minister to specific policy portfolios within the government
- **government departments** — the main administrative units of central government, each dealing with a particular area of policy

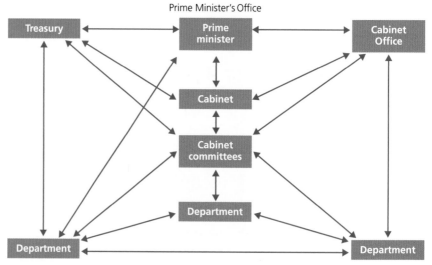

Figure 6.1 The UK executive

The first three of these institutions make up the political executive — they are politicians who enter office as MPs or peers from the political party (or parties) that won the last general election. Government departments, which are staffed by civil servants, are the administrative executive and oversee the daily administration of government. Civil servants are not political appointments and remain in post when the government changes.

In focus

Core executive

The core executive is the heart of government, consisting of those organisations and actors who coordinate central government activity, along with the activities themselves. The core executive includes: the prime minister, cabinet, cabinet committees, bilateral meetings between the prime minister and ministers, the Prime Minister's Office, coordinating departments (e.g. the Cabinet Office and Treasury) and top civil servants. The core executive model claims that the prime minister and senior ministers all have resources, and that power is based on dependence rather than command.

What is the role of the executive?

The executive has a number of core functions:

- **Making policy decisions.** The prime minister and cabinet set political priorities and determine the country's overall policy direction. They also make day-to-day decisions on policy. The administrative executive is responsible for policy implementation and oversees the day-to-day administration of the state.
- **Proposing legislation.** The executive devises and initiates legislation. Most primary legislation (i.e. bills) is proposed by the executive. Government bills put into effect the policies proposed in the manifesto of the governing party. The executive itself has law-making powers on **secondary legislation**.
- **Proposing a budget.** The executive makes key decision on economic policy and proposes a budget. The chancellor sets out proposed levels of taxation and public spending in the budget, following negotiations in cabinet and with government departments.

> **Key term**
>
> **Secondary legislation** A form of legislation which allows the provisions of an Act of Parliament to be brought into force or altered by ministers without requiring additional primary legislation.

What are the powers of the executive?

The executive has a number of powers that place it at an advantage over parliament in the policy-making process.

Prerogative powers

These are powers exercised by ministers that do not require parliamentary approval. They are collectively known as the **royal prerogative** and date from the time when the monarch had direct involvement in government. The monarch still has some personal prerogative powers, including the appointment of the prime minister and giving royal assent to legislation, but in exercising these, the monarch seeks to avoid controversy and acts under the direction of ministers.

Most prerogative powers are exercised by ministers acting on behalf of the Crown. These include:

- making and ratifying treaties
- international diplomacy, including recognition and relations with other states
- deployment of the armed forces overseas
- the prime minister's patronage powers and ability to recommend the dissolution of parliament
- the organisation of the civil service
- the granting of pardons

> **Key term**
>
> **Royal prerogative** A set of powers exercised by government ministers, or by the monarch, which do not require parliamentary approval.

Some prerogative powers have been clarified and limited in recent years. It has become a constitutional convention that parliament votes on the deployment of the armed forces overseas. Parliament voted against airstrikes on Syria in 2013 and then gave its approval in 2015. Prior to the Fixed-term Parliaments Act 2011, the prime minister could ask the monarch to dissolve parliament and call an early general election. Now, an early election can only be called if two-thirds of MPs approve in a vote in the House of Commons. In April 2017, MPs approved a motion for an early general election by 522 votes to 13. The prime minister's powers to award honours and make public appointments have also been restricted.

Control of the legislative agenda

Most bills are proposed by the government and it controls the legislative timetable (e.g. it can limit debate on bills). Most government bills are approved by parliament and become law. Private members' bills that do not enjoy government support are unlikely to succeed. Government control of the legislative process is also seen in its imposition of party discipline on important votes and the requirement that all ministers must support the government in parliament.

Powers of secondary legislation

Also known as delegated legislation, this is a form of legislation which allows the provisions of an Act of Parliament to be brought into force or amended by ministers without requiring a further Act. Acts confer on ministers the power to make more detailed rules and regulations through statutory instruments (SI). These vary from being largely technical (e.g. stating when parts of an Act come into force) to providing greater detail on broad provisions of an Act. Some 3,500 SIs are issued per year (see Figure 6.2). They are scrutinised by parliamentary committees but most are not debated and it is unusual for SIs to be rejected. However, the House of Lords amended two regulations on tax credits in 2015.

Figure 6.2 Volume of secondary legislation, 1990–2016

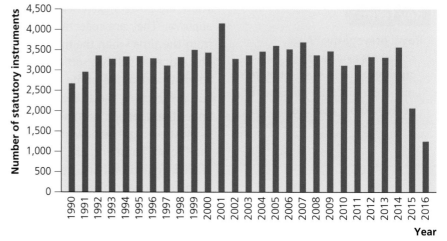

Source: data from www.legislation.gov

The prime minister and cabinet

Activity

Research the careers of postwar British prime ministers. Can you identify trends in the background and experience of prime ministers? Tony Blair and David Cameron, for example, had never held ministerial office before becoming prime minister, and Cameron had only been an MP for 9 years. Was this unusual?

The prime minister

The prime minister is the head of the UK government. He or she provides political leadership within the cabinet system and the country at large, chairs the cabinet, appoints ministers and is leader of the largest party in the House of Commons. The office of prime minister emerged in the early eighteenth century and became the accepted title for the First Lord of the Treasury. Robert Walpole (1721–42) is recognised as the first prime minister because he commanded majority support in the Commons and cabinet. Postwar prime ministers are listed in Table 6.1.

Table 6.1 Postwar British prime ministers

Prime minister	Period in office	Governing party	Reason for leaving office
Clement Attlee	1945–51	Labour	Election defeat
Winston Churchill	1951–55	Conservative	Resigned — ill health and some pressure from party
Anthony Eden	1955–57	Conservative	Resigned — ill health and reputation damaged by Suez Crisis
Harold Macmillan	1957–63	Conservative	Resigned — ill health
Alec Douglas-Home	1963–64	Conservative	Election defeat
Harold Wilson	1964–70	Labour	Election defeat
Edward Heath	1970–74	Conservative	Election defeat
Harold Wilson	1974–76	Labour	Resigned — feared ill health
James Callaghan	1976–79	Labour	Election defeat following House of Commons defeat on confidence motion
Margaret Thatcher	1979–90	Conservative	Resigned — failed to win Conservative leadership election
John Major	1990–97	Conservative	Election defeat
Tony Blair	1997–2007	Labour	Resigned — decided early date for departure after pressure from party
Gordon Brown	2007–10	Labour	Election defeat
David Cameron	2010–16	Conservative–Liberal Democrat (2010–15) Conservative (2015–16)	Resigned — led the losing 'Remain' campaign in EU referendum
Theresa May	2016–	Conservative	

Activity

When the result of the 2016 EU referendum became clear, David Cameron is reported to have said that 'all political lives end in failure'. Do you agree with this statement? Which, if any, postwar British prime ministers left office at a time of their choosing and/or with their legacy assured?

What is the role of the prime minister?

The *Cabinet Manual*, a government paper on the workings of the executive, describes the prime minister as 'the head of government'. But the precise role of the prime minister is not set out in statute law. The key functions are generally accepted to be:

- **Political leadership.** The prime minister decides the political direction taken by the government, setting its priorities and strategy. He or she determines (or at least shapes) policy on high-profile issues.
- **National leadership.** The prime minister is the predominant political figure in the UK and provides national leadership at times of crisis. He or she is responsible for national security. The prime minister also acts as a communicator-in-chief for the government.
- **Appointing the government.** The prime minister determines the membership of the government by appointing and dismissing ministers.
- **Chairing the cabinet.** The prime minister chairs meetings of the cabinet, sets its agenda and steers its decisions. He or she creates cabinet committees and holds bilateral meetings with ministers.
- **Managing the executive.** The prime minister is responsible for the overall organisation of the government and is head of the civil service.
- **Prerogative powers.** The prime minister exercises prerogative powers such as deploying the armed forces oversees and recommending some public appointments.
- **Managing relations with parliament.** The prime minister makes statements to, and answers questions in, the House of Commons. He or she also shapes the government's legislative programme.
- **Representing the UK in international affairs.** The prime minister represents the UK in high-level international diplomacy.

Who becomes prime minister?

Three main requirements must be fulfilled for a person to become prime minister. First, he or she must be a member of parliament. Until the late nineteenth century, the prime minister was usually a member of the House of Lords. As the House of Commons emerged as the dominant chamber, it became a constitutional convention that the prime minister should be an MP in the Commons. When Harold Macmillan resigned as prime minister in 1963, the Earl of Home succeeded him as Conservative Party leader and thus prime minister. He renounced his hereditary peerage to be known as Alec Douglas-Home, and stood successfully in a by-election for the Commons.

Second, he or she must be leader of a political party. The prime minister must command the support of their party. If forced to step down as party leader, they also relinquish the office of prime minister. In 1990, Margaret Thatcher had to resign as prime minister after failing to win the Conservative Party leadership election. Three of the last five prime ministers — John Major, Gordon Brown and Theresa May — took office when the incumbent resigned (see Table 6.1). In these cases, a leadership contest within the governing party determines who becomes prime minister. The new prime minister is not required to call an immediate general election.

Third, the political party that he or she leads will normally have a majority in the House of Commons. Most postwar prime ministers

Key terms

Coalition government A government consisting of two or more political parties formed after an agreement between them on policy and the allocation of ministerial positions.

Majority government A government consisting of members of one political party which has an absolute majority of seats in the House of Commons.

Minority government A government consisting of members of one political party which does not have an absolute majority of seats in the House of Commons.

Prime Minister's Office The senior civil servants and special advisers, based at 10 Downing Street, who provide advice and support for the prime minister.

10 Downing Street The residence and office of the prime minister. 'Number 10' and 'Downing Street' are sometimes used to refer to the Prime Minister's Office.

entered office by winning a general election. Prime ministers defeated in a general election must resign.

The monarch invites the leader of the party that can command a majority in the Commons to form a government. The prime minister accepts office at a private audience with the sovereign. There is no investiture vote in parliament to confirm the prime minister.

Majority governments are the norm at Westminster. A 'hung parliament' occurs when no party has an absolute majority of seats. The incumbent prime minister is not required to resign immediately but is given the chance to negotiate with other parties to form a **minority government** or a **coalition government**. The 2010 general election produced a hung parliament and a Conservative–Liberal Democrat coalition government was formed. The Conservatives formed a minority government after losing their parliamentary majority at the 2017 general election.

The Prime Minister's Office

The prime minister does not head a government department, nor is there a formal prime minister's department. However, within **10 Downing Street** is the **Prime Minister's Office** and this has grown in importance. Its staff of around 190 people are a mix of career civil servants and special advisers.

Two important aspects of the work of the Prime Minister's Office are:

■ **Policy advice.** It provides the prime minister with policy advice, which may differ from that given by ministers. The Prime Minister's Office also helps to set the future direction of government policy. Since Tony Blair's premiership, the Prime Minister's Office has had an important role in coordinating policy making and implementation across government. David Cameron initially scaled back this role but then strengthened Number 10's oversight of Whitehall by establishing a Policy and Implementation Unit.

Prime ministers appoint their own senior advisers. The Chief of Staff is the most influential adviser and works at the centre of operations in Downing Street.

■ **Communications.** The Prime Minister's Office is responsible for the presentation of government policy. This function has grown in importance with the intensification of the media focus on the prime minister. Following criticism of the politicisation of communications under Blair's communications director, Alastair Campbell, responsibility for government communications was transferred to a senior civil servant.

How powerful is the prime minister?

The functions allocated to the prime minister give him or her greater resources than other ministers. However, they do not automatically produce prime-ministerial power. The resources available to the prime minister are subject to important constraints and vary according to circumstances. The main resources available are:

■ patronage
■ authority within the cabinet system
■ policy-making input
■ party leadership
■ public standing

Patronage powers

The prime minister has special powers of **patronage**. The most significant
is the power to appoint government ministers (see below). Other
patronage powers include:

- **Life peers.** The prime minister can appoint people to the House of
Lords as life peers. They may include former MPs or party supporters
who have made significant contributions in other areas of public life.
An independent Appointments Commission makes recommendations
on non-party appointments to the Lords, but the prime minister makes
political nominations.

  The power to nominate life peers enables prime ministers to alter the
party balance within the Lords. Blair increased Labour's representation
in the Lords by appointing162 Labour peers (see Figure 6.3). The prime
minister may nominate life peers with a view to giving them ministerial
positions. Gordon Brown gave government portfolios and life peerages
to five prominent public figures who were not politicians, including
former Confederation of British Industry (CBI) head Sir Digby Jones.

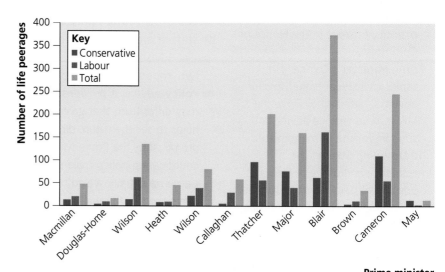

Figure 6.3 Life peerages created
1958–2017 (total includes Liberal/Liberal
Democrats, other parties and crossbench)

Source: www.parliament.uk

Contains public sector information licensed under the Open Government Licence v3.0.

- **The honours system.** A police inquiry into allegations of 'cash for
honours' — that donors to the Labour Party were rewarded with
peerages — ended in 2007 without criminal charges being brought.
But it led to changes to the prime minister's role in the honours
system. Nominations are now considered by honours committees
made up of civil servants and people independent of government.
The prime minister accepts their list. In cases where a nominee has
donated to a political party, the committee considers whether they are
deserving of an honour regardless of the donation.

Powers of patronage in other areas have also been curtailed. The prime
minister now plays no role in judicial appointments and is given only one
name to approve for ecclesiastical appointments.

Appointing cabinet ministers

The prime minister's power to appoint and dismiss government ministers, particularly at cabinet level, provides a crucial advantage over colleagues. In theory, prime ministers can create a cabinet in their own image, rewarding supporters and penalising disloyal MPs. In practice, the prime minister does not have a free hand.

The 2010 coalition agreement required Cameron to appoint five Liberal Democrats to his cabinet but all prime ministers face informal constraints on their choice of ministers. A prime minister is, for example, unlikely to overlook senior party figures, some of whom may be rivals for their job. Brown agreed not to stand against Blair in the 1995 Labour leadership election and in return received assurances that he would become chancellor of the exchequer in a future Labour government. Blair was required by Labour Party rules to select his first cabinet (in 1997) from those previously elected to the shadow cabinet by Labour MPs.

In 2016, 15 ministers who had attended cabinet under Cameron, including George Osborne and Michael Gove, were not appointed to May's first cabinet. Some commentators saw this as a sign of May's authority, while others noted that those dismissed could make trouble on the backbenches.

Ideological considerations are also important when the prime minister is appointing cabinet positions. A cabinet that contains politicians from only one wing of a party may not have the full support of that party. Margaret Thatcher included both economic 'dries' (Thatcherites) and 'wets' (one-nation Conservatives) to her first cabinet, but gave the key positions to her allies. New Labour politicians dominated Blair's cabinets but Old Labour was appeased by the appointment of John Prescott as deputy prime minister. Most ministers in Theresa May's first cabinet had campaigned to remain in the EU in the 2016 referendum, but Leave campaigners Boris Johnson, Liam Fox and David Davis were put in charge of departments that would deliver Brexit.

It may also be desirable to appoint ministers from different parts of the country and to include both MPs with significant experience or expertise and younger rising stars. Overall, the choice of ministers will be constrained by the talent available and a party that has had a long spell in power may become stale.

Cabinet reshuffles

Prime ministers can also reshuffle cabinet portfolios. Some ministers might be moved to another post and others dismissed entirely. This allows the prime minister to promote successful ministers, demote those who have underachieved, and freshen up the team. The prime minister decides the timing of a **cabinet reshuffle** but a sudden resignation may force an unwanted reshuffle.

The power to dismiss cabinet ministers can backfire. A botched reshuffle may raise questions about the prime minister's judgement, reveal cabinet divisions and highlight policy failings. This was true of Harold Macmillan's 1962 reshuffle, dubbed the 'night of the long knives', in which he sacked seven cabinet ministers. Margaret Thatcher's demotion of foreign secretary Sir Geoffrey Howe in 1989 had damaging consequences because his resignation a year later triggered Thatcher's downfall.

Key term

Cabinet reshuffle A series of changes to the personnel of the cabinet and the positions they occupy, instigated by the prime minister.

Activity

Examine media coverage of a recent cabinet reshuffle. Why were some cabinet ministers dismissed? Did commentators argue that the reshuffle had strengthened or weakened the position of the prime minister?

Key term

Core executive The heart of government, consisting of those organisations and actors who coordinate central government activity.

Key term

Bilateral meeting A meeting between the prime minister and a departmental minister in which policy is agreed.

Occasionally, senior ministers may thwart a prime minister's plans by refusing to change posts. Gordon Brown planned to make Ed Balls chancellor of the exchequer in 2009, but the incumbent, Alastair Darling, let it be known that he would refuse to accept another post and Brown relented. Weakened after losing seats in the 2017 general election, May shelved plans to dismiss senior ministers.

In the coalition government, David Cameron nominated Conservative ministers and Nick Clegg Liberal Democrats. Given this complexity, Cameron carried out only two major reshuffles.

Authority in the cabinet system

With the post of prime minister comes specific authority within the **core executive**. The prime minister:

- chairs cabinet meetings
- manages the agenda of cabinet meetings and determines their frequency and length
- directs and sums up cabinet discussions
- creates cabinet committees and appoints their members
- holds bilateral meetings with ministers
- appoints senior civil servants
- organises the structure of government

As chair of the cabinet, the prime minister steers and sums up discussions. Skilful prime ministers ensure that their favoured position prevails. However, if a group of senior ministers promotes an alternative viewpoint, the prime minister may not get his or her way so easily. Poor management of the cabinet by a prime minister who is either too domineering or too indecisive will weaken their authority. An effective prime minister will act as coordinator or broker on disputed issues. It is the prime minister's role to direct the government's general strategy, giving a sense of purpose, cohesion and direction.

The prime minister can establish cabinet committees to drive forward their agenda. In 2016, May established (and chaired) a new Economy and Industrial Strategy Committee. The prime minister can also reshape the structure and top personnel of central government. For example, May merged the functions of two former departments into the Department for Business, Energy and Industrial Strategy.

Agenda setting

The prime minister can determine the agenda of cabinet meetings by:

- controlling the information presented to ministers by determining which issues and papers should be brought before cabinet
- keeping potentially difficult issues off the cabinet agenda by dealing with them in a cabinet committee or in a **bilateral meeting** with the relevant minister
- deciding the chair, membership and remit of cabinet committees

Policy-making input

The prime minister's policy-making role is not confined to a specific field. Instead, he or she has licence to get involved in issues across the political spectrum. A prime minister with a strong interest in an issue can give it a central place in the government's programme.

The prime minister is the most important actor when crises occur and takes an active interest in economic and foreign policy. The chancellor and foreign secretary are powerful positions but the prime minister is likely to set objectives, and direct and coordinate policy in these crucial areas. However, the prime minister needs the backing of senior ministers on major issues. Chancellor Nigel Lawson and foreign secretary Geoffrey Howe forced Margaret Thatcher to shift government policy on the European Exchange Rate Mechanism (ERM) in 1989 by threatening to resign if she continued to rule out Britain's entry into the system.

Thatcher played an active role in many policy fields. Instances of policy success (e.g. the 1982 Falklands War) strengthened her position but in the case of the poll tax, policy failure undermined her authority. The 2003 invasion of Iraq undermined Blair's position when doubts about the government's case for war raised questions about his judgement and trustworthiness. In domestic politics, Blair became frustrated that increased public spending in health and education delivered only gradual improvement. Brown forged a reputation for competence as chancellor but the financial crisis undermined his economic credibility when he was prime minister. The 2010 coalition agreement limited Cameron's room for manoeuvre, but he set the overall agenda (e.g. the deficit reduction strategy) and determined responses to emerging issues (e.g. military intervention in Libya in 2011).

Party leadership

The prime minister is leader of the largest party in the House of Commons. A working majority in parliament strengthens their position because they are better able to enact the government's programme. However, the increased incidence of rebellion by backbench MPs means that a prime minister cannot always rely on party support. The Conservative–Liberal Democrat coalition government's proposals on reform of the House of Lords were dropped after a rebellion by Conservative MPs, and Conservative rebellions on EU issues contributed to Cameron's decision to promise an in/out referendum on membership.

Labour and Conservative leaders are elected by their MPs and party members and this legitimises their position. The length and cost of the leadership election process makes the sudden removal of a prime minister by the party less likely but a party's support for its leader is not unconditional. Margaret Thatcher was forced out of office after failing to win the 1990 leadership contest. John Major resigned as Conservative leader — but not as prime minister — in 1995, calling a leadership contest to reassert his authority. He won, but one-third of the party failed to support him. And both Blair and Brown survived efforts by Labour MPs to force them out of office.

Public standing

The prime minister has a high public profile. He or she provides political leadership at home and represents the UK in international affairs. Thatcher and Blair made a significant impact on the world stage and had a strong relationship with the president of the United States.

> ### Activity
>
> What policy initiatives are most associated with recent prime ministers? Carry out some research to find out if these policies are generally regarded as successful or unsuccessful.

Do the resources available to the prime minister bring him or her significant power?

Patronage

Yes

- They can appoint ministers.
- They can place allies in key roles.
- They can dismiss ministers.
- They can appoint outsiders to government.

No

- Senior colleagues might have claims to posts.
- They can be restricted by desire for an ideological balance across all parts of the party.
- Botched reshuffles can create rivals.
- Their choice is limited by the availability of talent.

Authority in the cabinet system

Yes

- The prime minister chairs and manages cabinet meetings.
- They steer and sum up cabinet discussions.
- They create cabinet committees and appoint members to them.
- They can use bilateral meetings with ministers to steer policy.

No

- Problems can arise if senior ministers feel ignored.
- Senior ministers may challenge the prime minister's policy preference.
- The prime minister is not involved in detailed policy making in cabinet committees.
- Ministers represent departmental interests, seeking additional resources and influence.

Party leadership

Yes

- The prime minister has authority as party leader.
- They have been elected as leader by MPs and party members (Conservative and Labour parties).
- The party normally has a majority in the House of Commons.

No

- Support of the party is not unconditional.
- Party rules allow for a leadership challenge.
- Backbench rebellions have become more frequent.

Public standing

Yes

- The prime minister has a higher public profile than other ministers.
- They are communicator-in-chief for the government.
- They provide national leadership in times of crisis.

No

- Unpopularity with voters can undermine their authority.
- They are blamed for the government's failings.
- They are expected to represent the public mood.

Policy-making role

Yes

- The prime minister directs government policy and sets agenda.
- They can direct policy in areas of their choosing.
- They represent the UK in international affairs.

No

- They are expected to be able to articulate a vision.
- They lack the time and expertise to have any significant involvement in this.
- Globalisation has reduced the scope for action.

Prime Minister's Office

Yes

- The Office provides advice and support to the prime minister.

No

- It has limited resources available to it.

The prime minister has taken on the role of communicator-in-chief for the government, articulating its policy programme and objectives. Twice-yearly appearances before the House of Commons Liaison Committee are a formal expression of this part of the role.

Public satisfaction with the prime minister strengthens their position (see Figure 6.4). A prime minister regarded as strong and effective has greater authority than one perceived as weak or out of touch. Thatcher polarised opinion but was widely regarded as a strong leader. This image was profitable for much of her premiership, but at the end she was viewed as autocratic. Blair enjoyed high poll ratings until the Iraq war damaged his standing. Cameron's ratings fell as austerity took effect, but he was more popular than his party. May's poor performance in the 2017 general election campaign weakened her position.

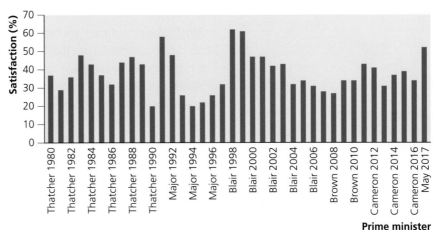

Figure 6.4 Public satisfaction with prime ministers

Note: data are for March each year

Source: Ipsos MORI (www.tinyurl.com/grwsc2z)

The cabinet

The traditional constitutional view is that executive power is vested in the cabinet, whose members exercise collective responsibility. But the importance of the cabinet has waned in the modern era. It now plays only a limited role in decision making as many key policy decisions are taken elsewhere in the executive. Suggestions that the cabinet has joined the ranks of Walter Bagehot's 'dignified institutions' — those with a symbolic role but no real influence — are premature. As Margaret

Theresa May holds her first cabinet meeting as prime minister, July 2016

Thatcher's resignation illustrated, a prime minister who fails to recognise his or her dependence on senior cabinet colleagues risks losing office.

Cabinet ministers

The cabinet consists of the senior ministers in the government. The number who can receive a cabinet minister's salary is limited to 22. The prime minister may also invite ministers to attend cabinet without making them full members of cabinet. Cameron gave 10 ministers this right to attend in 2012; May's 2017 cabinet had five such ministers. Eight of May's cabinet were women — equalling the record number appointed by Tony Blair in 2006.

Most cabinet ministers are heads of government departments. The most important departments are the Treasury, Foreign Office and Home Office. The ministers who head these departments have the highest profile and most influence (see Table 6.2). Some cabinet posts are more recent creations — for example, the Department for Exiting the European Union was established after the 2016 EU referendum. The position of deputy prime minister is not a fixed one in UK government and there are no specific powers or responsibilities associated with it. Blair gave the title to John Prescott, his deputy as party leader, while Nick Clegg became deputy prime minister as leader of the Liberal Democrats, the junior party in the 2010–15 coalition government.

Cabinet ministers must be members of parliament, to which they are politically accountable. Most sit in the House of Commons. It is unusual for members of the House of Lords to head major government departments. Two exceptions in the Brown government were Lord Mandelson, secretary of state for business, enterprise and regulatory reform (2008–10) and Lord Adonis, secretary of state for transport (2009–10).

Activity

Gordon Brown served as chancellor for the entirety of Tony Blair's premiership, as did George Osborne under David Cameron. Theresa May was the longest-serving home secretary in over 60 years. Turnover in other cabinet posts can be much higher. What might explain the variation in tenure?

Table 6.2 Senior ministers since 1997

	Tony Blair governments (1997–2007)	Gordon Brown government (2007–10)	David Cameron governments (2010–16)	Theresa May governments (2016–)
Chancellor of the exchequer	Gordon Brown (1997–2007)	Alistair Darling (2007–10)	George Osborne (2010–16)	Philip Hammond (2016–)
Foreign secretary	Robin Cook (1997–2001) Jack Straw (2001–06) Margaret Beckett (2006–07)	David Miliband (2007–10)	William Hague (2010–14) Philip Hammond (2014–16)	Boris Johnson (2016–)
Home secretary	Jack Straw (1997–2001) David Blunkett (2001–04) Charles Clarke (2004–06) John Reid (2006–07)	Jacqui Smith (2007–09) Alan Johnson (2009–10)	Theresa May (2010–16)	Amber Rudd (2016–)
Deputy prime minister	John Prescott (1997–2007)	—	Nick Clegg (2010–15)	—

Cabinet meetings

The frequency and length of cabinet meetings has fallen since the 1950s. Then it tended to meet twice per week but now it meets just once a week when parliament is in session. Cabinet meetings under Blair tended to last about an hour, with some over in half that time. Meetings were longer under Cameron because he adopted a more collegiate style in his first years in office but, like Blair, he came to prefer to do business outside of the cabinet.

Cabinet meetings are rather formal: there is a fixed seating arrangement, the agenda is settled in advance and items are introduced by departmental ministers, with interventions from senior ministers and relevant departmental ministers given priority.

Cabinet committees

Most decisions are taken within **cabinet committees**. These include:

- ministerial standing committees, which are permanent for the prime minister's term of office
- ministerial sub-committees, which report to a standing committee
- ad hoc committees, which are temporary committees set up to deal with a particular issue
- implementation taskforces, such as those used by Cameron and May to track progress on policies that cross departmental boundaries

Ministerial standing committees have considerable autonomy to determine the direction and detail of policy. Only where a final verdict has not been reached will the cabinet concern itself with the deliberations of a cabinet committee. The prime minister is responsible for the creation, membership, chairmanship and terms of reference of cabinet committees. He or she can establish cabinet committees to examine issues they wish to prioritise or which are pressing concerns.

Cabinet committees were given greater priority following criticism of Blair's preference for informal meetings. They were revived as important forums for discussion and resolution of differences in the Conservative–Liberal Democrat coalition and May streamlined the structure in 2016, having just five committees and ten sub-committees (see Figure 6.5). Long-standing cabinet committees dealing with home, economic and European affairs became sub-committees in the 2016 reorganisation. There were also seven implementation taskforces chaired by ministers.

> ### Key term
>
> **Cabinet committees** Sub-committees of the cabinet appointed by the prime minister to consider aspects of government business.

Figure 6.5 Cabinet committees and sub-committees, 2016

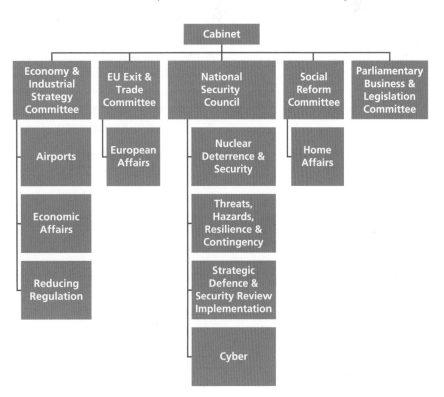

The prime minister chaired four committees, three sub-committees and three implementation taskforces. Cameron chaired only two committees and two sub-committees when he took office in 2010.

The detailed content of material entering the cabinet system is largely determined in government departments. Legislative proposals considered in cabinet committees must receive prior approval from the Treasury and Law Officers. If a proposal impacts upon the work of another department, the minister proposing the idea should seek the views of that department.

Policy decisions are also reached in bilateral meetings between the prime minister and a departmental minister. Blair conducted much government business in this manner, while meetings between Cameron and deputy prime minister Nick Clegg were crucial to the operation of the coalition government 2010–15.

The Cabinet Office

The **Cabinet Office** was created in 1916 to provide support for the cabinet system. The key unit is the Cabinet Secretariat, which regulates and coordinates cabinet business. It calls meetings, circulates papers, prepares the agenda and writes the minutes of meetings. The secretariat also coordinates work on issues that bridge departments, and acts as a facilitator in case of disputes. It is responsible to the prime minister and to committee chairs. The head of the civil service (Sir Jeremy Heywood since 2014) attends cabinet meetings as its secretary.

Under Blair, the Cabinet Office was given a leading role in policy delivery and public service reform. It was, in effect, brought within the remit of 10 Downing Street. Under the coalition, it led on political reform.

What role and powers does the cabinet have?

The *Ministerial Code* and the *Cabinet Manual* set out the role and functions of the cabinet and its committees, acting as authoritative guides to the **cabinet system** for ministers and civil servants. The functions of the cabinet are:

- registering and ratifying decisions taken elsewhere in the cabinet system
- discussing and making decisions on major issues
- receiving reports on key developments and determining government business in parliament
- settling disputes between government departments

Registering decisions

The main business of the cabinet and cabinet committees concerns:

- questions that engage the collective responsibility of government because they raise major policy issues or are of critical public importance
- matters on which there is an unresolved dispute between government departments

Decisions on most issues are taken in cabinet committees, in bilateral meetings between the prime minister and a minister, or in correspondence between departments. The cabinet acts as a clearing house for policy, registering or ratifying decisions taken elsewhere. If the prime minister and minister responsible for the policy in question are in agreement, other ministers have little chance of changing a decision. Ministers are discouraged from reopening issues where a decision has already been reached.

Key terms

Cabinet Office A government department responsible for supporting the cabinet system and the prime minister, and managing the civil service.

Cabinet system The cabinet and its associated bodies, including cabinet committees and the Cabinet Office.

Cabinet's ability to decide policy is constrained by the infrequency of meetings, its size and the detailed nature of policy. Cabinet ministers are primarily concerned with policy in their department. They have little time to study policy in other departments, lack expertise and may not see the relevant papers. This need not stop ministers offering their opinion on an issue outside of their brief, but it curbs their influence. The frequent turnover of ministers also limits their impact.

The cabinet takes fewer decisions than it did in the past. Diaries of cabinet ministers from the 1960s and 1970s reveal that on issues such as EEC membership and economic policy, the cabinet held lengthy discussions before reaching a decision. Thatcher and Blair avoided lengthy cabinet discussions and key decisions were instead taken by small groups of ministers and advisers.

Discussing or making decisions on major issues

Formally, the cabinet remains the ultimate decision-making body in the government. Yet for most areas of government activity, the cabinet is not an important actor in the decision-making process. Its role is more significant when:

- issues are especially important or sensitive
- major or unexpected developments require a rapid decision
- government departments and ministerial committees have been unable to reach agreement

Ministers can advise and warn, but it is the prime minister who must ultimately make a decision. The prime minister sums up the discussions and announces a verdict. Votes are rarely taken as they would reveal divisions.

Even when the cabinet does consider major issues, its role is largely advisory. In 2003, a special cabinet meeting was devoted to membership of the euro. Ministers aired their views, but in reality the cabinet was endorsing a decision — that the UK was not ready to adopt the euro — already taken by the prime minister and chancellor. The prime minister might also keep a sensitive issue away from cabinet to minimise the chance of their view being challenged. Thatcher opposed entry to the European Exchange Rate Mechanism (ERM) and did not want open discussion on it because other ministers were in favour of joining. But blocking discussion proved counterproductive as it widened the rift between the prime minister and her senior ministers. It will often be better for the prime minister to gauge the views of colleagues, assure them that they are being considered and persuade them of the worth of the policy and of cabinet unity.

Ken Clarke, who was a cabinet minister under Thatcher, Major and Cameron, noted that the level of cabinet discussion declined significantly during this period, and that much of the time in cabinet meetings under Cameron was taken up by departmental reports rather than discussion.

Reports on current issues

The cabinet hears reports on current developments, allowing ministers to keep abreast of events and discuss policy priorities. Cabinet meetings have a formal agenda, with the following reports as standard:

- parliamentary business
- economic and home affairs
- foreign affairs

133

In the parliamentary report, the leaders of the House of Commons and House of Lords outline the following week's business. This reflects the cabinet's formal role in timetabling government bills and ministerial statements.

On other issues, ministers may wish to clarify or question policy. They may offer their personal view, or that of a department or a section of their party. But the cabinet is not a debating society and time for discussion is limited. Only a small number of interventions, usually by senior ministers, are taken.

Settling disputes

If an issue cannot be settled in cabinet committee or bilateral meetings, it may be referred to the cabinet. Some appeals are straightforward matters of arbitration between competing departmental claims, for example over spending allocations or which department will lead on legislation. The cabinet judges the strength of the cases and reaches a binding decision.

This role as a court of appeal does not always work smoothly. In the 1985 Westland affair, secretary of state for defence Michael Heseltine resigned because he was unhappy with Thatcher's ruling that cabinet would not hear his appeal against a cabinet committee decision on the award of a defence contract.

Debate

Is the cabinet submissive to the prime minister?

Yes
- The prime minister can appoint his or her supporters to cabinet and dismiss ministers who disagree with his or her preferred policy.
- The prime minister has significant control over the cabinet agenda, steering and summarising discussions as they see fit and without having to call a vote.
- Many decisions are taken outside of the cabinet, often in bilateral meetings between the prime minister and a cabinet minister.
- The Prime Minister's Office has expanded and plays a greater role in directing and coordinating policy across government.
- The prime minister can claim a personal mandate from the public and their party.

No
- There are practical limits on the prime minister's patronage powers: potential rivals may have strong claims for inclusion in the cabinet.
- Senior ministers can frustrate the prime minister's policy preferences by working together to oppose them or by threatening to resign.
- Ministers with concerns about decisions that affect their department can refer issues to the cabinet as a final court of appeal.
- Government departments provide ministers with expertise and support.
- Senior ministers who are popular with the public or their party may gain additional influence.

Ministerial responsibility

Collective ministerial responsibility

The cabinet is theoretically a united body. Ministers are usually members of the same party who stood on an agreed manifesto at the general election. However, unity is undermined by departmental and personal rivalries. As well as being members of the government, ministers are also heads of government departments, whose interests they fight for in cabinet. Money and influence are scarce resources for which ministers must bargain. Departments provide ministers with authority, policy advice and technical information, so they may be tempted to act as departmental chiefs rather than members of a collegiate body.

Collective responsibility is a core principle of government. It has three main elements:

- **Secrecy.** Ministers must keep the details of discussions in the cabinet system secret. This ensures that sensitive information does not enter the public domain and prevents differences of opinion from being revealed.
- **Binding decisions.** Once a decision is reached in the cabinet system, it becomes binding on all ministers regardless of whether they had opposed it or were not directly involved in decision making. Those unable to accept this should resign or expect to be dismissed. Senior ministers who have resigned because they disagreed with government policy include Robin Cook (2003) and Iain Duncan Smith (2016) (see the case study on page 136). The Blair and Brown governments saw some ministers resigning in an attempt to force a change of leader (see Table 6.3).
- **Confidence vote.** The government must resign if it is defeated in a vote of confidence (i.e. one explicitly concerning the life of the government). This last happened in 1979 when James Callaghan's Labour government lost a vote of confidence after its bill on Scottish devolution was defeated in the Commons.

Table 6.3 Examples of ministerial resignations over collective responsibility

Date	Minister	Post	Reason for resignation
1986	Michael Heseltine	Secretary of state for defence	Opposed defence procurement policy (Westland affair)
1989	Nigel Lawson	Chancellor of the exchequer	Opposed prime minister's conduct of economic policy
1990	Sir Geoffrey Howe	Leader of the House of Commons	Opposed policy on Europe
1995	John Redwood	Secretary of state for Wales	Launched leadership challenge
1998	Frank Field	Minister of state for social security and welfare reform	Opposed welfare policy
2003	Robin Cook (and 2 junior ministers)	President of the Council and leader of the House of Commons	Opposed invasion of Iraq
2003	Clare Short	Secretary of state for international development	Opposed policy on Iraq
2006	Tom Watson	Under-secretary of state for defence	Signed letter calling on Blair to resign
2009	James Purnell	Secretary of state for work and pensions	Critical of Brown's leadership
2009	Caroline Flint	Minister of state, Foreign Office	Critical of Brown's leadership
2014	Norman Baker	Minister of state, Home Office	Opposed policy on home affairs
2016	Iain Duncan Smith	Secretary of state for work and pensions	Opposed cuts to disability benefits in budget

The resignations of Robin Cook and Iain Duncan Smith

Robin Cook resigned as Leader of the House of Commons the day before parliament was due to vote on the Blair government's decision to join the USA in the invasion of Iraq without a second United Nations resolution. He had expressed concerns about military action in cabinet and resigned when he could no longer accept collective responsibility for the decision. Cook, a former foreign secretary, delivered a powerful resignation speech in the House of Commons. Secretary of state for international development Clare Short had publicly threatened to resign from the cabinet over policy on Iraq, but supported the government's resolution in the Commons. She resigned 2 months later.

The 2016 resignation of Iain Duncan Smith was less clear-cut. He resigned as secretary of state for work and pensions in protest at cuts to disability benefits made in the budget. In a frosty reply to Duncan Smith's resignation letter, David Cameron declared that he was 'puzzled' because his minister had agreed to the cuts before the budget and the government had since agreed that the cuts would not go ahead. Duncan Smith said that he could not support government economic strategy and had only learned on the morning of the budget that benefits for wealthy pensioners would be maintained while those for the disabled would be reduced. He had been uncomfortable with government policy for some time and had joined the Leave campaign in the EU referendum.

Questions

- What impact did the resignations of Robin Cook and Iain Duncan Smith have on the Blair and Cameron governments respectively?
- Compare these resignations with others identified in Table 6.3. Which were the most significant?

Exceptions to collective ministerial responsibility

Formal exceptions to the concept of collective ministerial responsibility have been agreed by the prime minister and cabinet in exceptional circumstances. These are discussed below.

Temporary suspension during referendums

On rare occasions, prime ministers have suspended collective responsibility temporarily to prevent ministerial resignations. Harold Wilson allowed ministers to campaign for either a 'yes' or a 'no' vote during the 1975 referendum on the European Economic Community (EEC), despite the government supporting a 'yes' vote. This allowed a government that was divided on Europe to function in a more united fashion on other issues.

Conservative and Liberal Democrat ministers were permitted by the coalition agreement to campaign on opposite sides in the 2011 alternative vote referendum.

In the 2016 EU referendum, Cameron also allowed ministers to take a personal decision to campaign to leave the EU, even though the government's position was to support EU membership. They were, however, denied access to civil service resources to support their position on the EU and were required to support the government's position on all other issues. Five cabinet ministers (plus Boris Johnson, who attended cabinet but was not a full member) campaigned to leave the EU.

Coalition

The 2010 Conservative–Liberal Democrat coalition agreement identified four issues on which Liberal Democrat ministers would not be bound by collective responsibility. They were permitted to abstain on the construction of new nuclear power stations, tax allowances for married couples, and higher education funding, and to make the case against renewal of the Trident nuclear deterrent. Ministers were also free to campaign on different sides in the 2011 referendum on the alternative vote. But collective responsibility also broke down where significant differences emerged between the coalition partners. The Liberal Democrats responded to the abandonment of legislation on House of Lords reform by withdrawing support for constituency boundary changes, with their ministers voting against the changes in 2013. As the general election neared, the trade-off between government unity and party distinctiveness became more difficult to manage. Most Liberal Democrat ministers voted in favour of a 2014 private members' bill proposing exceptions to the government's 'bedroom tax', while Conservative ministers opposed it. Conservative ministers voted in favour of a private members' bill proposing that an EU referendum be held by the end of 2017 but Liberal Democrats did not.

Free votes

Free votes may be granted to ministers as well as backbench MPs on issues of conscience. Labour's 1997 election manifesto promised a free vote on legislation to ban fox hunting. Cameron allowed a free vote on the Marriage (Same Sex Couples) Bill in 2013. Two cabinet ministers voted against the bill.

Strain on collective responsibility

Collective responsibility has also come under strain for other reasons.

- **Leaks.** Disgruntled ministers and their advisers may leak information on cabinet discussions to the media. They may want dissatisfaction about the policy or the conduct of government to be aired, but do not want to go public with their criticism. Cabinet discussions have also been revealed in books written by former ministers such as Ed Balls and Nick Clegg.
- **Dissent and non-resignation.** Cabinet ministers who oppose important aspects of government policy have survived in office even when their concerns have been made public. 'Wets' (one-nation Conservatives) in Thatcher's first cabinet scarcely concealed their opposition to her economic policy. None resigned and Thatcher dismissed them only when her position was secure. Liberal Democrat ministers were openly critical of some coalition policies 2010–15, but only one junior minister (Norman Baker) resigned over policy differences.
- **Prime-ministerial dominance.** Some cabinet ministers who served under Thatcher and Blair claimed that the prime minister had undermined collective responsibility by ignoring the cabinet. Michael Heseltine, Nigel Lawson and Sir Geoffrey Howe all cited Thatcher's contempt for collegiality when resigning. Mo Mowlam and Clare Short complained that Blair did not consult cabinet sufficiently.

Collective responsibility

The principle that all members of the government are responsible as a group. It has three main elements:

- Discussions in government should be kept secret.
- Decisions made in government are binding on all ministers.
- The government as a whole must resign if defeated on a vote of confidence in parliament.

Individual ministerial responsibility

The principle that ministers are accountable to parliament for their personal conduct, the general conduct of their department and the policies they and their department pursue, and the actions of officials within their department. Governments have redefined the convention so that ministers should *not* be held personally responsible for:

- decisions made in their department without their knowledge
- operational matters handled by officials in departments or executive agencies

Key term

Individual ministerial responsibility The principle that ministers are responsible to parliament for their personal conduct and that of their department.

Individual ministerial responsibility

The principle of **individual ministerial responsibility** means that ministers are accountable to parliament for their own personal conduct, the general conduct of their department and the policies they and their department pursue. The convention is not a rigid one.

Governments have long drawn a distinction between ministerial accountability (i.e. a minister's duty to give an account to parliament) and their individual responsibility. In 1954, home secretary Sir David Maxwell-Fyfe stated that ministers cannot be held responsible for decisions taken by civil servants without their knowledge, or which they disagreed with. Ministers are not obliged to resign if failings are traceable to the action (or inaction) of civil servants, but they are constitutionally responsible for informing parliament of the actions of their department.

The 1996 Scott Report on the sale of arms to Iraq stated that ministers had a duty to be as open as possible, withholding information only when disclosure would not be in the public interest, but ministers were culpable only if they misled parliament 'knowingly'. The *Ministerial Code* states that ministers must give 'accurate and truthful information to Parliament … [those who] knowingly mislead Parliament will be expected to offer their resignation'. Immigration minister Beverley Hughes resigned in 2004 after admitting that she had unwittingly given parliament a 'misleading impression' on checks on migrants from eastern Europe.

A further distinction is that between policy and operations. Ministers are responsible for policy, but officials are responsible for day-to-day operational matters. The head of the UK Border Force, Brodie Clark, resigned in 2011 after border controls were relaxed without ministerial agreement. He went beyond a pilot scheme requiring fewer checks on passengers by also suspending some passport checks, action which had not been authorised by home secretary Theresa May.

The transfer of policy implementation functions from government departments to executive agencies has added to the complexity surrounding ministerial responsibility.

In what circumstances do ministers resign?

Four main categories of resignation on the grounds of individual ministerial responsibility can be identified, but in practice they may overlap (see Table 6.4).

- **Mistakes made within departments.** Agriculture minister Sir Thomas Dugdale resigned in 1954 when mistakes made by civil servants in the Crichel Down case came to light (see the case study). Such cases are rare. Reports into the sale of arms to Iraq (1996) and BSE (2000) uncovered mistakes in departments but ministers survived. Ministers also remained in post when errors by civil servants forced the cancellation of competition for the West Coast Main Line franchise in 2012.

Case study

The resignation of Sir Thomas Dugdale

In 1954, Sir Thomas Dugdale, minister of agriculture, resigned after an independent inquiry was critical of the government's role in the Crichel Down affair. It concerned the compulsory purchase by the government of 700 acres of privately-owned farmland in Crichel Down, Dorset, for use as a bombing range shortly before the Second World War. The government promised to return the land to its owners after the war, but when the previous owner then sought to repurchase it, the Ministry of Agriculture took it over and let it out to another tenant. When the inquiry reported, Dugdale accepted responsibility for the mistakes and inefficiency of officials in his department and resigned.

Dugdale's resignation was thereafter treated as the classic example of a minister resigning because of errors made by civil servants. However, the release of official documents decades later prompted a reassessment. It emerged that Dugdale bore some responsibility as he knew of the civil servants' actions and had not sought to stop them. Nonetheless, his resignation immediately led to a clearer exposition by the government of individual ministerial responsibility which states that ministers should rectify minor mistakes made by officials and should not resign if they did not know of or approve mistakes made within their departments.

Questions
- Should Sir Thomas Dugdale have resigned?
- Should ministers be held responsible for operational mistakes?

- **Policy failure.** Resignations following policy failure include that of chancellor of the exchequer James Callaghan after the 1967 devaluation of sterling, although he became home secretary in the ensuing cabinet reshuffle. However, Norman Lamont did not resign as chancellor when sterling was devalued after being forced out of the European Exchange Rate Mechanism (ERM) in 1992. Foreign secretary Lord Carrington resigned after Argentina invaded the Falkland Islands in 1982 (see the case study on page 140) but defence secretary John Nott remained in office as Thatcher refused to accept his resignation.

The resignation of Lord Carrington

The resignations of foreign secretary Lord Carrington and two foreign office ministers, Humphrey Atkins and Richard Luce, within days of the Argentine invasion of the Falkland Islands in April 1982 are often cited as an example of ministers standing down because of policy failure. But Carrington maintained that the situation had not been mishandled by the Foreign Office. In his resignation letter, he accepted that he had been responsible for the conduct of policy. Carrington later insisted that, having come under pressure from MPs and the press, he resigned to ensure national unity in the build-up to war.

By coincidence, Carrington had also been a junior minister in the Ministry of Agriculture during the Crichel Down affair. He had offered his resignation then, but it was not accepted.

Questions
- Should secretary of state for defence John Nott also have resigned?
- What were the main policy failures in this case?

- **Personal misconduct.** Ministers are expected to follow the 'seven principles of public life' set out by the 1995 Nolan Committee on Standards in Public Life and included in the *Ministerial Code*. They are selflessness, integrity, objectivity, accountability, openness, honesty and leadership. The Nolan Committee was set up after the 'cash for questions' case which led to the resignations of Neil Hamilton and Tim Smith. Ministers who break the *Ministerial Code* are expected to resign (as Liam Fox did in 2011). Peter Mandelson and David Blunkett both left the Blair cabinet twice after allegations about their private interests and/or conduct in office (see the case study on page 142). Expenses scandals and criminal investigations have also brought about resignations (see Table 6.4). A number of ministers have remained in office despite press revelations about their private lives, but exceptions include Cecil Parkinson (who resigned in 1983) and Brooks Newmark (who resigned in 2014).
- **Political pressure.** The interpretation of this category can be quite loose because it covers resignations that are not attributable to a single policy problem or scandal. Instead, they follow a period of sustained pressure from parliament, the party or the press about a minister's performance. Chief whip Andrew Mitchell resigned in 2012, weeks after he was alleged to have insulted police officers at the entrance to Downing Street, after pressure on his position escalated. A minister is unlikely to remain in office if the prime minister considers ongoing negative publicity to be too damaging to the government.

Select examples of ministerial resignations over individual responsibility from Table 6.4. What factors were most important in bringing about the resignation? Consider, for example, the scale and nature of media coverage and the attitude of the prime minister and senior MPs. In what circumstances should ministers resign?

Table 6.4 Examples of ministerial resignations over individual responsibility

Date	Minister	Post	Reason for resignation
1963	John Profumo	Minister of war	Personal misconduct — sex scandal and lying to House of Commons
1967	James Callaghan	Chancellor of the exchequer	Policy failure — devaluation of sterling
1972	Reginald Maudling	Home secretary	Personal misconduct — financial affairs
1982	Lord Carrington (and two junior ministers)	Foreign secretary	Policy failure — misjudgements before Argentina invaded the Falkland Islands
1983	Cecil Parkinson	Secretary of state for trade and industry	Personal misconduct — extramarital affair
1986	Leon Brittan	Secretary of state for trade and industry	Political pressure — leak of letter in Westland affair
1988	Edwina Currie	Minister of state, Department for Health	Policy failure — criticised for her warning about salmonella in eggs
1994	Neil Hamilton	Minister of corporate affairs, Board of Trade	Personal misconduct — 'cash for questions'
1998	Peter Mandelson	Secretary of state for trade and industry	Personal misconduct — financial affairs
2001	Peter Mandelson	Secretary of state for Northern Ireland	Personal misconduct — allegations of abuse of office
2002	Stephen Byers	Secretary of state for transport	Political pressure — disputes in Department for Local Government, Transport and the Regions, and policy problems
2004	David Blunkett	Home secretary	Personal misconduct — allegations of abuse of office
2005	David Blunkett	Secretary of state for work and pensions	Personal misconduct — broke *Ministerial Code* on private sector job
2008	Peter Hain	Secretary of state for work and pensions; secretary of state for Wales	Personal misconduct — police investigation into political donations
2010	David Laws	Chief secretary to the treasury	Personal misconduct — past expenses claims
2011	Liam Fox	Secretary of state for defence	Personal misconduct — working relationship with special adviser broke the *Ministerial Code*
2012	Chris Huhne	Secretary of state for energy and climate change	Personal misconduct — charged with perverting the course of justice
2012	Andrew Mitchell	Chief whip	Personal misconduct — accused of insulting policemen in Downing Street
2014	Maria Miller	Secretary of state for culture, media and sport	Personal misconduct — past expenses claims
2014	Brooks Newmark	Minister for civil society, cabinet office	Personal misconduct — sent explicit images to undercover reporter

The resignations of David Blunkett

David Blunkett resigned twice from the Blair governments on the grounds of individual ministerial responsibility

David Blunkett resigned from the Blair governments on the grounds of individual ministerial responsibility on two occasions, both as a result of alleged misconduct. He resigned as home secretary in 2004 after allegations emerged in the press that Blunkett had requested officials to fast-track a visa application for a nanny employed by his former lover. An independent inquiry subsequently found a chain of events linking Blunkett to a change in the decision on the visa application but did not find conclusive evidence that Blunkett had directly intervened on the decision. Press reporting of the case later featured in a phone-hacking trial.

Blunkett returned to the cabinet after the 2005 general election but resigned as secretary of state for work and pensions within 6 months. It was alleged that Blunkett had broken the *Ministerial Code* by accepting a position as director of DNA Bioscience while out of office without consulting the Advisory Committee on Business Appointments. Critics claimed that there was a potential conflict of interest as the company was bidding for government contracts which came under the remit of Blunkett's department. Blunkett was summoned to a meeting with the prime minister and resigned. However, after his resignation, Blunkett was exonerated by the head of the civil service.

Questions
- Blunkett returned to the cabinet within months of his first resignation. Was Tony Blair right to reappoint him so quickly?
- Both resignations followed political pressure and loss of support from the prime minister. Given that he was later exonerated, could Blunkett have resisted the pressure for him to resign in 2005?

The relative power of the prime minister and cabinet

Cabinet government or prime-ministerial government?

For much of the twentieth century, the main debate about executive power was whether the UK still had a system of **cabinet government** or had developed one of **prime-ministerial government**. In his classic text *The English Constitution* (1867), Walter Bagehot described a system of cabinet government in which the prime minister was 'first among equals' (or *primus inter pares*) but decision making was a collective endeavour. By the second half of the twentieth century, the cabinet had been weakened and the powers of the prime minister had expanded. Proponents of the prime-ministerial government thesis argued that the prime minister was now the dominant actor and bypassed the cabinet when taking key decisions.

Cabinet government

A system of government in which executive power is vested in a cabinet whose members exercise collective responsibility, rather than in a single office. Within the cabinet, the prime minister is 'first among equals'. Although the prime minister has institutional resources that other ministers do not have, he or she cannot act unilaterally.

The executive and devolution

The devolution of powers to the Scottish Parliament, Welsh Assembly and Northern Ireland Assembly has reduced the resources of the UK core executive. The UK government is no longer responsible for making policy on devolved matters (see Chapter 4). Some flagship policies introduced by the UK government, such as the creation of foundation hospitals under the Blair governments, apply only to England.

Prime-ministerial government

A system of government in which the prime minister is the dominant actor in the executive. The prime minister sets the direction of government, makes the major decisions and intervenes decisively in policy areas of his or her choosing. The cabinet is able to advise and warn the prime minister, but does not decide policy.

However, the debate on whether the UK has either prime-ministerial government or cabinet government is flawed. Power is not located inevitably in one or the other; instead it is shared. Decline in the power of the cabinet does not inevitably mean that the prime minister is dominant. Instead, the prime minister needs the support of cabinet ministers and officials to achieve his or her objectives.

Professor George Jones uses the image of an elastic band to explain prime-ministerial power. He argues that the power resources available to the prime minister are not static but vary over time. Thatcher stretched the elastic band with her dominant leadership and tendency to ignore the concerns of her cabinet. The elastic band initially stretched to accommodate her style of leadership but Thatcher eventually stretched it too far. Then the elastic band snapped back as some cabinet ministers resigned and others finally withdrew their support for the prime minister during the 1990 Conservative leadership election, bringing about her downfall.

The power of the prime minister also varies according to external factors (e.g. policy success, government popularity) and the leadership style and skills of the prime minister. Political context matters. Political success, public popularity (see Figure 6.4) and a large parliamentary majority (see Figure 6.6) strengthen a prime minister's position. But policy failure, divisions within their party and unforeseen crises can weaken them. For Harold Macmillan, it was 'events, dear boy, events' that a prime minister feared.

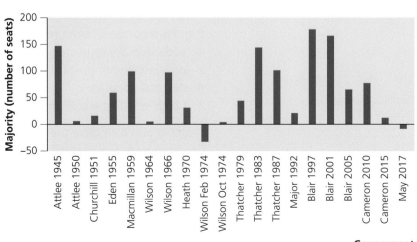

Figure 6.6 Government parliamentary majorities 1945–2017

A prime minister's **political leadership** skills are also important. Being a good communicator, having vision and political will, and being able to manage colleagues may all contribute to success in the role.

Case study

John Major and Gordon Brown: context and leadership style

John Major and Gordon Brown are judged unfavourably in comparison to their respective predecessors, Margaret Thatcher and Tony Blair. However, neither enjoyed the large parliamentary majorities or favourable political context of their predecessors. Both led unpopular and divided parties. The economic policy problems with which they are associated — sterling's exit from the European Exchange Rate Mechanism (ERM) in the case of Major, and the financial crisis

under Brown — resulted from external events as well as domestic policy failings.

However, the leadership style of both men was also criticised. Major's collegiate style was initially viewed as a welcome departure from Thatcher's dominance but he was soon regarded as weak and indecisive. Brown's communication skills, micro-management and temperament were all criticised.

Questions
- Why are John Major and Gordon Brown generally regarded as unsuccessful prime ministers?
- What is more significant in reaching this judgement — the difficult contexts they faced or the shortcomings of their leadership styles?

When is a prime minister predominant?

Richard Heffernan describes a system in which the prime minister is the *pre-eminent* figure because they automatically have four institutional power resources:
- legal head of the government (e.g. appointing ministers)
- leadership of the government (e.g. setting the policy agenda)
- the Prime Minister's Office
- setting the political agenda (e.g. through their party and the media)

The prime minister will be *predominant* (i.e. the stronger or main element) if they combine effective use of these institutional power resources with their own personal power resources:
- leadership ability and reputation
- association with political success
- electoral popularity
- a high standing within their party

Thatcher and Blair were predominant prime ministers, while Brown and Cameron were pre-eminent.

No prime minister has a monopoly of power: they have to work with ministers and must respond to parliamentary and public opinion. The prime minister leads but does not command the executive, and directs rather than controls its agenda.

In a 2016 survey, 82 political scientists and historians rated the success in office of postwar prime ministers on a scale of 0 to 10. The top three were: Clement Attlee (mean score of 8.5), Margaret Thatcher (7.2) and Tony Blair (6.7). David Cameron (4.0), Alec Douglas-Home (3.8) and Anthony Eden (2.4) made up the bottom three. The EU referendum was judged to be Cameron's greatest failure by 86% of those surveyed.

An earlier survey (2004) asked about the characteristics most important for prime-ministerial success. The top ones were: leadership skills (chosen by 64%), sound judgement (42%), good in a crisis (24%), decisiveness (22%) and luck (22%).

What do you think are the most important attributes for a successful prime minister? Use your list of core attributes to evaluate the strengths and weaknesses of recent prime ministers. How important are external factors and luck in determining whether a prime minister is successful?

Has the prime minister become presidential?

Professor Michael Foley argues that the office of prime minister has become more presidential: a *de facto* British presidency has emerged. There are three trends central to **presidentialisation**:

■ **Personalised leadership.** The prime minister is expected to be a dominant political personality who stamps his or her imprint on the government and imposes a personal vision. Thatcher was a conviction politician whose ideology set the political agenda, while Blair and Cameron modernised their parties. Thatcher and Blair were personally associated with major policy initiatives. The personalisation of leadership is also evident in election campaigns and party organisation. Election victory is treated as a personal mandate for the prime minister. The introduction of televised leaders' debates in the 2010 general election campaign reinforced the focus on party leaders.

■ **Public outreach.** Political leaders have become public commodities. The media spotlight falls on the prime minister to a greater extent than on any other minister. The prime minister is expected to connect with the popular mood. He or she claims to represent the public interest and takes their message directly to the public through the popular media (e.g. on 'soft format' chat shows). Blair and Cameron were especially effective communicators.

Key term

Presidentialisation The idea that UK prime ministers have taken on some of the characteristics of presidents.

Presidentialisation

This is idea that UK prime ministers have taken on some of the characteristics of presidents because of the emergence of a personalised form of leadership. It is characterised by spatial leadership (the distancing of the prime minister from his or her government) and public outreach (the tendency of the prime minister to reach out to the public directly). However, the concept of presidentialisation does not claim necessarily that the office of UK prime minister is becoming the same as that of US president.

The 'Quad' (Danny Alexander, David Cameron, George Osborne and Nick Clegg)

■ **Spatial leadership.** A sense of distance has been created between the prime minister and his or her government and party. The prime minister relies more on his or her own inner circle of advisers than on the cabinet system, as in Blair's 'sofa government' and the 'Quad' (Cameron, Nick Clegg, George Osborne and Danny Alexander) in the Conservative–Liberal Democrat coalition government. Blair and Cameron presented themselves as outsiders in their own parties.

The focus on the leader has strengthened the position of the prime minister but it also creates problems. Just as the prime minister gains credit for policy success, so they are blamed personally for policy or personal failings. Blair's position was weakened after the invasion of Iraq, Brown was criticised for his inability to connect with the public, and Cameron resigned after losing the EU referendum.

Debate

Has the prime minister become more presidential?

Yes

- Leadership in the executive has been personalised, with the prime minister expected to impose his or her personality and agenda.
- Prime ministers increasingly rely on a close circle of senior ministers and advisers.
- Prime ministers have created a 'strategic space' between themselves and their governments, distancing themselves from other actors in the executive.
- Prime ministers appeal to the public directly, through the media, and claim a personal mandate from the electorate.
- Prime ministers have additional authority as party leaders, where they are elected by MPs and members, and exercise personalised leadership.

No

- The prime minister leads but cannot command the executive, particularly in coalition, and directs rather than controls the agenda.
- Senior ministers have resources of their own, including support from government departments.
- The prime minister needs the support of ministers and officials to achieve his or her objectives.
- The prime minister's position is strong only if he or she enjoys policy success and popular approval, and makes effective use of his or her own personal abilities.
- Support from the party is not unconditional and unpopular leaders face concerted efforts to remove them.

Criticisms of the presidentialisation thesis

Critics argue that the notion of a British presidency misrepresents the nature of power within the core executive. It overstates the room for manoeuvre that a prime minister has and underestimates their dependence on cabinet ministers and their party. Crude versions of the thesis ignore the significant differences between the parliamentary system of government in the UK and the system of **presidential government** found in the USA.

Michael Foley's thesis does not claim, however, that the office of British prime minister is becoming the same as that of the US president. Nor has the UK become a presidential system of government.

Government ministers and departments

Government ministers

There are more than 100 ministers in the government. Ministers are allocated positions in government departments. Senior ministers often hold the rank of **secretary of state**, sit in the cabinet and head government departments. Below them in the hierarchy come the minister of state and parliamentary under-secretary. These junior ministers are given specific policy roles in a department. The Home Office has one secretary of state, four ministers of state (responsible for security, immigration, policing and the fire service, and devolution) and two parliamentary under-secretaries (responsible for internet security and tackling crime and extremism). Parliamentary private secretaries are unpaid assistants to ministers but do not have ministerial status.

The main roles performed by ministers are:
- **Policy leadership.** A minister does not have the time or knowledge to play a hands-on role in all detailed policy but plays an important role in policy initiation and selection. Cameron granted ministers greater policy autonomy than was the norm under Blair and Brown.
- **Representing departmental interests.** Ministers represent the interests of their department in the cabinet. They represent the government in the Council of the European Union.
- **Departmental management.** Ministers play a strategic role in managing their department, setting objectives and shaping the internal distribution of resources.
- **Relations with parliament.** Ministers steer bills through parliament. They are accountable to parliament for decisions taken in their department, answer questions in the House of Commons and appear before select committees.

Government departments

Government departments are the main administrative units of central government. They are located in the Whitehall area of London — hence the use of the term 'Whitehall' to describe the bureaucratic apparatus of central government. In major departments, a cabinet minister is the political head and the permanent secretary is the most senior civil servant.

The functions of government departments include:
- providing policy advice to ministers
- managing public spending
- fostering relationships with interested parties, such as pressure groups
- policy implementation

> **Key term**
>
> **Presidential government** A system of government in which a single, directly elected chief executive governs. The executive branch is constitutionally separate from the legislature.

> **Key term**
>
> **Secretary of state** A government minister in charge of a major government department, such as health or education.

Departments are organised according to the policy area they are responsible for (e.g. health) or the sections of society they serve (e.g. those receiving social security benefits). The territorial extent of their function varies. The work of some departments (e.g. the Ministry of Defence) covers the whole of the UK, but on devolved matters, some (e.g. the Department for Health) deal mainly with policy for England. Whitehall departments oversee the provision of public services, but responsibility for much day-to-day policy delivery has been transferred to semi-autonomous executive agencies (such as HM Prison Service).

The Treasury is the most powerful department. It controls public spending and other departments require its approval to undertake major new financial commitments. Spending reviews set out the spending limits for each government department and chancellors have used these to shape policy in high-spending departments such as health and social security. The contents of the budget are not revealed to the cabinet until hours before the chancellor's announcement.

The Attorney General's Office is the department responsible for providing legal advice to government. The two ministers within it, the Attorney General and the Solicitor General, are known as the Law Officers. The Attorney General is principal legal adviser on EU and international law, human rights and devolved powers. Draft legislation must be approved by the Law Officers. Advice provided by the Law Officers is occasionally controversial. The 2016 Chilcot Report stated that the circumstances in which decisions were taken about the legality of the 2003 invasion of Iraq were 'far from satisfactory'.

Civil servants

Government departments are staffed by **civil servants**: that is, officials appointed by the Crown. Some civil servants provide policy advice to ministers. In doing so, they may have advantages over ministers, such as experience, expertise and access to information. Civil servants are required to provide impartial advice but can define which policy options are practicable and affordable.

The civil service is a bureaucracy that has a hierarchical structure and has traditionally operated according to four principles:

- **Impartiality.** Civil servants serve the Crown rather than the government of the day. They are expected to be politically neutral and not become involved in overtly party political tasks.
- **Anonymity.** Individual civil servants should not be identified as the author of advice to ministers. Some may be called before parliamentary committees, but they give evidence under the direction of ministers.
- **Permanence.** Civil servants stay in their posts when there is a change of government.
- **Meritocracy.** Civil servants are not political appointments. Instead, the civil service is staffed by generalists, recruited through competitive exams and interviews.

The policy-making and policy implementation roles of the civil service were separated in the 1980s. Civil servants working in Whitehall continue to advise ministers but policy implementation functions and the delivery of public services were transferred to executive agencies. They operate at

Key terms

Special adviser A temporary political appointment made by a government minister.

Spin doctor A special adviser employed to promote the image of the minister and his or her policy in the media.

arm's length from government departments. The number of civil servants has been cut from 732,000 in 1979 to 385,000 in 2016.

Special advisers and spin doctors

Ministers employ **special advisers** to carry out policy advice or media liaison roles, the latter being known as **spin doctors**. Special advisers are political appointments employed as temporary civil servants. In 2015, there were 93 special advisers across government, more than double the number employed in the early 1990s. Of these, 32 worked for the prime minister.

The power of the prime minister and cabinet to dictate events and determine policy

Harold Wilson as prime minister

Harold Wilson served as prime minister in two non-consecutive terms, 1964–70 and 1974–76. In his first spell, Wilson appeared in tune with public opinion. He appeared at ease on television and was a technocrat who sought to modernise Britain. His Labour government increased welfare spending, reformed the education system and introduced liberal social reforms (see the case study below). It put its faith in economic planning, creating a (short-lived) Department for Economic Affairs and Ministry of Technology. But the government was forced to devalue the pound in 1967, damaging Wilson's credibility. As industrial relations worsened, government proposals for trade union reform were shelved after opposition from the Trades Union Congress.

Case study

Policy impact: social reform

The 1960s was a period of significant social and cultural change in Britain. Many of these changes occurred autonomously of government, but Wilson's Labour government also played a key role in changing the legal landscape. The Divorce Reform Act 1969 made divorce easier by introducing the principle of irretrievable breakdown: couples could divorce if they had been separated for 2 years and fault did not have to be established. Race relations legislation outlawed direct discrimination on the grounds of race, colour and ethnicity. Three landmark private members' bills abolished the death penalty, decriminalised sex between

men in private, and legalised abortion up to 24 weeks of pregnancy. Without government backing and Labour's large parliamentary majority after the 1966 general election, these changes would have been more difficult to achieve.

The government brought about important changes in education, encouraging local authorities to convert grammar schools into comprehensives — a key Labour commitment. It also established polytechnics, which focused on vocational education, and the Open University.

Question

Do governments tend to lead or follow public opinion on the social issues identified here?

Critics castigated Wilson for focusing on short-term tactics and lacking principles or vision. Party management became increasingly difficult as the left of the Labour Party flexed its muscles. It sought an extension of public ownership, but only steel was (re-)nationalised.

Wilson's 1974–76 government was dogged by difficulties. Labour formed a minority government after the February 1974 general election, then won a majority of 3 seats in the October 1974 contest. Intra-party divisions also saw Wilson hold a referendum on membership of the European Economic Community (EEC) in 1975 and suspend collective responsibility (see the case study below). With the economy performing poorly and industrial relations proving difficult, political commentators speculated that Britain was becoming 'ungovernable'.

Case study

Policy problems: European integration

The UK's relationship with the European Union (EU) and its predecessors has posed problems for UK prime ministers since the 1960s. In opposition, Harold Wilson had opposed Harold Macmillan's failed application to join the European Economic Community (EEC). But in government Wilson also applied to join, only to suffer the same fate as his predecessor when French president Charles de Gaulle vetoed the membership for a second time in 1967. When Labour returned to office in 1974, the UK was a member of the EEC having joined the previous year. But most Labour MPs opposed membership, viewing the EEC as a 'capitalist club'.

In an attempt to resolve the issue, Wilson undertook a limited renegotiation of the terms of EEC membership and then called a referendum on whether the UK should remain in the EEC under the new terms. In a highly unusual move, Wilson suspended collective responsibility during the referendum campaign. Most cabinet ministers campaigned to remain in the EEC but five campaigned to leave. Wilson himself played little role in the campaign. The result appeared decisive: a 2 : 1 vote in favour of membership. But within 6 years, Labour had split and the issue of European integration continued to trouble UK prime ministers.

Question
Why has the issue of European integration posed so many problems for British prime ministers?

Margaret Thatcher as prime minister

Margaret Thatcher is generally viewed as one of only two agenda-setting postwar prime ministers, the other being Clement Attlee whose Labour government (1945–51) created the modern welfare state. She was a conviction politician who gave her name to a new right ideology, Thatcherism, which overturned the postwar consensus by pursuing monetarism, privatising state-owned industries and reducing trade union power (see the case study).

Case study

Policy impact: trade union reform and privatisation

The industrial relations landscape was changed profoundly by the governments of Margaret Thatcher as five major pieces of legislation weakened the trade unions. But the initial approach was cautious as secretary of state for employment James Prior persuaded Thatcher of the case for gradual reform. The pace of change increased when Prior was replaced by Thatcher's ally, Norman Tebbit, in 1981. The government's victory in the miners' strike of 1984–85, a particularly bitter industrial dispute, also proved pivotal.

The Thatcher governments' privatisation programme saw the sale of shares in nationalised industries such as British Gas, British Airways and electricity and water companies. Again, a radical policy emerged gradually after the successful sale of shares in British Telecom in 1984 prompted the government to undertake further privatisations. Policy was motivated partly by ideology (the desire for greater competition and a smaller state), but political considerations (e.g. raising revenue and winning votes) were decisive.

Question
Were these policies driven by ideology or traditional political considerations?

Thatcher made less use of cabinet than her predecessors. She often began cabinet discussions by announcing the government's policy on an issue and kept some issues away from cabinet. Senior ministers accused her of paying greater attention to her advisers than to them.

Early in her premiership, Thatcher's skilful management of the cabinet enabled her to cement her authority at a time when many ministers doubted her policies. Her refusal, at a time of recession, to bow to pressure to tone down the monetarist budget of 1981 — and the unwillingness of her cabinet critics to seize the initiative — proved decisive. Thatcher was then able to construct a cabinet of ideological allies. Victory in the 1982 Falklands War was seen as a triumph for the 'Iron Lady' and, with the economy recovering, helped her to election victory the following year.

By 1990, Thatcher had few allies left in the cabinet. Chancellor John Major exploited her relative weakness to persuade Thatcher to agree entry into the European Exchange Rate Mechanism (ERM) — a policy she had long opposed. Within weeks, Thatcher failed to win on the first ballot of the Conservative leadership election. She then met her cabinet ministers one by one, but few offered their full support and Thatcher resigned. Economic problems, unpopular policies such as the poll tax (see the case study on page 152), cabinet divisions and low opinion poll ratings (see Figure 6.4 on page 129) contributed to her downfall. However, Thatcher was, in part, the author of her own misfortune. By ignoring the concerns of ministers and bypassing cabinet, she failed to recognise her dependence on her cabinet and alienated colleagues whose support she needed.

Policy problems: the poll tax

The poll tax, officially known as the Community Charge, is a prime example of a policy disaster — a policy that fails spectacularly to achieve its objectives and causes intensive disruption to the political process. A local tax that was paid by all taxpayers (with some exceptions), the poll tax replaced the domestic rates, which were based on property value and only paid by property owners. Advocates of the poll tax argued that if every person had to contribute towards the cost of local services through a flat-rate tax, local authorities would come under pressure to provide these services more efficiently. But the new tax proved hugely unpopular as millions of voters who had never before had to pay local taxes received large bills, and blamed the Thatcher government. The tax was also regressive, taking a higher percentage of the income of the poor than the rich, and many viewed it as unfair. Riots in London preceded the introduction of the tax in England in 1990. Councils then found the poll tax difficult to administer and collect, as many people refused to pay.

The roots of the policy disaster lay within government. Ministers had to act quickly on local taxation as a major review of the rates was due, but checks and balances within the cabinet system failed. In particular, warnings from the chancellor and Treasury were not given due consideration and local authorities were not consulted fully. Thatcher pushed the proposal through government and parliament without major amendment. By late 1990, many Conservative MPs recognised the electoral damage Thatcher's flagship policy was causing and voted against her in the Conservative leadership contest. The poll tax was replaced by the council tax under John Major.

A protest at the introduction of the poll tax, March 1990

Question
What part did the poll tax play in Thatcher's downfall?

Tony Blair as prime minister

In his first years in office, Tony Blair was viewed as a more dominant prime minister than Thatcher. He had little time for cabinet government, preferring to conduct government business through bilateral meetings in which he agreed policy objectives with individual ministers. Key decisions were reached in informal meetings of an inner circle of advisers. This style of government was dubbed 'sofa government'. Blair sought to command swathes of government policy from Downing Street and improve policy coordination and delivery.

In his first two terms, Blair enjoyed big parliamentary majorities, a strong position within his party and a largely loyal cabinet. He pursued a 'Third Way' that combined free market economics (privatisation, efficiency savings in the public sector, low taxes and control of inflation) with social justice (the national minimum wage, a reduction in child poverty and increased welfare spending). A programme of constitutional reform modernised the UK state, and Blair himself played a key role in the Northern Ireland peace process (see the case study).

Case study

Policy impact: constitutional reform

The Blair governments introduced the most extensive constitutional reforms of modern times — devolution, reform of the House of Lords, new electoral systems, the Supreme Court and the Human Rights Act. However, Blair did not play a great role in policy initiative or design. He inherited policy commitments from John Smith, his predecessor as Labour leader, and worked on them with Liberal Democrat leader Paddy Ashdown — including in a cabinet committee attended by Liberal Democrats.

Blair was not greatly interested in constitutional reform. His doubts helped kill off proposals for electoral reform for Westminster and devolution to the English regions. Changes to the role of the lord chancellor were botched and Blair also came to regret introducing the Freedom of Information Act 2000.

The prime minister did play a major role in the Northern Ireland peace process, notably in the negotiations on the 1998 Good Friday Agreement. He sidelined secretary of state for Northern Ireland, Mo Mowlam, who was distrusted by some unionists, and offered personal guarantees on weapons decommissioning and prisoner releases.

Question
How important was Blair's input to Labour's constitutional reform programme?

Problems came to the fore in Blair's second term in office. He faced rebellions by Labour MPs over Iraq, foundation hospitals and tuition fees, and his opinion poll ratings fell (see Figure 6.4 on page 129). The 2003 invasion of Iraq damaged his reputation (see the case study below). His announcement that he would step down during his third term weakened his authority and he had to fend off attempts by Labour MPs to remove him. By stepping down in June 2007, Blair may have jumped before he was pushed.

Case study

Policy problems: the invasion of Iraq

Blair's legacy is coloured by his decision to support US president George W. Bush and commit UK forces to the 2003 invasion of Iraq. While Bush made it clear that the removal of Iraq president Saddam Hussein was a core objective of US policy, Blair focused on removing weapons of mass destruction (WMD). Much of Blair's case rested upon intelligence assessments that Iraq could launch WMD within 45 minutes. But WMD were never found and the intelligence reports were later discredited. After the removal of Saddam, Iraq descended into anarchy. Opinion polls registered a sharp decline in public trust of Blair, and his standing in the Labour Party was badly damaged.

A series of official reports were highly critical of decisions taken in government prior to the invasion. The 2004 report by Lord Butler noted that although the cabinet was briefed on Iraq on 24 occasions in the year before the invasion, ministers were denied access to key papers. Blair's preference for 'sofa government' had also reduced the scope for informed collective judgement. The 2016 Chilcot Report concluded that other policy options had not been properly explored, that Blair had disregarded warnings about the intelligence and the potential consequences of military action, and that cabinet had not considered legal advice carefully enough. The report highlighted the need for frank and informed collective ministerial discussion in future.

Question
Why were independent inquiries on Iraq so critical of Blair's style of government?

The Blair government was unusual for the extent of chancellor Gordon Brown's influence. Blair and Brown had their own 'courts' and areas where they were influential — Brown had unparalleled influence over welfare and social policy that stretched beyond a chancellor's usual domain. It was Blair and Brown, rather than the cabinet, who decided to make the Bank of England independent (i.e. give it, rather than the Treasury, the authority to set interest rates) in 1997. The two bargained over policy but their relationship was often fraught. By Blair's third term, Brown's supporters were trying to force Blair out of office. But the relationship between Blair and Brown was one of mutual dependence: one could not maintain his position without the support of the other.

David Cameron as prime minister

David Cameron adopted a more collegial approach than Thatcher or Blair, in part because the coalition required regular negotiation between Conservative and Liberal Democrat ministers. Key decisions were taken in bilateral meetings between Cameron and Nick Clegg, and in meetings of the 'Quad' (Cameron, Clegg, George Osborne and Danny Alexander). But coalition constrained Cameron's powers of patronage and ability to dictate policy (see the debate).

Debate

Was coalition government a significant constraint on the power of David Cameron as prime minister?

Yes

- The Coalition Agreement for Stability and Reform set the number of Liberal Democrat cabinet ministers. Cameron could not dismiss or reshuffle Liberal Democrat ministers without Clegg's approval.
- The government's principal policies were set out in the Coalition Programme for Government, and the Liberal Democrats resisted deviation from it.
- Coalition required a more collective style of government, with key issues discussed in the cabinet system to ensure the agreement of both parties.
- The prime minister had to manage tensions between Conservatives and Liberal Democrats, in addition to dissent within the Conservative Party.

No

- The prime minister retained significant patronage powers, such as creating and making appointments to cabinet committees.
- The prime minister determined the overall direction of government policy and shaped its response to new issues.
- Key decisions were taken by the prime minister in consultation with Clegg or in the 'Quad', where relations were often smoother than those between Blair and Brown.
- Forming a coalition gave Cameron a healthy parliamentary majority, and the coalition proved stable.

Cameron appeared temperamentally suited to coalition and allowed ministers greater freedom to get on with their job. But this backfired as he was criticised for making a number of policy U-turns. Reorganisation of the NHS ran into trouble as problems with radical plans produced by secretary of state for health Andrew Lansley were not spotted early enough. Cameron thereafter beefed up Number 10's role in commanding policy.

Economic austerity was the defining position of the coalition. This was a Conservative position that marked a return to the Thatcherite vision of a free economy and small state. The Liberal Democrats accepted much of this and, despite implementing their policies on increasing the income tax allowance for the low paid, it proved electorally costly for them. Osborne cut public spending significantly as he sought to reduce the deficit and reassure the financial markets. Critics highlighted the social costs of spending cuts, and targets for deficit reduction were still missed. Despite this, and the 'omnishambles' budget of 2012, voters trusted the Conservatives more than Labour on the economy.

The coalition stayed in office for a full term, although growing tensions between the coalition partners stemmed the flow of policy initiatives. Intra-party divisions also proved difficult to manage and, in 2013, Cameron promised an in/out referendum on EU membership in an attempt to quell Conservative dissent. Many Conservatives also voted against one of Cameron's main initiatives, the legalisation of same-sex marriage.

Victory in the 2015 general election strengthened Cameron's position, but a small parliamentary majority, his announcement that he would retire before the next general election and the upcoming EU referendum suggested problems ahead. A year later, Cameron resigned when the UK voted for Brexit. His warnings of the dire consequences of Brexit damaged his relationship with many in his party and undermined his popularity with voters.

Theresa May as prime minister

There were signs early in May's premiership that she may be a strong prime minister:

- reorganisation of the cabinet system, with the prime minister carrying out an extensive cabinet reshuffle, chairing key cabinet committees and strengthening the Prime Minister's Office
- significant support within her party — 199 Conservative MPs (61%) voted for her on the second ballot of the 2016 leadership election
- strong performance in opinion polls
- her extensive ministerial experience before becoming prime minister

However, limits to her potential power as prime minister became apparent:

- the damage to her personal authority caused by calling an early general election, then performing badly in a campaign in which she chose to focus on her 'strong and stable' leadership
- losing her parliamentary majority in the election, and becoming a minority government reliant on support from the Democratic Unionist Party
- divisions within the cabinet and among Conservative MPs over her leadership and policy direction
- the scale of the domestic and foreign policy challenges posed by Brexit
- a sharp reduction in her standing in the opinion polls

The collapse in May's authority following the 2017 general election was so pronounced that it seemed highly unlikely that she could survive as prime minister for a full term.

What you should know

- The prime minister is the pre-eminent actor within the executive branch. He or she has significant institutional resources. The prime minister appoints and dismisses ministers, chairs the cabinet and directs discussion within it, and is supported by the Prime Minister's Office and Cabinet Office. Leadership of the largest party in the House of Commons brings additional authority.
- The powers of a prime minister are tempered by constraints, including the need to placate senior colleagues and the party when appointing the cabinet. The prime minister has the potential to be predominant, but this depends upon effective use of institutional resources, a favourable context and the prime minister's own leadership skills.
- The position of prime minister has been strengthened in recent decades, with some scholars talking of presidentialisation. Leadership has become personalised and prime ministers turn to their inner circle of ministers and advisers rather than to the formal institutions of the cabinet system.
- No prime minister can monopolise power. They can lead but not command, and direct rather than control policy. Other individuals (e.g. cabinet ministers) and institutions (government departments) also have resources. To achieve his or her goals, the prime minister needs the support of senior cabinet ministers.

UK/US comparison

The prime minister and the president

- The US president is head of state as well as head of government. The key formal source of the powers of the president is the US Constitution. It places significant limits on presidential power. Informal sources of presidential power (e.g. the use of executive orders and powers of persuasion) have also developed over time. The monarch is head of state in the UK. The powers of the prime minister are not set out in statute law.
- The US president is directly elected and can claim a personal mandate. Fixed-term elections take place every 4 years. The UK prime minister is not directly elected; he or she is leader of the largest party in the House of Commons. Fixed-term elections to the Commons take place every 5 years.
- In the USA, the separation of powers means that the executive does not dominate the legislature. The president cannot force Congress to accept his will: the president has some powers to veto legislation but Congress may override this. The legislature can only dismiss the president through impeachment. Divided government occurs when one political party holds the presidency but its rival controls Congress. In the UK, the executive exercises significant control over the legislature but the government must resign if it loses a vote of confidence in the Commons.
- The US executive branch serves the president. The US cabinet is an advisory body subordinate to the president; it does not share executive power with him or her. The Executive Office of the President provides strong institutional support. Presidents also appoint many of the officials working within their administration. In the UK, the prime minister is the predominant figure in the executive but needs the support of senior cabinet colleagues. The civil service is impartial and is not politically appointed.
- The US president's nominees for key posts, such as cabinet members and Supreme Court judges, are subject to approval by the legislature. In the UK, some appointments made by the prime minister (e.g. government ministers) do not require parliamentary approval.
- The US president is head of his or her political party but parties are loose organisations whose members often act independently. The UK prime minister is also leader of his or her party but enjoys much greater control over it.

Further reading

Bennister, M. (2015) 'The prime minister: has coalition government affected prime ministerial power?', *Politics Review*, Vol. 24, No. 3, pp. 8–11.

Bennister, M. (2016) 'Prime ministerial power: is it in decline?', *Politics Review*, Vol. 25, No. 3, pp. 24–27.

Bennister, M. (2017) 'The cabinet: is there still collective cabinet responsibility?', *Politics Review*, Vol. 26, No. 4, pp. 2–5.

Foley, M. (2009) 'The presidential controversy in Britain', *Politics Review*, Vol. 18, No. 3, pp. 20–22.

Heffernan, R. (2008) 'Prime ministerial predominance', *Politics Review*, Vol. 17, No. 3, pp. 2–5.

Cabinet Manual (2010) Cabinet Office: www.tinyurl.com/hs6fqqh

Ministerial Code (2015) Cabinet Office: www.tinyurl.com/nnns45m

10 Downing Street: www.number10.gov.uk

Cabinet Office: www.tinyurl.com/qf597gz

Cabinet committees: www.tinyurl.com/gkpmhpa

Institute for Government: www.instituteforgovernment.org.uk

BBC News report: 'The Blair Years 1997–2007': www.tinyurl.com/c787szv

BBC News report: 'Margaret Thatcher': www.tinyurl.com/hlq8su5

Exam-style questions

Short-answer questions

1 Explain, with examples, the role of a cabinet minister.

2 Explain, with examples, how a person may become prime minister.

3 Explain and analyse three considerations made when appointing cabinet ministers.

4 Explain and analyse three features of cabinet government.

Mid-length questions

1 Describe the main functions of the UK cabinet.

2 Describe the key features of prime ministerial government.

3 Analyse and evaluate the arguments that suggest prime ministers have become more presidential.

4 Analyse and evaluate the arguments in favour of collective ministerial responsibility.

Essay questions

1 Evaluate the extent to which the cabinet can act as a check on prime ministerial power.

2 Evaluate the extent to which prime ministers have become more presidential in recent years.

3 'The cabinet no longer plays a meaningful role in the UK political system.' Analyse and evaluate this statement.

4 'Prime ministers are free to follow the policies they want.' How far do you agree with this view of prime ministerial power?

In your answer you must:

- Refer to one pre-1997 prime minister and at least one post-1997 prime minister.

- Draw on relevant knowledge and understanding of UK politics.

Chapter 7

The Supreme Court

Key questions answered
- What is the role and composition of the Supreme Court?
- What are the key doctrines and principles that underpin the work of the Supreme Court?
- How does the Supreme Court use its powers to review the actions of other institutions and protect rights?
- What impact does the Supreme Court have through its work?
- What might Brexit mean for the jurisdiction, power and authority of the Supreme Court?

Supreme Court judges can establish new rules or 'precedents'

The UK Supreme Court's power to hear appeals and review the action of other public bodies allows it to establish new rules or 'precedents' that affect not only the case in question, but also all subsequent cases.

At 2.30 a.m. on 10 June 2011, Paul Fyfe was stabbed to death by a man later known in court as 'Hirsi'. A third man, known as 'Jogee', had been drinking and taking drugs with Hirsi on that evening. Although Jogee had not stabbed Mr Fyfe, he had been shouting encouragement to Hirsi at the time of the fatal attack.

At the Crown Court trial that followed, both Hirsi and Jogee were found guilty of murder, under the so-called 'joint enterprise' rule. This rule or precedent had been established in common law by the courts in earlier cases such as *Chan Wing-Siu* v *The Queen* (1985). It meant that any individual who was part of a group that committed an offence could be convicted for that crime, even if they had not themselves 'pulled the trigger'.

Jogee's appeal against his murder conviction eventually made its way to the UK's highest court, the Supreme Court. In the case of *R* v *Jogee* (2016), the court used its power to change the rules on joint enterprise. It was no longer enough simply to be present when a crime was committed in order to be convicted of that crime; there would also have to be 'intent', 'encouragement' or 'assistance'. Jogee's actions on the night of the murder meant that his sentence was only reduced from 20 to 18 years but the case had a wider importance because a new precedent had been established. In March 2016, just 1 month after the Supreme Court's ruling, the *Daily Telegraph* reported that two defendants in another murder case had walked free after a judge ruled that they no longer had any case to answer. Some commentators argued that the Supreme Court had, in effect, *changed* the law, rather than simply *applied* the law.

The role and composition of the Supreme Court

Key term

Judiciary In normal usage the term 'judiciary' refers collectively to all UK judges, from lay magistrates and those serving on tribunals right up to the 12 senior justices sitting in the UK Supreme Court. In a wider sense the term might be seen as encompassing all of those who are directly involved in the administration and application of justice.

The UK **judiciary** does not exist as a single body. Scotland and Northern Ireland operate under different legal arrangements from those in place in England and Wales. The one feature common to all three systems is the part played by the UK Supreme Court, which acts as the highest court of appeal from the Court of Appeal in England and Wales, the Court of Sessions in Scotland, and the Court of Appeal in Northern Ireland (see Figure 7.1).

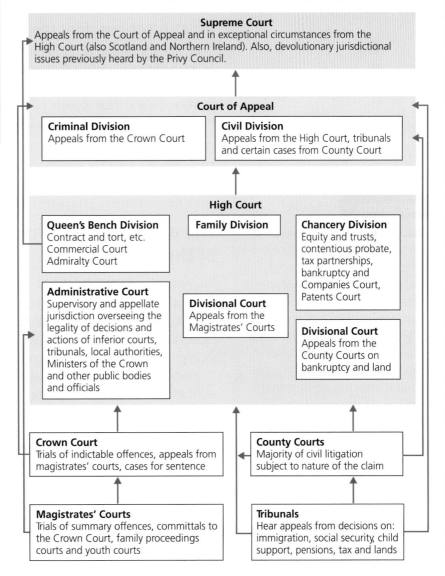

Figure 7.1 The judiciary in England and Wales

The origins and functions of the Supreme Court

Why was the UK Supreme Court established?

Before the UK Supreme Court began its work in October 2009, the highest court of appeal in the UK comprised the 12 Law Lords who sat in the Appellate Committee of the House of Lords. The UK Supreme Court was established under the **Constitutional Reform Act (CRA) 2005** in response to a number of longstanding concerns:

- concerns over the incomplete separation of powers, or partial 'fusion of powers', present in the UK system; specifically, the position of the lord chancellor and the presence of the Law Lords in the upper chamber of the legislature
- criticisms of the opaque system under which senior judges, such as the Law Lords, were appointed
- confusion over the work of the Law Lords — specifically, a widespread failure to understand the distinction between the House of Lords' legislative and judicial functions

What functions does the Supreme Court perform?

Under the Constitutional Reform Act 2005 the new UK Supreme Court took on most of those judicial roles previously performed by the Law Lords:

- to act as the final court of appeal in England, Wales, and Northern Ireland – and hear appeals from civil cases in Scotland
- to clarify the meaning of the law, by hearing appeals in cases where there is uncertainty

The creation of the UK Supreme Court, under the Constitutional Reform Act, is also discussed in Chapter 3 — in the context of New Labour's constitutional reform programme (1997–2010).

The appointments process and the composition of the court

How are Supreme Court justices appointed?

Appointments to all positions in the **senior judiciary** were traditionally made by the monarch on the advice of the prime minister and the lord chancellor. The lord chancellor would consult existing senior judges through a process known as **secret soundings**.

It was said that this system lacked transparency, undermined the separation of powers, and resulted in a senior judiciary drawn almost exclusively from a very narrow social circle: public school and Oxbridge educated, white, male and beyond middle age. Such criticisms were at the heart of the 2005 Constitutional Reform Act.

The founding justices of the new Supreme Court were those working Law Lords in post on 1 October 2009. Although these individuals remained members of the House of Lords, they were barred from sitting and voting in the upper chamber for as long as they remained justices of the new Supreme Court. Under the Constitutional Reform Act 2005 those appointed to the court after 1 October 2009 are not automatically awarded peerages.

Key term

Constitutional Reform Act (CRA) 2005 The CRA reduced the power of the lord chancellor and placed most senior judicial appointments into the hands of a new, independent Judicial Appointments Commission (JAC). It was hoped that this change would enhance the separation of powers and result in a senior judiciary that was more socially representative of the broader population. The Act also provided for the creation of the Supreme Court.

Key terms

Secret soundings The informal and secretive way in which most senior UK judges were once appointed. The phrase describes the way in which the lord chancellor consulted in secret with close associates and those already serving in the senior judiciary. The resulting lack of transparency in appointments led to accusations of elitism.

Senior judiciary The senior judiciary comprises justices of the Supreme Court (formerly the Lords of Appeal in Ordinary, or Law Lords), heads of divisions, Lords Justices of Appeal, High Court judges, and deputy High Court judges.

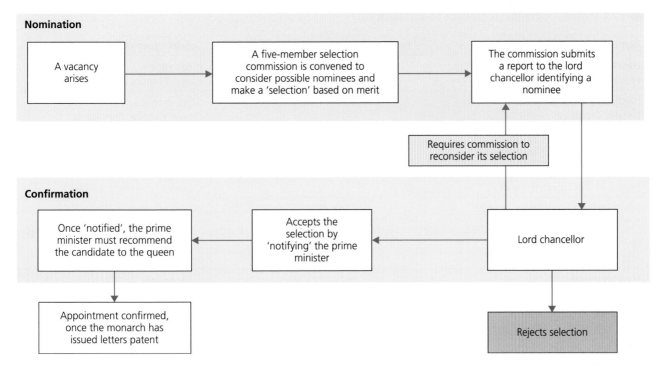

Figure 7.2 Appointing justices to the UK Supreme Court

In order to be considered for appointment as a justice of the Supreme Court today, candidates must have either held high judicial office for at least 2 years, or been a **qualifying practitioner** for a period of 15 years.

Vacancies in the UK Supreme Court are filled by an ad hoc selection commission, as opposed to the Judicial Appointments Commission (JAC) which deals with all other appointments to the senior judiciary. According to the Constitutional Reform Act 2005, this five-member, ad hoc commission should comprise: the president of the Supreme Court; the deputy president of the Supreme Court; one member of the JAC; one member of the Judicial Appointments Board for Scotland; and one member of the Northern Ireland Judicial Appointments Commission.

Although the appointments procedure (see Figure 7.2) still involves a government minister, their input is greatly reduced as they are not permitted repeatedly to reject names put forward by the selection commission.

Composition: does the Supreme Court 'look like the UK'?

Although one would hardly expect a superior court such as the UK Supreme Court to be entirely socially representative of the broader population — due to the qualifications for office and the importance of the role — the membership of the court has left it open to accusations of elitism (see Table 7.1). Such concerns have not been dispelled by appointments to the court between 2009 and 2016 (see Table 7.2).

Table 7.1 The make-up of the UK Supreme Court, March 2017

Justice, position	Birth date (age at end of March 2017)	School type, name of university
Lord Neuberger of Abbotsbury President of the Supreme Court	10/01/1948 (69)	Independent Christ Church, Oxford
Baroness Hale of Richmond Deputy President	31/01/1945 (72)	State grammar Girton College, Cambridge
Lord Mance Justice of the Supreme Court	06/06/1943 (73)	Independent University College, Oxford
Lord Kerr of Tonaghmore Justice of the Supreme Court	22/02/1948 (69)	State grammar Queen's University, Belfast
Lord Clarke of Stone-cum-Ebony Justice of the Supreme Court	13/05/1943 (73)	Independent King's College, Cambridge
Lord Wilson of Culworth Justice of the Supreme Court	09/05/1945 (71)	Independent Worcester College, Oxford
Lord Sumption Justice of the Supreme Court	09/12/1948 (68)	Independent Magdalen College, Oxford
Lord Reed Justice of the Supreme Court	07/09/1956 (60)	Independent Edinburgh; Balliol College, Oxford
Lord Carnwath of Notting Hill Justice of the Supreme Court	15/03/1945 (72)	Independent Trinity College, Cambridge
Lord Hughes of Ombersley Justice of the Supreme Court	11/08/1948 (68)	Independent University of Durham
Lord Toulson Justice of the Supreme Court	23/09/1946 (70)	Independent Jesus College, Cambridge
Lord Hodge Justice of the Supreme Court	19/05/1953 (63)	Independent Corpus Christi College, Cambridge

Table 7.2 The changing profile of Supreme Court justices

	2009 (October)	2017 (March)
Number of justices in post	11*	12
Number of justices who attended an independent secondary school	10	10
Number of justices who attended Oxford or Cambridge University	10	10
Number of female justices	1	1
Average age of justices (years)	67.8	69

(*one seat vacant in October 2009)

> **Activity**
>
> Using the material provided in Tables 7.1 and 7.2, as well as your own research, what criticism could be made of the composition of the current UK Supreme Court? In what ways could such a socially unrepresentative composition be explained or defended?

Key doctrines and principles that underpin the work of the Supreme Court

The rule of law

The rule of law is a key doctrine of the UK constitution under which justice is guaranteed to all. A. V. Dicey saw the rule of law as one of the 'twin pillars' of the constitution, the other being parliamentary sovereignty.

According to Dicey the rule of law has three main strands:

- **No one can be punished without trial.** While this principle makes good sense in theory, it is not always maintained in practice. For example, terrorist suspects have been subject to a range of punishments without trial under measures passed since 2001, including indefinite detention, the imposition of control orders and the freezing of their assets.
- **No one is above the law and all are subject to the same justice.** Again, while this would appear to be a principle that would hold true in all liberal democracies, there have always been those who are effectively above the law in the UK, including the monarch, foreign ambassadors and MPs. In the case of the latter, a number of MPs even tried to use parliamentary privilege as a way of ending legal proceedings taken against them over their expenses during the 2009 expenses scandal.
- **The general principles of the constitution (e.g. personal freedoms) result from the judges' decisions rather than from parliamentary statute.** While the decisions of judges (i.e. case law or common law) certainly have a part to play in defining the UK's constitutional arrangements, parliament remains sovereign and statute law reigns supreme. Any legal precedent can be overturned by the means of a simple Act of Parliament.

Judicial independence and judicial neutrality

The rule of law clearly demands that judges at all levels of the UK judiciary should operate with a high level of independence and dispense justice with a degree of neutrality. However, it is important to draw a clear distinction between judicial independence and judicial neutrality. The absence of judicial independence is a threat to judicial neutrality because the impartiality of judges is compromised if they are subject to external control. However, judicial independence does not guarantee judicial neutrality because judges may still allow their personal views to influence the way they administer justice.

Distinguish between

Judicial independence and judicial neutrality

Judicial independence
- Judicial independence is the principle that those in the judiciary should be free from political control.
- Such independence allows judges to 'do the right thing' and apply justice properly, without fear of the consequences.

Judicial neutrality
- Judicial neutrality is where judges operate impartially (i.e. without personal bias) in their administration of justice.
- Judicial neutrality is an essential requirement of the rule of law.

How is judicial independence maintained?

Judicial independence in the UK is based on six main pillars:

- **'Security of tenure' enjoyed by judges.** Judges are appointed for an open-ended term, limited only by the requirement that they must retire by the age of 75. This means that politicians cannot seek to bring influence to bear by threatening to sack or suspend them. Members of the senior judiciary can only be removed as a result of impeachment proceedings requiring a vote in both Houses of Parliament.

- **Guaranteed salaries paid from the Consolidated Fund.** Judges' salaries are classified as 'standing services' and are therefore paid automatically from the Consolidated Fund. This means that politicians are unable to manipulate judges' salaries as a way of controlling them.
- **The offence of contempt of court.** Under *sub judice* rules, the media, ministers and other individuals are prevented from speaking out publicly during legal proceedings. This requirement is designed to ensure that justice is administered fairly, without undue pressure being brought to bear by politicians or the public in general.
- **Growing separation of powers.** The downgrading of the post of lord chancellor and the creation of a new UK Supreme Court enhanced the separation between the senior judiciary and the other branches of government. Prior to these changes, the most senior judges, the Law Lords, sat in the House of Lords and the lord chancellor held significant roles in all three branches of government: executive, legislature and judiciary.
- **Independent appointments system.** The Constitutional Reform Act 2005 saw the creation of an independent Judicial Appointments Commission (JAC). This brought greater transparency to the process of judicial appointments and served to address concerns that the system in place previously had been open to political bias.
- **Training and experience of senior judges.** Most senior judges have served an 'apprenticeship' as barristers and come to the bench having achieved a certain status within their chosen profession. It is argued that such individuals take considerable pride in their legal standing and are therefore unlikely to defer to politicians or public opinion, where this would be seen to compromise their judicial integrity.

Debate

Has the UK judiciary become more politicised in recent years?

Yes

- The Human Rights Act 1998 has drawn senior judges into the political fray by requiring them to rule on the *merit* of an individual piece of statute law as opposed to its *application*.
- The *Factortame* case (1990) established the precedent that UK courts can suspend Acts of Parliament where they are thought to contradict EU law.
- The creation of the Supreme Court in 2009 and the physical relocation of those senior judges to Middlesex Guildhall has brought senior judges into the public arena and subjected them to greater scrutiny by the media.
- Politicians have broken with convention by publicly criticising rulings handed down by senior judges. 'Brexit minister' (Secretary of State for Exiting the European Union) David Davis, did this when he reacted to a November 2016 High Court ruling which stated that the government could not trigger Article 50 without parliamentary approval.

No

- The appointments process for senior judges has been made more transparent and less open to accusations of political interference through the creation of the JAC and the separate Supreme Court appointment process.
- Although 'politicisation' is often associated with political interference and/or control, the UK senior judiciary has, in fact, become more independent in the wake of the Constitutional Reform Act 2005, such as through the downgrading of the role of lord chancellor.
- Increased conflict between judges and politicians is a positive thing because it shows that the courts are prepared to challenge the government when it appears to be encroaching upon our civil liberties.
- The fact that senior judges still benefit from security of tenure and guaranteed salaries helps to insulate them from political pressure.

How is judicial neutrality guaranteed?

In simple terms, of course, it is impossible to guarantee judicial neutrality; judges are human, after all, and they will inevitably bring some degree of personal bias to their work. However, the promise of a universal application of the law under the doctrine of the rule of law requires that such bias is not allowed to colour judicial decisions.

There are four main ways in which this goal is achieved:

- **The relative anonymity of senior judges.** Judges have traditionally operated away from the public eye. Until recently, judges rarely spoke out publicly on issues of law or public policy, and senior judges are still expected to avoid being drawn into open defence of their rulings, or criticism of those in government.
- **Restriction on political activity.** As with many senior civil servants, judges are not supposed to campaign on behalf of a political party or a pressure group. Although judges retain the right to vote, their political views or outlook should not become a matter of public record.
- **Legal justifications of judgments.** Senior judges are generally expected to offer an explanation of how their decisions are rooted in law. This requirement that decisions be clearly rooted in the law makes it less likely that senior judges will be guided by personal bias. Note that in the case of the UK Supreme Court, decisions are published in full on the court's official website, along with press summaries of significant cases.
- **High-level training.** Judges are part of a highly trained profession, regulated by the Law Society. Senior judges have commonly served for many years as barristers before taking to the bench, and their elevation to the higher ranks of the judiciary would normally reflect a belief that they are able to put any personal bias they might hold to one side when administering justice. Although the security of tenure enjoyed by senior judges makes it difficult to remove those whose neutrality is open to question, additional guidance and training can be required in such cases, and individual judges might also be moved away from more serious cases while their performance is monitored.

Judges are required to dispense justice with a degree of neutrality

Threats to judicial neutrality

The main question mark over judicial neutrality comes from the narrow recruiting pool from which senior judges have traditionally been drawn, with most of those appointed to the higher tiers of the judiciary being privately schooled, Oxbridge-educated, white, middle-class men who are beyond middle age. How, it is argued, can judges be truly neutral when their own life-experiences are so very different from most of those who are brought before them? As we will see later in this chapter, the creation of the Judicial Appointments Commission (JAC) appears to have done little to address this problem, and the composition of the UK Supreme Court, although determined under entirely different procedures, is similarly unrepresentative.

Critics also point to the way in which senior judges have been drawn into the political fray in recent years, with the suggestion that the passage of measures such as the Human Rights Act (1998) has resulted in the **politicisation** of the judiciary. However, while some see this growing public profile and increased conflict between senior judges and politicians as a threat to judicial neutrality, it could just as easily be seen as evidence of growing independence and neutrality — not least because senior judges appear increasingly willing to take on the political establishment in defence of civil liberties.

The power of the UK Supreme Court

While the US Supreme Court can declare Acts of Congress unconstitutional, thereby striking them down, the UK Supreme Court has no such power in respect of parliamentary statute. This is because statute law remains the supreme source of constitutional law in the UK. Despite this, the UK Supreme Court wields considerable influence through its use of **judicial review**.

The importance of judicial review

While it is helpful to have an awareness of the judiciary in its broader sense, the Supreme Court and the Courts of Appeals that operate directly below it are of most interest to students of politics. This is because it is these higher tiers of the judiciary that have the power to set legal precedent, establishing **common law** through their use of judicial review. In short, these higher courts clarify the meaning of the law as opposed to simply applying the letter of the law.

Common law, specifically judge-made law, is also discussed in Chapter 3 as one of the five main sources of the UK constitution.

The changing character of judicial review in the UK

Judicial review often requires senior judges to clarify the legal meaning of a particular law or regulation. Judicial review may also involve reviewing appeal cases heard previously at lower (inferior) courts.

As we have noted, the doctrine of parliamentary sovereignty and supremacy of statute law means that judicial review in the UK is generally seen as being less significant than in the USA, where the US Supreme Court can strike down pieces of regular statute that are judged to have violated the provisions of the US Constitution.

In the UK context, the phrase 'judicial review' was once taken to mean little more than the courts assessing the actions of those in power to ensure that they had not acted beyond the authority given to them in law; so-called **ultra vires** cases. Although the ability to make ultra vires rulings is still an important weapon in the Supreme Court's armoury, judicial review in the UK has grown significantly in both scope and scale due to two key developments:

- the growing importance of European Union law
- the elevated status given to the European Convention on Human Rights (ECHR) under the Human Rights Act 1998

Factortame A case in which the European Court of Justice (ECJ) established the precedent that UK courts can suspend UK statute law where it appears to violate EU law, at least until the ECJ is able to make a final determination as to the legality of the statute in question. The case took its name from a Spanish-owned fishing company, Factortame Limited, which had challenged the legality of the Merchant Shipping Act 1988 under European law.

European Union law and the Supreme Court

Under the European Communities Act 1972, the UK incorporated the Treaty of Rome into UK law. The effect of this simple change was to give European laws precedence over conflicting UK statutes, whether past or present.

> Supreme Court Justice Lord Mance said that Parliament gave the ECJ [European Court of Justice] a blank cheque when it drafted the 1972 European Communities Act in such a way as to give the EU a higher status. 'No explicit constitutional buttress remains against any incursion by EU law whatever', he said.
>
> *Daily Telegraph*, 8 June 2016

For many years this simply meant that the UK government could be called to account at the European Court of Justice (ECJ). However, in the wake of the *Factortame* case (1990), UK courts have also been able to suspend UK statutes that appear to be in violation of EU law. This power will naturally disappear when the UK leaves the European Union in the wake of the Brexit vote.

Case study

The UK Supreme Court hearing a case relating to EU Law

United States of America v *Nolan* (2015)

This case resulted from a claim against the US government under the Trade Union and Labour Relations Act 1992. Nolan, who had been employed by the US Army at a base in Hampshire, had argued that there should have been more consultation with workers' representatives before making her redundant. The US government argued that the Secretary of State had acted ultra vires under the European Communities Act (1972), because the 1995 regulations under which Nolan had made her original claim went beyond the basic rights given under EU Law. The Supreme Court found in Nolan's favour, arguing that the Secretary of State had not exceeded his powers when issuing regulations in 1995.

Questions
- Why did the US government feel that giving an employee a right to proper consultation before making them redundant was ultra vires?
- What does this case tell us about the nature and complexity of the Supreme Court's work?

European Convention on Human Rights (ECHR) 1950
The ECHR was established by the Council of Europe, an intergovernmental body that is separate from the European Union and not to be confused with the EU's Council of Ministers or European Council. Alleged violations of the ECHR are investigated by the European Commission on Human Rights and tried in the European Court of Human Rights, based in Strasbourg. Again these bodies are not to be confused with the EU's European Commission and European Court of Justice.

The Human Rights Act (1998) and the Supreme Court

Before 1998, cases brought under the **European Convention on Human Rights (ECHR)** were heard at the European Court of Human Rights (ECtHR) in Strasbourg. The Human Rights Act (HRA) 1998 came into force in October 2000. It incorporated most of the articles of the ECHR into UK law, thereby allowing citizens to pursue cases under the ECHR through UK courts as opposed to having to go directly to the ECtHR in Strasbourg.

The Human Rights Act 1998 came into force in October 2000

In focus

The Human Rights Act

- **Article 1** commits all signatories to protecting the rights included in the European Convention on Human Rights (ECHR).
- **Article 2** protects the right to life.
- **Article 3** prohibits torture and degrading or inhuman treatment.
- **Article 4** outlaws slavery and involuntary servitude.
- **Article 5** secures liberty and security of the individual against arbitrary arrest and imprisonment.
- **Article 6** guarantees a fair trial.
- **Article 7** prevents legislation that criminalises acts retrospectively.
- **Article 8** promotes respect for the individual's private and family life.
- **Article 9** protects the freedom of thought, conscience and religion.
- **Article 10** enshrines the right to freedom of expression.
- **Article 11** protects the rights of association and assembly: for example, the right to form a trade union.

- **Article 12** protects the right of men and women to marry and start a family.
- **Article 13** allows for the redress of grievances where convention rights have been violated.
- **Article 14** prohibits discrimination in the application of rights guaranteed in the ECHR.
- **Article 15** allows for suspension or 'derogation' of some of the rights guaranteed by the ECHR in times of national emergency.
- **Article 16** permits restrictions on the political rights of foreign nationals.
- **Article 17** prevents rights protected in the ECHR from being used to limit other convention rights.
- **Article 18** holds that the 'get-out clauses' included in some articles of the ECHR should not be abused as a way of limiting those rights protected in more general terms.

As the Human Rights Act is based on the Council of Europe's ECHR, rather than on EU law, it is not superior to parliamentary statute. Under the HRA, the Supreme Court is only able to issue a declaration of incompatibility where a parliamentary statute appears to violate the rights guaranteed — and parliament is not obliged to amend the offending statute. That said, the HRA (like the ECHR) has a 'persuasive authority' that has enhanced the protection of individual rights in the UK.

The following case study illustrates both the extent of the ultra vires power and its limitations, while also demonstrating the extent of the judiciary's power under the European Convention on Human Rights (and the Human Rights Act that incorporates that convention into UK law).

Case study

Ultra vires and the ECHR

R. (Reilly) v Secretary of State for Work and Pensions (2016)

Reilly argued that, in requiring her to work for a private company in order to receive her benefit payments, the Department of Work and Pensions (DWP) had infringed the protection against slavery provided in Article 4 of the European Convention on Human Rights (ECHR).

On appeal in 2013, the Supreme Court concluded that while the DWP had not infringed the ECHR in introducing 'welfare to work', the scheme was unlawful because the department had operated ultra vires, i.e. beyond the authority given to it by parliament.

By then the government had already passed the Jobseekers (Back to Work Schemes) Act, which changed the law retrospectively so that no offence had been committed. In 2016, the Court of Appeal eventually ruled that changing the law retrospectively in this way was incompatible with Article 6 of the ECHR (which guarantees the right to a fair trial) but confirmed that it was up to the government and parliament to decide how to proceed in light of that declaration of incompatibility.

In this case the Court of Appeal ruled that the government department in question (the DWP) had not established slavery, which is prohibited under the ECHR, but had acted beyond the authority given to it by parliament under statute law.

Questions

- Does it really make any difference *why* the department in question lost the case? Explain your answer.
- What does the final paragraph in the case study tell us about the power of parliament and the status of the ECHR (and the Human Rights Act)?

The extent of the Supreme Court's power under the HRA

As we have seen, the HRA does not have the same legal status as EU law or the US Bill of Rights, with the latter being both entrenched and superior to regular statute. As a regular piece of statute, the HRA can be amended, suspended (**derogated**) — in its entirety or in part — or simply repealed, like any Act.

While the courts cannot strike down parliamentary statute under the HRA, they can make a declaration of incompatibility and invite parliament to reconsider the offending statute. Furthermore, where statute law is silent or unclear, the courts can make even greater use of the HRA by using its provision to establish legal precedent in common law (see Table 7.3). In addition, we should remember that the HRA also has a hidden influence through the process by which draft legislation is now examined by parliament's Joint Committee on Human Rights in order to ensure that it is compatible with the HRA.

Key term

Derogation A process by which a country is exempted, perhaps temporarily, from observing a law or regulation it has previously agreed to abide by. Under Article 15 of the European Convention on Human Rights (ECHR), national governments are permitted to derogate some of the convention's articles in times of national crisis.

The Supreme Court sits in Middlesex Guildhall

Debate

Has the UK judiciary had a greater impact on the work of the executive and parliament in recent years?

Yes

- In diminishing the role of lord chancellor and removing the UK's most senior judges from the House of Lords, the Constitutional Reform Act 2005 inevitably enhanced judicial independence, making it more likely that judges would feel able to hold the executive and parliament to account.
- By allowing cases under the European Court of Human Rights (ECHR) to be heard in UK courts, the Human Rights Act 1998 allowed the UK's most senior judges to directly question Acts of Parliament — as well as the actions of those working in the executive.
- The precedent established under the *Factortame* case (1990) allows senior judges to suspend the actions of both parliament and the executive, where either branch appears to have breached EU law.
- The extension of EU law in the wake of the Maastricht Treaty (1992) brought senior UK judges into conflict with both the executive and parliament across a far wider range of policy areas than had previously been the case.
- This growth in judicial action has had a further, indirect, impact. Those in the executive and in parliament now look to head off potential conflict in the courts by ensuring that all legislation complies with the HRA and EU law.

No

- The physical relocation of the UK's top court to its new accommodation in Middlesex Guildhall in 2009, though highly symbolic, did little to change the legal–constitutional relationship between the judiciary, the executive and the legislature (parliament).
- Although the Human Rights Act gives judges the right to issue a 'declaration of incompatibility' where an Act of Parliament appears to have violated the ECHR, parliament is under no legal obligation to fall into line with court rulings.
- While senior judges have the ability to rule that ministers in the executive have acted beyond their statutory authority (i.e. ultra vires), those very ministers can use the executive's control of parliament to pass retrospective legislation which legitimises their earlier actions.
- Although the scope and scale of EU law has grown significantly since Maastricht, many areas of public policy remain largely in the hands of parliament, thus limiting the scope of judicial action.
- Any move to review the status of the Human Rights Act and/or complete Brexit would massively reduce the ability of the Supreme Court to have a significant impact on the operation of the executive or parliament.

> **Activity**
>
> Using the information provided in the section above, as well as material drawn from your own research, write two paragraphs evaluating the significance of the Human Rights Act in relation to the power of the Supreme Court. One paragraph should argue that the HRA has only a limited impact on the power of senior judges such as those who sit in the UK Supreme Court. The other paragraph should argue that the HRA has seen the UK Supreme Court develop into an institution more akin to its US counterpart.

The overall impact of the UK Supreme Court

The UK does not have an entrenched, codified and supreme constitutional document — a set of 'fundamental laws' akin to the US Constitution. As we have seen, therefore, it is impossible for the UK Supreme Court to strike down Acts of Parliament or move against the government in the style in which its US counterpart can tear up Acts of Congress and force the president to back down.

The UK Supreme Court's power is therefore limited to the four main areas identified over the course of this chapter:

■ revisiting and reviewing earlier legal precedent established under common law and case law (judge-made law)
■ making ultra vires rulings where the court judges that public bodies have acted beyond their statutory authority
■ addressing disputes arising under EU law
■ issuing 'declarations of incompatibility' under the Human Rights Act 1998

While the court has certainly developed a more public profile since its creation in 2009, Lord Philips' prediction that the change would essentially be one of 'form rather than of substance' has largely been borne out. In an article marking the first 5 years of the court, Lord Neuberger identified 'key cases' that clearly do not represent a significant departure from what the Law Lords might have done previously (see Table 7.3).

Table 7.3 Five key cases from the first 5 years of the Supreme Court

	Case	Focus	Significance
2009	*R* v *Horncastle &others*	Hearsay evidence	Hearsay evidence — evidence from others that is not given under oath in court and cannot be substantiated — could be used as a basis for conviction
2011	*Al Rawi* v the *Security Service*	Secret hearings	Outlawed the use of secret evidence by the intelligence services in court
2013	*Prest* v *Petrodel Resources Ltd*	Company law and divorce law	Property belonging to a company (i.e. company assets) should normally be seen as separate from property belonging to individuals
2014	*R (HS2 Action Alliance Limited)* v *Secretary of State for Transport*	EU directives and the monitoring of parliament	EU directives did not require government to consult more widely over HS2 (planned high-speed railway)
2014	*R (Nicklinson)* v *Ministry of Justice*	Right to die	Article 8 of the ECHR could not be used over the Suicide Act (1961) as a means of justifying assisted suicide

Source: Cases identified in 'Lord Neuberger on the Supreme Court: five key cases from its first five years', *Independent*, 11 October 2014

In the years since Lord Neuberger selected his 'top five', the kinds of rulings that the court has handed down continue to be similar in character to those that the Law Lords might have issued in the years prior to the establishment of the Supreme Court. This was certainly true in the case of *R v Jogee* (2016), as we have seen, where the precedent of joint enterprise was reviewed and refined.

Is the Supreme Court too powerful?

Such a question is generally rooted in the notion that there has been a blurring of the traditional distinction between those politicians who *make* the law and the judges who should simply *apply* it: that senior judges have become little more than 'politicians in robes'.

Such a distinction will clearly always be flawed as a result of the role that senior judges play in interpreting and clarifying the law when resolving disputes that arise under it. The Supreme Court's ability to establish precedent through common law could therefore be seen as a **quasi-legislative** power.

The unelected nature of the Supreme Court

Criticism of the Supreme Court on the grounds that it is too powerful for an entirely unelected body is clearly misguided. As we have already established, the UK Supreme Court has no more power than the Appellate Committee of the House of Lords that it replaced back in 2009. Although it is often said that the House of Lords wields too much power for an unelected body, that was never a criticism levelled at the Law Lords who sat in the Appellate Committee. Moreover, we should remember that it is rare for those in senior judicial positions worldwide to be elected to office. Judicial independence requires that senior judges are free to interpret the law and dispense justice fairly, without fear of being arbitrarily removed from office through the ballot box (or by any other means).

The Roman poet Juvenal asked the rhetorical question *'Quis custodiet ipsos custodes?'* ('Who is to guard the guards themselves?') From the perspective of the UK Supreme Court, it is clear that judicial independence demands a degree of unaccountability. It is an essential feature of democracy that we must at times place our trust in those who are not directly accountable to the citizenry at large.

The growing authority of the Supreme Court

While power can be seen as the ability to do something or make something happen, authority can be defined as the right to take a particular course of action. The German sociologist Max Weber (1864–1920) identified three sources of authority:

- **traditional authority** based on established traditions and customs
- **charismatic authority** based on the characteristics of leaders
- **legal–rational authority** granted by a formal process, such as an election

Although the UK Supreme Court has no more formal power than that held previously by the Appellate Committee of the House of Lords, and could not really be said to 'tick' any of Weber's boxes, it could be argued that the new court nonetheless possesses greater authority than the body it replaced. This is because the very nature of its institution and its operation has changed the way in which it is perceived as an institution, thus transforming the way in

Key term

Quasi-legislative Where the impact of differences in the Supreme Court's interpretations over time can appear tantamount to a legislative change, even though parliament has made no change to statute law.

which other institutions, the media and the wider public have come to view and accept its rulings. Factors which have enhanced its authority include:

- a more independent and less opaque appointments process than that which applied to the Law Lords
- a clearer separation of powers accompanied by a clear physical separation between legislature and judiciary
- an ongoing process of 'demystification' — with public visits, an intelligible website and enhanced coverage in the mainstream media

The potential impact of Brexit on the jurisdiction, power and authority of the UK Supreme Court

The UK's departure from the European Union will inevitably have an impact on the status, power and authority of the Supreme Court. It is important, however, to distinguish between those institutions and processes which are part of the EU, and those which are not.

Brexit and the Supreme Court's power under the Human Rights Act 1998

Those who argued in favour of the UK leaving the EU have often also been the fiercest critics of the European Court of Human Rights (ECtHR), the body established in 1959 to hear cases arising under the 1950 European Convention on Human Rights (ECHR). That convention, incorporated into British law under the Human Rights Act (HRA) 1998, is problematic for those who see it as a threat to the independence and sovereignty of the Westminster Parliament. Irrespective of the merits or demerits of that view, the reality is that the ECHR was established not by the European Union, but by the Council of Europe — an entirely separate organisation, founded in 1949 by Britain and nine other European states (see Figure 7.3 on page 174).

Thus leaving the EU would not, in itself, remove our obligations under the ECHR, any more than repealing the HRA would. The only way to remove ourselves from the jurisdiction of the ECtHR would be to withdraw from the ECHR itself — an almost unthinkable act, given that all European states (with the exception of the Vatican City, Belarus and Kazakhstan) are current signatories.

Leaving the EU would not remove our obligations under the ECHR

European Court of Human Rights (ECtHR) and European Court of Justice (ECJ)

European Court of Human Rights
- It was established by the Council of Europe.
- It hears cases brought under the European Convention on Human Rights.
- It is based in Strasbourg but is not an EU institution.

European Court of Justice
- It is the 'supreme court' of the European Union.
- It hears cases arising under EU law.
- It is based in Luxembourg.

Figure 7.3 The European Union and the Council of Europe

European Union (EU)	Council of Europe (CoE)
Foundation and size • Originally founded as the EEC, under the Treaty of Rome (1958) • 6 founding states • 28 member states in 2016 • Based in Strasbourg, Brussels and the City of luxembourg	**Foundation and size** • Founded under the Treaty of London (1949) • 10 founding states • 47 members in 2016 • Based in Strasbourg
Aims • Originally designed to promote economic cooperation and peace • Developed into a stronger political and economic union under the 1992 Maastricht Treaty	**Aims** • To promote democracy • To protect human rights and uphold the rule of law
Status • Establishes European Law which, under the Treaty of Rome, is superior to national laws • Enforced by the European Court of Justice (ECJ)	**Status** • Established the European Convention on Human Rights (ECHR) to which all signatories agree to abide • Enforced by the European Court of Human Rights (ECtHR)

Brexit and the Supreme Court's power under EU law

While leaving the EU will have little or no direct impact on the status of the HRA, the ECHR or the ECtHR, Brexit would involve withdrawing from the Treaty of Rome, meaning that EU law would no longer take precedence over UK law and the European Court of Justice (ECJ) would no longer have jurisdiction over the UK. This would impact on the work of the UK Supreme Court in two ways because:

- A proportion of its current caseload relates to EU law.
- The removal of a court that is, in theory, superior to the Supreme Court in some aspects of law would enhance the Supreme Court's status and authority.

A decision to withdraw from the ECHR as well as the EU (removing the UK from the jurisdictions of both the ECtHR and the ECJ) would obviously leave the UK Supreme Court in a greatly enhanced position.

The European Court of Justice is also discussed alongside the other main European Union institutions in Chapter 8.

Conclusions

Those comparing the UK Supreme Court with its US counterpart often assume that the power of the latter must be clearly set out in the US Constitution, but that is simply not the case. Article 3 of the US Constitution, concerns itself more with the organisation of the federal judiciary court than with its power. Indeed, the constitution makes no explicit mention of the US Supreme Court's primary tool, judicial review. That power was instead *discovered* by the court; developed over time through the court's own rulings — and by the willingness of other key players to accept them.

In a sense, therefore, while the UK has no codified constitution, no fundamental law for the UK Supreme Court to interpret, and it has been granted no new powers beyond those previously held by the Appellate Committee of the House of Lords, its status and authority are developing along a similar trajectory to that followed by its US counterpart. Just how far the UK Supreme Court will travel down the US path in the absence of a codified constitution will depend upon the extent to which it can sustain the confidence and support of other key players, and of the wider public.

What you should know

- The term 'judiciary' refers collectively to all judges in the UK, from lay magistrates all the way up to justices of the UK Supreme Court. However, students of politics are primarily concerned with the work of the Supreme Court.
- Under the doctrine of the rule of law, judges are expected to operate under the twin principles of judicial independence and judicial neutrality. Judicial independence requires that judges are able to apply the law as they see fit, free from external political controls. Judicial neutrality demands that justices set aside personal bias when applying the law.
- In recent years, the independence of the UK judiciary has been enhanced as a result of reforms to the judicial appointments process and the greater separation of powers achieved following reforms to the role of the lord chancellor and the creation of a new Supreme Court.
- The Supreme Court can defend the rights of citizens by making ultra vires rulings where government officials have acted beyond their authority, by issuing a declaration of incompatibility under the Human Rights Act 1998, or by finding that UK law violates EU law — for as long as the UK remains a member of the EU.
- The Supreme Court has the power to establish legally binding precedent or common law using the power of judicial review. This role is particularly significant where statute law is ambiguous or unclear, or where the laws passed by parliament conflict with European law or are deemed incompatible with the Human Rights Act.
- Although it was not afforded any significant powers beyond those held by the Appellate Committee of the House of Lords, which it replaced in October 2009, the Supreme Court has grown in status and authority in recent years, and may well continue to do so.

The judiciary

- Under the US Constitution, individual US states are free to organise their own state-level judiciary largely as they see fit. As a result, UK/US comparisons tend to focus on the higher levels of the US federal judiciary in the USA and the senior judiciary in the UK.
- The US judiciary, like the UK judiciary, is broadly hierarchical in structure. The US Supreme Court sits above 13 US Federal Circuit Courts of Appeal, with US District Courts, the US Claims Court and the US Court of International Trade at the lowest tier.
- Whereas the UK Supreme Court comprises 12 members (the president of the court, the deputy president of the court and ten justices of the court), the US Supreme Court has numbered 9 justices since 1869 (with one chief justice and eight associate justices).
- US courts, like their UK counterparts, are expected to operate with high levels of judicial independence and judicial neutrality. Judges on both sides of the Atlantic must rely on other state institutions to enforce their judgments.
- The UK Supreme Court inherited its main powers from the Law Lords who sat in the Appellate Committee of the House of Lords, which the Supreme Court replaced in 2009.
- The role and powers of the US Supreme Court are set out in Article 3 of the US Constitution but the court's main power — that of judicial review — is not clearly enumerated. This power was instead *discovered* by the court in the case of *Marbury* v *Madison* (1803) and extended in a number of landmark cases thereafter.
- The power of judicial review allows the US Supreme Court to strike down regular Acts of Congress where they violate constitutional provisions. This makes the US Supreme Court significantly more powerful than its UK counterpart — which, in the absence of a codified and supreme constitution, has the doctrine of parliamentary sovereignty and the supremacy of statute law to contend with.
- The US Bill of Rights is far harder to change or ignore than the UK Human Rights Act 1998, which can easily be repealed or derogated in times of national emergency. Subsequent amendments to the US Constitution have offered citizens further entrenched guarantees. For example, the 14th Amendment (1868) guarantees equal protection under the law.

Further reading

Fairclough, P. (2017) 'The UK Supreme Court: too much power for an unelected body?', *Politics Review*, Vol. 26, No. 3, pp. 26–29.

Moelwyn-Hughes, O. T. and Murphy, T. (2016) 'Debate: Is the UK judiciary too powerful?', *Politics Review*, Vol. 25, No. 3, pp. 22–23.

Munce, P. (2016) 'The Human Rights Act: why is it difficult to reform?', *Politics Review*, Vol. 25, No. 4, pp. 10–13.

Tomes, A. (2017) 'AS focus on: judicial review', *Politics Review*, Vol. 26, No. 4, pp. 28–29.

Exam-style questions

Short-answer questions

1 Explain, with examples, how Supreme Court justices are appointed.

2 Explain, with examples, the role of the Supreme Court.

3 Explain and analyse three ways in which judicial independence is maintained.

4 Explain and analyse three criticisms of the Supreme Court.

Mid-length questions

1 Describe the main functions of the Supreme Court.

2 Describe the main features of judicial independence in the UK.

3 Analyse and evaluate the arguments in favour of replacing the Human Rights Act with a British Bill of Rights.

4 Analyse and evaluate the criticisms of the Supreme Court.

Essay questions

1 Evaluate how far the British judiciary is effective at defending the rights of British citizens from the government.

2 Evaluate how far the Supreme Court remains truly independent.

3 Analyse and evaluate the factors that may undermine judicial neutrality.

4 'The British judiciary is neither independent nor neutral.' Analyse and evaluate this statement.

In your answer, you must:

- Consider judicial independence and judicial neutrality.

- Draw on relevant knowledge and understanding of UK politics.

Chapter 8

The European Union

Key questions answered
- How did the European Union develop?
- What are the aims of the European Union and to what extent has it achieved them?
- What are the roles and functions of the European Union institutions?
- How does the European Union political system work?
- What impact has membership of the European Union had on British politics and policy?
- What happened in the 2016 European Union referendum?

The 2016 UK referendum vote on membership of the European Union (EU), in which 52% voted to leave, was one of the most dramatic and significant events in modern British politics. In the immediate aftermath, prime minister David Cameron resigned. In the longer term, withdrawal from the EU (Brexit) will reshape both domestic politics and Britain's place in the world. Since joining in 1973, membership of the EU has had a profound effect on the British political system — challenging core principles of the constitution, transforming policy and shaping the party system. Within the EU, the UK has often been a semi-detached member, opposing further **integration** and not participating in core policies such as economic and monetary union.

Key term

Integration The process of coordinating the activities of different states through common institutions and policies.

Membership of the EU has had a profound effect on the British political system

The development of the European Union

Key terms

Supranational Having authority independent of national governments.

Key terms

Supranational Having authority independent of national governments.

Activity

Identify the states that have recently applied to join the EU. What do they have to do to join, and when might they become EU members?

Key terms

Enlargement The expansion of the EU to include new member states.

Economic and monetary union (EMU) The creation of a single currency, central bank and common monetary policy.

Qualified majority voting A voting arrangement in which proposals must win a set number of votes (over 50%) to be approved.

Unanimity A voting arrangement in which all states must be in agreement for a proposal to be passed.

The stages of the development of the European Union (EU) are outlined below.

- **The European Coal and Steel Community was established in 1952.** The founding members were France, West Germany, Italy, Belgium, the Netherlands and Luxembourg. It was a **supranational** organisation which had decision-making authority independent of its member states. By contrast, in intergovernmental organisations states cooperate voluntarily and can veto proposals.
- **The European Economic Community (EEC) was formed in 1958.** The 'Six' founding members of the European Coal and Steel Community formed the EEC under the Treaty of Rome (1957). The Common Agricultural Policy (CAP) began in 1962 and a customs union followed in 1968 when internal tariff barriers were removed and a common external tariff was created.
- **Enlargement occurred when the UK, Ireland and Denmark joined the EEC in 1973. Enlargement** continued when Greece (1981), Spain and Portugal (both 1986) also joined.
- **The Single European Act was agreed in 1985.** It came into force in 1987. It created the single European market and prompted a greater Community role in social and regional policy. **Unanimity** was replaced by **qualified majority voting** on single market legislation.
- **The Maastricht Treaty was agreed in 1991.** It came into force in 1993. It created the European Union (EU) and set a timetable for **economic and monetary union (EMU)**. It also increased intergovernmental cooperation in foreign and security policy, and in justice and home affairs.
- **The Amsterdam Treaty was agreed in 1997.** It came into force in 1999 and established an 'area of freedom, security and justice'.
- **An economic and monetary union was established in 1999.** Eleven states abolished their national currencies and adopted the euro. The Eurozone had expanded to 19 states by 2016.
- **The Nice Treaty was agreed in 2001.** It came into force in 2003 and created a European security and defence policy and introduced institutional reforms.
- **Enlargement occurred when ten states joined in 2004.** Cyprus, the Czech Republic, Estonia, Hungary, Latvia, Lithuania, Malta, Poland, Slovakia and Slovenia all joined. EU membership reached 28 states after Bulgaria and Romania (2007) and Croatia (2013) joined (see Figure 8.1).
- **The Lisbon Treaty was agreed in 2007.** This followed the rejection of the EU Constitutional Treaty in referendums in France and the Netherlands. The treaty came into force in 2009 and further reformed the EU institutions.
- **A sovereign debt crisis began in 2009.** After running up large debts, Greece, Ireland, Spain, Portugal and Cyprus were bailed out by the EU and International Monetary Fund. In turn, they were required to introduce austerity measures.

- **A migrant crisis began in 2015.** Large numbers of people, many of them refugees fleeing conflict, began crossing the Mediterranean or travelling through southern Europe to reach countries of the EU. Thousands have died making the journey. New EU measures to tackle migrant smuggling and relocate the record number of asylum seekers (1.2 million in 2015) have had a limited impact.
- **In 2016, the UK voted for Brexit in a referendum.** The UK will become the first member state to leave the EU.

Figure 8.1 Map of the European Union

EU countries

D	Denmark
N	Netherlands
B	Belgium
L	Luxembourg
S	Switzerland
SK	Slovakia
SV	Slovenia
BS	Bosnia
SB	Serbia
M	Macedonia
AB	Albania
MV	Moldova
MN	Montenegro
K	Kosovo

The aims of the European Union

The aims of the EU are set out in Article 3 of the EU treaty. They include:
- promoting peace and the EU's values
- establishing a single European market
- promoting economic, social and territorial cohesion
- establishing an economic and monetary union

- establishing an area of freedom, security and justice without internal frontiers
- combating discrimination and promoting equality

The European Union's values

The EU is founded on the values of 'human dignity, freedom, democracy, equality, the rule of law and respect for human rights, including the rights of persons belonging to minorities' (www.tinyurl.com/7wzpdnb). These form part of the accession criteria for prospective new members. EU membership has helped to embed liberal democracy in states that have recently been under authoritarian or communist rule. **Eurosceptics** claim that the EU has ignored popular concerns about integration. They believe that democracy is rooted in the nation state.

A single European market

The single European market, or internal market, is 'an area without internal frontiers in which the free movement of goods, services, persons and capital is ensured' (Article 26, Treaty on the Functioning of the European Union). The **four freedoms** involve:

- **Free movement of goods.** Member states cannot impose duties or taxes on goods from another EU state, or directly discriminate against them. Under a system of 'mutual recognition', goods that meet minimum standards in one EU state can be freely traded in others. Physical and technical barriers, such as border checks and restrictive national regulations, have been removed.
- **Free movement of services.** Professionals, businesses and self-employed people can establish or offer their services across the EU. Qualifications from one EU state are recognised in others.
- **Free movement of people.** Any national of an EU member state has the right to seek employment in another EU state without discrimination of the grounds of their nationality. They have the same rights as national workers in recruitment, pay, social security and housing. Free movement was a key issue in the UK's 2016 EU referendum (see the case study on page 182).
- **Free movement of capital.** Many restrictions on capital movements (e.g. on buying currency and foreign investment) between EU member states have been removed.

The single European market is widely regarded as one of the EU's successes. It is estimated to have created more than 2.5 million jobs across the EU and helped to increase GDP by 15%. However, some sectors (e.g. energy and public procurement) have proved difficult to open up. Critics in the UK note that EU regulations are costly for small and medium-sized enterprises, and financial services.

Key terms

Eurosceptic Someone who is critical of the extension of supranational authority in the EU and hostile to further integration.

Four freedoms The principles of the free movement of goods, services, people and capital within the EU's single market.

Free movement is a core principle of the EU

European Union migration and the UK

The free movement of people is one of the EU's core principles. EU citizens have the right to move to, reside in and work in any member state without discrimination. In 2014, 268,000 citizens of other EU states moved to the UK, while 98,000 emigrated from the UK. At that time, 2.5 million EU citizens resided in the UK, with Poland being the main country of origin, and 1.8 million UK citizens resided elsewhere in the EU.

The coalition government's 2014 *Review of the Balance of Competences between the UK and the European Union* reported that the impact of freedom of movement of skilled workers had been largely positive, but noted concerns about the impact on wage levels caused by the movement of low-skilled people.

Migration from other EU states became a salient issue in British politics after the 2004 eastward enlargement. Temporary restrictions on free movement were imposed on citizens of Bulgaria and Romania after they joined the EU in 2007. Ahead of the 2016 referendum, David Cameron negotiated a 4-year 'emergency brake' on paying in-work benefits to EU migrants. But this fell short of what he had asked for. The Leave campaign focused on immigration, claiming that the UK could only regain control of its borders by leaving the EU. The migrant crisis added another dimension to the issue, despite only a fraction (3% in 2015) of asylum applications made in the EU being received in the UK.

Questions
- Why was immigration such a salient issue in the EU referendum?
- How might Brexit change UK immigration policy?

Economic, social and territorial cohesion

The creation of the single market prompted a greater EU role in social, employment and regional policy. The objective is to reduce disparities between and within member states. Much social policy is made at national level but the EU promotes employment, social protection and workers' rights. Poorer regions receive money from the EU Structural Funds. EU economic and social policy has been criticised by the right for imposing costs on businesses and not doing enough to improve competitiveness, and by the left for imposing public spending cuts and failing to tackle inequality.

An economic and monetary union

States that meet the Maastricht Treaty's 'convergence criteria' (e.g. on low inflation and levels of debt) can abolish their national currencies and replace them with a single currency, the euro. The European Central Bank (ECB) implements monetary policy for the Eurozone, seeking to maintain low inflation.

Eleven states — Austria, Belgium, Finland, France, Germany, Ireland, Italy, Luxembourg, the Netherlands, Spain and Portugal — joined Economic Monetary Union (EMU) in 1999. The UK and Denmark **opted out**. By 2016, 19 of the EU's 28 states were in the Eurozone, the later entrants being Greece (2001), Slovenia (2007), Cyprus and Malta (2008), Slovakia (2009), Estonia (2011), Latvia (2014) and Lithuania (2015). This is an example of **differentiated integration**.

EMU brings a number of benefits, including an end to exchange rate uncertainty and the elimination of transaction costs on cross-border trade. But it also involves a loss of sovereignty as national governments cede control over their currency. The ECB's 'one-size-fits-all' policy on interest rates may not suit all states and rules designed to ensure budgetary discipline were not implemented fully, leading to the sovereign debt crisis. The EU created new funds to bail out five member states and required them to cut public spending. The 2012 fiscal compact treaty — officially called the Treaty on Stability, Coordination and Governance in the Economic and Monetary Union — established stricter rules and sanctions on budget deficits, and paved the way for further economic integration.

An area of freedom, security and justice

In the border-free single market, EU citizens enjoy freedom of movement. This requires common measures on issues such as external border controls, asylum and immigration, criminal justice, policing and judicial cooperation. Cross-border cooperation mechanisms include the European Arrest Warrant and Europol.

Combating discrimination and promoting equality

The EU has created new rights for citizens. EU citizenship applies to citizens of member states. It affords rights to vote in European Parliament elections and local elections. EU citizens have the right to move to

Key terms

Opt-out An exemption set out in a treaty or law, which means that a state does not have to take part in a specific EU policy.
Differentiated integration A form of integration in which states move at different speeds or towards different objectives.

another member state in order to work or reside. They can acquire the right to permanent residence in another EU country if they have lived there legally for 5 years. Discrimination against EU citizens on the grounds of their nationality is prohibited. EU law has also extended workers' rights by limiting working hours, improving health and safety, and prohibiting discrimination in the workplace.

The EU Charter of Fundamental Rights was proclaimed in 2000 and became legally binding within the Lisbon Treaty. It entrenches rights established by case law of the Court of Justice and enshrined in the European Convention on Human Rights. These rights cover dignity (e.g. right to life), freedoms (e.g. liberty), equality (e.g. prohibition of discrimination), solidarity (e.g. workers' rights) and citizens' rights (e.g. free movement).

Debate

Has the European Union achieved its aims?

Yes

- The single market of 500 million consumers is the largest in the world and has promoted trade, investment and prosperity.
- It has protected and extended the rights of workers, and promoted the economic development of its poorer regions.
- It has extended citizens' rights, notably through the right to live and work in another EU state.
- Economic and monetary union has eliminated transaction costs within the Eurozone.
- Increasing political union has delivered coordinated action on cross-border issues such as criminal justice and immigration.
- It has cemented democracy and the rule of law in European states that had previously been under authoritarian rule.

No

- The single market is incomplete and over-regulated.
- Economic growth in the EU is weak and socioeconomic inequality is growing.
- The free movement of people and EU migration policy have proved controversial.
- Economic and monetary union has experienced significant difficulties, with less prosperous states running up significant debts and then being required to introduce austerity measures.
- It has not been able to resolve major challenges such as the migration crisis.
- There is significant popular opposition to increasing political union and the democratic deficit, as seen in the rise of populist parties and Brexit.

The roles and functions of European Union institutions

The EU's institutional architecture is unique. It includes intergovernmental bodies in which national governments meet (the Council of the European Union and the European Council) and supranational bodies with their own authority (the European Commission, the European Parliament and the Court of Justice).

European Commission

The Commission is the executive body of the EU, with political and administrative functions. As a supranational body, the Commission acts in the general interests of the Union and is independent of member states. It is based in Brussels.

The President of the Commission is nominated by the European Council and then elected by the European Parliament. Commissioners are nominated by national governments and approved by the European Parliament. The president allocates policy portfolios to them within the College of Commissioners.

The European Commission:

■ has the sole right to initiate draft legislation in most areas of EU activity
■ executes EU legislation and ensures it is applied correctly
■ administers EU expenditure and collects revenue
■ represents the EU on the world stage, notably in trade negotiations

Council of the European Union

This is the main decision-making body of the EU and was previously known as the Council of Ministers. Based in Brussels, it is where government ministers from the 28 member states take key decisions on EU legislation. The Council consists of ten sectoral councils dealing with specific areas of EU activity. The presidency of the council is held by member states for a 6-month period.

The Council of the European Union:

■ shares legislative power with the European Parliament
■ coordinates the economic policies of member states
■ develops the common foreign and security policy of the Union

Many decisions are made by consensus but votes are held regularly. There are two main voting procedures:

■ **Unanimity.** A proposal will fail if at least one member state vetoes it. Unanimity applies only to major or sensitive policies.
■ **Qualified majority voting (QMV).** A qualified majority is achieved if 55% of member states vote in favour and the proposal is supported by states representing at least 65% of the EU population. A blocking minority must comprise at least four states representing at least 35% of the EU population. QMV applies to most areas of EU activity.

European Council

This is where heads of government (or in the case of France and Finland, heads of state) and foreign ministers meet. The presidents of the European Council and European Commission also attend. It meets at least four times per year. The president of the council is an individual selected by EU states for a renewable 2½ year term.

The European Council has established itself as the EU's key strategic body, enhancing the power of member states and reducing the influence of the European Commission. It:

■ discusses major issues
■ sets the political direction for the EU
■ makes key decisions on foreign policy and the EU's economic situation
■ launches new initiatives and agrees changes to treaties

European Parliament

A meeting of the European Parliament in Strasbourg

This is the EU's directly elected institution. Elections take place at 5-year intervals. There are 751 Members of the European Parliament (MEPs) with seats allocated to member states roughly according to their population. MEPs sit in transnational party groups based on ideology rather than nationality.

The European Parliament has three locations: Strasbourg (where most plenary sessions are held), Brussels (where committee meetings are held) and Luxembourg (where its secretariat is based).

The European Parliament has a number of powers:

- **Legislative power.** It shares legislative power with the Council of the European Union. It cannot, however, initiate legislation. Parliament's power is greatest under the ordinary legislative procedure, as it can both amend and veto proposed legislation. Most of the parliament's amendments are accepted in whole or in part. This procedure of vetoes and amendments is used for most areas of EU activity.
- **Budgetary power.** It shares budgetary authority with the Council of the European Union and can request amendments to the budget or veto it.
- **Democratic supervision.** It elects the president of the European Commission after nomination by the European Council. The parliament also holds hearings for nominated commissioners and, by expressing concerns, has caused the withdrawal of some. Once they are in the post, the parliament can question commissioners and Council members.

Court of Justice of the European Union

This upholds EU law and ensures that it is applied uniformly and effectively. It is located in Luxembourg. The court decides cases involving member states, EU institutions, businesses and individuals. National courts ask it for preliminary rulings on matters of EU law. Decisions by the court have extended the EU's competences and strengthened its institutions.

The Court of Justice should not be confused with the European Court of Human Rights, an intergovernmental organisation which was created in 1949 and which is associated with the Council of Europe and not the EU.

The European Union political system

The EU's institutions do not fit as neatly into the categories of executive, legislature and judiciary as do national institutions (see Figure 8.2). The Court of Justice is the EU's independent judicial branch. On economic and related policies, the EU legislative branch has the equivalent of two 'houses'. The Council of the European Union is the equivalent of an upper house where national governments are represented, and the European Parliament is the equivalent of a lower house with member states represented roughly according to their population.

The European Commission is the executive branch of the EU. It does not have the power of national cabinets but resembles them in that each commissioner has a policy portfolio. It also makes proposals to the legislative branch and is responsible for implementing laws. But the Council of the European Union also performs some executive functions (e.g. influencing the EU's strategic direction).

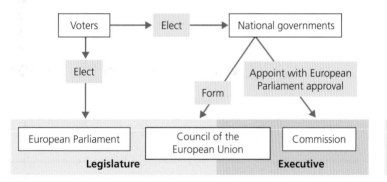

Figure 8.2 The EU system of government

Figure 8.3 The EU legislative process

When considering where power lies in the EU, it is helpful to distinguish between two different types of EU activity:

- 'History-making decisions' (e.g. treaty changes) are the result of bargains between the EU's most powerful member states and are decided in the European Council.
- 'Day-to-day decisions' (e.g. legislation on mobile phone roaming charges) involve the European Commission, Council of the European Union and European Parliament in decision making (see Figure 8.3).

The democratic deficit

The **democratic deficit** refers to the erosion of democratic accountability that occurs when decision-making authority is transferred from national governments that are directly accountable to voters and national parliaments, to EU institutions that are less accountable. It also refers to the distance between the EU and its citizens. Citizens do not identify with or fully understand the EU and have opposed important developments in the integration process. Turnout in European Parliament elections has declined (see Figure 8.4).

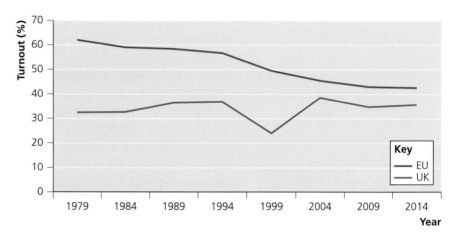

Figure 8.4 Turnout at European Parliament elections, 1979–2014

Source: European Parliament (www.tinyurl.com/hkwwewk)

It is worth noting, however, that the EU's supranational institutions have most autonomy in technical areas which also operate at arm's length from the democratic process in nation states. Decisions on interest rates, for example, are made by the European Central Bank in the EU and by the Bank of England in the UK. The EU has little power over taxation and spending, and its budget is relatively small. It also relies on national governments to implement EU policy.

Debate

Is there a democratic deficit in the European Union?

Yes

- Legislation is initiated by the European Commission, which is not directly elected.
- National governments can be outvoted under qualified majority voting, and this may mean that the will of the electorate is thwarted.
- The directly elected European Parliament is not sufficiently powerful.
- Elections to the European Parliament are dominated by national issues and turnout is low.
- Citizens do not understand or identify with the EU — it is too distant and complex — and have opposed key developments.

No

- The European Commission, which initiates legislation, is accountable to the European Parliament, and its key personnel are nominated by national governments.
- The EU's supranational institutions have greatest autonomy in technical matters (e.g. competition policy, central banking).
- National governments are represented in the Council of the European Union and the European Council, where bargaining is the norm.
- The European Parliament shares legislative power with the Council of the European Union in most policy areas — there is a system of checks and balances.
- The EU does not have power in key areas of national life, such as taxation, social security and education.

European Union policies

The powers of the EU are set out in the treaties of the Union. A treaty is a binding agreement between member states setting out the EU's objectives, institutional framework, decision-making procedures and policy competences. The original Treaty of Rome has been amended on a number of occasions, with the most recent major revision being the Lisbon Treaty.

What policy competences does the European Union have?

The EU is the main actor in many areas of public policy (see Table 8.1). It has only the **competences** conferred on it by the treaties — it cannot act in other areas. Competences not conferred upon the EU remain with member states.

In areas of exclusive competence, only the EU is permitted to make law. In areas of shared competence, member states can only make laws where the EU has chosen not to. Where it has supporting or special competence, the EU can only intervene to coordinate or support actions taken by national governments.

In exercising its competences, the EU must act according to two key principles:

- Proportionality — any action taken by the EU should not go beyond what is necessary to achieve the objectives of the treaties.
- Subsidiarity — outside of its exclusive competences, the EU does not act unless it is more effective than action taken at national, regional or local level.

> **Key term**
>
> **Competence** The legal capacity to act in a particular area.

Table 8.1 Policy competences of the EU (selected)

Exclusive EU competence	Shared EU and member state competence	Supporting or special competence	Exclusive member state competence
Customs union	Single market	Industry	Many areas of taxation, including income tax
External trade	Social and employment policy	Culture	Many areas of public spending, including social security
Monetary policy (in the Eurozone)	Economic, social and territorial cohesion	Education	
Competition policy	Environment, transport and energy	Health	
Marine conservation	Area of freedom, security and justice	Macroeconomic policy	
	Agriculture and fisheries	Common foreign and security policy	

The impact of the European Union on British politics

Membership of the EU has had a significant impact on British politics and policy. The EU's policy impact varies from sector to sector according to the extent of EU competence. The impact of the EU is significant in trade, agriculture, business and the environment, but it is less apparent in health and defence. While the UK remains in the EU, government departments and local authorities implement EU laws, and the British courts enforce them.

Activity

Using the publications and websites recommended in the Further reading section at the end of this chapter, examine the impact of Brexit on selected policy areas.

Key terms

Legal sovereignty Supreme legal authority — the theoretical exercise of sovereignty.

Multilevel governance A system of decision making in which subnational, national and supranational institutions all have policy competences.

Parliamentary sovereignty Where ultimate authority resides with parliament, which is the supreme law-making body.

Political sovereignty The political ability to exercise sovereignty — sovereignty in practice.

Synoptic links

The European Union and the British constitution

EU membership is one among a number of challenges to parliamentary sovereignty (see Chapter 3). Others include devolution, the Human Rights Act and the use of referendums on constitutional issues — including EU membership.

EU membership has contributed to the development of **multilevel governance** in the UK. Central government remains a crucial actor in decision making but the British state is less centralised than it was. Decision making authority has been transferred upwards from central government to the EU, and downwards to devolved institutions and local government.

Sovereignty

An institution is sovereign if it has final legislative authority and can act without undue external constraint. National sovereignty is the idea that final decision-making authority is located within the nation state, with the national government determining law for its own territory.

It is helpful to distinguish between **legal sovereignty** and **political sovereignty**. Legal sovereignty concerns ultimate decision-making authority— it is sovereignty in theory. In the UK, eurosceptics often focus on legal sovereignty, arguing that EU membership means a loss of sovereignty because EU law has primacy over national law and the EU has exclusive competence in some policy areas. 'Soft' eurosceptics sought opt-outs from some EU policies and the repatriation (i.e. the return to national governments) of some competences. 'Hard' eurosceptics regarded only withdrawal from the EU or a fundamental renegotiation of British membership as sufficient to restore sovereignty.

Political sovereignty concerns the ability to exercise sovereignty. It regards sovereignty as a political resource rather than a legal position. For pro-Europeans, sovereignty thus means effective influence and a practical capacity to act. On joining the EU, the UK pooled sovereignty, sharing its sovereignty with other EU states in order to increase its influence and capacity to act.

Parliamentary and popular sovereignty

Parliamentary sovereignty is a central element of the British constitution. It has three elements:

- Legislation made by parliament cannot be overturned by any higher authority.
- Parliament can legislate on any subject of its choosing.
- No parliament can bind its successors.

EU membership has challenged parliamentary sovereignty in the UK. EU law has primacy: in cases of conflict between national law and EU law, the latter takes priority. The European Communities Act 1972 gave future EU law legal force in the UK and denied effectiveness to national legislation which conflicts with it. This was illustrated in the 1990 *Factortame* case. The Merchant Shipping Act 1988 had prevented non-British citizens from registering boats as British in order to qualify for the UK's quota under the Common Fisheries Policy. But the House of Lords, following a ruling from the Court of Justice, decided that the Act was incompatible with EU law and should be 'disapplied'. This undermined parliamentary sovereignty because it showed that laws made by parliament can be overturned by another authority. However, it did not render parliamentary sovereignty meaningless because parliament

Activity

Follow the debate on parliament's role in the Brexit process. What role does parliament have — and what role should it have?

retained ultimate legislative authority and could repeal the European Communities Act.

Parliamentary sovereignty has also been challenged by the increased use of referendums, which have shifted the focus to **popular sovereignty**. The European Union Act 2011 introduced a 'referendum lock' under which any future treaty transferring powers from the UK to the EU must be put to a binding referendum in the UK. Ultimately, this 'lock' will not be used because of another expression of popular sovereignty — the 2016 EU referendum.

The EU referendum result produced competing claims of sovereignty. Supporters of popular sovereignty warned that parliament should not frustrate Brexit, whereas adherents to parliamentary sovereignty argued that referendums are not binding and that Brexit requires the consent of parliament. In January 2017, the Supreme Court ruled that the government could not trigger Article 50 without an Act of Parliament.

Debate

Will departure from the European Union restore British sovereignty?

Yes

- Parliamentary sovereignty will be restored. Parliament will have supreme authority and the UK will no longer be subject to EU law.
- Policy competences will be returned to the UK government and parliament. They, not the EU, will make law in these areas.
- Voters will have greater opportunity to hold the government to account for policy decisions in areas where the EU had competence.

No

- **Globalisation** means that no state can act independently on issues such as the environment, migration and economic policy.
- By pooling sovereignty in the EU, the UK was able to achieve policy objectives that it might not be able to achieve outside of the Union. It also gave the UK greater influence in European and world affairs.
- A post-Brexit deal with the EU might still entail some loss of sovereignty if the UK–EU relationship is similar to those between the EU and Norway or Switzerland.

Is the UK an awkward partner in the European Union?

Writing in 1990, Professor Stephen George described the UK as an 'awkward partner' within the EU. The UK has been less enthusiastic about European integration than other states and has been a semi-detached member of the EU. The idea of British 'awkwardness' persists today and includes elements such as:

- **Distinctive history and culture.** The UK's historical development differs from that of continental Europe. It has had a global outlook and close relationship with the USA, and has not experienced the major political upheavals seen in other European states.
- **Late entry.** French President Charles de Gaulle vetoed the UK's membership applications in 1961 and 1967 and it wasn't until 1973 that membership was accepted. By this time, policies that the UK finds problematic, such as the Common Agricultural Policy (CAP) (see the case study on page 192), were already in place.

Agriculture and fisheries

The Common Agricultural Policy (CAP) is an EU system of agricultural subsidies and price interventions. Famers receive direct subsidies from the EU for producing crops or livestock and the EU intervenes to buy farm outputs if prices fall below an agreed level. It also taxes agricultural imports and subsidises exports.

The CAP is controversial but has been difficult to reform given the support it enjoys from some states (notably France) and powerful farming interests. It is the largest area of EU expenditure, covering some 38% of the EU budget. It previously used 70% of the budget but the link between subsidies and production has been weakened and more attention is now paid to environmental protection. In the UK, which has a small and efficient agricultural sector, the CAP is viewed as wasteful and bureaucratic.

The EU's Common Fisheries Policy (CFP) sets quotas for the amount and types of fish that can be caught. It also sets minimum prices and rules for external trade. Critics in the UK argue that, by giving all European fishing fleets access to UK waters, British fishermen have been put out of business. The CFP has not reversed the long-term decline of fish stocks.

Questions
- Why has CAP reform proved so difficult?
- How will Brexit impact UK agriculture and fisheries?

- **Wariness of further integration.** British governments have tended to be less enthusiastic about (and often hostile to) further integration. They have supported intergovernmental cooperation rather than extensive supranational authority; and a single market rather than EMU.
- **EU policy exemptions.** The UK has negotiated a series of special arrangements and opt-outs that mean it does not participate in some EU policies (see Table 8.2).

Table 8.2 UK EU policy exemptions (selected)

EU policy area	UK exemption
EU budget	An EU budget rebate, first negotiated in 1981, that reduced UK contributions (see the case study).
The Exchange Rate Mechanism	Non-participation in the ERM. The UK was briefly a member of the system between 1990 and 1992 but was forced out when sterling came under pressure from financial speculators.
Economic and Monetary Union	An opt-out from EMU in the Maastricht Treaty, so that the UK does not have to join the single currency unless approved by Westminster. The Conservatives and Labour also pledged that joining the euro would have to be approved in a referendum. In 2003, the Blair government decided that the UK had not met the 'five economic tests' it had set for euro membership.
'Social chapter' of the Maastricht Treaty	An opt-out from the 'social chapter' of the Maastricht Treaty, though the Labour government reversed this in 1997 (see the case study).
Justice and home affairs measures	Opt-outs from various justice and home affairs measures, including much EU legislation on criminal justice and policing that originated in the 1985 Schengen Agreement (to which the UK did not sign up).
Protocol to the Lisbon Treaty	An opt-out from a protocol to the Lisbon Treaty stating that the courts could not use the EU Charter of Fundamental Rights to create rights that do not already exist in national law, or find UK laws to be inconsistent with human rights.
2012 fiscal compact treaty	Non-participation in the 2012 fiscal compact treaty and in some EU bailout mechanisms.

Case study

The UK and the European Union budget

The UK is a net contributor to the EU budget, meaning it pays in more than it receives back. Only Germany pays more. In 2015, the UK paid around £18 billion into the EU budget, got a rebate of £5 billion, and received back £4.4 billion in public sector income. This meant a net contribution of £8.5 billion which equates to 1.5% of public spending. By comparison, the UK spent £130 billion on health. Of the money that the UK receives back from the EU, £3 billion per year is from the CAP and £1 billion is funding for poorer regions (e.g. Cornwall and Northern Ireland). In addition, the private sector also receives some £1 billion per year in EU research funding. The UK government will come under pressure to make up funding shortfalls after Brexit.

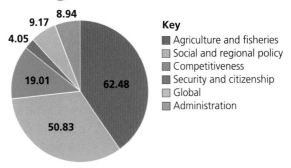

Key
- Agriculture and fisheries
- Social and regional policy
- Competitiveness
- Security and citizenship
- Global
- Administration

Source: European Commission (www.tinyurl.com/hjzocpw)

Figure 8.5 The EU budget, 2016 (in € million)

Questions
- Using Figure 8.5, identify the largest areas of EU spending.
- Who are the main contributors to the EU budget?

Case study

European Union social policy

The EU does not have extensive competences in social policy. It does not, for example, have responsibility for social security. Instead, EU social policy has focused on correcting perceived market failures (e.g. by protecting workers' rights) and promoting employment. But EU social policy has been controversial in the UK. John Major's opt-out from the Maastricht Treaty's 'social chapter' ended when Labour took office in 1997, yet the Blair government opposed a greater EU role in social policy. The UK is exempt from parts of the Working Time Directive. This sets a maximum working week of 48 hours but British workers can choose to work more than this. It also gives workers the right to rest breaks at work and to paid holidays. Trade unions fear that Brexit could weaken workers' rights but employers have highlighted the costs of complying with EU regulations.

The UK has traditionally favoured the free market Anglo-Saxon model of capitalism rather than the European social model of regulation, strong welfare states and bargaining between trade unions and employers.

Questions
- Why has EU social policy been controversial in Britain?
- To what extent do debates about EU social policy reflect a left–right ideological divide?

- **Limited influence in EU negotiations.** The UK has often been in a minority of states opposed to change and has not developed durable alliances to rival the Franco-German partnership. Despite this, it has been influential in areas such as the single market and defence.
- **Weak elite consensus.** The UK has not experienced the strong elite consensus on the benefits of the EU found in other member states. The two main parties have swapped positions on Europe. Labour

opposed membership at various times from the 1960s to the early 1980s, before becoming more supportive of EU social and regional policies from the late 1980s. The Conservatives advocated membership in the 1960s and championed the single market in the 1980s, but were eurosceptics from the 1990s when they saw further integration as a threat to national sovereignty and the free market. By the time Cameron took office in 2010, euroscepticism had moved from the margins to the mainstream of British politics. Both main parties have also suffered serious internal divisions on the issue of European integration. Harold Wilson held a referendum on EEC membership in 1975 in an attempt to resolve Labour's divisions but in 1981, Labour's policy of withdrawal prompted the defection of pro-European MPs to the Social Democratic Party. Conservative prime ministers Major and Cameron faced a series of rebellions by eurosceptic MPs.

■ **Popular euroscepticism.** Levels of public support for EU membership (see Figure 8.6) and integration have long been lower in the UK than in other member states. UK citizens are also less likely to feel European. Newspapers like the *Sun* and the *Daily Mail* take populist eurosceptic positions. UKIP has both tapped into and fuelled euroscepticism within the British electorate. The extent of popular euroscepticism was made apparent in the 2016 referendum, as shown in Figure 8.6.

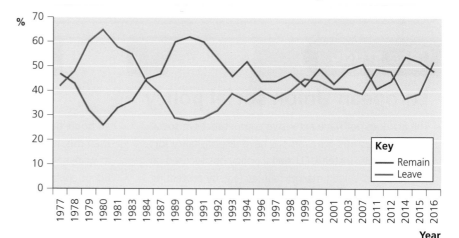

Figure 8.6 Popular support for EU membership in the UK, 1977–2016

Source: Ipsos MORI (www.tinyurl.com/hrw8hw2) and 2016 referendum

The decision to leave the European Union

In 2013, David Cameron promised to hold an in/out referendum on EU membership should the Conservatives win the 2015 general election. He also promised to renegotiate relations with the EU before the referendum. Cameron's decision was largely shaped by domestic politics. The Conservatives were divided on the EU issue, with eurosceptic MPs rebelling frequently. Cameron also hoped that the referendum pledge would reverse the flow of voters from the Conservatives to UKIP.

The EU referendum, held on 23 June 2016, asked 'Should the United Kingdom remain a member of the European Union or leave the European Union?' The result saw 51.9% vote to leave and 48.1% vote to remain. Turnout was 72%, the highest UK-wide figure since the 1992 general

The EU referendum, held on 23 June 2016, asked 'Should the United Kingdom remain a member of the European Union or leave the European Union?'

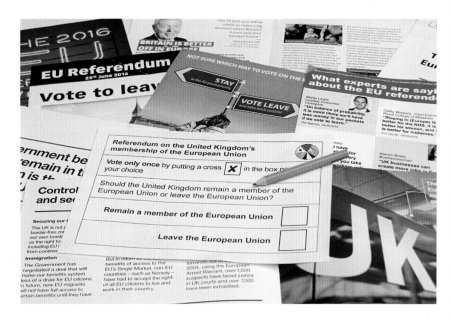

election. The use and impact of referendums in the UK is examined in Chapter 9. The roots of the vote for Brexit run deep in British politics, but short-term effects were also significant.

The 2016 European Union referendum

The campaign

The Remain campaign appeared to have a number of advantages. It was supported by the government and endorsed by senior figures from business, the Bank of England, the military and security services, and by US President Obama. But these interventions did not shift public opinion significantly. The Remain campaign focused on the economic case for EU membership (see the case study) and Remain voters believed that Brexit would be economically costly. But many Leave voters did not believe that the economic costs of Brexit would affect them and were more concerned by cultural issues. Stark warnings about the costs of Brexit also damaged Cameron's credibility.

Case study

Costs and benefits of European Union membership

The EU is the UK's main export market (45% of UK exports in 2014), some 3.5 million jobs are linked to trade in Europe, and the single market makes the UK more attractive to foreign direct investment. But EU regulation is costly, with the Open Europe think-tank putting the cost at £33 billion a year. The UK is also a net contributor to the EU budget.

The economic impact of Brexit is difficult to quantify. Much will depend on whether the UK has preferential access to the single market — including in financial services, a key part of the UK economy — and a comprehensive free trade agreement. If it does not, the EU could impose tariffs on British goods. Outside the EU, the UK will be free to negotiate bilateral trade details, but even as the world's fifth-largest economy, it may not have the same clout in trade negotiations as the EU.

Questions
- What have been the main benefits of EU membership?
- What are the potential benefits of Brexit?

In the 1975 EEC referendum, Harold Wilson persuaded voters that he had secured a good deal when renegotiating British membership. But Cameron's renegotiation did not convince enough Conservative MPs or voters that real change had been secured.

In referendums, voters often follow cues provided by the party they support, but in this case, with the exception of UKIP, many supporters did not follow the lead provided by party leaders. Most Conservative supporters voted to leave. They had received mixed messages: Cameron and most ministers urged them to remain, but 140 Conservative MPs campaigned to leave. Most Labour supporters voted to stay in the EU, but Jeremy Corbyn was accused of being disengaged.

The Leave campaign enjoyed support from much of the tabloid press. Nigel Farage played a key role in getting the core eurosceptic vote out, but Boris Johnson was crucial in broadening Leave's appeal. The Leave campaign had a clear message ('take back control') and it persuaded its supporters that Brexit would reduce immigration. Turnout was higher in areas that voted to leave.

Boris Johnson was crucial in broadening the Leave campaign's appeal

A divided Britain

The referendum exposed old and new fault lines in British politics. England (except London) and Wales voted to leave the EU, but Scotland and Northern Ireland voted to remain (see Figure 8.7). Sharp demographic differences were evident (see Figure 8.8). A clear majority of young people voted to remain, but most older voters backed the Leave campaign. Middle-class voters supported Remain while working-class voters supported Leave. Voters with a university degree were strongly in favour of remaining in the EU while those with qualifications no higher than GCSE were strongly in favour of leaving. The result reflected divisions between the advantaged and disadvantaged, with people and regions that felt 'left behind' by economic and social change voting to leave.

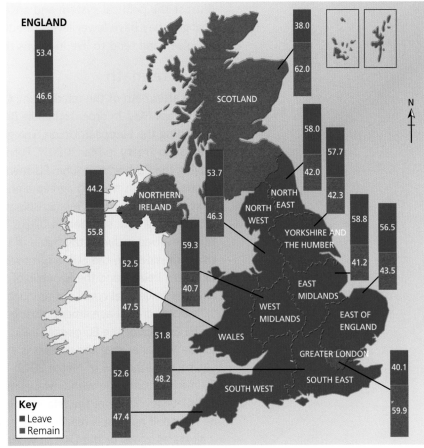

Figure 8.7 2016 EU referendum results by region

Source: Electoral Commission

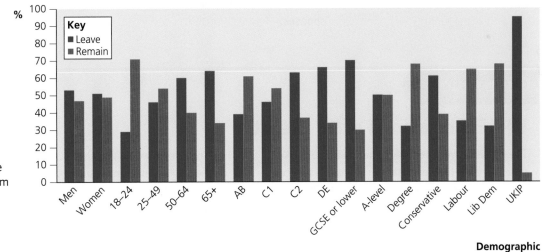

Figure 8.8 How Britain voted in the 2016 EU referendum

Demographic

Source: YouGov (www.tinyurl.com/zvsb5bb)

The division is also about values. The referendum provided further evidence of a cleavage between cosmopolitans and non-cosmopolitans. Cosmopolitans have social liberal attitudes and are pro-immigration and positive about social and cultural change. They are university educated, have professional occupations, are younger and disproportionally found in London and university towns. Non-cosmopolitans (or communitarians) have social conservative attitudes, are negative about immigration, distrust the political system and are suspicious of social and cultural change. They have lower levels of education, are in manual occupations, are older, and tend to live in towns that are in economic decline.

The aftermath

In the aftermath of the referendum, Cameron resigned and was succeeded by Theresa May. In order to handle Brexit, she created the Department for Exiting the European Union. The government triggered Article 50 of the Lisbon Treaty in March 2017. Formal negotiations on the terms for leaving the EU began in June. EU member states meeting in the European Council (without the UK) agreed a phased approach to negotiations with talks on the UK's future relationship with the EU (e.g. a free trade deal) not commencing until sufficient progress is made on the exit terms. Key issues to be resolved included the rights of EU citizens resident in the UK (and UK citizens resident in the EU), a financial settlement, and the border between Northern Ireland and the Republic of Ireland. Both sides recognised that any free trade deal could not amount to membership of the single market.

The withdrawal agreement must be approved by a qualified majority in the Council of the European Union, and by the European Parliament. Article 50 states that the process is expected to be completed within two years (i.e. by the end of March 2019). If it is, the UK will cease to be an EU member once the withdrawal agreement is approved. Rather than a complete severance of the relationship, transitional arrangements may be agreed. If no deal is reached, the negotiation period can be extended if all states agree, or the UK can withdraw unilaterally. Domestically, the government will introduce legislation (a 'great repeal bill') to incorporate existing EU law into UK law, and then amend or repeal those laws it opposes.

Case study

UK–EU relations after Brexit

The Conservative government wants a bespoke UK–EU deal that gives the freest trade in goods and services but restricts the free movement of people. The terms 'hard Brexit' and 'soft Brexit' refer to alternative post-Brexit scenarios. 'Hard Brexit' would see the UK end free movement of people, leave the single market and not contribute to the EU budget. The UK would trade with the EU based on World Trade Organization rules (e.g. applying tariffs on EU goods), unless a deal was reached to eliminate many tariffs. Canada has negotiated a free trade deal with the EU, but it needs to be ratified by all EU states.

'Soft Brexit' would give the UK a form of membership of the single market in return for accepting (limited) free movement of people. Norway and Switzerland have this sort of relationship with the EU. Norway is a member of the European Economic Area, while Switzerland has a looser relationship with the EU based on a series of bilateral treaties. Both enjoy access to the single market and are members of the border-free Schengen Area. But they do not take part in the EU customs union, common trade policy, CAP, or foreign and security policy. However, both contribute to the EU budget and are not represented in negotiations on EU laws that they must implement.

Questions
- What are the main differences between the 'hard' and 'soft' options outlined above?
- What is the UK government seeking?

Synoptic links

Devolution

Brexit creates further tensions within the Union. Scotland's first minister Nicola Sturgeon argues that it creates the conditions for a second referendum on Scottish independence. In Northern Ireland, the status of the border with the Republic of Ireland has also emerged as an issue.

What you should know

- The European Union has changed significantly since the UK joined in 1973. It has 28 members and has extended its policy competence into areas such as economic, internal security and foreign policy. The EU's supranational institutions have also grown in importance.
- The UK has been regarded as an 'awkward partner' in the EU. Successive governments sought to defend national sovereignty and opted out of major EU policy developments such as EMU.
- EU membership has had a significant impact on British politics. Many areas of public policy are now determined by the EU. EU law takes priority over national law. Political parties have experienced damaging internal divisions. Euroscepticism is more prevalent in the British party system, public opinion and the media than in many other EU member states.
- The 2016 referendum vote reflected long-term dissatisfaction with the UK's relationship with the EU. It also revealed sharp demographic and attitudinal fault-lines within British politics.

Further reading

Geddes, A. (2013) *Britain and the European Union*, Palgrave Macmillan.

Miller, V. (ed.) (2016) *Briefing Paper: Brexit: impact across policy areas*, House of Commons Library.

Moxon, K. and MacEwan, I. (2012) 'Debate: should the UK remain within the EU?', *Politics Review*, Vol. 22, No. 1, pp. 16–17.

Whitaker, R. (2014) 'The European Parliament: does it matter?', *Politics Review*, Vol. 23, No. 3, pp. 30–33.

Whitaker, R. and Lynch, P. (2009) 'Where does power lie in the European Union?', *Politics Review*, Vol. 18, No. 1, pp. 10–13.

Department for Exiting the European Union: www.tinyurl.com/zl673yf

European Union: www.tinyurl.com/j62s3mn

The UK in a Changing Europe: http://ukandeu.ac.uk

What UK thinks EU: www.whatukthinks.org/eu/

Exam-style questions

Short-answer questions

1 Explain, with examples, the four freedoms of the single European market.

2 Explain, with examples, the Common Agricultural Policy.

3 Explain and analyse three of the freedoms of the single market.

4 Explain and analyse three treaties that have altered the work of the European Union since 1985.

Mid-length questions

1 Describe the main features of the European Union.

2 Describe the main functions the European Council.

3 Analyse and evaluate the arguments in favour of the UK leaving the European Union.

4 Analyse and evaluate the arguments in favour of membership of the single European market.

Essay questions

1 Evaluate how far membership of the European Union affected British sovereignty.

2 Evaluate how far economic concerns explain the result of the referendum to leave the European Union in 2016.

3 Analyse and evaluate the criticisms of the European Union.

4 'The European Union is, fundamentally, an undemocratic organisation.' How far do you agree with this statement?

In your answer you must:

- Refer to the institutions of the European Union and the impact of the European Union on member states.

- Draw on relevant knowledge and understanding of UK politics.

SECTION
2

POLITICAL PARTICIPATION IN THE UK

Chapter 9

Democracy and political participation

Democracy takes many forms and can be interpreted in many ways

Why has there been such debate over the nature of decision making in the wake of the EU referendum result? With 17 million people voting in favour of leaving, and a majority of 52%, it would seem a pretty clear-cut case of a democratic decision being made. Yet some have claimed that such a decision should never have been left to the British public. Some, looking at who was allowed to vote and how different regions of the UK voted, believe the result to be unfair. Others believe that, like it or not, the majority vote has to be respected and followed, no matter what.

The divided opinions about what should have happened next reflect the different aspects of democracy and the fact that democracy takes many forms and can be interpreted in many ways. The arguments about the role of the EU referendum in British politics reveal different attitudes to democracy in the UK and the way perceptions of democracy have changed in recent years. Democracy is fundamental to all aspects of modern politics and understanding the issues surrounding it is essential to your study of the subject.

What is democracy?

Key term

Democracy A system where power is held by 'the people'.

Democracy is an idea fundamental to our understanding of politics, yet it is a term often misunderstood. In the modern world, particularly in the west, democracy is seen as the purest and most effective way of ruling a state, but this has not always been the case. Indeed, for centuries democracy was seen as an insult and something to be feared.

In modern democracies, checks are put in place to limit the power given to the people. In America, the Declaration of Independence declared all men to be created equal and a founding principle of the constitution was the establishment of democracy, but various institutions were created to limit and check the power of the people and initially it was only wealthy, white men who could vote.

In Britain, often seen as the oldest of the modern democracies, the extent of power given to the people has always been limited. Never mind the House of Lords and the power of the monarch, for centuries only wealthy, male landowners had the right to vote for MPs. The franchise has been extended over time to include property owners, all men, women and eventually those over the age of 18. Yet even today, there are concerns about further extending the right to vote to other groups of people, such as 16- and 17-year-olds and those in prison. The argument is always the same — are these groups intelligent enough, capable enough and responsible enough to make decisions in the best interests of everyone in society?

The definition of the term 'the people' varies from country to country and has changed over time. Equally, how 'the people' exercise their power varies from state to state, with some relying on majoritarian democracy and others on liberal democracy. There are **direct** and **representative democracies** and some that rely on a mixture of the two. Some democracies are presidential while others are parliamentary, or even rely on a constitutional monarchy. All are democracies, but how effectively they allow the people to exercise power, and whether or not people power is in the national interest, is a matter of debate for each type.

Key terms

Direct democracy A system where the people are able to make decisions directly on an issue, usually in the form of a 'yes' or 'no' response.

Representative democracy A system where the people elect a person or group of people to represent their interests and make decisions on their behalf.

Case study

Can the people be trusted?

In the referendum on the UK's membership of the EU, turnout was 72.2%, of whom 52% voted to leave. As a result, the British government is pursuing a policy that will fundamentally change the way Britain works — politically, socially and economically. Such a monumental decision was effectively made by only 37.7% of the voting population.

Many of the people who voted based their decisions on issues such as parliamentary sovereignty and immigration, or on their dissatisfaction with the government at the time. It is claimed there was a lack of understanding of the issues involved. Much had been made of a claim that £350 million that was sent to the EU every week could instead be spent on the NHS. The claim was contested before the vote and, after the vote, UKIP leader Nigel Farage said the claim should never have been made, because there is no guarantee that the money could be redirected in this way. Arguably, people had therefore made a decision based on emotion, lack of understanding, poor education or misinformation.

Questions

- In the 1979 referendums on Scottish and Welsh devolution, at least 40% of the voting population had to vote 'yes' for devolution to proceed. Should there be a similarly high standard of acceptance for all referendums dealing with constitutional reform?
- If a campaign uses false information, should the result of the vote be ignored?
- Assess two criticisms of the use of referendums in a parliamentary democracy.

Spend some time thinking about these issues:
- Should a decision made by a majority always be followed, even at the expense of the minority?
- Should important decisions be left to an educated few who will act in the best interest of society, or to the popular will of the many, who might not understand the issues?
- Can the many be relied on to act in the interest of society, or will they always act in their own interests?

Forms of democracy

It is important to be able to identify the different forms that democracy can take.

- **Liberal democracy.** In this form of democracy, the right to vote will be widespread and representatives will act in the interests of everyone in society.
- **Majoritarian democracy.** This is a system whereby the will or desires of the majority of the population are the prime considerations of the government.
- **Parliamentary democracy.** This is a system where parliament stands as the highest form of authority. The executive branch will be drawn from and accountable to the people's representatives in parliament.
- **Presidential democracy.** This is a system where the executive will be elected separately from the legislative body and is therefore chosen by and directly accountable to the people.
- **Direct democracy.** This refers to any occasion when the citizens are directly involved in the decision-making process.
- **Representative democracy.** This describes any system where the people transfer the power to make decisions to an elected representative.

Distinguish between

Parliamentary and presidential democracy

Parliamentary democracy
- The government is drawn from members of parliament.
- The government is held to account by parliament.
- There is a unified system, whereby the executive and legislature are from the same party.
- The head of state and head of government are likely to be separate.

Presidential democracy
- The government is elected separately from members of the legislature.
- The electorate holds the government to account.
- There is the possibility of a divided government when different parties control the executive and legislature.
- The head of state will usually be the head of government as well.

In focus

Pluralist democracy

Pluralism is the broad idea that there is competition between different groups who represent different concerns, either as parties or as pressure groups. In a **pluralist democracy**, power is widely and evenly distributed across society rather than concentrated in the hands of an elite. The government should remain neutral in a pluralist system and make decisions based on the merits of the competing arguments, making it an alternative to majoritarian and parliamentary democracy.

In a pluralist democracy:

- there will be a wide dispersal of power among competing groups
- there will be no elite groups
- groups will be internally democratic
- group leaders will be accountable to their members
- there will be a range of access points
- the government should be politically neutral

Activity

The UK has elements of most of the forms of democracy listed on page 204. Try to identify the examples that demonstrate the existence of a particular type of democracy.

Based on what you know about UK politics, try to rank the different forms of democracy in order of relevance to the UK: the one at the top should be the one that best describes the UK's system of democracy and the one at the bottom should be the least relevant to the UK's system. Then write a short paragraph explaining why you believe your top choice is the best description of democracy in the UK.

In small groups, compare your lists and explain why you think your top choice is more convincing. If your top choice is the same, compare your second choices. Do you feel your top choice is the best form of democracy for the UK? If so, why? If not, which one would you change it to and why?

What are the functions of democracy?

Having established what makes a state a democracy, we need to ask ourselves what is the point of having a democracy? In the West, we tend to assume that democracy is the best form of government and the only way in which a civilised state can operate. But what makes democracy so great and so appealing? How can we judge the health of a democracy?

To answer these questions and allow us to answer questions about the state of democracy in the UK, we need to understand the purpose of democracy. In other words, what are its functions?

- **Representation.** There must be a means of the people being able to put their views to the government of the day.
- **Accountability.** There must be a process by which the government of the day can be made to explain and take responsibility for its actions.
- **Participation.** There must be a way in which the people can be engaged and take part in the political process.
- **Power dispersal.** There should be a system that ensures power is spread across different political bodies to avoid one body becoming overly dominant.
- **Legitimacy.** The process for the selection of the different branches of government should have legal authority and fairly represent the will of the people.
- **Education.** The political process should be open to all and there should be an educated and informed citizenry who are able to understand the issues and make informed decisions.

Direct democracy

Direct democracy refers to a system where the eligible citizens make the political decisions themselves without operating through anyone else, such as representatives (see Table 9.1). Typically, decisions will be made by a majority vote on a simple for or against basis. In such a system the process of decision making is continuous and on-going, requiring a high level of education and engagement from the people.

Direct democracy is seen as the purest form of democracy, as the people are able to express their opinions directly, without being misinterpreted. While some modern states employ a level of direct democracy, the classical idea is just not possible with the geographic and population sizes of modern countries. However, elements of direct democracy are evident in most countries and are becoming more common in the UK.

The most common form of direct democracy is the use of referendums, whereby the public vote directly on an issue presented to them. Referendums are called by representatives or those in charge. Other countries and regions, especially some of the United States, have **initiatives**, which are similar to a referendum but are proposed and called by a percentage of the population. This allows the public more direct control over the issues being considered. In addition, the USA also adopts a system of town hall meetings where members of the public can attend and put their views directly to the people in power.

Other elements of direct democracy used in the UK include citizens' juries and public **petitions**, both of which allow the people to express their opinion on a particular policy or area of government, although these are still tempered by representatives.

Key terms

Initiative A means by which the people, rather than the government, can call for a vote on a specific issue.

Petition An appeal to make something specific happen, usually by demonstrating a high level of popular support.

Table 9.1 Arguments in favour of and against direct democracy

Arguments in favour of direct democracy	Arguments against direct democracy
A pure form of democracy. The system is a true form of democracy because everyone has a say on an issue rather than having their views expressed through representatives.	**It is not practical.** In a modern state the number of issues, plus the size of the population, means a system of direct democracy would be unresponsive and impractical.
Increased legitimacy. Decisions have greater democratic legitimacy because they have the support of the majority of the people.	**Tyranny of the majority.** Minority groups and interests may have their needs and concerns overlooked when decisions are based on a majority vote.
Improves participation. Participation is greater when people have more opportunities to be involved in issues that directly affect them.	**Undermines elected representatives.** Having direct democracy in a representative system undermines the role of those representatives and allows them to pass the responsibility for difficult decisions to the public. Representatives are less accountable and have less responsibility for their policy decisions.
Increases public engagement. Regular public debates and discussion of issues help to improve public engagement in the running of the country.	**Low turnouts.** A low turnout means that only a small group of people make decisions which affect everyone. This undermines the legitimacy of the decisions being made.
Improves political education. Political education is improved because people need to be informed in order to make decisions.	**Emotional responses.** People can tend to vote on the basis of emotion rather than the practical considerations of major issues.
It works. Countries like Switzerland regularly use direct democracy to make decisions and are seen to function effectively.	**Populist outcomes.** People can tend to vote on popular short-term measures that will benefit them, rather than consider what will be in the national interest and good for everyone.

Complete your own version of the following table, identifying how the increased use of direct democracy might improve or worsen each function of democracy in the UK.

How might direct democracy improve democracy in the UK?

Function	How direct democracy might improve democracy in the UK	How direct democracy might worsen democracy in the UK
Representation		
Accountability		
Participation		
Distribution of power		
Legitimacy		
Education		

Look over the section on referendums in Chapter 10 (pages 274–79) and carry out your own research to find examples and explanations of direct democracy improving or failing to improve each of these functions. The following websites may be helpful:

www.paparty.co.uk

www.tinyurl.com/ofbncxh

www.tinyurl.com/jboc62t

www.iniref.org

www.tinyurl.com/gmhkl34

Should a referendum, such as that on membership of the EU, be advisory or binding on politicians?

Representative democracy

In a representative democracy the people elect someone to represent them in a legislative body. The nature of the representation can take many forms but essentially the elected representatives will debate and discuss laws on behalf of the people who have elected them. They may act on what their constituents want or on what they think would be best for their constituents, or they may represent wider groups when debating and creating laws.

How effectively does democracy operate in the UK?

Positive aspects of democracy in the UK

Free and fair elections

The UK has a wide variety of elections, allowing citizens to choose representatives for a range of local and national bodies, and providing many opportunities for the public to participate in the democratic process and be educated by political campaigns.

Key term

Purdah A phrase used to describe the period before an election or vote where members of local councils or government are not allowed to make any new statements or proposals that could affect the way in which people vote. The period is usually between 4 and 6 weeks.

Elections in the UK are free from government manipulation because they are conducted by the Electoral Commission, which is independent of any particular party. There are laws in place about campaigning in and around the ballot stations on the day of an election.

Other measures designed to make sure elections are fair include campaign spending limits and a ban on campaigning during the period of **purdah**. Furthermore, the UK restricts the amount of broadcast campaigning for each party by ensuring that party political broadcasts are allocated according to previous electoral support, are given the same amount of time and are broadcast at the same time each day.

In focus

The Electoral Commission

The Electoral Commission was created in 2000 by the Political Parties, Elections and Referendums Act. The Commission is independent from government and party influence and has the key responsibility of overseeing and strengthening democracy in the UK. Responsibilities include:
- registering political parties
- advising and explaining the rules relating to campaign finance and election spending
- ensuring political parties comply with legal requirements
- setting the criteria by which elections are run
- reviewing and reporting on how well elections are run
- reviewing and reporting on all UK elections and referendums, with suggestions for improvements
- advising parliament and being consulted on changes to election laws and regulations
- approving the wording of referendum questions to ensure fairness
- educating the public on how to register to vote and on the importance of registering

People queuing to vote in the EU referendum, 23 June 2016

Turnout

After hitting a historic low of 59% in the general election of 2001, turnout in UK general elections has been steadily increasing. Turnout was 62% in 2005, 65% in 2010 and 66% in 2015 before rising to 69% in 2017. Furthermore, turnout at the Scottish independence referendum was 84.6% and at the EU referendum was 72%, showing that more people are participating in the political process.

Universal suffrage

Building on the idea of fairness, the UK has a system of universal suffrage. This means that everyone over the age of 18 who is not a prisoner, mentally incapable or a peer, has the right to vote, on the basis of one person, one vote. This means that all votes are equal in value and that there is no distinction based on wealth, race, gender, class or any other grounds.

The party system

The UK has a wide variety of political parties and the number has grown greatly in the past 50 years. Currently, there are eight parties represented in the House of Commons, with many more contesting elections and 11 having held seats in the last parliament. This variety provides a wide range of options for voters with different views and visions for the country, as well as a greater degree of representation.

Furthermore, it is the parties who drive public education. With so many political parties contesting elections and scrutinising each other, the parties raise the profile of political issues and help to create a better informed and educated population.

Pressure groups

The UK has thousands of **pressure groups**, covering every issue possible. Pressure groups provide an alternative avenue of representation, particularly on small or minority issues, that might not concern a majority of the electorate or the parties seeking majority support. With such a large number of groups, the UK provides a mouthpiece for any minority interest as well as providing a variety of ways in which the public can participate.

Pressure groups will investigate issues, raise public awareness and help to develop government policies in order to educate the electorate and ensure that the needs of people who may not be able to vote are taken into consideration. Pressure groups are legally equal and are free to compete with each other in order to allow the government and the public to make an informed and balanced decision.

Parliamentary sovereignty

Parliament holds legal sovereignty, which means that the chosen representatives of the people hold the ultimate power in making, amending and repealing laws. As such, government is drawn from members of parliament and is accountable to parliament. In trying to pass policies or on issues of taxation and spending, the government must get consent from the House of Commons, thereby gaining consent indirectly from the people.

Devolution

The process of devolution has allowed the constituent parts of the UK (apart from England), along with many cities, to make decisions on a local basis. Representatives are closer to the community in which they serve. This allows for better quality representation and ensures that policies are appropriate to each area, rather than being imposed by a remote and disconnected central government.

Negative aspects of democracy in the UK

While the UK has many democratic elements, there is a concern that many of these elements do not work well, resulting in a **democratic deficit**.

Unelected elements

An unelected hereditary monarchy and an unelected House of Lords undermine the concept of representative democracy in the UK. The monarch and peers have not been selected to represent any specific section of society and they can only be removed by death or, following the House of Lord Reform Act 2014, resigning or being expelled for failing to attend an entire annual parliamentary session or committing a serious criminal offence. This means there is no way for the public to hold them to account.

Although the powers of the monarch and Lords are theoretically limited, this is only by convention, such as the Salisbury Doctrine, and can be ignored by the Lords if they choose to do so.

Furthermore, even after reform, 92 hereditary peers remain and the system of appointment is often criticised for cronyism, making the undemocratic House of Lords appear even less democratic.

Case study

Tax credits: money or welfare?

In October 2015, the House of Lords rejected a series of proposed cuts to the tax credit system by 289 to 272 votes. The proposals had recently been passed by a narrow vote in the House of Commons. The government then dropped the plans to make the cuts but the situation raised questions over the nature and democratic legitimacy of the Lords.

- The tax credit cuts were set out in the Conservative manifesto and therefore the government had a mandate from the British people to carry them out. Under the terms of the Salisbury Doctrine, the Lords should not have rejected the cuts.
- The government presented the cuts as a financial measure, or money bill, which, by convention, the

House of Lords is not allowed to reject. The Lords claimed it was a welfare bill, rather than a money bill, and so they were entitled to reject it.

- The Lords also saw it as a piece of delegated legislation, rather than primary legislation, which meant they had the power to veto it.
- The 289 peers who rejected the tax credit cuts were mainly a coalition of Labour and Liberal Democrat peers, the two parties that had just lost the general election and therefore had no party mandate.
- Lord Andrew Lloyd Webber, a Conservative peer who resides in the USA and rarely attends parliament, flew to the UK to vote in favour of the government's plans, despite not being affected by any of the issues.

Questions

- Do you believe the cuts to tax credit were a welfare bill or a financial bill? Explain your choice.
- To what extent do you agree with the view that the Lords should not be allowed to defeat measures passed by the House of Commons?

Turnout

While the UK has many elections, turnout is often quite low, leading to claims of a **participation crisis**. Recent general election turnouts are still below the historic average of 75% or the 71% achieved in 1997.

Below elections at the national level, turnout drops significantly, as shown in Table 9.2. Turnout at most referendums is also far below that of general elections. This raises questions about the legitimacy of the decisions made and the representatives elected.

Key term

Participation crisis A term used to describe a failure of the public to participate in the political process, which can undermine democratic legitimacy.

Table 9.2 Turnout in UK elections, 2016

Election	Turnout (%)
Local council	34.33
Scottish Parliament	55.8
Welsh Assembly	45.44
London Mayoral	46.1
Police and Crime Commissioner (PCC)	27.31
Northern Irish Assembly	45.60

The West Lothian Question and EVEL

Devolution has created an imbalance in UK politics, known as the West Lothian Question. The question relates to the fact that Scottish MPs (and Welsh, Northern Irish and London MPs, depending on the issue) can vote on issues that do not affect their constituents but do impact other people. For example, the increase in student tuition fees in England and Wales in 2004 was only passed with the votes of Scottish MPs, while the extension to Sunday trading was defeated in 2016 with the votes of SNP MPs, despite the fact that neither issue would directly affect residents in Scotland. This means that MPs are making decisions about things that affect people who cannot hold them accountable.

Attempts to address this imbalance with 'English votes for English laws' (EVEL) have been limited and run the risk of creating two tiers of MPs, which would undermine the principle of a parliamentary chamber.

In focus

English votes for English laws

In order to address the West Lothian Question, the 2015 Conservative Party manifesto contained a proposal for an extra stage in the legislative process for legislation that would only affect England — 'English votes for English Laws' or EVEL. This additional stage gives English MPs (or English and Welsh MPs, depending on the issue) the power to strike down legislation that would affect their constituents. This means that an issue such as the 2004 increase in tuition fees would be prevented from going to a vote of the whole house. However, it does not address the issue of Scottish MPs being able to strike down legislation which is supported by English MPs, as was shown in the case of the Sunday Trading Bill in 2016.

In focus

The West Lothian Question

During debates over Scottish devolution in the 1970s, the MP for West Lothian, Tam Dalyell, asked why Scottish MPs should be able to vote on matters that relate only to England, when English MPs could not vote on the same matters that had been devolved and therefore affected only people in Scotland. This has become known as the West Lothian Question and reflects the fact that Scottish MPs are able to vote on issues that do not affect their constituents. In 2003–04, Labour passed legislation for the creation of foundation hospitals and increases in student tuition fees, matters that would not affect anyone in Scotland. In both cases, the legislation only passed with the votes of Scottish MPs.

Although the number of Scottish seats at Westminster was reduced from 72 to 59 in 2005 to counter this problem, the issue has become more prominent since 2010 because the vast majority of Scottish MPs have represented a different party from the one in government. Since 2015, there has been a Conservative majority in Westminster but only one Conservative MP from Scotland.

The voting system

The first-past-the-post (FPTP) electoral system has a number of flaws:

- **Wasted votes**. Any votes cast for a candidate who does not win in a constituency play no role in the selection of representatives in parliament, meaning they are effectively wasted.
- **Safe seats.** Some constituencies elect a candidate from the same party in every election and the level of support required to win the constituency is so high that voters see no point in voting for a different party.
- **Unrepresentative.** Differences in the concentration of support across the UK mean that the result of elections does not reflect the way the public voted, with UKIP winning 13% of the vote in 2015 but only 1 seat, while the SNP gained 56 seats with only 2% of the national vote.
- **Winner's bonus.** The system exaggerates the support received by the most popular party, which means the party receives more seats than is proportional to the number of votes it received, thus boosting its majority in parliament.

- **Discriminates against parties with widespread support.** Parties with support spread across the UK but not concentrated in a geographic area will find it difficult to gain seats and therefore representation, such as the Greens, Liberal Democrats and UKIP.
- **Minority constituencies.** In these constituencies, an MP wins the most votes but does not gain more than 50% of the total vote, meaning a majority of the public did not vote for their representative.
- **Two-party system.** It favours parties with a lot of support spread evenly across the country and generally results in one of the two main parties forming the government and the other forming an opposition or 'government in waiting'.

Alternative systems have been tried but even when they have solved some of the problems of FPTP they have also had problems of their own, leading to extremist parties gaining representation, confusion at the polls, spoiled ballot papers and a lack of clear representation.

Lack of meaningful choice

Despite the range of parties competing, only two have a realistic chance of gaining power in Westminster. As a result, many people vote for one of the two main parties, which often have similar polices, especially in the period of post-Thatcherite consensus.

Even in devolved areas, the contest tends to centre on a two-party system, with the SNP first competing with Labour, and then more recently against the Conservatives, while in Northern Ireland there is a straight contest between Sinn Féin and the DUP. The English regional mayoral elections reflected a battle between the Conservatives and Labour.

Elitist pressure groups

Pressure groups do not compete on an equal footing. A small number of pressure groups tend to dominate any political debate at the expense of other interests. This results from a number of factors:
- insider status
- size of membership
- wealth
- public profile

Consequently, British pressure group participation is based on elitism rather than a pluralist system of representation.

Weaknesses of the Electoral Commission

Although the Electoral Commission oversees the elections, it is often a reactive, rather than proactive, body. In terms of comments, adverts and spending, it tends to pass judgement and sanctions after an event, meaning the message has already had its impact. Furthermore, there are loopholes over spending and the use of social media that the Commission has no power to regulate or ability to control.

Lack of entrenched rights

Without a codified constitution, key rights can easily be overturned by the government without effective redress through the judicial system. This undermines a key principle of democracy that citizens' rights are protected from government abuse (see Table 9.3).

Table 9.3 Evidence of the weaknesses in rights protection

Right	How it is undermined
Freedom of speech	The creation of 'safe spaces' in universities has been criticised in parliament for restricting forums for debate and discussion.
Freedom of protest	Additional measures have been taken to restrict protests outside of parliament.
Right to vote	Despite repeated judicial instructions, governments have not granted any prisoners the right to vote.
Right to due process	Governments have been able to extend the period of detention without charge under the Terrorism Act to 28 days in 2006 (reduced to 14 days in January 2011) and suspend part of the Human Rights Act, as in the Belmarsh case.

Table 9.4 Positive and negative aspects of representative democracy in the UK

Positive aspects of representative democracy in the UK	Negative aspects of representative democracy in the UK
Everyone is represented through a constituency MP.	Due to the FPTP electoral system, there are many minority MPs who were not voted in by a majority of their constituents.
The FPTP electoral system is simple and provides a clear winner for each seat.	The electoral system leads to wasted votes and unrepresentative outcomes in parliament.
Britain has a variety of parties that contest elections, with 11 parties in parliament and many others contesting elections.	Safe seats across the UK mean that there is a lack of real choice in many constituencies. In addition, the fact that only two parties are in a realistic position to form a government reduces the level of choice.
Everyone over the age of 18, who is not a prisoner, mentally incapable or a peer, has the right to vote.	There are issues concerning the denial of the franchise to 16- and 17-year-olds as well as prisoners. There are also many groups who are effectively disenfranchised by the process of registration, such as the homeless. There is relatively low turnout, with only around two-thirds of people voting in general elections, raising concerns about the democratic legitimacy of the government.
There are thousands of pressure groups representing a wide variety of interests and groups which can compete.	Due to a variety of factors, including wealth, size and status, the competition between pressure groups is often unfair and elitist, giving some groups much greater power than others.
New groups and parties can easily be created to take on new issues.	In a situation of hyperpluralism, important issues can be drowned out by the sheer number of campaigns.
The Electoral Commission works hard to ensure that parties adhere to rules on spending and campaigning.	Parties are able to find ways around the regulations to spend more. The increasing use of the internet has effectively allowed parties to by-pass the broadcasting restrictions imposed in other areas.

Activity

Democratic Audit UK is an organisation that investigates and analyses the state of UK democracy. Visit its website to read its annual report and various articles relating to the state of democracy in the UK.
www.democraticaudit.com

Extending the franchise

Key term

Franchise The right to vote in elections.

The **franchise** is the right to vote, so those who hold the franchise are those who are eligible to vote in elections. As elections are conducted by law in the UK, those who hold the franchise, or the automatic right to vote, are determined by legislation. The franchise can be extended in a one-off event, as it was in the Scottish independence referendum in 2014, but this is done on a case-by-case basis. For all representative elections in the UK, the franchise is currently extended to everyone over the age of 18 who is not a criminal, mentally incapable or a peer. This is known as universal suffrage and covers approximately 71.5% of the current UK population.

While many take universal suffrage for granted today, 200 years ago only about 2.7% of the UK population had the franchise. The growth in the franchise reflects the changing nature of democracy in the UK, as attitudes to class, gender and age have evolved. As the franchise has been extended, previously excluded groups have been granted a more equal say in British politics and the way the country is run. It is therefore the extension of the franchise that has made Britain a modern representative democracy (see Table 9.5).

The essential argument over the franchise is that those who pay tax should have a say in how that tax is spent, hence the rallying cry of the colonies in the American War of Independence: 'No taxation without representation'. While other factors have also played a role, reform of the franchise has often been driven by the desire of those who pay taxes to determine how those taxes are raised and spent.

Table 9.5 The extension of the franchise in the UK

Year	Development
1832	Voting rights extended to property owners
1867	Voting rights extended to skilled workers
1918	Voting rights extended to all men over 21 and women over 30
1928	Voting rights extended to all women over 21
1969	Voting rights extended to everyone aged 18 or above

The Great Reform Act 1832 and middle-class voting

Before 1832, the right to vote was based on the amount of land owned, essentially limiting it to members of the upper class. However, during the eighteenth and nineteenth centuries, Britain underwent rapid economic change during the Industrial Revolution, shifting from a rural, land-based economy to a more urban, industrial one. This led to the rise of the middle class as a major economic force in the UK, who contributed more to the economy than the land-owning nobility but held most of their wealth in property. As a result, the most important economic group in the country was denied representation.

Public discontent, led by middle-class campaigners, as well as other issues, eventually led to the passing of the Great Reform Act in 1832. The Act extended the right to vote to an additional 300,000 people as the value of property, rather than of land, became the key factor for awarding the franchise.

In truth, this extension of the franchise to the middle class was relatively modest, as still only 5.6% of the population could vote (about 20% of adult men), but it showed that reform was possible and demonstrated how future groups might be able to persuade parliament to make further changes.

The Representation of the People Act 1918 and women's right to vote

By 1900, many aspects of life for women in the UK were changing. These included:

- New jobs, such as typists and telephone exchange workers, teachers and nurses, even doctors and architects, which gave women from all backgrounds more opportunity to earn money and pay taxes.
- Changes to marriage laws which meant that women could divorce their husband for cruelty, desertion or bigamy, could keep their own property and leave their husband (i.e. they were free to live where they chose, even if still married).

Such changes had given women a greater sense of independence and personal responsibility but it was believed that they would need to be given the franchise in order to achieve full gender equality with men (see Table 9.6).

Table 9.6 Arguments in favour of and against giving women the vote in the 1900s

Arguments in favour of giving women the vote	Arguments against giving women the vote
It would help to end other inequalities.	Men and women had separate roles.
Men would treat women with more respect.	Women did not want the vote.
Women had proven themselves politically capable.	Women's focus should be on local, not national, affairs.
It was happening elsewhere.	It would undermine a system that worked.
It was a fundamental right, especially if based on property.	Women had not fought to defend their country.
It would make Britain a true democracy.	Women were represented by their husbands.

By 1918 the situation had changed considerably:

- The issue of voting rights had to be considered in 1918 because many men had lost the right to vote as a result of serving overseas during the First World War. It was also felt that as men from all classes had fought in the war, all should be rewarded. This provided an opportunity to discuss women's voting rights at the same time.
- Women had contributed to the war effort at home and in non-combat roles overseas, proving they could take part in the defence of the country.
- Women had provided invaluable work during the war and should be rewarded.
- With many men away at war, women had proven themselves responsible and capable of maintaining a safe country.
- The suffragettes had stopped their violence and aided the war effort. The government was worried that they might start up a violent campaign again now that the war was over.
- David Lloyd-George had replaced Herbert Asquith as prime minister and he was much more supportive of women's right to vote than Asquith had been.

The Representation of the People Act 1918 extended the franchise to all women over the age of 30, as well as all men over the age of 21, giving some degree of female enfranchisement and full universal suffrage to adult men.

The Representation of the People Act 1928

Following the 1918 Representation of the People Act, the National Union of Women's Suffrage Societies (NUWSS) and the Women's Social and Political Union (WSPU) disbanded. The NUWSS become the new National Union of Societies for Equal Citizenship (NUSEC), with Eleanor Rathbone replacing Millicent Fawcett as leader of the group. Although some women now had the right to vote, the NUSEC began to campaign for more equal treatment, with six key aims:

- equal pay for equal work
- equality in sexual conduct and morals
- benefits to provide for widows with children
- equality in the franchise
- equal recognition of mothers as guardians
- equal access to the legal profession

The NUESC continued to campaign peacefully and, despite a failure to equalise the franchise under the Labour government of Ramsay MacDonald in 1924, equality of the franchise was passed by the Conservative government of Stanley Baldwin in 1928. The Representation of the People Act 1928 extended the franchise to all citizens over the age of 21, regardless of gender.

The Representation of the People Act 1969

Unlike previous efforts to extend the franchise, the extension to 18–20-year-olds in 1969 came about as a result of MPs reacting to social changes, rather than to a campaign or public demand.

Since the Second World War, the role and status of 18–20-year-olds had been changing, with more gaining employment, higher education and financial independence, even though the law still regarded anyone under 21 as a minor.

The 26th Amendment

While the extension of the franchise to 18-year-olds in the UK came from parliament, in the USA it came about as the result of war. There had already been campaigns to extend the franchise but it was the role of young men in the Vietnam War (American involvement 1961–73) that persuaded a large majority of Americans of the need to grant the franchise to those who were serving the country and fighting a war in which they had no say. A common rallying cry was 'Old enough to fight, old enough to vote.'

As part of their new status, 18–20-year-olds were trying to get married earlier, buy or rent their own home, secure bank accounts and make a will, but the law did not recognise them as capable adults. This led to some notable cases where 19- and 20-year-olds were classed as orphans and made a ward of the court, despite being financially independent. In addition, without parental consent, young adults were unable to access civil recognition for things that should have been commonplace.

In 1965, a committee was set up under Justice John Latey to consider whether or not to lower the age of majority to 18, in order to reflect the changing nature of society. The focus of the Latey Committee was to review issues relating to marriage, wardship, contracts and property. However, when the committee reported in 1967, it went further by suggesting the voting age should be lowered to 18 for a number of reasons:

- 18-year-olds were more financially astute and independent than in previous generations
- 18-year-olds were more physically developed than in previous generations
- 18-year-olds were increasingly mature and better educated than in previous generations
- radio and television meant that young people were better informed than in previous generations
- the age of 21 was an arbitrary anachronism that no longer served any valid purpose

Based on the Latey Committee's suggestions and the passage of other legislation, notably the Marriage Act 1949 which lowered the age at which a person could marry without parental consent to 18, the Representation of the People Act 1969 was introduced and passed, meaning that anyone over the age of 18 could vote, regardless of race, gender or wealth.

Campaigns to extend the franchise to women

The Suffragists

In 1866, the first petition to give women the right to vote was presented to parliament. Following its failure to extend the franchise to women, a variety of movements across the country were created, beginning with the Manchester Society for Women's Suffrage.

These various movements were eventually unified in 1897 by Millicent Fawcett under the title the National Union of Women's Suffrage Societies (NUWSS), nicknamed the 'Suffragists'.

The NUWSS was an internally democratic group with members electing their president and decisions being made through elected committees. Most of the members were middle class and would usually campaign for other women's rights issues, such as marriage rights and employment rights. Anyone could join the NUWSS and some men did join the group.

The methods of the NUWSS were peaceful, looking to apply pressure to politicians and the public through persuasion. Their activities tended to involve:

- writing letters
- writing pamphlets and other material for publication
- giving educational lectures
- organising petitions
- holding peaceful marches and protests

The Fawcett Society is a modern pressure group that campaigns for women's rights, named in honour of Millicent Fawcett. Visit its website and compare the aims and methods used by the Fawcett Society with those of the NUWSS. How much has changed over the past 100 years?
www.fawcettsociety.org.uk

By 1914, the NUWSS had more than 100,000 members in 400 branches spread across the whole country.

The Suffragettes

The Women's Social and Political Union (WSPU) was nicknamed the 'Suffragettes'. The organisation was founded by Emmeline Pankhurst and her daughters, Christabel and Sylvia, in 1903. It was initially based in Manchester and drew much of its support from working-class women, though it started to recruit more middle- and upper-class women when it moved to London in 1906.

The aims of the WSPU were very clear and focused:

- to secure equal voting rights for women
- to have a female-only membership
- to be a group of deeds or action, not words
- to focus only on the issue of political equality and nothing else

The WSPU campaigned for equal voting rights for women

The Pankhursts had been frustrated by the slow pace of change of the NUWSS and founded the WSPU with a view to using violent and illegal protest methods to draw attention to the cause and put pressure on the government. Methods the organisation used included:

- disrupting political party meetings
- chaining themselves to public railings
- smashing windows
- attacking or fighting police officers
- blowing up buildings
- burning buildings
- destroying letters in post boxes
- going on hunger strike in prison

On 18 November 1910, known as Black Friday, a WSPU protest resulted in a fight with police that saw many women assaulted, both physically and sexually, by the police. Some members of the public felt the police had acted inappropriately but many thought the women had brought it upon themselves.

The government was fearful that a woman on hunger strike in prison might die and become a martyr to the cause, thus gaining public sympathy. A policy of force feeding led to criticism of the government. In 1913, the government passed the Cat and Mouse Act, whereby a woman on the brink of death would be temporarily released from prison in order to regain her strength at home and then be returned to jail when she was strong enough.

The work of the Suffragettes certainly raised the public profile of the cause of women's voting rights, but at a cost. Having worked with the WSPU to organise a procession in London in 1908, the NUWSS became alarmed that the violent actions of the suffragettes were causing hostility from the government towards the cause. By 1914, public opinion was firmly against the WSPU and its cause, making it easy for the government to ignore its demands.

When war broke out in 1914, the WSPU promised to end violent methods for the duration of the war and began to help the government to organise women workers. They put pressure on men to volunteer to fight by shaming them in public.

Debate

Did violent methods help get women the right to vote?

Yes

- The violence was sensational and meant the media reported on these acts, raising public awareness of the issue of women's suffrage.
- Regular violent actions kept the public fearful of an attack and therefore kept the issue in the public eye.
- The violent methods led to brutal suppression by the police, which created sympathy for the suffragettes.
- People who were already opposed to giving the vote to women were not going to be any more put off by the use of violence, so there was little to be lost by its use.

No

- The violence seemed to prove that women were not responsible enough to vote.
- The government could not be seen to be giving in to terrorists, which prevented them from extending the right.
- The violence turned many moderate men and women away from the cause.
- Membership of the WSPU was decreasing by 1913 as people turned to the peaceful NUWSS.
- The peaceful work of women during the First World War played the crucial role in gaining the right to vote, rather than earlier violent actions.

Distinguish between

Suffragists and Suffragettes

Suffragists

- Membership was open to all.
- The organisation was internally democratic.
- They used peaceful methods of protest.
- They tried to work with the government.
- The organisation had a national network of committees.

Suffragettes

- Membership was open to women only.
- The organisation was run by the Pankhursts, with no involvement of the members.
- They used violent and illegal methods of protest.
- They tried to intimidate the government.
- The organisation was centred around London (after 1906).

Synoptic links

Prison voting rights in the USA

Prison, or felon, voting rights in the USA have become a major issue in recent years. Some states, like Maine, allow all prisoners to vote. In other states, people may vote while released on parole, while others must wait for their sentence to finish. However, in ten states, including Florida, felons lose the right to vote for ever. As a disproportionately high percentage of prisoners are African-American and Hispanic, this has been seen as a means of denying the vote to these minority groups, who tend to support the Democrat Party. The issue has therefore become political, rather than moral.

Current moves to extend the franchise

Prisoners and the right to vote

Traditionally in the UK, criminals have lost the franchise and been denied the right to vote when they are incarcerated. With the loss of the right to vote, prisoners can no longer participate as full members of society and, in effect, lose part of their citizenship.

A small but persistent campaign has attempted to have the franchise extended to at least some prisoners. This was begun by the legal challenges of John Hirst (see the case study on page 220) and, following the ruling of the European Court of Human Rights (ECtHR) in *Hirst* v *UK* (2005), which declared that the blanket ban on all prisoners was a violation of their human rights, other groups, including the Howard League for Penal Reform, the Prison Reform Trust and Amnesty International, have campaigned to put pressure on the government to recognise its legal obligations and give at least some prisoners the right to vote. These groups have:

- supported more than 2,000 legal challenges from prisoners denied the right to vote
- produced articles
- set up petitions
- used their insider status to lobby politicians

The goal of the campaign is to extend the franchise to prisoners serving less than 1 year, in order to comply with the ECtHR ruling and ensure the full rights of prisoners are recognised so that, while they lose their liberty, they do not lose their citizenship or basic human rights.

With approximately 48,000 prisoners affected in the UK, this is a small but important issue that addresses the nature of voting in the UK. Is the right to vote a fundamental right that should not be denied, or is it a privilege for those who contribute to society?

Case study

Hirst v *UK*

John Hirst was born in Yorkshire and raised in a Barnardo's children's home. He entered into a life of crime as a young man and in 1979 beat his landlady to death. In 1980, he was convicted of manslaughter on the grounds of diminished responsibility and sentenced to 15 years in prison.

In total, Hirst spent 24 years in jail, with the additional sentences mostly for violent protests and rioting as he fought against life and conditions in prison. In the 1990s, he began a legal campaign to restore prisoners' right to vote.

The High Court dismissed his challenge in 2001 but Hirst launched a new appeal under the Human Rights Act which was successfully upheld by the European Court of Human Rights in 2005.

Questions

Carry out some research to identify the arguments for and against giving prisoners the right to vote.

- To what extent do you agree with the view that prisoners should be given the right to vote?
- Given that the UK has voted to leave the EU, do you think that the issue of prisoner voting will end? Explain your answer.

Debate

Should prisoners be given the right to vote?

Yes
- The denial of the right to vote removes a sense of civic responsibility, making rehabilitation harder.
- There is no evidence that loss of the franchise acts as a deterrent.
- The right to vote is fundamental and cannot be removed.
- Removal of the vote makes a prisoner a non-person and further alienates them from society.
- The European Court of Human Rights has ruled that the blanket ban on prisoners is a violation of the Human Rights Act.

No
- Those who commit a custodial crime against society should lose the right to have a say in how that society is run.
- The threat of losing the right to vote prevents crime and enhances civic responsibility.
- Giving convicted criminals the right to have a say in how laws are made would undermine the principle of justice.
- Prisoners are concentrated in certain constituencies where they are unlikely to remain once free, so they should not be able to choose the local representatives for those communities.

Extending the franchise to 16-year-olds

Votes at 16 is a coalition of a number of different groups that believe the franchise should be extended to 16- and 17-year-olds. The campaign believes that 16- and 17-year-olds should be granted the vote on the basis of the principle of Engage, Empower and Inspire (see Figure 9.1):

> Engage: 'Votes at 16 will engage 16 and 17 year olds, who hold many responsibilities in our society, to influence key decisions that affect their lives and ensure youth issues are represented'

> Empower: 'Votes at 16 will empower 16 and 17 year olds, through a democratic right, to influence decisions that will define their future'

> Inspire: 'Votes at 16 will inspire young people to get involved in our democracy'

Source: www.votesat16.org/about

Figure 9.1 Things that 16-year-olds in the UK can legally do

There are several places where 16-year-olds have the right to vote:
- the Isle of Man, Jersey and Guernsey
- Austria
- Nicaragua
- Brazil
- Ecuador
- in *Länder* or state elections in Germany
- Hungary, if married

- Slovenia, if employed
- Argentina, if they choose to (it is compulsory after 18)
- Scotland, for the Scottish independence referendum of 2014

Votes at 16 is an umbrella group made up of other groups including:
- British Youth Council
- Children's Rights Alliance for England
- National Union of Students
- Public Achievement
- Scottish Youth Parliament

In addition, the organisation has the support of a number of politicians from all political parties and provides these individuals with evidence and support to change legislation, as shown in Table 9.7.

Table 9.7 Timeline for votes at 16

Date	Action
1999	Simon Hughes MP proposes an amendment to give 16-and 17-year-olds the right to vote: it is defeated by 434 to 36.
2000	The Young People's Rights Network is established.
2001	Representatives of the Young People's Rights Network meet with the Electoral Reform Society to discuss jointly campaigning for votes at 16. The Liberal Democrats publicly support the campaign for votes at 16.
2005	Stephen Williams MP introduces a private members' bill — Representation of the People (Reduction of Voting Age) Bill. The bill is supported by 128 MPs, with 136 MPs voting against it.
2007	The Scottish National Party (SNP) passes a resolution at its annual conference in support of votes at 16.
2009	The SNP passes a resolution to allow 16- and 17-year-olds the right to vote in an independence referendum.
2011	'Votes at 16' launches a new, interactive website to allow supporters to share its work.
2015	Votes at 16 Private Members' Bill, proposed by Vicky Foxcroft MP, has its second reading in the House of Commons.
2017	Liberal Democrats' manifesto contained a commitment to lowering the voting age to 16

Source: adapted from www.votesat16.org/about/campaign-history

There are many resources on the Votes at 16 website to encourage people to join the campaign, including:
- **The opportunity to adopt a lord.** Applicants are awarded a lord to adopt and pressurise into supporting extending the franchise.
- **The opportunity to email your MP.** There is a draft document that can be sent under your own name to your local MP.
- **Suggestions of how to spread awareness of the campaign.** Advice for using social networks, local media, press releases, case studies and letters is provided.
- **Passing a model motion.** Information and support materials are provided to allow someone to set up a debate and discussion about the issue.

- **Resources for schools.** There are resources to raise awareness in schools as well as advice on how to lobby school leaders and fellow students to support the cause.
- **Engaging community groups.** There are suggestions and advice on how to encourage other local campaigns to promote the cause.
- **Planning a campaign.** There is advice on the practicalities and legalities of running a local campaign to allow supporters to grow local support.
- **Advice on lobbying representatives.** Going beyond e-mail, there is advice and support to encourage people to meet with and lobby their local representatives at all levels. A chart of current members who support the cause is posted to indicate the progress and size of the task left.

Impact of the campaign

The campaign to extend the franchise to 16- and 17-year-olds has been gaining strength, with 16 local councils, the Scottish Parliament, Welsh Assembly and Northern Irish Assembly all voting to support votes at 16, while repeated debates and motions in parliament show that the number of MPs and peers supporting the extension is rising, though still not at a majority.

Political participation

One of the fundamental aspects of democracy is that it allows citizens to participate in the process. Participation can take many forms, but it should be about the citizen taking an active role and doing something to contribute to a political debate or process.

Methods of participating

When it comes to participation, a citizen must be active and actually doing something; watching a television programme is not active or participation, but contributing to an online discussion forum is active and therefore is participation. As such, there are many ways to participate.

Traditional methods of participation

Traditional methods of participation include:

- voting — general elections, referendums, elections for devolved bodies, local council elections, local mayoral elections, police and crime commissioner (PCC) elections
- joining a party and helping it to campaign
- joining a pressure group and helping to promote it
- organising or signing a petition
- going on a march
- going on strike
- writing a letter
- standing for public office

Crowds gathered in London to protest against the renewal of Trident, February 2016

Modern developments in participation

With the development of the internet and digital communication, more methods of participation and opportunities exist than ever before, including:

- e-petitions
- blogging
- protesting on social media
- organising a demonstration via social media

Is there a participation crisis in the UK?

Concerns have been raised that the UK may be experiencing a participation crisis, with fewer people taking part in political activities, leading to widespread public apathy. This is mainly due to decreasing turnout in elections and a fall in membership of UK political parties.

Yes: there is a participation crisis

Electoral participation

The most important form of participation is voting, where citizens transfer power to elected officials and hold them to account. Given the role of parliamentary sovereignty, the most important elections are the general elections to the Westminster Parliament.

General election turnout from 1945 to 1992 was usually above 75%, and reached 84% in 1950, suggesting a reasonably high level of participation on a par, if not above, many equivalent states.

However, in 1997, Tony Blair won the general election on a turnout of 71%, which meant that the 'landslide' Labour win by 179 seats was achieved with half a million fewer votes than John Major's narrow 22-seat win in 1992.

Since 1997, general election turnout has been at historically low levels, despite the seemingly close and uncertain contests in 2010 and 2015:

- 2001: 59% — the lowest ever turnout for a general election
- 2005: 61%
- 2010: 65%
- 2015: 66%
- 2017: 69%

So, fewer people are turning out to vote in general elections. Things get even worse below the national level when other electoral systems are analysed:

- Scottish Parliament election 2011: 50%
- European Union election 2014: 34%
- Police and crime commissioner (PCC) elections 2012: average 12–14%, lowest 8%
- Alternative vote (AV) referendum 2011: 42%

As elections are the main method of participation, if people are not voting they are not involved in the process and are therefore not engaged. This raises the question of legitimacy of elected officials. The Labour Party won a landslide majority in 2001 with only 26% of all registered voters actually voting for it. To put it another way, 74% of registered voters did not bestow a mandate on the government that launched the invasion of Iraq.

Low turnout can allow small extremist parties to gain a larger share of the vote, raise their profile and even obtain representation. It also leads to a lack of accountability, as politicians do not need to fear an electorate that does not turn out to hold them to account.

Party membership

Another common form of participation is to join a political party and get involved with the activities and campaigns it organises.

In the 1950s, Labour had more than 1 million members, thanks, in part, to its trade union affiliation, while the Conservative Party had 2.8 million members. As recently as 1983, 3.8% of the UK population was a member of a political party, reflecting a strong level of participation at the heart of British politics, as well as ensuring that party activists reflected a reasonable proportion of society.

Table 9.8 UK political party membership, March 2017

Party	Membership
Conservative	149,800
Labour	517,000
SNP	120,000
Liberal Democrats	82,000
UKIP	39,000
Green	55,500
Plaid Cymru	8,273

Source: www.parliament.uk

Contains public sector information licensed under the Open Government Licence v3.0.

In focus

Corporatism

Corporatism refers to the process of 'incorporating' different groups into the workings of government. In the 1970s, this was used to describe the close working relationship, or partnership, between the government, business and the trade union movement (or workers).

Since the 1980s, there has been a rapid decline in party membership, with less than 1% of the population currently a member of any political party and membership of all parties below the postwar totals. However, since the 2015 general election, Labour Party membership has been growing rapidly, thought to be due to the introduction of cheap membership fees and the buzz created by Jeremy Corbyn's leadership bid (see Table 9.8).

The decline in party membership suggests that people are disillusioned with the main parties in the UK and are not engaged by them. It also shows a lack of participation in the political process. This is a problem for the parties as it reduces their funds and their pool of committed activists who campaign for them. It also means there is a much more limited choice of candidates to put up for election at all levels. For the public, it means there is a smaller group of people influencing the direction of party policy, which has an impact on everyone.

The end of corporatism

As prime minister, Margaret Thatcher distrusted group activity and tended to favour individual and free market policies. As such, she weakened the power of the trade union movement and reduced the role of key economic groups, such as the Confederation of British Industry (CBI), in working closely in the processes of government. The result of this has been a decline in the power of group activity, particularly in trade union activity, and a decline in participation, as well as union membership.

With the decline in power and influence of trade union groups, workers are left with a much weaker voice to represent their concerns or needs to the government. The result is that there has been a decline in the number of people willing to fight for collective interests and hold the government to account.

No: there is not a participation crisis

Increasing turnout

Since 2001, general election turnout has been increasing in the UK, suggesting that people are increasingly engaging and participating. The very high levels of turnout in the Scottish independence referendum and the EU referendum show that when opinion is divided, and the issue is one that people care about, they will engage and vote.

The population of the UK is much larger than it has been in the past. Turnout percentages may be lower, but in terms of numbers, more people are voting than ever before.

More parties

Through much of the period of high party membership, two major parties dominated the electoral landscape, typically receiving about 80–90% of the vote between them.

The UK had 11 parties represented in the last parliament and still has eight since the 2017 general election, with a sizeable third party and a far greater range of manifestos to choose from.

New initiatives, such as Labour's £3 membership fee to be a registered supporter and be allowed to vote for the party leader, have made joining parties easier and driven up membership.

Pressure group membership

Even though party membership is declining, membership of pressure groups has increased markedly since the 1980s. People will often be members of a variety of groups and participate through these, rather than the traditional party system. The largest pressure groups have memberships in the millions and there are thousands of groups operating across the UK, which shows that the public are still finding ways to participate in group activities. Rather than there being a participation crisis, the nature of participation has changed.

Social campaigns

The internet and social media have provided a means for more people to participate in campaigns and to share information. In the past, getting people to sign a petition, raising awareness through a protest or vigil, or holding a mass rally, took time, effort and a lot of organisation. By making it easier and cheaper to get involved in campaigns, more people have the opportunity to participate in a way that suits them. For example, the 'Justice for the 96' campaign was able to promote and encourage people to participate by signing an online participation to reopen the inquest into the Hillsborough disaster, and the 'Occupy' movement was able to use social media to coordinate and encourage supporters to occupy London in 2011.

More than anything, if there is a public outcry over an issue, people will tend to turn to an online petition to raise awareness, express their opinions and put pressure on the government. None of this would have been possible without the development of social campaigns.

How do pressure groups and other organisations promote democracy and political participation?

Pressure groups are organisations that usually have a single interest or goal. Some groups campaign for a cause that their members believe in, such as ending the abuse of human rights (Amnesty International), or they may be sectional groups, where they campaign for the interests of their members, or a section of society, such as supporting doctors (the British Medical Association).

Unlike political parties, pressure groups do not look to gain power, but want to influence those in power by generating public support and persuading the government to support their point of view. In this sense, pressure groups are a great example of pluralism in the UK.

Types of pressure group

There are two main types of pressure group: sectional and causal.

Sectional groups

Sectional groups look after their own section of society. Often these are professional associations, like the British Medical Association (BMA) or a trade union such as the National Union of Rail, Maritime and Transport Workers (RMT). The members of these groups will usually have the same or a similar occupation and shared interests. Sectional groups tend to have closed membership, so only workers in a particular occupation can join a specific group.

Sectional groups act in the best interests of their members, usually trying to pressure those in power to get the best deal possible for their members. While sectional groups may campaign on a number of issues, their interest is with the benefit of a single section of society.

Causal groups

Causal groups campaign for a particular cause or issue, often one that does not directly affect its members. Causal groups are therefore campaigning on behalf of other people — usually those who are unable to campaign for themselves.

Members of causal groups often come from a wide variety of backgrounds and the particular cause may be the only thing they have in common. These groups are relatively easy to join and membership is open to everyone.

Causal groups often aim to improve society in some way and may take the form of a charity, such as the Royal Society for the Prevention of Cruelty to Animals (RSPCA) or Oxfam. They will often perform a wide variety of activities, from fundraising and raising awareness, to research and education, as well as putting pressure on those in power.

Insider and outsider status

A further distinction is made between groups with insider and outsider status. Insider groups have a special relationship with the government and are given access to officials and decision-makers. Outsider groups do not have such close links with the government and may resort to activities that generate attention from the press in order to publicise their cause and put pressure on the government to take the action they desire.

Distinguish between

Sectional and causal pressure groups

Sectional groups
- Sectional groups advance or protect the interests of their members.
- Sectional groups have closed membership.
- Members of sectional groups tend to be motivated by self-interest.

Causal groups
- Causal groups tend to promote a value, ideal or principle.
- Causal groups are open to all.
- Members of causal groups tend to be motivated by altruistic considerations.

Taking strike action can put pressure on those in power and may force them to accept the group's demands

Table 9.9 Pressure group methods

Method	Why they do it
Lobby (as an insider)	Groups meet with politicians and civil servants in order to argue their case and try to persuade them to adopt their ideas.
Research and publish reports	Research can provide evidence to support a group's argument and can be used to inform politicians and raise public awareness of the cause.
Give evidence at hearings	Public consultations, legislative committees and select committees will hold hearings to help them determine a decision or action. By giving evidence and speaking on behalf of their members, groups can exert influence on those in a position of power.
Organise publicity campaigns	Groups may organise publicity campaigns to raise public awareness of their cause. This might be to raise awareness of a particular issue and encourage the public to take action themselves, or it might be to encourage the public to put pressure on elected officials.
Organise public demonstrations	Groups may organise large demonstrations, such as marches and rallies, to demonstrate to those in power the strength and scale of support for their cause. A large demonstration is also likely to gain publicity and help spread awareness of the cause.
Publicity stunts	Small groups without the resources to pay for a media campaign may use publicity stunts in order to attract media attention and thereby gain publicity and generate awareness of their cause.
Civil disobedience	Some groups may use illegal methods as a form of civil disobedience, by disrupting public events or staging a sit-in in order to cause disruption and bring attention to their cause. This usually happens because they feel they have no other option.
Go on strike	Workers may go on strike to put pressure on those in power in order to try to reach an agreement with them. A strike can be damaging and unpopular for a government or organisation and may force them to accept the group's demands.
Use a celebrity spokesperson	Groups may recruit a celebrity spokesperson in order to raise the profile of the group, gain media attention and attract more support by sharing in the popularity of the celebrity.
Bring test cases to court	Some groups provide legal expertise and bring a case or help to bring a case to court. In this way they can look to secure the rights of their members and ensure those rights are protected.
Digital campaigns	Groups may set up websites to promote their cause and use social media to publicise events and create viral campaigns.

Why do people join pressure groups?

Pressure groups are a key means of representation in the UK. While political parties try to appeal to and represent a wide cross section of society, pressure groups focus on a single issue and are able to represent the interests of a small group on a single cause. As there are many different types of pressure group and different causes, there are many factors that motivate people to join pressure groups (see Table 9.10).

Table 9.10 Motivation for joining a pressure group

Motivation	Reason behind the motivation
Representation	People may join a pressure group if they feel they are not being represented by the main political parties. This is often the case with minority interests, such as gay rights, where membership of a group offers the individual the representation they feel they cannot get elsewhere.
Personal beliefs	People may join a pressure group because it reflects their beliefs. People who believe passionately in an issue or cause will look to join a group whose members think the same and share the same goals.
Participation	Some people join a pressure group for the opportunity to get involved in a political issue. This may be by, for example, attending a public demonstration or responding to a discussion group. It allows the individual to get involved and to express their beliefs.
Material benefits	Many people join a pressure group in order to get something out of it, rather than for the cause itself. People who take out breakdown cover will become a member of the AA, while people wishing to visit historic buildings may join the National Trust. While this boosts membership, it can mean the members are not particularly passionate about the issues and causes that are central to the group.
Need	Some people may join a pressure group because they feel they have to, either for job protection (by joining a trade union), or because they see it as the only way to achieve a desired goal.

Debate

Is the internet good for pressure groups?

Yes

- An online campaign can be a cheap way of spreading information and raising awareness, particularly if it goes viral.
- The internet makes it easier and cheaper to coordinate a large group or an event.
- The internet gives people an easier and more convenient means of participation.

No

- The marketplace can be swamped with groups, making it difficult to stand out. If a campaign does go viral, there is no way of guaranteeing that people will understand the message behind it.
- To be really successful, a group needs a professional website and expertise, which can be expensive.
- The internet can lead to 'slacktivism' where people might 'like' something but fail to engage with the wider issue, making them less likely to get involved or join the group.

Activity

Think back to the section on the extension of the franchise. Imagine the NUWSS and WSPU are modern pressure groups and try to describe each group using modern political terms, such as insider or outsider. Which of the two would have been more likely to achieve success today?

Why do pressure groups succeed or fail?

The success or failure of a pressure group can be judged on whether or not the group achieves its goals. A pressure group that looks to change government policy on an issue is successful if it achieves this change, whereas a pressure group that seeks to prevent a government action, such as going to war, will have failed if war is declared. There are many ways in which pressure groups may be successful and many reasons why a pressure group may fail to achieve its goal(s).

Success

In order to achieve its goals, a pressure group will try to persuade those in power to adopt its position. They may try to persuade government ministers directly through lobbying or try to build public support in order to put pressure on those in power. There are a number of factors associated with pressure group success, shown in Table 9.11.

Table 9.11 Reasons for pressure group success

Reason for success	Example
Insider status. Having close links to the government, insider pressure groups are able to advise and influence ministers directly as events are happening.	In 2014, the Howard League for Penal Reform successfully campaigned to end the ban on prisoners receiving books sent to them by family or friends.
Wealth. Financial resources allow pressure groups to pay for things that may help promote their cause, such as lobbyists, adverts and websites.	In 2012, the British Bankers' Association paid lobbyists to persuade ministers to cut corporation tax and taxes on banks' overseas subsidiaries.
Large membership. Having a lot of members means you control a large section of the electorate and also have a number of people ready to take action in terms of signing petitions and organising protests.	In 2015, the RSPB utilised over 500,000 members for its Big Garden Birdwatch.
Organisation. Effective management and coordination will allow a group to maximise its resources and target them effectively to help achieve its goals.	In 2012, the RMT Union organised a series of strikes to secure a bonus for members during the Olympics.
Expertise. A pressure group that has knowledge and expertise over a particular policy area is more likely to be listened to and respected by the government and the public.	In 2016, the AA provided evidence and statistics to persuade the government to increase the penalties for using a mobile phone while driving.
Celebrity endorsement. A popular celebrity will generate press interest and raise the profile of a cause, and may help to draw members to the group.	In 2009, Joanna Lumley and the Gurkha Justice Campaign secured equal rights for British and Commonwealth soldiers.

Case study

Gurkha Justice Campaign

Gurkhas are Nepalese soldiers who serve in the British army. Until 1997, they were based in Hong Kong, but they had to relocate to the UK when Hong Kong was returned to China. In 2004, the Labour government said that all Gurkhas who had served since 1997 would be allowed to settle in Britain.

The Gurkha Justice Campaign spent 4 years trying to persuade the Blair and Brown governments to give equal rights to all Gurkhas. It was not until the celebrity Joanna Lumley joined the campaign in November 2008 that the media began to take notice and, due to her campaigning, in May 2009 Gordon Brown announced that all Gurkhas would be given equal settlement rights.

Questions
- Explain why celebrity backing might help a campaign to succeed.
- In a democracy, should celebrity backing make a difference to the discussion?
- Do celebrities have a duty to lend their support to political campaigns? Explain your answer.

A number of factors may limit the success of a pressure group:

- Chequebook membership — people may join a group for the material benefits and so be less likely to get involved in a campaign.
- 'Slacktivism' — people may be willing to click 'like' or forward an online post, but they may have no more than a superficial engagement with the issue, making them less committed to a campaign.
- Small membership — limited numbers can make it difficult to organise public demonstrations, raise funds or gain media attention.
- Outsider status — being an outsider can make it much more challenging for a group to gain access to the people in power.

Failure

There are a number of reasons why a pressure group might fail to achieve its goals. The absence of any of the factors required for success (see Table 9.11) may make it difficult for a pressure group to succeed, but need not necessarily lead to failure. Key reasons why pressure groups fail are given in Table 9.12.

Table 9.12 Reasons for pressure group failure

Reason for failure	Example
The goal contradicts a government policy. If the government is determined to follow a particular policy then it will be very difficult for a pressure group to persuade the government to change its mind.	The Conservative government (2015–) is determined to introduce new polices for a 7-day NHS, therefore the BMA campaign against the proposals has largely failed.
The government can resist pressure from the group. If those in power are in a strong enough position, they will feel able to resist a group's campaign and effectively ignore it.	The Stop the War Coalition organised mass rallies and activities to stop the invasion of Iraq in 2003. However, with a large majority and cross-party support in parliament, the Blair government was able to resist the pressure and ignore the group's demands.
Countervailing forces. A pressure group may find itself campaigning against another, more powerful or more popular, pressure group which 'wins' the debate.	The pro-smoking group Forrest has failed to prevent restrictions on smoking in the UK, largely because it has lost out to the group ASH, which has successfully campaigned for restrictions on smoking.
The goals of the group act against popular opinion. A group is more likely to fail if it is campaigning for a cause that is not popular with the public, as governments will be more inclined to follow popular feelings on an issue.	Groups such as the Coalition for Marriage failed in their campaign against the legal recognition of gay marriage because most public opinion was in favour of it. The group was therefore campaigning against a change that had public support.
The group alienates the public. A group may make itself unpopular by committing acts that alienate public opinion. A groups that partakes in violent or criminal action will be regarded unfavourably and lose support for its goals.	Violent groups such as ALF and PETA fail to achieve their goals because the public are opposed to their methods, even if they might support their causes. The same can be true of strike action if the public begins to blame the trade unions for the disruption caused.

Case study

The RMT Union

What is it?

The National Union of Rail, Maritime and Transport Workers was founded in 1990, following a merger between the National Union of Railwaymen (NUR) and the National Union of Seamen (NUS). Its members are concentrated in London transport, particularly the Tube network.

Aim and methods

It aims to promote and defend the rights and conditions of all members employed in the transport industry. The methods it uses are shown in Table 9.13.

Table 9.13 Methods used by the RMT Union

Method	Detail
Insider status	Until 2004, the union was part of the Labour Party and could exert insider influence. Since 2004 the RMT has been regularly consulted on transport issues, though its status as an insider has been reduced, particularly with a Conservative government.
Putting up candidates for election	In 2009, the union put up anti-EU candidates for election to the European Parliament and went on to create its own left-wing party, the Trade Unionist and Socialist Coalition, which contested the UK general elections in 2010 and 2015.
Lobbying politicians	The union lobbies key politicians and consults with them to secure a transport policy that works for its members.
Strikes	The union routinely uses strikes, or the threat of strikes, to pressure Transport for London into adopting its policies.
Social media	The union uses social media to raise awareness of its campaigns and to gain public support and sympathy.

Success

Throughout 2011 and 2012, the RMT Union lobbied Transport for London, London Underground and the mayor of London over their concerns about the additional workload that would be placed on all London Underground staff during the 2012 Olympics.

In January 2012, London Underground offered each member of staff a £500 bonus but this was rejected by the union. In March 2012, London Underground offered each member of staff a bonus of £850, subject to certain requirements, including customer satisfaction scores and flexible working periods. This was also eventually rejected by the union.

At the end of May 2012, London Underground offered drivers a bonus of up to £1,000 and all other staff a bonus up to £850, with no conditions. The RMT general secretary at the time, Bob Crow, said he was happy to have agreed a deal with his members for their work 'in recognition of what we all know will be the biggest transport challenge ever faced by this city [London]' (quoted in *Metro*, 30 May 2012).

There were four key reasons for the success of the RMT Union in securing these bonuses for its members:

■ The importance of the Olympics and the international spotlight on London put pressure on London Underground and the government.
■ The union's large membership covered a vital sector of the London economy (Underground transport), which meant it could effectively close the Tube during the Olympics.
■ The two factors above made the threat of a strike by a unified membership too great a risk.
■ The general secretary of the union, Bob Crow, was able to raise the media profile of the issue to pressurise the government and ensure the membership stayed unified in its actions.

Failure

Throughout 2015 and early 2016, London Underground began to close ticket offices across the Tube network. Staff were to be moved to work on platforms, but the RMT raised concerns over passenger safety and the job security of its members. The union launched a series of 48-hour strikes to disrupt the Tube network, as well as taking a legal case to the High Court.

By June 2016, Transport for London had closed 289 ticket offices, meaning the RMT had failed to achieve its goal. The failure was due to:

■ the strikes failing to gain public support
■ a lack of public sympathy over the issue
■ the commitment to the programme of closures by Transport for London, the mayor of London (at the time) and the government
■ the court case being rejected

Question

Carry out some additional research into the RMT Union. Does the union promote or undermine democracy in the UK? Explain your answer.

Greenpeace

What is it?

Greenpeace is a non-governmental organisation (NGO) that operates on an international scale. It was founded in Canada in 1971 and now has 2.9 million members worldwide.

Aim

Greenpeace's stated aim is 'to ensure the ability of the Earth to nurture life in all its diversity', thus making it a causal group (www.tinyurl.com/cj5k429).

Under this broad goal, the group has a number of specific campaigns which centre around:

- climate change
- forests
- oceans
- agriculture
- toxic pollution
- nuclear

Methods used

Initially, Greenpeace relied on direct action campaigns to raise awareness of activities it believed to be wrong. Over time, the group has been seen to move from 'the wetsuit to the business suit' as it increasingly uses insider methods to achieve its goals (see Table 9.14).

Success

In 2011, Greenpeace launched a campaign to stop the practice of tuna fishing using aggregating devices and purse-seine nets, which catch and kill many other fish at the same time. These other fish can end up in canned tuna and the practice can lead to unsustainable fishing.

A combination of direct and indirect action resulted in all the UK supermarkets announcing that they would provide clearer labelling on their tuna products and stop purchasing tuna caught using unsuitable methods by 2014. After UK success, the campaign was launched in New Zealand and Canada and has become a global movement.

Failure

In 2011–12 Greenpeace failed to prevent Cairn Energy, an oil and gas exploration company, from exploring gas reserves on Greenland.

Aggressive insults from Greenpeace protestors about the eating of whale and seal meat (traditional foods of the Inuit population) insulted members of the Greenland community. Greenlanders had previously suffered from the ban in the trade of sealskin, the result of an earlier Greenpeace campaign.

Furthermore, the people of Greenland wish to become fully independent of Denmark and if natural gas was to be found and could be converted into a revenue stream, this would make their dream a reality.

The failure to prevent drilling for gas in Greenland was due to:

- methods that alienated the local population and turned them to the oil company
- previous campaigns that had also alienated the local population
- the financial and political considerations of the Greenland population, which were far more important to the local population than environmental considerations
- lack of support from the UN for Greenpeace to do anything more than protest, despite its insider status

Greenpeace's attempts to prevent drilling for gas off the coast of Greenland in 2011–12 failed

Table 9.14 Methods used by Greenpeace

Method	Detail
Direct action	The group raises public awareness by actions such as boarding a whaling ship or publicly destroying GM crops in order to gain media attention.
Lobbying politicians	The group lobbies politicians to ensure a green agenda, such as lobbying British MPs over the building of the Hinkley Point nuclear power station.
Insider status	The group holds consultative status at the UN and its views are sought on environmental issues.
Media campaigns	The group has set up online petitions around the world to encourage the public to pressure politicians into keeping to the Paris Agreement on climate change.
Research	The group routinely conducts surveys and research to inform people about environmental issues and possible solutions to problems.

Question

Carry out some additional research into the methods used by Greenpeace. Has Greenpeace become more or less democratic since the 1970s? Explain your answer.

Other organisations

Think-tanks

A think-tank is a group that has been formed with the specific purpose of formulating and developing policy ideas.

The role of developing policy was traditionally done by the parties, but think-tanks offer an alternative that is based on focused and academic research rather than partisan ideals. Consequently, the use of think-tanks grew markedly under Tony Blair's leadership of the Labour Party, as he sought to develop his Third Way policy ideas, which were not widely supported by the party membership.

Think-tanks may be single issue groups, such as the Adam Smith Institute, which focuses on free market issues, or they may pursue a general agenda, such as Reform, which develops proposals to better deliver public services and economic prosperity.

Think-tanks are privately funded by a group or individual that wishes to have workable ideas made into government policy. Like pressure groups, think-tanks attempt to persuade the government to adopt their policy goals, but unlike many pressure groups their methods rely on working with the government of the day or aligning themselves with a particular party, rather than on a populist campaign.

Lobbyists

In the 1870s, the US President Ulysses Grant would often visit his favourite hotel for a drink. When he entered the lobby, people would begin petitioning him for jobs and favours. He called them the 'lobbyists' and the term stuck.

Lobbying is the process of meeting with key political figures and trying to persuade them to support your aims. Today, there are professional lobbying firms which employ people who have contacts with, and access to, key political figures. Corporations and other groups employ lobbying firms and lobbyists to gain this level of access.

Access does not guarantee the desired outcome but a face-to-face meeting adds a personal element, while having a minister's friend represent your interests can give a group a distinct advantage.

Lobbying in the USA

In the USA, the 'lobbying industry' is based on K Street in Washington, DC, and is a $3.5 billion industry that directs approximately $3.5 trillion of government spending, as well as influencing legislation. It has also led to a phenomenon called 'Revolving Door Syndrome', where members of Congress or their staff leave their political jobs and go to work for a lobbying firm, while maintaining contact with their old colleagues.

Lobbying in the UK has not reached this scale, but it has grown markedly since 1997, with 114 lobbying firms now registered in the UK. A sign of the increasing practice of politicians becoming lobbyists was revealed by a scandal in 2015 involving two former foreign secretaries, Jack Straw and Sir Malcolm Rifkind. Rifkind claimed to be able to gain special access to global diplomats, through which he could represent the views of firms that paid him a fee, while Straw claimed to have been able to change EU rules on behalf of a commodity firm which had paid him £60,000. Although neither had done anything illegal, the impression generated by this story further undermined trust in politicians and suggested major figures were acting on behalf of interest groups that paid them, rather than in the public interest. These widely publicised incidents show that lobbying is increasingly becoming an issue in UK politics, especially as it effectively allows wealthy groups to buy insider status.

There is no definitive proof that lobbying works, as there is no way to measure this sort of influence, but the growth of lobbying in the UK and the size of the lobbying industry in the USA suggest that organisations believe that it is effective.

Corporations

Corporations often work closely with government in order to develop practical legislation. Government consults corporations on certain policy ideas to check that they are practical and also to get help to implement key proposals.

Corporations also look to exert pressure on those in charge in order to gain an advantage. While this may be through lobbying themselves, or employing lobbyists, corporations are also able to exert influence and pressure through control of a key sector of the economy.

Corporations may pressurise the government to give them more favourable legislation or financial assistance by threatening to relocate. For example, motor corporations, such as Nissan or Ford, might propose to relocate their manufacturing plants to elsewhere in the world, which would result in increased unemployment and a loss of economic strength for the UK.

Other corporations, such as those in the banking sector, might threaten to relocate their main offices from London to another country. Not only would this weaken the British economy, it would also lead to the loss of a major source of employment, partly through those employed directly by the corporation but also from support industries that sell services to those employees, such as cleaners, coffee shops, IT companies, restaurants and taxis.

Synoptic links

Corporations and political campaigning

In the US Supreme Court's decision of *Citizens United* v *Federal Election Commission (FEC)*, the court ruled that corporations should be classed as people and were therefore subject to constitutional protections, including freedom of speech. As such, corporations regularly campaign on behalf of favoured candidates and issues in the USA.

In the UK, corporations are tightly regulated in what they can and cannot do in terms of political campaigning.

Which system is better for political education? Why do you think this?

Case study

Corporations and referendums

During the referendum on the UK's membership of the EU, the majority of major corporations, such as HSBC, Ford and Burberry, campaigned for the UK to remain in the EU, suggesting that jobs, wages and economic stability would be threatened by a vote to leave. A minority of corporations, such as Dyson, campaigned to leave. The 'Leave' campaign dismissed the claims made by the majority of corporations and the public ultimately ignored them by voting to leave.

Questions

- What does the result of the referendum suggest about the influence of corporations on the public in the UK?
- Should corporations be involved in the political decision-making process?

The protection of rights in a democracy

What are rights?

Human rights, sometimes known as 'natural rights', are those rights and liberties that all people are automatically entitled to. Human rights are:

- **absolute**, meaning they cannot be compromised or diminished in any way
- **universal**, meaning they are applied to everyone equally, regardless of any other considerations, such as race or gender
- **fundamental**, meaning they are an essential part of life and cannot be removed for any reason

The main protection that citizens have from government intrusion is their individual rights, or civil liberties. These are the basic freedoms that allow people to express themselves and live without fear of oppression or a police state.

These rights and liberties can take two distinct forms, being either a fundamental right to do something — such as live — or a fundamental freedom from government oppression — such as freedom of speech, which means you cannot be penalised for speaking against the government.

Until the Human Rights Act was passed in 1998, rights were characterised in a negative way, meaning a person had a right to do anything as long as it was not expressly forbidden by the law. The Human Rights Act gave rights a degree of codification and for the first time clearly set out the positive rights that a citizen holds.

Many of the rights that people in Britain took for granted were simply based on common law and therefore had limited legal authority and could easily be superseded by statute law. With the introduction of the Human Rights Act, much of common law was replaced by clear statute law, giving citizens much greater legal protection and securing more democratic freedoms for the people (see Table 9.15).

Table 9.15 The development of rights in the UK

Year	Milestone	Summary
1215	Magna Carta	Imposed various restrictions on the monarchy in order to prevent the arbitrary abuse of power by the monarch.
1689	Bill of Rights	Imposed greater limits on the power of the monarchy and set out the rights of parliament, including regular parliaments, free elections and parliamentary free speech.
1953	European Convention on Human Rights (ECHR)	The UK had signed the ECHR in 1950 and it became effective in 1953. Government actions had to comply with the ECHR but could only be challenged in the European Court of Human Rights, not in UK courts.
1973	European Court of Justice	The UK joined the European Economic Community in 1973, which meant that the European Court of Justice had the power to protect workers' rights in the UK.
1984	Data Protection Act	Established protections surrounding personal information held by public institutions. It was updated in 1988 and 1998.
1998	Human Rights Act	Codified the ECHR into British law, replacing much common law and allowing citizens to access rights protection through the UK legal system.
2000	Freedom of Information Act	Ensured political transparency by allowing citizens to access any non-security related information held by public institutions.
2010	Equality Act	Consolidated and codified all anti-discriminatory measures into one document.

Case study

Legal highs

Before May 2016, drugs were only illegal if they had been specifically banned by UK legislation. New psychoactive substances (NPS), or legal highs, are substances which contain various chemicals, not all of which are illegal. The drugs have similar effects to illegal drugs such as cocaine and cannabis. Until legislation was passed, the authorities had no legal power to arrest or charge anyone for possession or selling of these products, hence they were termed 'legal highs'.

In May 2016, the government passed legislation creating a blanket ban on all psychoactive drugs that had not been made legal, thus ending the negative right to use them.

Questions

- Do you think things should be legal until they are clearly made illegal?
- Should people have the right to do things which are not illegal, even if it causes them harm?
- In a democracy, does the government have a responsibility to protect people from making a mistake? Explain your answer.

In focus

Human Rights Act 1998

The Human Rights Act was passed in 1998 and came into force in 2000. It incorporated many of the provisions of the ECHR. The ECHR was judged by the European Court of Human Rights (which is completely separate from the EU), which meant only people with the resources and means could challenge a government action, as they had to bring it to a foreign court. When the Human Rights Act was passed many of these provisions were effectively codified into statute law, meaning that they could be judged under British law in British courts. This has made it much easier for ordinary citizens to seek legal redress in local courts if they believe their rights have been infringed. For this reason, there has been a rapid development of 'rights culture' in the UK since the Human Rights Act was implemented in 2000 (see Table 9.16).

Table 9.16 Examples of the Human Rights Act defending individual rights in the UK

Date	Example
2004	A law that prevented a gay partner from inheriting a council flat was struck down as discrimination under the HRA.
2011	A special court ruled that local councils cannot force a vulnerable adult to live in a care home as it undermines their right to a family life.
2012	Home secretaries were repeatedly prevented from deporting Abu Qatada, a Jordanian national who was accused of having links to terrorist organisations, on the basis that the evidence against him was obtained through torture.

Civic responsibilities

Along with rights, British citizens are given a number of key responsibilities. Although not often written down, these are duties which a citizen is expected to perform or abide by, in return for the rights and liberties that have being granted. These include the responsibility to:

- respect and obey the law
- pay taxes
- ensure you do not act in a way that causes harm to others, either deliberately or negligently
- perform specific duties in certain relationships, such as parents or public figures
- show respect for parliament and government institutions (such as the police)
- vote
- serve on a jury

Political thinkers, like John Stuart Mill in the nineteenth century, considered civic responsibilities to be an integral part of civil rights and liberties. This view was further established in the European Convention on Human Rights. However, with the move to a more individualist society since the 1980s, there is a concern that civil responsibilities have been overlooked. As many civic duties are not expressly written down, proponents have argued that a British Bill of Rights would help to enshrine and make clear the civil responsibilities of a citizen, as well as their rights (see Table 9.17).

Table 9.17 Arguments in favour of and against individual rights

Arguments in favour of individual rights	Arguments against individual rights
Ensures protection from government abuse	Can come at the expense of wider society
Leads to civil responsibilities	Can hinder the effective operation of government
Necessary for a free society	

Rights conflicts

Since 1997, there have been a growing number of conflicts between governments and the judiciary, for the following reasons:

- The introduction of the Human Rights Act has given judges more power to challenge government ministers.
- The introduction of the Human Rights Act has made it easier for ordinary people to use the judicial system to challenge government measures.
- The increased threat of terrorism has caused governments to take actions on the basis of national security which conflict with individual rights.
- There is a perception that ministers are attempting to expand their powers at the expense of civil rights and liberties.

Five key areas have seen significant conflicts between the judiciary and the government over rights protection:

- anti-terrorism
- deportation
- detention
- free speech and the right to protest
- anti-social behaviour

Who can better defend rights?

With the growing rights consciousness in the UK, the issue of whether the judiciary, the government or parliament is best placed to defend citizens' fundamental rights is one that needs serious consideration (see Tables 9.18 and 9.19).

Table 9.18 Is the judiciary best placed to defend the rights of citizens?

Strengths	Weaknesses
Judges exercise the rule of law and can use the Human Rights Act and their power of judicial review to ensure rights in the UK are fully respected.	Judges are undemocratic and unaccountable so may abuse their position. They have no incentive to promote controversial cases.
Enhanced measures for judicial independence have meant the judiciary is independent of the other two branches of the political system and can defend rights based only upon the law, without political pressure.	While independent, senior judges work with parliament to advise on the legality of legislation. This means that judges have played a role in the creation of legislation and are less likely to approach issues over human rights with true independence or neutrality.
Judges are neutral and can therefore protect a person's rights without discrimination or considerations of their beliefs, character or other traits, making them more effective at upholding individual rights.	The lack of a codified constitution means the judiciary cannot strike down primary legislation. This means that, even if they decide there is an abuse of human rights, they are powerless to do anything about it, if it is enshrined in primary legislation. Judges can only apply the law as it stands.
	Judges are unrepresentative and from a narrow social and gender background, making them less aware of the issues facing most people. There is a belief that judges naturally favour conservative and privileged groups over other individuals.

Table 9.19 Is parliament best placed to defend the rights of citizens?

Strengths	Weaknesses
Parliament holds sovereignty, therefore it can determine what rights are in the UK and whether or not they should be enforced.	Short-term political considerations may be more important than defending human rights.
Parliament is more representative of the people and so is better able to reflect the values of society and understand different individuals.	Parliament has the ability to suspend the Human Rights Act to achieve its goals.
Parliament introduced and passed all of the Acts relating to human rights, so it has a history of being the institution that has promoted and defended human rights in the UK.	Parliament is usually dominated by the governing party, leading to a tyranny of the majority and leaving very few effective checks on government actions that contradict human rights.
Members of Parliament represent their constituents and are in a position to raise the issue of citizens' rights with government ministers, where they feel those rights are at risk or have been violated.	The role of the House of Lords undermines the democratic arguments for parliament.
Parliament is democratically elected and so is more accountable to the people for its defence of human rights.	MPs may be reluctant to champion the cause of human rights if it benefits an unpopular element, such as terror suspects or criminals.

Pressure groups and rights

There are many pressure groups in the UK and around the world that have taken on the role of defending rights. These groups raise awareness of threats to civil rights, promote the application of rights and put pressure on the government to ensure rights are protected. Key groups include:

- Liberty
- Amnesty International
- Centre on Housing Rights and Evictions
- Equality Now
- Witness

Liberty has a campaign to 'Save Our Human Rights Act', in opposition to the government's proposals for a British Bill of Rights, and previously campaigned (unsuccessfully) against the introduction of the Investigatory Powers Act — nicknamed the 'Snooper's Charter'.

Other groups, like Stonewall, have campaigned hard to end discrimination against homosexuals and ensure equal rights. Stonewall has fought legal battles, provided education and organised campaigns and demonstrations to make the age of consent for homosexuals the same as that for heterosexuals, as well as lobbying to persuade parliament to legalise gay marriage.

What could be done to improve democracy in the UK?

Compulsory voting

Compulsory voting could be introduced to the UK in order to increase public participation at all levels. A system that fines people who do not vote, perhaps £20–£50 a time, would encourage more people to vote in elections and referendums. By adding a 'none of the above' option to ballot papers, people would not be forced to vote for something against their wishes.

This system has been proven to work in Australia and Belgium, where turnout rates are typically between 93% and 96%. By increasing turnout, participation and legitimacy would also be improved.

People might take a greater interest in political issues if voting was compulsory and might be more inclined to join a pressure group or political party, leading to improved education and participation. The money raised from fines could be spent on public education programmes.

Despite these arguments, there is a strong belief that the right to vote also includes the right not to vote and any attempt to force people into voting would undermine a fundamental British value. There is a risk that people might not educate themselves and might simply select a candidate at random. Repeated forced voting could lead to public apathy and resentment.

Reform of the voting system

In the 2015 general election, the Conservatives won a majority of MPs with 36% of the vote. UKIP gained 1 MP with nearly 4 million votes, while the SNP gained 53 seats with fewer than 1.5 million votes.

Changing the voting system to a more proportional one, such as single transferable vote (STV) or closed party list, would distribute votes more fairly, end the problem of safe seats and reduce the number of wasted votes. There might be greater engagement in the political process if everyone believed their vote mattered.

However, alternative systems can be confusing and far more complicated than the first-past-the-post (FPTP) system. Proportional systems can lead to extremist parties gaining seats, and can weaken the link between a representative and their constituency. Evidence from places in the UK where alternative systems are used also suggests that they do not increase turnout.

Voting systems are discussed in more detail in Chapter 10.

Reform of the House of Lords

There are a number of proposals for making the House of Lords more democratic. The simplest of these would be to remove the remaining hereditary peers. This might not increase democracy but would improve

243

In focus

Burkean representation

Edmund Burke was an eighteenth-century MP and political writer who proclaimed a trustee model of representation. For Burke, the job of a representative was to make judgements in the best interests of their constituents, not simply to do what they wanted them to do. In this view, MPs sometimes have to make decisions and take action that they believe is right, even though it may not be popular or represent the wishes of their constituents.

legitimacy. There are also proposals for a fully or partially elected House of Lords, which would improve democratic representation and give the second chamber greater authority in dealing with the House of Commons.

However, it is possible that an elected second chamber would simply mirror the House of Commons, while a more powerful second chamber could lead to gridlock politics with nothing being decided or passed. An elected House of Lords would see a reduction in the number of experts and an increase in professional politicians, losing a source of advice and expertise that currently informs legislation.

Greater recall of MPs

A system for recalling MPs was introduced just before the 2015 general election but it remains quite limited. A more rigorous method of recall would make MPs more responsive to the demands of their constituents for fear of being recalled and removed. It would also ensure that all MPs worked hard to keep in touch with their constituents.

However, the continued prospect of being recalled and defeated might hinder MPs in the other aspects of their role. It would also undermine 'Burkean representation' and the idea that MPs should be able to use their judgement and not just follow the wishes of their constituents. A tougher system of recall might lead to on MP simply acting as a spokesperson for their constituency.

Reform of the House of Commons

The House of Commons has a number of issues that undermines its image as the home of British democracy. Reforms to make Prime Minister's Question Time less adversarial, to make all members of select committees elected by the whole house, to bestow more power on the speaker to control debates and behaviour, and to introduce more modern technology for online questioning and public scrutiny stages would all make the House of Commons more collegiate, less adversarial and more open to the public.

However, many of these traditional elements of the Commons are popular and do not face serious or broad calls for reform. Any issues over the adversarial nature of British politics would need to be tackled at a fundamental level, not just by reforming parliament.

Reforming the devolved system

The West Lothian Question underlies the most pressing need for reform of the House of Commons because representatives from Scotland are able to vote on issues that do not affect their constituents, such as university tuition fees or an extension to Sunday trading in England and Wales.

The Conservative government tried to reform the system by introducing 'English votes for English laws' (EVEL) in 2015. There is now an extra stage in the legislative process where only MPs representing English (or English and Welsh) constituencies can vote on an issue which affects only England (or England and Wales). However, the whole chamber still votes on the final stages of a bill and which parts of the UK are affected by a bill is often not clear-cut. The process also runs the risk of creating two types of MPs, which undermines the principle of a legislative chamber.

Another possible reform would be to introduce further devolution to England, either through regional assemblies or through an English assembly

Synoptic links

Gun rights in Britain and the USA

In 2016, a gunman in Florida killed 49 people in a nightclub in Florida. This was the biggest in a long line of massacres committed in the USA. Each time, calls for greater gun control fail to result in changes to legislation.

In 1996, a gunman in Dunblane, Scotland, killed 16 schoolchildren and their teacher. Following this, the UK government quickly passed legislation to tighten restrictions on handguns and introduce a ban on many of them.

Which system is more democratic — the one that protects an individual's right to own a gun even if it results in mass shootings, or the one that removes the rights of all gun owners as a result of the actions of one person?

Key term

E-democracy A term used to describe any electronic or digital method that can lead to greater democracy.

Synoptic links

Democracy and constitutional reform

Many of the reforms that could make the UK more democratic would also be constitutional reforms. That is because the elements that make the UK a democracy are part of the constitutional framework. Therefore, democratic reforms will also involve constitutional reform and any constitutional reforms will also change UK democracy.

or parliament, to mirror the powers of those in Scotland, Wales and Northern Ireland. This would leave Westminster as a federal government overseeing national affairs, such as defence and foreign relations. But there is currently little demand for English devolution and when regional devolution was proposed for the northeast in 2004, it was rejected by 77.93%.

Reform of the monarchy

While currently popular and with limited power, an unelected hereditary monarchy is undemocratic. Introducing an elected head of state, whether by having an elected monarchy or by replacing the monarchy with a presidency, would make the UK more democratic, but there is little popular will for this reform and the costs of a president would be far more than the system of monarchy. In addition, an elected head of state would have more power and authority, and would therefore create a rival centre of power, undermining the principle of parliamentary sovereignty.

Codifying the constitution

Individual rights can too easily be reformed and changed by the government of the day. The introduction of a codified constitution would help to entrench citizens' rights and may lead to greater public education, but by transferring sovereignty to a codified constitution rather than an elected parliament, much more power would be transferred to an unelected and unaccountable judiciary. In addition, an entrenched constitution might make it harder for the government of the day to carry out desirable reforms.

E-democracy

Many of the problems with participation and democracy in the UK could be solved by a greater use of **e-democracy** (see Table 9.20).

Table 9.20 Advantages and disadvantages of e-democracy

Type of e-democracy	Advantage	Disadvantage
Online voting	Would make it easier for people to vote	Would be difficult to monitor and ensure free votes
Online questioning of ministers	Would allow people to ask questions directly	Would undermine the role of MPs
Digital campaigning	Would reduce costs and make it easier for people to access information	Would disadvantage people unable to get online and risk increased partisanship
Online public consultation of a bill	Would allow the public to give their thoughts on legislation before it is passed	Would undermine the legislative role of parliament and risk a tyranny of the minority

In focus

E-democracy

E-democracy refers to any electronic or digital method used to enhance democracy. It can take many forms, from creating a website to promote information and make it easier to access information, to more complicated measures such as online or text voting. The aim of e-democracy is to make it easier and more accessible for the population to engage with the democratic process.

Case study

Banning Donald Trump

In conjunction with the creation of the Backbench Business Committee (BBBC) in 2010, a new version of the government's online petition service was launched in August 2011. For any official petition gaining 100,000 or more signatures, the BBBC would discuss whether or not to allow time for a parliamentary debate on the matter. Following 570,000 signatures on a petition to ban Donald Trump from entering the UK, after his comments about banning all Muslims from the USA, a debate was held in Westminster Hall in January 2016. This raised the public profile of parliament as people tuned in to watch, but as the power to ban a person from entering the UK lies with the home secretary, not parliament, it was essentially a meaningless, if symbolic debate.

Questions
- What other arguments could be given to justify banning a person from the UK?
- Assess the arguments for preventing people from entering the UK.
- Given that Donald Trump has been elected president of the USA, do you believe that the Backbench Business Committee made a mistake in holding this debate? Explain your answer.

What you should know

- Democracy is of central importance to modern politics, but it comes in many forms, the main ones being direct, representative and pluralist. Each system has different ways of conferring legitimacy on decisions made, which can alter the results.
- The UK political system has elements of all types of democracy, which brings with it advantages and disadvantages. There are many proposals to reform the democratic process in the UK, ether by improving the system of representative democracy or by increasing the amount of direct democracy, but for every benefit there is a corresponding cost.
- The franchise refers to the right to vote and this has evolved since 1832 to grant almost all adults in the UK the right to vote, although lords, prisoners and those who are mentally incapable are unable to vote.
- There have been various campaigns to increase the franchise, including the work of the suffragettes and suffragists, as well as recent group activity to extend the right to vote to 16-year-olds and prisoners. For each campaign, you should know the arguments for and against their cause.
- UK politics relies on group activity, mostly in the form of pressure groups. Such groups have a variety of motives, either sectional or causal, and several methods for achieving their goals. As well as representing people, these groups also play an important role in allowing people to participate in politics.
- There have been several attempts to establish legal protection for civil rights and liberties in the UK. There has been a conflict between the rights of the individual and the rights of society and this, in turn, has led to a clash between the executive and parliament on one side and the judiciary on the other.

UK/US comparison

Democracy and participation

- Democracy was a fundamental principle in the writing of the US Constitution, although the people who drafted it were also concerned about a tyranny of the masses. For this reason, several anti-democratic measures were introduced to act as a check on the popular will, such as indirectly elected senators, the Electoral College and the presidential veto.

- There has never been a national referendum in the USA, but many of the individual states regularly use direct democracy in the form of initiatives and propositions to allow the people a greater say in decision making.

- The USA fought for independence on the basis of 'no taxation without representation', along the same lines as the demand to extend the franchise in the UK. Later, a key aspect of the American Civil War was granting citizenship and the right to vote to former slaves. Elsewhere in the world, the extension of the vote by class developed much earlier than in Britain, though the extension of the franchise to women and those aged 18 and over occurred at similar times around the world.

- There is a much wider range of access points to the political process in the USA than in the UK and this has allowed group activity to play a more prominent role in politics. The cost of US elections has also meant that politicians are reliant on donations, meaning the culture of lobbying is more prevalent and well established.

- The democratic rights of Americans are firmly entrenched in the Bill of Rights and the other amendments to the constitution. However, the interpretation of these rights has led to conflict across the states, most notably in the civil rights conflict of the 1950s and 1960s. There is also concern about the power of the US Supreme Court, which has been accused of creating rights through its interpretation of the constitution. Such judicial tyranny is seen to undermine the role of the executive and legislature, and to be fundamentally undemocratic.

Further reading

Batchelor, A. (2012) 'Referendums: without a consensus, the answer is no', *Politics Review*, Vol. 21, No. 3, pp. 24–27.

Cairney, P. (2014) 'Pressure groups: is pressure group power in decline?', *Politics Review*, Vol. 24, No. 1, pp. 30–33.

Cooper, T. (2016) 'Why do UK pressure groups fail?', *Politics Review*, Vol. 25, No. 3 pp. 6–7.

Fairclough, P. (2016) 'Democratic participation: has the nature of political participation changed?', *Politics Review*, Vol. 26, No. 2, pp. 12–15.

Heffernan, R. (2012) 'Pressure groups: do promotional groups strengthen democracy?', *Politics Review*, Vol. 22, No. 1, pp. 24–27.

McNaughton, N., Fairclough, P. and Magee, E. (2012) 'Pressure groups: how democratic are direct action and mass protest?' in *UK Government and Politics Annual Update 2012*, Phillip Allan.

Rathbone, M. (2015) 'Pressure groups: do they strengthen pluralist democracy? *Politics Review*, Vol. 25, No. 2, pp. 2–5.

Stoker, G, 'The UK political system: is it democratic?', *Politics Review*, Vol. 22, No. 1 pp. 2–5.

Democratic Audit: www.democraticaudit.com

Prospect: www.prospectmagazine.co.uk

Unlock Democracy: www.unlockdemocracy.org

Exam-style questions

Short-answer questions

1 Explain, with examples, the concept of pluralist democracy.

2 Explain, with examples, the role of pressure groups in British politics.

3 Explain and analyse three arguments against the greater use of direct democracy in the UK.

4 Explain and analyse three ways in which rights are protected in UK politics.

Mid-length questions

1 Describe the main features of representative democracy.

2 Describe the main functions of pressure group activity in the UK.

3 Analyse and evaluate the arguments in favour of extending the franchise in the UK.

4 Analyse and evaluate the arguments against rights protection being left to parliament.

Essay questions

1 Evaluate the view that democracy in the UK is suffering from a participation crisis.

2 Evaluate how far the UK system of representative democracy remains in need of improvement.

3 Analyse and evaluate the factors that determine the success of pressure groups in the UK.

4 'Judges, rather than politicians, are better able to protect and defend rights in the UK.' Analyse and evaluate this statement.

Chapter 10

Electoral systems

Elections to public office are a central feature of the democratic process in the UK

> **Key questions answered**
> - How do elections and electoral systems contribute to democracy?
> - How does the first-past-the-post electoral system work?
> - What are the advantages and disadvantages of the first-past-the-post electoral system?
> - What are the strengths and weaknesses of the other electoral systems used in the UK and how do they compare with the first-past-the-post system?
> - What impact does the electoral system have on government, party representation and voter choice?
> - What functions do referendums play in the UK and what are the arguments in favour of and against their use?

On the evening of 8 June 2017, prime minister Theresa May awaited the verdict of some 47 million voters in the general election she had called. Opinion polls had predicted that May would increase her parliamentary majority. Then at 10 p.m. the exit poll forecast that the Conservatives would remain the largest party but lose seats. Both main parties increased their share of the vote, but the first-past-the-post electoral system translated the narrowing of the gap between them into a net loss of seats for the Conservatives and a net gain for Labour. May formed a minority government but her authority was diminished. Labour had lost its third general election in a row, but a large increase in its vote share strengthened Jeremy Corbyn's position.

Elections and democracy

An election is a competitive process in which a designated group of people, known as the electorate, select individuals to serve in specified positions. Elections to public office are a central feature of the democratic process. Members of legislatures, and members of the executive in presidential systems, are chosen and held accountable through elections. Voting in an election is the main form of political activity for many people. For UK general elections, the electorate consists of almost all of the adult population.

Elections in the UK have a number of functions:

- **Representation.** In a representative democracy, elections enable a large group (the electorate) to select a smaller group (representatives) to act on their behalf.
- **Choosing a government.** General elections determine the composition of the House of Commons, but as the majority party in parliament

forms the government, elections also normally determine which party takes power.

- **Participation.** Voting is the key act of political participation for most citizens.
- **Influence over policy.** Elections allow citizens to voice their policy preferences. Political parties issue **manifestos** outlining the policies they would introduce in government. The victorious party then claims a **mandate** to deliver those policies.
- **Accountability.** The government and individual MPs are held accountable and will be removed from power if the electorate is unhappy with their record.
- **Citizen education.** Election campaigns provide citizens with information on major political issues and the policies of the main parties. In theory, this enables citizens to make an informed decision on how to vote, but in practice the information provided is imperfect.
- **Legitimacy.** Elections give **legitimacy** to the winning party and to the political system as a whole. By voting, even for a losing party, citizens give their consent to the system.
- **Elite recruitment.** Political parties nominate candidates for election and provide them with campaign resources — and, in return, expect loyalty from them if they become MPs.

Free and fair elections

In a liberal democracy, elections should be competitive, free and fair. A competitive election requires that voters have a meaningful choice between different political parties. Free elections require basic civil liberties such as freedom of speech and association, the right to join and stand for a party of one's choice, and a free press. The maxim 'one person, one vote, one value' is a key criterion for a fair election: each citizen should have one vote that is worth the same as everyone else's. Electoral law should be free from bias and overseen by an impartial judiciary. The electoral system should also translate votes cast into seats won in the legislature in a reasonably accurate manner, but as we will see, the first-past-the-post electoral system used in the UK falls short on some of these criteria: not all votes are of equal value, and election outcomes are disproportional.

Democratic and elitist theorists hold different views on the role of elections within liberal democracies. The former prioritise the role of the people in the political process. They focus on bottom-up functions such as policy influence, participation and accountability. In a representative democracy, the government should act in accordance with the wishes of the people.

For elite theorists, elections provide authority and stability for the political system, allowing elites to get on with the task of governing, with only limited recourse to the expressed wishes of the people. They highlight top-down functions such as legitimacy and elite recruitment. In a representative democracy, the political elite decides what is in the best interests of the people.

Elections in the UK

Elections take place at different levels in UK politics:

- **General elections.** These elect all 650 MPs who make up the House of Commons. The Fixed-term Parliaments Act 2011 introduced fixed 5-year terms for governments. Before 2011, the prime minister could call a general election at a time of his or her choosing within their 5-year term (see Chapter 5). Prime ministers must now seek a two-thirds majority in the Commons if they wish to trigger an early general election.
- **Elections to the devolved assemblies.** Elections to the Scottish Parliament, Welsh Assembly and Northern Ireland Assembly are now held every 5 years.
- **Local elections.** Local councillors are elected for fixed 4-year terms. In some local authorities, all councillors face the electorate at the same time; in others, only a proportion of members (normally a quarter) are elected each year. Some towns and cities also have directly elected mayors. In London, there is an elected mayor and assembly. Police and crime commissioners (PCCs) are also elected in England and Wales.
- **European Parliament elections.** The UK has elected Members of the European Parliament (MEPs) every 5 years since 1979. However, the UK is unlikely to take part in the 2019 elections given the 2016 referendum vote to leave the European Union (EU).
- **By-elections.** A **by-election** is held to choose a new representative if a **constituency** seat in the House of Commons, devolved assembly or English local authority becomes vacant because of the death or resignation of an elected member.

Three significant parts of the UK polity are not elected:

- the head of state — the hereditary monarch
- the upper chamber of parliament — the House of Lords
- the judiciary

Electoral systems

Electoral systems translate votes cast by citizens into seats in an assembly or a political office. There are four main types of electoral system.

Majoritarian system

The winning candidate must secure an absolute majority of the vote (i.e. 50% + 1 vote). Candidates are usually elected in single-member constituencies. The first-past-the-post system used for UK general elections is often described as a **majoritarian system** but this is not strictly accurate because the term is being used to reflect the output of the system rather than its mechanics.

Plurality system

First-past-the-post is a **single-member plurality system** in which the winner needs only a plurality of votes cast (i.e. one more than their closest rival), not an absolute majority. Plurality systems share characteristics of majoritarian systems. MPs are elected in single-member constituencies and both systems are non-proportional.

Key terms

By-election A one-off election that takes place in an individual constituency when a vacancy arises between scheduled elections.

Constituency A geographical area that elects one or more representatives to a legislative assembly.

Activity

Research the results of recent by-elections for the House of Commons. How do the outcomes differ from the general election results for these constituencies?

Key terms

Majoritarian system An electoral system in which the winning candidate must achieve an absolute majority of votes cast in a single-member constituency.

Single-member plurality system An electoral system in which the candidate with the most votes in a single-member constituency wins.

Proportional representation

Proportional representation (PR) covers many systems that produce a close fit between votes and seats, although no system can deliver perfect proportionality. The **district magnitude** (i.e. the number of legislative seats per constituency) is crucial — the larger the constituency, the more proportional the result. PR systems use multi-member constituencies and electoral formulas. Some (e.g. the single transferable vote) allow electors to vote for as many candidates as they wish in order of preference, whereas others (e.g. the closed list system) permit only a single vote.

Mixed system

A **mixed system** combines elements of the plurality or majoritarian systems with elements of proportional representation (e.g. in the additional member system, AMS). Some representatives are elected in single-member constituencies using first-past-the-post. The remainder are elected by proportional representation in multi-member constituencies — seats are allocated to parties on corrective lines to represent their share of the vote proportionally.

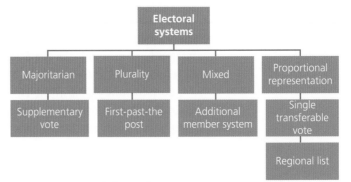

Figure 10.1 Types of electoral system

Majoritarian and proportional representation electoral systems

Majoritarian systems
- A candidate must secure an absolute majority of the vote to win; in a plurality system, they need only win more votes than the second-placed candidate.
- Candidates are elected in single-member constituencies.
- The outcome is not proportional — large parties take a higher proportion of seats than their share of the vote merits, while smaller parties are often under-represented.
- The systems tend to produce single-party governments with working parliamentary majorities.

Proportional representation systems
- Candidates are elected in multi-member constituencies.
- Electoral formulas are used to allocate seats in the legislative assembly.
- The outcome is proportional — there is a close fit between the share of the vote won by a party and the share of the seats it is allocated.
- The systems tend to produce coalition governments as no single party wins a majority of seats.

A range of electoral systems has been used in the UK — majoritarian, proportional representation and mixed systems — since the late 1990s (see Table 10.1).

Table 10.1 Electoral systems in the UK

Electoral system	Use in UK	Key features
First-past-the-post	General elections to the House of Commons	Plurality system; single-member constituencies; disproportional outcome
Supplementary vote	Mayor of London, directly elected mayors, police and crime commissioners	Majoritarian system; used to elect individuals; voters record two preferences; winning candidate has a majority
Regional list	European Parliament elections in Great Britain; list seats for the Scottish Parliament, Welsh Assembly and London Assembly	Proportional representation system; electors vote for a party in multi-member regions; proportional outcome
Single transferable vote	Assembly, local and European Parliament elections in Northern Ireland; local elections in Scotland and Northern Ireland	Proportional representation system; electors rank candidates in multi-member constituencies; proportional outcome
Additional member system	Scottish Parliament, Welsh Assembly, London Assembly	Mixed electoral system; electors cast two votes — one for a constituency candidate elected by FPTP and one for a regional list candidate elected by closed list PR; list candidates are allocated to parties on a corrective basis to produce a proportional outcome

Activity

Research the mechanics and pros and cons of different electoral systems by visiting the websites of the Electoral Reform Society (www.tinyurl.com/po2kpex) and Democratic Audit UK (www.democraticaudit.com).

The first-past-the-post electoral system

The first-past-the post (FPTP) system is the most significant electoral system in the UK because it is used for general elections. A variant of it, known as the block vote — in which constituencies elect more than one candidate — is used in local elections in England and Wales.

FPTP operates as follows:

- MPs are elected in single-member constituencies. Each constituency in the UK elects one representative to the House of Commons.
- Electors cast a single vote by writing a cross (X) on the ballot paper beside the name of their favoured candidate.
- A candidate requires a plurality of votes to win: that is, one more vote than the second-placed candidate. There is no requirement to obtain a majority of the votes cast. In contests involving three or more candidates, the winner may fall well short of an overall majority. Table 10.2 shows the extreme case of Belfast South in the 2015 general election where the victorious candidate secured fewer than one in four votes.

The results are read out for the 2015 general election in Belfast South in which the victorious candidate secured fewer than one in four votes

Table 10.2 General election result in Belfast South, 2015

Candidate	Party	Vote	% vote
Alasdair McDonnell	Social Democratic and Labour Party	9,560	24.5
Jonathan Bell	Democratic Unionist Party	8,654	22.2
Paula Bradshaw	Alliance Party	6,711	17.2
Máirtín Ó Muilleoir	Sinn Féin	5,402	13.9
Rodney McCune	Ulster Unionist Party	3,549	9.1
Other (4)		5,081	13.1

Activity

Find information about the electoral geography of the area in which you live. What changes are being proposed by the Boundary Commission? Why might the changes be viewed as enhancing democracy — or undermining it?

Key term

Safe seat A constituency in which the incumbent party has a large majority, and which is usually retained by the same political party at election after election.

Constituencies

Constituency boundaries are determined by independent boundary commissions which review the size of the electorate in each constituency every 8–12 years. Differences in size are permitted if there are significant geographical factors. The most populous constituency at the 2017 general election, the Isle of Wight, had an electorate five times larger than the smallest constituency, Na h-Eileanan an Iar (the Western Isles) — 110,700 compared to 21,300. Urban constituencies tend to have fewer electors than suburban and rural seats. The geographical size of constituencies also varies. The smallest are inner city seats while the largest are rural seats in Scotland.

In 2016, the Conservative government confirmed its plans to reduce the number of MPs from 650 to 600 and reduce disparities in constituency size. With the exception of two constituencies in Scotland (Orkney and Shetland, and the Western Isles) and two in England (the Isle of Wight will elect two MPs), all constituencies will have electorates that deviate by no more than five percentage points from the UK average of 74,769.

Safe and marginal seats

The competitiveness of elections varies significantly across constituencies. In **safe seats**, the same party wins at election after election because the incumbent party's majority is so large. The safest seat in 2017 was Liverpool, Walton, where Labour won 86% of the vote.

Marginal seat A constituency where the incumbent party has a small majority and which may thus be won by a different party at the next election.

Swing The extent of change in support for one party to support for another party from one election to another.

Turnout The percentage of registered voters who voted at an election.

Marginal seats are the most competitive. Here, the incumbent party has a small majority which their nearest rival(s) has a realistic chance of overturning. Parties focus resources here as the results determine the overall election outcome. **Turnout** tends to be higher in marginal seats because votes are more likely to make a difference to the result. The most marginal seat in 2017 was North East Fife, where the SNP won by just two votes.

The number of marginal seats has been in long-term decline, making it less likely that the winner of a close election would have a sizeable parliamentary majority. In 2015, there were 87 seats held by either Labour or the Conservatives in which the gap between them was under 10%, compared to 121 in 2010. However, the 2017 general election produced a larger number of marginal, including eleven 'super-marginals' with majorities of fewer than 100 votes. A **swing** of 2% to Labour at the next election would make it the largest party in the House of Commons, but the Conservatives would win a parliamentary majority on a swing of 1%.

Case study

2017 general election

The 2017 general election saw a reversal of some long-term trends. The Conservatives and Labour polled a combined 82% of the vote, the highest figure since 1970. It was the first general election since 1951 in which both main parties gained votes. The election outcome was the least disproportional since 1955. More MPs secured a majority of votes in their constituencies, but the tight contest also brought an upturn in the number of marginal seats. Regional disparities narrowed as Labour made gains in southern England, and the Conservatives in Scotland.

Despite the strong performance of the two main parties, FPTP did not deliver a clear parliamentary majority. The share of seats won by the Conservatives was higher than their share of the vote, but the closing of the gap between them and Labour denied the Conservatives a 'winners' bonus'. Parties other than the Conservatives and Labour won 70 seats and the DUP held the balance of power.

Questions
■ To what extent did the 2017 election see changes in the way FPTP operates?
■ Did the election confirm or refute the perceived advantages and disadvantages of FPTP?

Features of first-past-the-post elections

Characteristic features or outcomes of FPTP elections are:
■ a two-party system
■ a winner's bonus
■ bias to a major party
■ discrimination against third and smaller parties
■ single-party government

Having been evident in many postwar general election results, some of these features are now becoming less apparent.

Two-party system

FPTP tends to foster a two-party system in which two major parties compete for office (see the case study). It favours major parties that have strong nationwide support, which gives them a good chance of securing a parliamentary majority. There is little incentive for a faction within a major party to split and form a new party because small parties find it very difficult to win seats. The Social Democratic Party (SDP) was formed by disaffected Labour MPs in 1981. It fought the 1983 general election in an Alliance with the Liberals, winning 25% of the vote but only 23 seats. New 'outsider' parties also find it difficult to break through. The UK Independence Party (UKIP) won its only seat at a general election in 2015 but this was poor reward for 12.6% of the national vote.

The two-party system has, however, been in failing health and the UK began to resemble a multi-party system. In 2010, the Conservatives and Labour together received only 65% of the vote — a postwar low. Support for parties other than the Conservatives, Labour and Liberal Democrats reached a record 25% in 2015. The 2017 general election reversed this trend as the two main parties won a combined vote share of 82%, the largest since 1970. The two-party system had made a comeback, particularly in England. But the SNP remained the largest party in Scotland and the Conservatives relied on the support of the Democratic Unionist Party in the House of Commons.

Winner's bonus

FPTP tends to exaggerate the performance of the most popular party, producing a **winner's bonus** or landslide effect. A relatively small lead over the second-placed party is often translated into a substantial lead in parliamentary seats. The Conservatives won landslide victories in 1983 (see the case study on page 258) and 1987, with Labour doing likewise in 1997 (see the case study on page 263) and 2001 (see Table 10.3).

Table 10.3 UK general election results, 1945–2017

Year	Conservative vote (%)	Conservative seats (%)	Labour vote (%)	Labour seats (%)	Liberal Democrat vote (%)	Liberal Democrat seats (%)	Other vote (%)	Other seats (%)
1945	39.6	31.1	48.0	48.0	9.0	1.9	3.4	3.9
1950	43.4	47.7	46.1	50.4	9.1	1.4	1.4	0.5
1951	48.0	51.4	48.8	48.8	2.6	1.0	0.6	0.5
1955	49.7	54.8	46.4	44.0	2.7	1.0	1.2	0.3
1959	49.4	57.9	43.8	41.0	5.9	1.0	0.9	0.2
1964	43.4	48.3	44.1	44.1	11.2	1.4	1.3	0.0
1966	41.9	40.2	48.0	57.8	8.6	1.9	1.5	0.2
1970	46.4	52.4	43.1	43.1	7.5	1.0	3.0	0.9
1974 (Feb)	37.9	46.8	37.2	47.4	19.3	2.2	5.6	3.6
1974 (Oct)	35.8	43.6	39.2	50.2	18.3	2.0	6.7	4.1
1979	43.9	53.4	36.9	42.4	13.8	1.7	5.4	2.5
1983	42.4	36.1	27.6	32.2	25.4	3.5	4.6	3.2
1987	42.3	57.8	30.8	229	22.5	3.4	4.4	3.5
1992	41.8	51.6	34.2	41.6	17.9	3.1	6.1	3.7
1997	30.7	25.0	43.4	63.4	16.8	7.0	9.3	4.5
2001	31.7	25.2	40.7	62.7	18.3	7.9	9.3	4.2
2005	32.3	30.5	35.2	55.1	22.1	9.6	10.4	4.8
2010	36.1	47.2	29.0	39.7	23.0	8.8	11.9	4.3
2015	36.8	50.8	30.4	35.7	7.9	1.2	24.9	12.3
2017	42.4	48.9	40.0	40.3	7.4	1.8	10.2	8.9

Note: Liberal Democrat includes Liberals (1945–79) and SDP/Liberal Alliance (1983–87). Northern Ireland MPs are included as 'Other' from 1974 onward

Bias to one major party

Rather than simply favouring the winning party, FPTP is biased towards one of the two major parties. The system favoured Labour from the 1990s until 2010. Between 1997 and 2005, the proportion of seats won by the Conservatives was lower than their share of the vote. Then in 2010, the Conservatives led Labour by 7% but fell 19 seats short of an overall majority (see the case study on page 259).

There are a number of reasons for this bias, some of which persist today:

- **Tactical voting.** Labour benefited from anti-Conservative tactical voting between 1997 and 2005.
- **Differences in constituency size.** The electorate in constituencies won by Labour in 2015 was, on average, 3,850 lower than in those won by the Conservatives. This is largely because of population movement from urban constituencies to suburban and rural ones.
- **Differential turnout.** Turnout is lower in Labour-held seats: 62% in 2015, compared to 69% in seats won by the Conservatives. Labour needed fewer votes to win seats between 1997 and 2010 (see Table 10.4).

Table 10.4 Votes per seat at general elections, 1992–2017

Party	1992	1997	2001	2005	2010	2015	2017
Conservative	41,943	58,188	50,347	44,531	34,989	34,243	42,978
Labour	42,659	32,340	25,968	26,895	33,350	40,290	49,141
Liberal Democrats	299,980	113,977	92,583	96,487	119,788	301,986	197,647
UKIP	—	—	—	—	—	3,881,129	—
Green	—	—	—	—	285,616	1,157,613	525,371
SNP	209,854	103,592	92,863	68,711	81,898	25,972	27,930
Plaid Cymru	39,199	40,257	48,973	58,279	55,131	60,564	41,116

Labour retained its advantages in constituency size and turnout in 2015 and 2017 but the Conservative vote was more efficiently distributed. The Conservatives were the main beneficiaries of the collapse in support for the Liberal Democrats in 2015, whereas Labour lost 40 seats to the SNP. The Conservatives performed best in marginal seats in 2015, with their new incumbent MPs enjoying an average 4.5% increase in support compared to a 1.4% increase nationally. In 2017, the Conservatives gained 12 seats in Scotland, helped by anti-SNP tactical voting, while Labour's share of seats in Scotland was significantly lower than its share of the vote.

Discrimination against smaller parties

FPTP discriminates against third parties and smaller parties whose support is not concentrated in particular regions. Smaller parties are disadvantaged by:

- **Mechanics.** FPTP makes it more difficult for smaller parties to win seats. There are no rewards for coming second.
- **Psychology.** Smaller parties have a credibility problem because voters believe that a vote for them is a 'wasted vote'.

The Liberal Democrats and their predecessors have been consistent losers under FPTP, most notably in 1983 (see the case study). Effective targeting of seats, intensive local campaigning and incumbency helped them reach 62 seats in 2005, but this was still a disproportionate outcome.

Case study

1983 general election

The Conservatives won a landslide victory in 1983, gaining 37 seats despite a 1.5% fall in their share of the vote. A parliamentary majority of 144 reflected the party's 15 percentage point lead over Labour. The government also benefited from the split in the anti-Conservative vote between Labour, who recorded their worst result of the postwar period, and the Liberal–SDP Alliance. Labour polled only 660,000 more votes than the Alliance but won 186 more seats. The Alliance's 25% of the vote translated into 3.5% of seats. Votes for Labour were distributed efficiently, with the party holding its safe seats despite the collapse in its national vote, while the Alliance chalked up a series of second and third place finishes without reward.

Question

What role did FPTP play in (i) helping Labour survive as Britain's second party and (ii) halting the Liberal–SDP Alliance's political momentum?

In 2015 Douglas Carswell was the only UKIP candidate to win a seat at Westminster despite a dramatic increase in UKIP's share of the vote

In 2015, despite a dramatic increase in UKIP's share of the vote, only Douglas Carswell in Clacton emerged victorious. UKIP came second in 120 constituencies but was only within 10% of the votes of the winning party in two of these.

Parties whose support is concentrated in a particular region, such as Plaid Cymru in Wales, fare better in terms of matching seats to share of the vote. The SNP showed how a party with strong regional support can prosper under FPTP, winning 50% of the vote and 95% of the seats in Scotland in 2015.

Single-party government

FPTP tends to produce single-party **majority governments** with working parliamentary majorities. **Coalition governments** and **minority governments** are relatively rare at Westminster. In the postwar period, only the February 1974, 2010 and 2017 general elections did not deliver a majority of seats for one party. A minority Labour government took office after the first of these, while the 2010 Conservative–Liberal Democrat coalition was the first coalition government since the Second World War. In 2017, a Conservative minority government negotiated a confidence and supply deal with the Democratic Unionist Party (DUP).

The 2015 election saw a brief return to single-party government. But the Conservative majority of 12 was small by postwar standards. Majority governments were less common in the first half of the 20th century. Four of the seven general elections held between 1910 and 1929 did not produce a majority government, and a multiparty National Government held power from 1931 to 1940.

Key terms

Minority government
A government consisting of members of one political party which does not have an absolute majority of seats.

Coalition government
A government consisting of two or more political parties, usually with an absolute majority of seats in parliament, formed after an agreement on policy and ministerial posts.

Majority government
A government consisting of members of one political party which has an absolute majority of seats.

Case study

2010 general election

This was the first general election since February 1974 to produce a hung parliament in which no party had an absolute majority of seats. The Conservatives were the largest party but fell 19 seats short of a parliamentary majority. They achieved a net gain of 97 seats, their highest since 1931, and led Labour by 7%, but their 36% of the vote was well short of that won by Margaret Thatcher and John Major between 1979 and 1992. Labour fell below 30% of the vote for only the second time since 1945 but it benefited from disparities in constituency size and turnout.

Questions
- Was the 2010 election an anomaly?
- Did it reflect longer-term trends?

2015 general election

For supporters of FPTP, the 2015 election showed that it can still deliver single-party government. The party that won most votes formed a majority government, could deliver its manifesto commitments and would be held accountable to voters for its record in office. Some voters may have switched to the Conservatives because they wanted to avoid a hung parliament.

Critics of FPTP claimed that their case had been strengthened. The Conservatives could not convincingly claim democratic legitimacy: their vote share was up by less than 1% and they performed poorly in parts of Britain. The 2010–15 coalition government had been stable, but a Conservative government with a parliamentary majority of just 12 may not enjoy the same stability. The 2015 election was also particularly disproportionate: the SNP were major beneficiaries and UKIP major losers of the way FPTP operates.

Questions
- Did the 2015 election signal a return to normality in the way FPTP operates?
- Did the election strengthen or weaken the case for FPTP?

Advantages and disadvantages of the first-past-the-post electoral system

Arguments in favour of the first-past-the-post system

Supporters of the FPTP system point to a number of advantages.

Simplicity

FPTP is easy to understand and operate. The ballot paper is simple: electors only vote once and counting the votes is straightforward and speedy. Voters are familiar with the current system and, for the most part, view it as legitimate and effective.

Clear outcome

FPTP elections normally produce a clear winner. The party securing the largest number of votes often achieves a majority of seats.

Strong and stable government

By favouring the major parties and giving the winning party an additional bonus of seats, FPTP produces strong government. Single-party governments with working majorities exercise significant control over the legislative process. They can fulfil their mandate by enacting the policy commitments they made in their manifestos, and can act decisively in times of crisis.

Responsible government

Voters are given a clear choice between the governing party, which is held responsible for its record in office, and the main opposition party, which is a potential alternative government. The doctrine of the mandate obliges the winning party to put its proposals into effect.

Effective representation

Single-member constituencies provide a clear link between voters and their elected representative, with one MP representing the interests of the area.

Keeps out extremist parties

Parties on the far right and far left have not prospered in the UK, in part because FPTP makes it difficult for them to win seats at Westminster.

Arguments against the first-past-the-post system

Critics of the FPTP system respond by noting its disadvantages.

Disproportional outcomes

The number of parliamentary seats won by parties at a general election does not reflect accurately the share of the vote they achieved. As we have seen:

- The two main parties tend to win more seats than their vote merits, with the lead party given an additional winner's bonus. A party can form a majority government having won only 35% of the vote.
- Third parties and small parties whose votes are spread thinly are significantly under-represented in parliament.

Since 1945, the party coming second in the popular vote has twice won more seats than its opponent. In 1951, the Conservatives won more seats than Labour, despite winning fewer votes, while in February 1974, Labour won more seats and the Conservatives most votes.

Figure 10.2 shows the disproportionality of elections. Deviation from proportionality calculates the difference between each party's percentage vote-share and percentage seat-share, summing all deviations (ignoring minus signs) and halving the total. The 1983 general election was notably disproportionate but 2017 much less so.

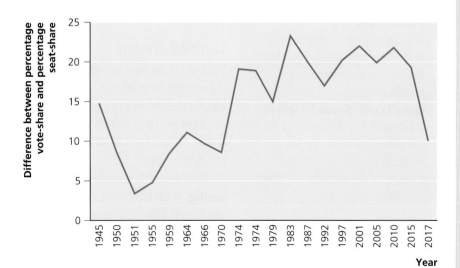

Figure 10.2 Disproportionality of general election outcomes, 1945–2017

Electoral 'deserts'

FPTP creates electoral 'deserts': that is, parts of the country where a party has little or no representation. The Conservatives won 34% of the vote in north east England in 2017 but only 10% of seats; Labour's

28% vote share in the south east gave them 10% of the region's seats. In south west England, the Liberal Democrats won 15% of the vote but just one of 55 seats.

Overall, the Conservatives perform more strongly in southern and rural England than in northern and urban England, while Labour does significantly better in northern England and Wales than in the south. But Labour gained ground on the Conservatives in southern England in 2017, while the Conservative vote rose dramatically in Scotland.

Plurality rather than majority support

Victorious candidates do not need to secure a majority of the votes cast. In 2010, a record two-thirds of MPs did not achieve a majority in their constituency. Low turnout meant that most MPs were supported by less than one in three of the electorate. The proportion of MPs winning a majority of votes rose to 73% in 2017 as support for smaller parties collapsed.

In 2005, Labour won a parliamentary majority with 35% of the UK vote. The general election of 1935 was the last time that the governing party won a majority of the popular vote. In 2010, the Conservatives and Liberal Democrats, who formed a coalition, won a combined 59% of the vote.

Votes are of unequal value

FPTP does not meet the 'one person, one vote, one value' principle. Disparities in constituency size mean that votes have different values. A vote cast in a small constituency is more likely to influence the outcome than one cast in a larger constituency. Many votes are wasted because they do not help to elect an MP. A **wasted vote** is:

- any vote for a losing candidate — this amounted to 50% of all votes cast in 2015
- a vote for a winning candidate that was not required for him or her to win, i.e. where the candidate had already secured enough votes to win — this amounted to 24% of votes in 2015

Limited choice

Voters are denied an effective choice because only one candidate stands for each party: voters cannot choose between different candidates from the same party. Furthermore, many constituencies are safe seats in which one party has a substantial lead over its rivals. Supporters of other parties have little prospect of seeing their candidate win.

Voters whose favoured party is unlikely to win may engage in **tactical voting**. A tactical vote is one cast not for the voter's first-choice candidate, but for the candidate best placed to prevent a party they dislike from winning the seat. Tactical voting was particularly evident at the 1997 general election (see the case study).

Activity

Find the 2017 general election result for the constituency in which you live. Did the victorious candidate win a majority of votes cast? What proportion of the electorate in your constituency voted for the winning candidate?

Key terms

Tactical voting Voting for the candidate most likely to defeat the voter's least favoured candidate.

Wasted vote A vote for a losing candidate in a single-member constituency, or a vote for a winning candidate that was surplus to the plurality required for victory.

Case study

1997 general election

In 1997, Tony Blair's Labour Party achieved a swing of 10.2% from the Conservatives, giving it a record tally of 418 Labour MPs and a parliamentary majority of 179. Labour advanced across the country, gaining not only countless marginal seats but also some apparently safe Conservative seats. The Conservatives received 30% of the vote, their worst result since 1832, and were left without MPs in Scotland, Wales and big cities in the north.

The Liberal Democrats won 46 seats, the highest third-party total since 1929. Despite a 1% decline in their share of the vote, the Liberal Democrats doubled their tally of seats. They and Labour benefited from tactical voting, which cost the Conservatives some 50 seats. Labour voters switched to the Liberal Democrats in seats where they, rather than Blair's party, were best placed to defeat the Conservative incumbent. Voters recognised that Labour and the Liberal Democrats were ideologically similar and had worked together on constitutional reform.

Questions
- Why did Labour win a landslide victory in 1997?
- Why did the Conservatives win fewer seats than their share of the vote merited?

Key term

Adversarial politics A situation often found in two-party systems in which the governing party is confronted by an opposition party that offers a different policy programme and is hostile towards the government even when in broad agreement with it.

Divisive politics

In the 1960s and 1970s, critics argued that FPTP brought **adversarial politics**. Small shifts in voting produced frequent changes of government and this led to instability because parties were able to overturn policies introduced by their rivals. Then, from 1979 to 2010, FPTP contributed to long periods of one-party rule, first by the Conservatives and then by Labour, without them winning majority support.

FPTP no longer does what it is supposed to

Professor John Curtice argues that FPTP has become less effective at delivering what its supporters view as some of its key strengths, notably single-party government and a winner's bonus. He identifies a number of reasons for this:

- FPTP is less effective in persuading electors not to vote for smaller parties. The combined vote for Labour and the Conservatives was lower in 2010 and 2015 than in other postwar elections. Support for the Liberal Democrats hit 23% in 2010, then the SNP, UKIP and the Greens recorded their best ever performances in 2015. But the combined vote for the two main parties rose to 82% in 2017.
- Parties other than Labour and the Conservatives are winning more seats in the House of Commons. The Liberal Democrats had over 50 seats between 2001 and 2010, and the SNP won 56 seats in 2015. Even in 2017, parties other than Labour and the Conservatives won 70 seats.
- Regional differences in support for parties are more pronounced. This makes it more difficult for one party to win a parliamentary majority. In 2015 and 2017, different parties topped the poll in each nation of the UK: the Conservatives won most votes in England, Labour in Wales, the SNP in Scotland and the DUP in Northern Ireland.
- The number of marginal seats has declined (until 2017), so fewer seats change hands at general elections.

Debate

Should the first-past-the-post system be retained for general elections?

Yes

- It is simple to use and voters are familiar with it.
- It tends to produce strong and stable majority governments which can deliver their manifesto commitments.
- The governing party is held accountable by voters who have a clear choice between two major parties and can remove unpopular governments.
- It rarely produces unstable minority governments or coalitions that emerge from secretive negotiations.
- There is a clear link between an MP and the constituency he or she represents.
- Extremist parties are kept out of parliament and government.

No

- Votes are not translated into seats fairly — larger parties get more seats than they merit and many smaller parties get fewer than they deserve.
- A party can win a parliamentary majority with as little as 35% of the vote — this is far from a democratic mandate.
- Regional differences in support are exaggerated, creating electoral deserts.
- Most MPs do not have the support of a majority of voters in their constituencies.
- Many votes do not influence the election outcome, particularly in the growing number of safe seats.
- FPTP is becoming less likely to deliver what its supporters claim is its key strength, i.e. strong, single-party government.

Other electoral systems used in the UK

Supplementary vote

The supplementary vote (SV) is used to elect the mayor of London (see Table 10.5) and directly elected mayors in other towns and cities. It is also used to elect police and crime commissioners (PCCs) (except in contests with only two candidates, where single-member plurality is used). Its key features are:

- The voter records their first and second preferences on the ballot paper (though they are not required to make a second choice if they do not wish to).
- If no candidate wins a majority of first preferences, all but the top two candidates are eliminated and the second preference votes for the two remaining candidates are added to their first preference votes.
- The candidate with the highest total is elected.

Table 10.5 Mayor of London election results, 2016

Candidate	Party	First preference (%)	Second preference (%)	Final (%)
Sadiq Khan	Labour	44.2	65.5	56.9
Zac Goldsmith	Conservative	35.0	34.5	43.1
Siân Berry	Green	5.8		
Caroline Pidgeon	Liberal Democrats	4.6		
Peter Whittle	UKIP	3.6		
Other (7)		6.8		

Advantages of supplementary vote

The advantages of SV are:

- The winning candidate must achieve broad support, giving them greater legitimacy.
- Supporters of smaller parties can use their first preference to express their allegiance and their second preference to indicate which major party candidate they prefer.
- The votes of people who use both their first and second preferences to support minor parties do not influence the election outcome.

Disadvantages of supplementary vote

The disadvantages of SV are:

- The winning candidate may be elected without winning a majority of votes if second preference votes are not used effectively. Voters need to use either of their preferences for one of the top two candidates in order to affect the outcome.
- The winning candidate does not need to get a majority of first preference votes. The candidate who secures most first preference votes may not be elected after second preferences are distributed — the least unpopular, rather than most popular, candidate may be elected.
- The system would not deliver a proportional outcome if used for general elections.

Single transferable vote

The single transferable vote (STV) is used in Northern Ireland for elections to the Assembly (see Table 10.6 on page 266), local government and the European Parliament. It is also used for local elections in Scotland — and for general elections in the Republic of Ireland. The main features of STV are:

- Representatives are elected in large multi-member constituencies. In Northern Ireland Assembly elections, 18 constituencies each elect six members.
- Voting is preferential — electors indicate their preferences by writing '1' besides the name of their first preference, '2' next to the name of their second choice and so on.
- Voting is ordinal — electors can vote for as many or as few candidates as they like.
- A candidate must achieve a quota, known as the Droop quota, in order to be elected. Any votes in excess of this quota are redistributed on the basis of second preferences. The quota is calculated as follows:

$$\left(\frac{\text{total valid poll}}{(\text{seats available} + 1)} \right) + 1$$

- If no candidate reaches the quota on the first count, the lowest-placed candidate is eliminated and their second preferences are transferred. This process of elimination and redistribution of preferences continues until the requisite number of seats is filled by candidates meeting the quota.

Activity

Find the constituency results of the 2017 Northern Ireland Assembly elections (e.g. at www.tinyurl.com/y9ze2yw) and trace the progress of the count stage by stage. At what stages were successful candidates elected?

Table 10.6 Elections to the Northern Ireland Assembly 2017

Party	First preference votes (%)	Number of seats	Share of seats (%)
Democratic Unionist (DUP)	28.1	28	31.1
Sinn Féin	27.9	27	30.0
Ulster Unionist (UUP)	12.9	10	11.1
Social Democratic and Labour Party (SDLP)	11.9	12	13.3
Alliance	9.1	8	8.9
Traditional Unionist	2.6	1	1.1
Green	2.3	2	2.2
People Before Profit	1.8	1	1.1
Others	3.4	1	1.1

Advantages of single transferrable vote

The advantages of STV are:
- It delivers proportional outcomes and ensures that votes are largely of equal value.
- The government is likely to consist of a party or group of parties that win over 50% of the vote.
- Voters choose between a range of candidates, including different candidates from the same party, meaning there is greater choice.

Disadvantages of single transferrable vote

The disadvantages of STV are:
- It can be less accurate in translating votes into seats than proportional representation list systems.
- Large multi-member constituencies weaken the link between individual MPs and their constituency.
- It is likely to produce a coalition government that may be unstable and can give disproportional influence to minor parties that hold the balance of power.
- The counting process is lengthy and complex.

Additional member system

The additional member system (AMS) is a mixed electoral system which includes elements of FPTP and the regional list (closed list) system of proportional representation. It is sometimes referred to as a mixed-member proportional system. AMS is used to elect the Scottish Parliament, Welsh Assembly and London Assembly. (The structure and power of the devolved bodies are examined in Chapter 4.) It is also used for general elections in Germany. The main features of AMS are:
- A proportion of seats in the legislative assembly are elected using FPTP in single-member constituencies: 73 out of 129 members (57%) of the Scottish Parliament are elected in single-member constituencies, as are 40 of the 60 members (67%) of the Welsh Assembly.
- A smaller number of representatives, known as additional members, are elected in multi-member constituencies using the regional list system of proportional representation. This regional list system is used to elect

56 members (43%) of the Scottish Parliament and 20 members (33%) of the Welsh Assembly.

- Electors cast two votes: one for their favoured candidate in a single-member constituency and one for their favoured party from a closed party list in a multi-member constituency.
- For the regional list seats, political parties draw up a list of their candidates and decide the order in which they will be elected. It is a *closed list* system, meaning electors can only vote for a party or an independent candidate. The list of candidates for each party appears on the ballot paper, but electors cannot choose between candidates representing the same party. (In an *open list* system, voters can choose between candidates from the same party.)
- Regional list seats (additional members) are allocated on a corrective basis to ensure that the total number of seats for parties in the assembly is proportional to the number of votes won. So a party that has won a disproportionately high number of constituency seats may not win many list seats, even if it also polls more list votes than other parties.
- Regional list seats are allocated using the d'Hondt formula. The total number of votes for each party is divided by the number of seats it already has, plus the next seat to be allocated. So the party totals are divided first by 1 (0 seats plus 1), then by 2 (1 seat plus 1) and so on. The first seat goes to the party with the largest number, the next seat to the next highest number, and so on. Candidates are elected in the order they appear on the party list.
- To win seats in the London Assembly, a party must also pass a threshold of 5% of the vote. There is no threshold for Scottish Parliament and Welsh Assembly elections.

Advantages of additional member system

The advantages of AMS are:

- It combines the best features of FPTP and proportional representation, e.g. balancing the desirability of constituency representation with that of fairness of outcomes.
- Results are broadly proportional and votes are less likely to be wasted.
- Voters have greater choice. **Split-ticket voting** is allowed: a voter may use their constituency vote to support a candidate from one party and their list vote to support a different party.
- Some parties have used the system to improve the representation of women: e.g. by 'zipping' — alternating male and female candidates on party lists.
- Votes are easy to count and it is not difficult for voters to understand how the outcome is reached.

Disadvantages of additional member system

The disadvantages of AMS are:

- It creates two categories of representative, one with constituency duties and one without. This may create tensions within the legislative assembly.

Key term

Split-ticket voting The practice of voting for candidates from different parties in an election where an elector is permitted to cast more than one vote.

Find the results of the 2016 Welsh Assembly election (e.g. at www. tinyurl.com/ze3hrwo). How proportional was the outcome? How different were the results in the constituency and regional list sections?

- Parties have significant control over the closed lists used to elect additional members and voters cannot choose between candidates from the same party.
- Smaller parties are often under-represented because in many multi-member seats, only a few representatives are elected. Larger parties are also over-represented if other votes are split evenly between many small parties.
- Proportional outcomes are less likely where the number of additional members is low, as in the Welsh Assembly.

Case study

2016 Scottish Parliament election

In 2016, the SNP dominated the constituency contests, winning 59 of the 73 seats (see Table 10.7), but added only four list seats (which are allocated in a corrective way). The party fell two seats short of a parliamentary majority and formed a minority government. For the first time, the Conservatives won more seats than Labour in the Scottish Parliament. The Greens contested only three constituency contests, but secured six list seats.

This was the second time that AMS had produced an SNP minority government. The 1999 and 2003 contests both resulted in a Labour–Liberal Democrat coalition. Yet in 2011, AMS delivered a majority government when the SNP won 73% of constituency seats.

Questions
- Why does the Green Party focus on regional list rather than constituency contests?
- Why have Welsh Assembly election outcomes been less proportional than elections to the Scottish Parliament?

Table 10.7 Scottish Parliament election results, 2016

Party	Constituency contests		Regional lists		Total seats
	Share of vote (%)	Seats won	Share of vote (%)	Seats won	
Conservative	22.0	7	22.9	24	31
Labour	22.6	3	19.1	21	24
Liberal Democrats	7.8	4	5.2	1	5
SNP	46.5	59	41.7	4	63
Green	0.6	0	6.6	6	6
Other	0.5	0	4.5	0	0

The impact of the electoral systems used in the UK

Comparing UK electoral systems

Table 10.8 compares the first-past-the-post, single transferable vote and additional member systems as they operate in the UK. The systems have produced different outcomes in terms of type of government, party representation and voter choice.

Table 10.8 Comparing UK electoral systems

	FPTP	STV	AMS
Where it is used	House of Commons	Northern Ireland Assembly	Scottish Parliament Welsh Assembly
Type of constituency	Single-member constituencies	Multi-member constituencies	Mix of single-member and multi-member constituencies
How the vote is cast	Single vote for one candidate	Rank candidates	Two votes: one for an individual candidate; one for a party
How the winner is decided	Candidate with the most votes	Counting and redistribution of preferences until sufficient number of candidates meet a quota of votes	Constituency seats won by candidate with most votes; list seats distributed to give proportional outcome
Result: single-party majority government	4 out of 6 elections	0 out of 6 elections	Scotland: 1 out of 5 elections Wales: 0 out of 5 elections
Result: minority government	1 out of 6 elections	0 out of 6 elections	Scotland: 2 out of 5 elections Wales: 4 out of 5 elections*
Result: coalition government	1 out of 6 elections	4 out of 6 elections**	Scotland: 2 out of 5 elections Wales: 1 out of 5 elections*
Effective number of electoral parties (mean)	3.4	5.2	Scotland: 4.4 Wales: 4.5
Effective number of parliamentary parties (mean)	2.0	4.5	Scotland: 3.3 Wales: 3.1
Deviation from proportionality (mean)	20.6	7.1	Scotland: 10.5 Wales: 14.8
Turnout (mean)	65.4%	61.8%	Scotland: 53.4% Wales: 43.1%

Note: The figures for single-party government, majority government, effective number of electoral parties, effective number of parliamentary parties, deviation from proportionality and turnout are mean figures from 1997 to 2017 for FPTP, 1998–2017 for STV, and 1999–2016 for AMS.

*In 2016, the sole Liberal Democrat Additional Member joined Labour in government after reaching a 'progressive agreement'. There have been two other periods of coalition government in Wales (2000–03 and 2007–11), but each followed an initial period of minority government after the preceding election. Only the 2007–11 Labour–Plaid Cymru coalition had a majority of seats in the Assembly.

**The Northern Ireland devolved institutions were suspended from 2003–07 so no government took office after the 2003 elections. By June 2017, no government had been formed following the March 2017 Assembly election

The impact on the type of government

Minority governments and coalition governments are the norm in the devolved assemblies but the exception at Westminster. Only one of the devolved elections — the 2011 Scottish Parliament elections, which produced an SNP majority government — delivered an outright winner. FPTP is becoming less likely to deliver a majority government at Westminster, with the 2010 election leading to the formation of a Conservative-Liberal Democrat coalition and the 2017 election producing a Conservative minority government.

Of the last three UK general elections, only the 2015 contest produced a majority government. Had STV or the closed list PR system been used, the Conservatives would have fallen well short of a parliamentary majority and UKIP would have been their most likely coalition partner (see Table 10.9). In 2017 they would have given Labour a better prospect of forming a minority government.

Table 10.9 Outcome of the 2015 UK general election under different voting systems

Party	Number of seats		
	First-past-the-post	List PR	Single transferable vote
Conservative	331	242	276
Labour	232	208	236
Liberal Democrats	8	47	26
UKIP	1	80	54
Green	1	20	3
SNP	56	30	34
Plaid Cymru	3	5	3

Source: Electoral Reform Society (www.electoral-reform.org.uk)

Distinguish between

Majority, minority and coalition government

Majority government
- One political party has an absolute majority of seats in parliament and forms the government.
- All government ministers are members of this one party.

Minority government
- No political party has an absolute majority of seats in parliament.
- A party without a majority (often, but not necessarily, the largest party) forms a government but must try to secure support from other parties in order to pass key measures.
- All ministers are members of this governing party.

Coalition government
- No political party has an absolute majority of seats in parliament.
- Two or more parties agree a deal to form a government, following negotiations and a formal agreement on policy.
- Ministerial positions are shared between the two or more governing parties.

The impact on party representation

Elections to the devolved assemblies and European Parliament better reflect the development of multiparty politics across the UK. The SNP has been in power in Scotland since 2007. Parties such as UKIP and the Greens are better represented than at Westminster because the number of seats better reflects the share of the vote.

However, the UK's two-party system was in failing health until 2017. Political scientists measure the 'effective number' of parties. Figure 10.3 shows that the 'effective number of electoral parties' (ENEP), a weighted measure of the share of the vote won by parties at general elections, was close to 2 in the 1950s — i.e. the UK had a two-party system — but this rose to almost 4 by 2015 only to fall back to 2.8 in 2017. The 'effective number of parliamentary parties' (ENPP), which is based on the share of seats in the House of Commons, has only increased from 2 to 2.5. FPTP acted as a life support machine for the two-party system, holding back but not halting the advance of multiparty politics.

The big increase in support for the two main parties in 2017 meant that the distribution of seats was less disproportionate than in 2015. Then UKIP won 13% of the vote but only one seat and the SNP's 50% of the vote in Scotland brought 95% of the seats.

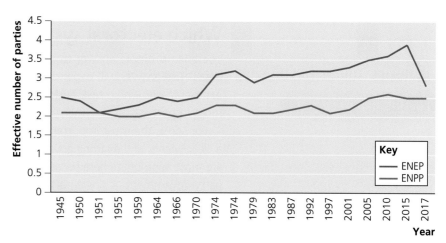

Figure 10.3 The effective number of parties in UK general elections, 1945–2017

Source: data from election indices dataset (www.tinyurl.com/d8gcnz3)

The 2015 general election was one of the most disproportionate in the postwar period. The Conservatives won a majority of seats with 38% of the vote, UKIP won a single seat despite winning almost 13% of the vote, and the SNP won 95% of Scottish seats with 50% of the vote in Scotland.

Elections conducted under STV and AMS are more proportional than Westminster elections (see Table 10.8) but they also produce results that reward larger parties and penalise smaller ones. The outcome of the 2016 Welsh Assembly election, for example, was notably disproportional. The large number of constituency seats delivered to Labour by FPTP could not be corrected fully by the distribution of the smaller number of regional list seats.

The impact on voter choice

Voters have greater choice under AMS, SV and STV than under FPTP. They allow for split-ticket voting in which an elector uses one of their votes or preferences to support their first-choice party (or candidate), but uses their second vote to back a different party (or candidate). This has allowed voting behaviour to become more sophisticated. Electors recognise that a vote for a minor party is less likely to be wasted under AMS and STV. In return, smaller parties gain a higher profile and, having become accustomed to voting for a smaller party, electors are more likely to vote for one in general elections as well.

Evidence from other countries shows that turnout in general elections conducted under PR is higher than where FPTP is used. Low turnout is common in 'second-order' elections that do not determine who forms the national government. Turnout in elections to the devolved institutions in the UK and the European Parliament has been significantly lower than for general elections, but turnout at general elections has declined since the early 1990s, and turnout at local elections in England — which use a version of FPTP — is often poor.

AMS, SV and STV give voters greater choice but some have found the different electoral systems complex and difficult to understand. The design of ballot papers was changed after the 2007 Scottish Parliament elections, when 146,000 ballots were completed incorrectly. At the 2016 London mayoral election, 382,000 electors did not use their second preference vote and 220,000 cast it for the same candidate as their first preference. Another 1.5 million second preference votes that were not for the top two candidates did not affect the result.

Which electoral system is best?

There is no simple answer to the question 'Which electoral system is best?' The answer will depend upon which element of representative democracy or which task performed by an electoral system is viewed as most important — and there is no consensus on this.

For some, the most important task of an electoral system is to produce a clear winner and a strong government. Majoritarian and plurality systems are most appropriate here because they are more likely to produce single-party government. A single-party government is, in turn, more likely to be effective in implementing its manifesto commitments and more accountable, as voters can easily identify which party is responsible for government policies and reward or punish them accordingly in the next election. In contrast to majoritarian and plurality systems, proportional representation is often associated with unstable governments in which fringe parties exercise influence that is disproportional to their popular support.

Electoral systems using single-member constituencies, such as FPTP and SV, also score highly for those who value a clear link between an elected representative and their constituents. Under FPTP, MPs have incentives to represent the interests of their geographical constituency (e.g. their support may include a 'personal vote' which results from their record or activities in office) and voters can easily identify their parliamentary representative.

For those who most value fairness to smaller parties and a high degree of proportionality in the way votes are translated into seats, proportional representation systems such as STV and the regional list are the most attractive. These systems tend to produce coalition governments and promote cooperation between parties. Under STV and the regional list system, the government often consists of parties that have collectively secured more than 50% of the vote. Large multi-member constituencies produce the most proportional outcome.

Voter choice is also regarded as a valuable feature of electoral systems. If a straightforward choice between the government and opposition party is desired, then FPTP might be preferred. If there is a choice from a range of parties then the closed regional list might be favoured, but if a choice between candidates from the same party is also viewed as desirable then STV is the optimal system. There is also evidence that parties are more likely to select women and minority candidates under AMS and STV. Finally, comparative research shows that turnout is higher in general elections that use proportional representation.

Mixed systems such as AMS combine elements of both plurality and proportional representation systems. They provide a degree of proportionality while still rewarding the major parties and offer a link between MPs and constituencies. They might, then, be regarded as providing the best of both worlds, but the experience of AMS can vary, as has been seen in Scotland and Wales. In Scotland, it has resulted in both stable government and representation of smaller parties. In Wales, election outcomes have not been

Activity

If asked to recommend an electoral system for Westminster, how would you decide? You might start by deciding what an electoral system should do. Rank the following in order of importance:

- allows voters to unseat the government
- provides a clear link between MPs and constituents
- enhances the representation of minority groups
- provides choice between parties and candidates
- produces stable government
- ensures proportionality of outcome
- is easy to understand

Now consider how three of the electoral systems used in the UK — FPTP, AMS and STV — perform these tasks. You could give each electoral system a score (e.g. 5 = performs very well; 1 = performs very poorly). On this basis, which of these electoral systems would you recommend?

proportional because there are too few list seats. Labour has remained in power after every election, despite fluctuations in its vote share, but has never won a parliamentary majority — which suggests that the electoral system is not effective at rewarding or penalising governing parties.

Choosing which electoral system is best might be regarded as a trade-off between different criteria, notably between strong accountable government and the representativeness of parliament. Yet it is not as simple as that. For example, FPTP did not produce single-party governments with commanding parliamentary majorities in either 2010, 2015 or 2017. Nor have the coalition and minority governments in the devolved assemblies been weak and unstable. And PR and AMS systems can be designed to deny representation (and influence over government formation) to fringe parties, so, for example, parties much achieve a threshold (5% of the vote) to get seats in the London Assembly.

Electoral reform

Labour embraced **electoral reform** after the Conservatives won four successive general elections between 1979 and 1997. The Blair government then introduced new electoral systems for the European Parliament and devolved institution elections, and established the Jenkins Commission to examine the case for electoral reform at Westminster. Jenkins recommended using alternative vote plus (AV+), a hybrid of the AMS and alternative vote systems, for general elections but Blair did not support the change. Like the supplementary vote, AV is a majoritarian system in which voters rank their preferred candidates. If no candidate wins a majority, the lowest-placed candidate is eliminated and their second preferences are redistributed. This continues until one candidate achieves a majority of votes cast.

David Cameron agreed to hold a referendum on AV as part of the coalition agreement with the Liberal Democrats. The 2011 referendum produced a 68% vote against AV. This appeared to end the prospect of electoral reform for Westminster in the medium term, even though FPTP was becoming less effective in delivering its supposed benefits. At the 2017 general election, the Liberal Democrats proposed using STV for general elections but neither the Conservatives nor Labour supported the replacement of FPTP.

The 2011 referendum produced a 68% vote against AV

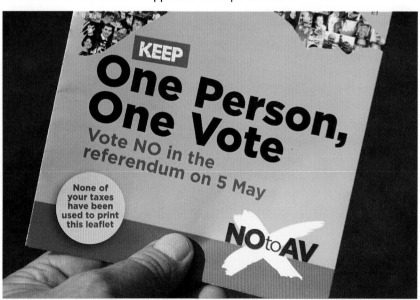

Have the additional member system, supplementary vote, single transferable vote and regional list been effective in the UK?

Yes

- Election results have been more proportional, translating votes cast into seats won more effectively.
- The rise of multiparty politics is reflected in election outcomes with smaller parties winning seats and taking office.
- Voters have a greater choice as votes for small parties are less likely to be wasted.
- Minority and coalition governments in the devolved assemblies have been stable.
- The new electoral systems have helped to produce more representative political systems.
- Voters have become more sophisticated, often engaging in split-ticket voting.

No

- The new systems have not always delivered highly proportional outcomes.
- Extremist parties have gained seats — the British National Party (BNP) won two seats in the 2009 European Parliament elections.
- The closed list element of AMS restricts voter choice and gives party bosses a significant say over the composition of the legislature.
- The relationship between representatives and constituents has been weakened by using large multi-member constituencies or, in AMS, creating two classes of representative.
- Turnout has been low.
- Some voters appear confused by the different systems, evidenced in the relatively high number of spoiled ballot papers and wasted second preference votes.

Referendums in the UK

Key term

Referendum A vote on a single issue put to a public ballot by the government.

A **referendum** is a popular vote on a single issue. It is the major modern-day example of direct democracy. In states such as Switzerland or the Republic of Ireland, referendums are used widely to resolve major political and constitutional issues.

Referendums are a relatively modern phenomenon in the UK. The first nationwide referendum did not take place until 1975 and most have been held after 1997. Before then, referendums were regarded as alien to a British political tradition that emphasised the sovereignty of parliament rather than popular sovereignty. The absence of a codified constitution meant that there was no formal list of circumstances in which a referendum must be held.

Distinguish between

Elections and referendums

Elections

- They are a feature of representative democracy — citizens choose representatives to make decisions on their behalf.
- They determine who holds political office and, in the case of a general election, who forms the government.
- Citizens vote for candidates who stand in geographical constituencies.
- An election campaign covers many issues of public policy.
- They are required by law and must take place at a specified time.

Referendums

- They are an example of direct democracy — citizens make the decisions themselves.
- A referendum is a one-off vote on a specific issue of public policy.
- The choice offered to voters is normally a simple 'yes' or 'no' in response to a proposal.
- The decision to hold a referendum in the UK is taken by the government.

There have been only three UK-wide referendums:

■ the 1975 referendum on continued membership of the European Economic Community
■ the 2011 referendum on using the alternative vote system for Westminster elections
■ the 2016 referendum on whether the UK should remain a member of the European Union

Each of these referendums was authorised by parliament. The other ten referendums sanctioned by parliament concern the devolution of power (see Table 10.10).

Table 10.10 UK referendums, 1973–2016

Date	Who voted	Question (paraphrased)	Yes (%)	No (%)	Turnout (%)
1973	Northern Ireland	Should Northern Ireland remain part of the UK?	**98.9**	1.1	58.1*
1975	UK	Should the UK stay in the EEC?	**67.2**	32.8	63.2
1979	Scotland	Should there be a Scottish Parliament?	**51.6**	48.4	63.8
1979	Wales	Should there be a Welsh Parliament?	20.3	**79.7**	58.3
1997	Scotland	Should there be a Scottish Parliament?	**74.3**	25.7	60.4
		With tax-varying powers?	**63.5**	36.5	
1997	Wales	Should there be a Welsh Assembly?	**50.3**	49.7	50.1
1998	Greater London	Should there be a London mayor and London Assembly?	**72.0**	28.0	34.0
1998	Northern Ireland	Do you support the Good Friday Agreement?	**71.1**	28.9	81.0
2004	Northeast England	Should there be a regional assembly for the northeast?	22.0	**78.0**	48.0
2011	Wales	Should the Welsh Assembly have primary legislative powers?	**63.5**	36.5	35.6
2011	UK	Should the alternative vote replace first-past-the-post for elections to the House of Commons?	32.1	**67.9**	42.2
2014	Scotland	Should Scotland become an independent country?	44.7	**55.3**	84.6
2016	UK	Should the UK remain a member of the EU or leave the EU?	Remain 48.1	Leave **51.9**	72.2

Note: The 'Yes' or 'No' figures in bold indicate the outcome.

*This referendum was boycotted by nationalists.

Source: House of Commons Library, *Briefing Paper: Referendums* (www.tinyurl.com/h6cqaze)

Local referendums

Referendums have been used more frequently at local level since the 1990s, both to approve (or reject) structural changes to local government and to authorise local policies.

■ **Establishing directly elected mayors.** By 2016, 52 referendums had been held on moving to the directly elected mayor model, with only 16 approving the move. The referendums were triggered by central government, a decision by the local authority or a petition by local citizens.

■ **Congestion charges.** Two cities, Edinburgh in 2005 and Manchester in 2008, held referendums on introducing congestion charges. In both cases, some three-quarters of voters rejected the proposals and so they were dropped.

- **Council tax increases.** A local authority proposing to increase council tax above a threshold set by central government must hold a referendum to approve it. In 2015, voters in Bedfordshire rejected an increase proposed by the police and crime commissioner (PCC).
- **Neighbourhood plans.** The Localism Act 2011 requires local authorities to hold referendums on neighbourhood plans for housing development. By the end of 2015, 126 such referendums had been held and all of them approved the plans. Turnout averaged 33%.
- **Parish polls.** The Local Government Act 1972 allows voters to request that a parish council holds an advisory referendum on a local issue. The regulations were tightened after criticism that the system was being used to hold votes on issues that were not local matters (e.g. EU treaties).

National referendums

The government usually decides whether and when to call a referendum. Key factors influencing the decision have included:

- **Constitutional change.** The Blair governments held referendums to approve their proposals for constitutional change, particularly devolution.
- **Coalition agreement.** A referendum on replacing first-past-the-post with the alternative vote system was a central feature of the 2010 Conservative–Liberal Democrat coalition agreement. It also included commitments to referendums on Welsh devolution, directly elected mayors and future EU treaties.
- **Party management.** By calling the 1975 and 2016 EEC/EU referendums, Harold Wilson and David Cameron hoped to resolve long-running internal party divisions on the issue of European integration. Neither was successful.
- **Political pressure.** The momentum for a Scottish independence referendum became unstoppable following the SNP's victory in the 2011 Scottish Parliament elections. The rise of UKIP and media campaigns for a vote influenced Cameron's decision to hold an EU referendum. However, governments are unlikely to hold referendums that they believe they will lose and they have the advantage of controlling the timing of the referendum. Governments have also promised referendums — e.g. on joining the euro and approving EU treaties — that, in the end, they did not hold because of a change in circumstances.

Referendum regulations

The Political Parties, Elections and Referendums Act 2000 gave the Electoral Commission specific responsibilities on regulating referendums:

- **Wording.** The Commission comments on the intelligibility of proposed referendum questions. The government is not required to accept these recommendations, but tends to do so.
- **Campaign participation.** Groups and individuals who expect to spend more than £10,000 on referendum campaigning must register as participants with the Electoral Commission. The Commission designates the lead organisations for each side of the campaign. These

Synoptic links

EU referendums and collective responsibility

The principle of collective responsibility — i.e. that ministers must support the position of the government or resign — was suspended during the 1975 and 2016 referendums on European integration (see Chapter 6). The EU referendum is considered in more detail in Chapter 8.

Activity

Research the 2011 AV referendum and 2016 EU referendum. How much did each side of the campaigns spend? To what extent did each side of the campaigns educate the electorate on the issues involved?

organisations have a higher spending limit, receive public money and are entitled to television broadcasts.

- **Campaign spending.** The Commission ensures that organisations and individuals adhere to limits on funding and spending.
- **Conduct of the campaign.** After the referendum, the Commission issues a report on administration and spending. Its report on the 2016 EU referendum questioned the rules regarding spending by the UK government.

Case study

2014 Scottish independence referendum

The Yes Scotland campaign group was fronted by the SNP, while Better Together was supported by Labour, the Conservatives and Liberal Democrats. The campaign saw debate over the costs and benefits of the Union and independence, but Better Together was criticised for a negative campaign focused on the dangers of independence. In the final stages of the campaign, when opinion polls suggested a vote for independence was possible, the leaders of the three main UK parties made a vow to deliver further devolution in the event of a 'no' vote.

The referendum was a success in terms of political participation and education. Turnout was very high (84.5%), and 16- and 17-year-olds were permitted to vote. In the end, 55.3% said 'no' to an independent Scotland while 1.6 million voters (44.7%) supported independence. The result did not settle the issue of

Scottish independence and the SNP supports a second vote, particularly in the wake of the outcome of the EU referendum in 2016.

16- and 17-year-olds were permitted to vote in the Scottish independence referendum in 2014

Questions
- Does the Scottish independence referendum strengthen or weaken the case for referendums?
- Why did the referendum not resolve the independence issue?

The impact of referendums

Referendums have had an impact on UK political life in three main areas:
- direct democracy
- parliamentary sovereignty and representative democracy
- constitutional convention

Direct democracy

An element of direct democracy has been injected into a political system previously wedded to representative democracy. However, the extent to which referendums have enhanced UK democracy is debatable (see the debate). Referendums have extended political participation and made government more responsive to the people on major constitutional issues, but they have created competing legitimacies (e.g. should parliament or the people have the final say?) and some of the information presented by referendum campaign groups has been misleading.

Have referendums enhanced representative democracy in the UK?

Yes

- They have introduced direct democracy, ensuring that citizens, not politicians, have the final say on major issues.
- They have checked the power of government, making it more responsive to the wishes of the people.
- They have enhanced political participation, notably in the Scottish independence referendum.
- They have educated people on key issues and improved popular understanding of politics.
- They have legitimised important constitutional changes such as devolution.

No

- They have undermined representative democracy, taking decision making on complex issues away from those with the most political knowledge or experience.
- They have undermined parliamentary sovereignty and, in the case of the 2016 EU referendum, created tensions between parliament and the people.
- Governments take advantage of their authority to decide whether and when to call referendums in order to strengthen their position, e.g. to legitimise their policies or resolve internal divisions.
- Turnout in referendums is often poor, with decisions taken on the basis of votes cast by a minority of eligible electors.
- Referendum campaigns have been ill-informed and distorted by inaccurate claims made by rival camps and media bias.

Parliamentary sovereignty and representative democracy

The doctrine of parliamentary sovereignty is the cornerstone of the British constitution. It states that parliament is the highest legal authority and can make law on any matter of its choosing. The predominance of parliament is also central to representative democracy. Citizens elect MPs to take decisions on their behalf: MPs are representatives who make up their own mind on issues rather than delegates who must follow instructions from voters.

The use of referendums on major constitutional issues marks a shift towards popular sovereignty in which the people, rather than parliament, take the ultimate decision. This has created competing claims of legitimacy. Most UK referendums are not legally binding and parliament retains the authority to respond as it sees fit — though legislation meant the government would have been required to change the electoral system in the case of a 'yes' vote in the 2011 AV referendum. A clash of competing claims of legitimacy was evident after the 2016 EU referendum. It was followed by debate on whether and how the government should invoke Article 50 of the Lisbon Treaty in order to leave the EU. Some people prioritised parliamentary sovereignty, arguing that the referendum had not authorised the terms of Brexit and that parliament must be asked to give its consent for the country to leave the EU. Others warned that attempts to bypass or dilute the referendum result would damage the legitimacy of the government and political system.

Chapter 3 examines how a number of developments, including devolution, EU membership and referendums, have weakened parliamentary sovereignty.

Constitutional convention

Since the 1997 devolution referendums, it has become a constitutional convention that further changes to the devolved settlement would require approval in a referendum. The Government of Wales Act 2006 permitted the Welsh Assembly to gain new powers if they were approved in a referendum — as happened in 2011. The Scotland Act 2016 states that the Scottish Parliament and government cannot be abolished unless approved in a referendum in Scotland.

What you should know

- Elections are central to politics in a liberal democracy. Their main functions include determining and legitimising the government, holding politicians to account, and ensuring the democratic participation and representation of the people.
- The first-past-the-post electoral system is used for general elections in the UK. A candidate in a single-member constituency needs only a plurality to win (i.e. one more vote than their nearest rival). Supporters of FPTP claim that it produces strong, stable and responsible government. Critics argue that it is disproportional, results in wasted votes and denies voters real choice.
- Four other electoral systems are used for elections beyond Westminster: the supplementary vote, the closed list system, the single transferable vote and the additional member system.
- These new electoral systems have produced more proportional outcomes than FPTP, although smaller parties may still be under-represented. They have also led to minority and coalition governments, reflecting the development of multiparty systems in the UK.
- The impetus for electoral reform for Westminster stalled when the 2011 referendum delivered a decisive 'no' to the question of introducing the alternative vote system.
- A series of referendums have been held in the last 20 years. This raises questions about the relationship between parliamentary and popular sovereignty.

UK/US comparison

Electoral systems

- There are separate elections for the president and for Congress in the USA. Presidential elections take place every 4 years. Members of the House of Representatives are elected every 2 years. Senators serve a 6-year term but there are rolling elections, with one-third of the Senate elected every 2 years. Hundreds of thousands of other positions (from judges to local officials) are subject to election. In the UK, the prime minister is not directly elected.
- Members of the House of Representatives are elected in single-member constituencies known as districts. Each of the 50 US states sends two representatives to the Senate. In the UK, the House of Lords is unelected.
- The single-member plurality system is used for Elections to Congress. In presidential elections, the candidate who secures a plurality of votes in a state receives all the Electoral College votes for that state. As in the UK, single-member plurality can deliver a winner's bonus and may produce the 'wrong' result — Republican candidates won the 2000 and 2016 presidential elections despite polling fewer votes than their Democratic opponents.
- The USA retains a classic two-party system while it is in decline in the UK. The Republicans and Democrats win the vast majority of votes and seats in Congress. Since the 1850s, the presidential election has been won by either a Republican or Democratic candidate — a candidate from a third party has not taken office.

Further reading

Curtice, J. (2015) 'A return to normality? How the electoral system operated', *Parliamentary Affairs*, Vol. 68, No. 4, pp. 25–40.

Hawkins, O., Keen, R. and Nakatudde, N. (2015) *Briefing Paper: General Election 2015*, House of Commons Library.

Johnston, R. (2011) 'Which electoral systems are best for Westminster?', *Politics Review*, Vol. 21, No. 2, pp. 2–5.

Kelly, R. (2014) 'Britain's European elections 2014: party list vindicated?', *Politics Review*, Vol. 24, No. 1, pp. 2–5.

Kelly, R. (2015) 'Assessing the UK's electoral system: first-past-the-post revalidated?', *Politics Review*, Vol. 25, No. 1, pp. 28–31.

Lundberg, T. (2013) 'UK electoral systems: are they all flawed?', *Politics Review*, Vol. 23, No. 2, pp. 30–33.

Electoral Commission: www.electoralcommission.org.uk

Electoral Reform Society: www.electoral-reform.org.uk

Political Science Resources (UK general election results): www.politicsresources.net/area/uktable.htm

Exam-style questions

Short-answer questions

1 Explain, with examples, proportional representation.

2 Explain, with examples, the workings of referendums in the UK.

3 Explain and analyse three arguments in favour of retaining the first-past-the-post electoral system for general elections.

4 Explain and analyse three reasons for holding referendums in the UK.

Mid-length questions

1 Describe the main functions of elections in the UK political system.

2 Describe the main features of the first-past-the-post electoral system.

3 Analyse and evaluate the arguments in favour of reforming the Westminster electoral system.

4 Analyse and evaluate the arguments against the greater use of referendums in the UK.

Essay questions

1 Evaluate the view that elections promote democracy and participation in the UK political system.

2 Evaluate how far alternative electoral systems introduced since 1997 have benefited the UK political system.

3 Analyse and evaluate criticisms of the various electoral systems used in the UK.

4 'The first-past-the-post electoral system is no longer fit for purpose.' Analyse and evaluate this statement.

Chapter 11

Voting behaviour and the role of the media in politics

> **Key questions answered**
> - How do different regions of the UK vote?
> - How do class, gender, age and ethnicity affect voting?
> - Why have voting trends changed in the UK?
> - How can voting choices be explained?
> - What role do party leaders play in determining voter choice?
> - How have voting trends changed across elections?
> - What role do the media play in politics?

John Major's victory in the 1992 election defied expectations and opinion polls

On Saturday, 11 April 1992, the *Sun* newspaper published the headline 'It's the Sun Wot Won It'. In what turned out to be an extraordinarily close election, John Major's Conservative Party defied expectations and opinion polls to win a slim 21-seat majority. The final result saw the Conservatives gain 14,093,007 votes to Labour's 11,560,484, or 41.9% to 34.4%. The turnout for the election was 77.7%, the highest it had been for 18 years, and the number of votes for the Conservatives remains the highest won by a single party in any election.

So, was it 'the Sun Wot Won It'? Certainly a number of Conservative MPs credited the *Sun* with at least part of their victory and the losing Labour leader, Neil Kinnock, blamed the newspaper for defeat after it ran a negative personal campaign against him.

The 1992 election reflects some of the most important issues in UK politics:
- Which groups of voters turned out and who did they vote for?
- How did turnout affect the result?
- What issues kept the Conservatives in power?
- What role did the personalities of the main leaders play?
- Why did the opinion polls get it wrong?
- What role did the media play in the election?

Many of these issues raise themselves repeatedly in UK elections. There are always multiple issues at play in an election, with each one contributing to the outcome.

How do different regions of the UK vote?

The geographic breakdown of the UK (see Table 11.1) helps to explain recent electoral results.
- The Conservatives have continued to do well in areas that are predominantly white, rural or suburban and socially conservative.
- Since 2005, Labour Party support has contracted to industrial urban areas in south Wales, the industrial north and London.

Table 11.1 Recent regional voting trends in the UK

Region	Voting preferences	Reasons
Scotland	Left wing, traditionally Labour, but since 2015 there has been an SNP dominance but with a return of unionist parties in 2017, particularly the Conservatives	Opposition to London-centred policies and New Right policies Specific social and economic problems in Scotland The impact of devolution
Wales	A heavy Labour bias, but with strong levels of support for the Conservatives	Industrial areas favour Labour Rural areas vote Conservative or Liberal Democrat The far west is more likely to vote nationalist
Northern Ireland	Has its own party system, with a split between unionist and nationalist parties	The party votes reflect religious and cultural divisions in the region
London	Majority Labour	Increasing ethnic diversity Greater economic disparity across the city Reliance on public services More socially liberal than other regions
Rural England	Overwhelmingly Conservative	Mostly white Economically conservative Socially conservative
Industrial north of England	Mostly Labour	Higher levels of unemployment than elsewhere in the country Greater rates of poverty and urban decay Greater ethnic diversity
The Home Counties	Predominantly Conservative	London commuter belt, made up of C1, B and A classes (see Table 11.2) Mostly white More conservative than London Economically prosperous

- Urban areas are now increasingly Labour strongholds and less inclined to vote Conservative, compared to the period before the 1980s.
- Scottish voters have very different concerns and priorities from the rest of the UK.
- Labour has lost its dominance in Scotland after concentrating on winning seats in England, while 2017 saw the establishment of the Conservative Party as the main opposition in Scotland.
- In southeast England, traditional party politics is becoming far more divided, with votes for UKIP and the Green Party reducing support for the three traditional parties.

How do class, gender, age and ethnicity affect voting?

Class

Traditionally, British society was divided into three classes based on wealth and how money was earned:
- upper class — landowners (the nobility)
- middle class — property owners
- working class — labourers

As British society has evolved, the class system has also developed into a more diverse set of groups (see Table 11.2).

Table 11.2 Modern class categories

Class	Nature of employment
A	Higher managerial and professional workers, such as business owners and judges
B	Middle managers and professionals, such as store managers, teachers and lawyers
C1	Clerical workers, such as office clerks and secretaries
C2	Skilled manual workers, such as builders, electricians and plumbers
D	Semi-skilled and unskilled workers, such as day labourers and factory workers
E	The unemployed, pensioners and those unable to work

Key terms

Class dealignment Where people no longer vote according to their social class.

Class voting The idea that people will vote for a party based on the economic interests of their class.

Core voter Any group of voters who will loyally vote for a party, regardless of any personal issues.

Floating (swing) voters Voters who are not loyal to a party and are therefore open to persuasion.

Partisan dealignment The idea that people are less committed or loyal to one particular party.

Social class A way of categorising people based on their status in society, usually by occupation or income.

Until the 1980s, class often determined how a person would vote. This is known as **class voting**. Classes A, B and C1 would usually be described as middle class and tended to vote Conservative. Classes C2, D and, to a large extent, E would be described as working class and tended to vote Labour.

This meant each party had a set of **core voters** from a distinct **social class**, reflecting the fact that economic factors, such as employment and inflation, were the top concern of many people. As a result, the two main parties presented a clear, class-based choice to the electorate. This explains why, in 1970, 88% of all votes went to the two main parties.

Since the 1970s, economic reforms and changing attitudes in society have resulted in a decline in the importance of economic issues and greater concern about social issues, including:

- immigration
- civil and human rights
- crime
- welfare provision
- attitudes to sex and sexuality
- Britain's position in the world

Many of these issues have an economic dimension but they tend to be considered from an emotional and social point of view. As they cross the class-based divisions, they have resulted in **class dealignment** which has seen people less likely to vote according to their class.

This widening of the issues considered important by the electorate has also led to **partisan dealignment**, with voters less likely to be loyal to one party and taking into consideration multiple issues before casting their vote. This in turn has led to an increase in **floating (swing) voters**.

The weakening of the class system across the UK has seen the emergence of a more diverse set of political struggles between the parties, particularly at election time. While elections from 1945 to 1992 were more or less a straight contest between Labour and the Conservatives, by 2015 the contest involved at least six key parties, all dealing with issues that crossed class lines.

Then again, despite the competition between many parties during the election campaign and leadership debates, the results seemed to show a emergence of the Conservative/Labour division, with 82.4% of the vote going to these two parties, the highest proportion since 1970. However, this alone does not prove the re-emergence of the class system because education, rather than class, proved to be the major factor in determining how people voted.

In April 2013 Professor Mike Savage published a new way of defining class distinctions, reflecting the growing diversity and lack of clarity in the class system since the 1960s.

Using the link below, visit the BBC report and take the online quiz to see what class you are.
www.tinyurl.com/ozbfq25

Then answer the following questions:
- How does the new model differ from the traditional model?
- Under the new system, which classes would be the most important? Why?
- How could this new system be used to explain general election results in 2010 and 2015?
- What social class were you? Do you agree or disagree with this result? Explain your reasons.

2017 general election

The results from the 2017 election (see Table 11.3) show that:
- The share of Conservative and Labour votes increased markedly
- Smaller party votes declined dramatically, particualrly UKIP
- The Conservative vote share remained constant in the AB and C1 categories, but increased dramtically among the C2 and DE voters, usually associated with Labour
- Labour's vote share with the DE groups remained stable, but they saw a significant increase in vote share among the C1 and AB groups, usually associated with the Conservatives
- The Liberal Democrat vote remained fairly stable
- The Green vote fell typically by 3% by class, most likely moving to Labour
- It appears that the collapse in UKIP votes was due to these going to the Conservatives in the C2 and DE categories

Table 11.3 Voting by class in 2015 and 2017 (status of vote %)

Social Class	2015					2017				
	Conservative	Labour	Liberal Democrats	UKIP	Green	Conservative	Labour	Liberal Democrats	UKIP	Green
AB	45	26	12	8	4	46	38	10	1	2
C1	41	29	8	11	4	41	43	8	1	2
C2	32	32	6	19	4	47	40	6	2	1
DE	27	41	5	17	3	41	44	5	4	2

Source: Ipsos MORI

Using Table 11.3 and any other sources, explain the effects of class turnout in the 2017 general election.

Case study

Case study

The 'left behind' voters in 2015

Working-class people, or C2, D and E class, vote Labour, do they not? People from these groups usually:

- oppose austerity measures
- object to benefits for the wealthy
- support welfare spending

So why did Labour do so badly in the general election of 2015?

The answer lies in the rise of the 'left behind' voters. These traditionally working-class voters would have voted for Labour in the past, but cultural concerns over immigration and income inequality, as well as a perception that politics is dominated by a socially liberal, educated and urban elite, have alienated them from the Labour Party. Instead, they have gravitated towards UKIP, which reflects their concerns. This reveals partisan dealignment and the fact that Labour cannot rely on class as a means of getting votes.

Questions

- As leader of the Labour Party, has Jeremy Corbyn appealed to these 'left behind' voters, or alienated them further?
- It appears that, in 2017, the Conservatives won the support of the 'left behind' voters. Explain why you think that would be.

In focus

'Left behind' voters

This is a term used to identify a group of voters who feel left behind by the social and economic reforms that have occurred in the UK over the past 50 years and who believe that their lives and the country have changed for the worse. They tend to be economically left-wing but culturally right-wing.

Left-behind voters also tend to be:

- older
- white
- financially poorer
- less educated (typically only to GCSE level)
- live in deprived areas, outside major cities

Debate

Does the class system still matter in UK politics?

Yes

- Issues of tax and benefits remain a key distinction between the two main parties.
- Many voters do still identify with a party based on their perceived class.
- Geographic voting trends still reflect the relative wealth and class make-up of a region or constituency.
- Class inequality and a lack of social mobility remain major concerns for many voters.

No

- Major issues, such as immigration, cross class divisions.
- The size and role of the working class has declined by more than a half, making it less of a political presence.
- Increasing property ownership and improved education make it more difficult to categorise classes.
- Successful parties have to appeal across a wide range of issues, not just those relating to class.

- With the Conservative vote remaining the same in the AB and C1 categories, it appears that former UKIP voters did vote Conservative, but that a number of Conservatives (as well as Greens and Liberal Democrats) switched their votes to Labour, giving Labour a significant boost in these usually strong Conservative areas.
- The end result shows that class was not a major dividing line in the 2017 general election, with the AB and C1 groups voting 44% Conservative and 40% Labour and the C2 and DE classes voting 44% Conservative and 42% Labour
- Instead of class, education is now a factor, with 55% of those with GCSEs or below voting Conservative and 49% of those with a degree or above voting Labour.

Gender

Gender is clearly an important issue for political parties, which have been making concerted efforts to appeal to women over the course of recent elections:

- In 2015, Labour's Woman to Woman pink minibus visited 75 constituencies, targeting women who did not vote in the previous election.
- In 2014, David Cameron declared that Britain would 'lead the change on women's equality'.
- In 2014, Jo Swinson launched the Liberal Democrats' campaign to push for equal pay and increased childcare provision.
- In 2010, David Cameron worked to increase the number of female Conservative MPs.
- In 1997, Tony Blair introduced all-women shortlists to increase the number of women in parliament.
- In 2017, Labour committed to conducting a gender impact assessment on all policies and legislation.

These approaches show that the issue of who women vote for has shaped some of the policies of the parties and the campaign methods they use. However, there is some debate over whether there is such a thing as 'the woman's vote'.

Traditionally, women are believed to favour the Conservatives, with Labour only winning a larger share of the female vote under Tony Blair. In 1970, Ted Heath's Conservatives won a surprise victory over Harold Wilson's Labour Party. It was believed that the 'housewives' had swung the election for Heath. His promise of economic stability, protection for the price of the weekly shop and a stable society were believed to have appealed to mothers with family concerns, from all classes.

Table 11.4a Voting by gender in 2015

	Share of vote (%)					
Gender	Conservative	Labour	Liberal Democrats	UKIP	Green	Other
All	38	31	8	13	4	6
Male	38	30	8	14	4	6
Female	37	33	8	12	4	6

Source: Ipsos MORI

Table 11.4b Voting by gender in 2017

Gender	Share of vote (%)				
	Conservative	Labour	Liberal Democrats	UKIP	Green
All	42.5	40	7.5	2	2
Male	45	39	8	2	2
Female	43	43	7	1	2

Source: yougov.com

The general election of 2015 appeared to show that gender was not, in fact, a crucial factor in determining votes, with only a small male bias toward the Conservatives and UKIP and slight female bias towards Labour but the difference relatively small. In the 2017 general election, the female vote split evenly for the two main parties, but crucially the Conservatives won the male vote by 6%, giving them the national advantage over Labour.

On most issues, there is little difference in opinion between men and women. The exceptions to this are:

■ Foreign intervention (war)
■ Nuclear power
■ Nuclear weapons

Men tend to prioritise these factors, while women tend to prioritise health and education. The clear divisions between Jeremy Corbyn and Theresa May over international relation and nuclear power and weapons perhaps explain the Conservative victory with male voters and why they remained the largest party in Westminster in 2017. However, gender does not explain why the Conservatives lost their majority and Labour made substantial gains.

Age

Age plays two significant roles in the way UK voters cast their votes:

■ Younger voters lean left, while older voters lean right.
■ The older the voter, the more likely they are to vote.

Table 11.5 shows that the percentage of Conservative and UKIP voters increases with age, while the percentage of Labour and Green Party voters drops with age.

In theory, this should balance out, but the parties of the left have two disadvantages:

■ The younger the voter, the less likely they are to vote.
■ Britain's ageing population means the elderly population is growing as a percentage of the total population.

This means there are more older people and they are more likely to vote. Social platforms and online polling tend to focus on the young, which distorts the reality of what happens in the polling stations and might explain why the Labour Party often does worse than expected while the Conservative Party quite often does better.

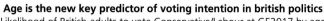

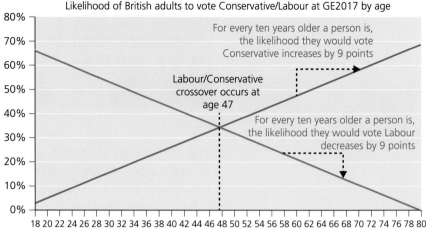

Age is the new key predictor of voting intention in british politics
Likelihood of British adults to vote Conservative/Labour at GE2017 by age

For every ten years older a person is, the likelihood they would vote Conservative increases by 9 points

Labour/Conservative crossover occurs at age 47

For every ten years older a person is, the likelihood they would vote Labour decreases by 9 points

Age

Source: YouGov

Figure 11.1 The percentage of Conservative voters increases with age, while the percentage of Labour voters decreases with age

Parties know the significance of age to voting and tend to tailor their policies accordingly. A substantial increase in university fees will hit the young, who do not vote, but promising to protect or even increase pensions will please the elderly, who do vote. Pension reforms, the NHS, law and order and limited social reform are areas of particular concern to the elderly and these are the areas the parties tend to focus on in their manifestos and campaigns. Issues about housing for the young, youth unemployment, university fees and reform of drug laws are given far less priority because the people whom these issues appeal to are not likely to vote — a lesson Ed Miliband learned in the 2015 election.

Table 11.5 Voting by age in 2017

Age	Share of vote (%)					Turnout
	Conservative	Labour	Liberal Democrats	UKIP	Green	
18–19	19	66	9	1	2	57%
20–24	22	62	9	1	2	59%
25–29	23	63	7	1	2	64%
30–39	29	55	8	1	2	61%
40–49	39	44	8	2	2	66%
50–59	47	37	7	3	2	71%
60–69	58	27	7	2	1	77%
70+	69	19	7	2	1	84%

Source: Ipsos MORI

As Table 11.5 shows, age is perhaps the key determining factor in how a person will vote, with 47 proving to be the age at which voters are most likely to move their support from Labour to the Conservatives. Although much was made in the wake of the 2017 general election of Jeremy Corbyn's ability to enthuse the young and motivate them to vote, they still remained far less likely to vote than older voters. Clearly there was a significant increase in the turnout of the under-30s in 2017, but more importantly, Labour was able to win a signficantly higher percentage of the under-30 vote (around two-thirds), which the Conservatives couldn't quite match with the 50–70 age bracket.

Ethnicity

As with age, race seems to point to a clear partisan divide in the UK, with white voters leaning more to the right and ethnic minority voters leaning more to the left.

The tendency for voters from an ethnic minority to favour Labour has two possible sources:

- The legacy of anti-minority campaigning by the Conservative Party, such as Enoch Powell's 'Rivers of Blood' speech (1968), where he criticised the Labour government's immigration and anti-discrimination legislation, and Norman Tebbit's 'Cricket test' (1990), where he criticised South Asian and Caribbean immigrants for their lack of loyalty to the England cricket team.
- The concentration of many ethnic minority groups into industrial urban centres, such as London, Birmingham, Manchester, Leeds and Bradford.

The mass immigration that began in the 1950s brought a new wave of workers to the UK, who often found themselves in urban areas doing industrial labouring. Although there were tensions within the Labour movement, these new citizens benefited from Labour polces of social equality. During the 1960s and 1970s, many Conservative Party members played on 'white fright' and fears about the changing nature of British society to win elections. These actions and the Conservative Party's association with a rural and higher-class electorate have meant that Labour has continued to hold a great deal of support among ethnic minority voters. However, 87.1% of the UK population is white British, and minority voters are less likely to turn out to vote (see Table 11.6).

Table 11.6 Voting by ethnicity in 2015

Social class	Share of vote (%)						Turnout
	Conservative	Labour	Liberal Democrats	UKIP	Green	Other	
White	39	28	8	14	4	7	68%
All black and minority ethnic (BME)	23	65	4	2	3	3	56%

Source: Ipsos MORI (www.tinyurl.com/h99wm86)

> ### Activity
>
> Discuss the impact of race on the MPs who are elected. In the 2015 general election, all ethnic minority Labour MPs were elected in constituencies that had a majority of voters from the same ethnic background. In contrast, ethnic minority Conservative MPs came from the safest Conservative seats, with the least number of ethnic minority voters.
>
> What does this suggest about the nature of race for these parties?

Changes in voting trends

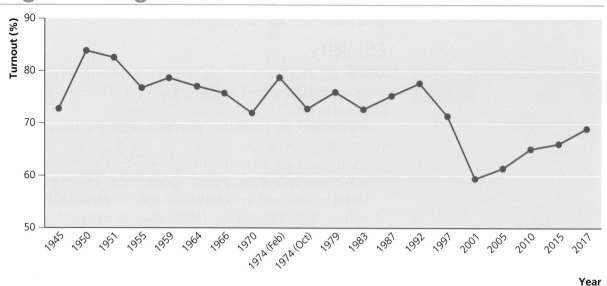

Figure 11.2 Declining turnout, 1945–2017

Source: UK Political Info

Since 1992, there has been a sharp drop in voter turnout in the UK (see Figure 11.2). This has raised concerns over democtratic legitimacy and public engagment in politics. It also has an effect on which party wins in an election and who forms the government. There is no clear reason to explain why voter turnout has declined but there are some theories as to why it has happened (see Table 11.7 on page 290).

Table 11.7 Theories about the decline in voter turnout

Theory about the decline in voter turnout	Reason why the theory is not convincing
A decline in **social capital** means that people are less inclined to feel they are part of society.	There has been a growth in rights culture and media engagement.
Declining standards in education mean people are less aware of their civic responsibilities.	Citizenship lessons mean citizens are better educated than ever before.
The first-past-the-post (FPTP) electoral system alienates the electorate because the number of seats won does not accurately reflect the number of votes received by a party.	An alternative voting system was rejected in a referendum vote in 2011 and turnout is even lower in UK elections which use other voting systems.
Partisan dealignment means people are less motivated to vote.	Party loyalty may have declined but people still engage through pressure groups and campaigns, yet they do not vote in elections.
An increase in ethnic minority citizens, who are less likely to vote, might explain a decline in turnout.	There has been an increase in the number of ethnic minorities in the UK but the increase began as far back as the 1950s and does not explain the scale of the fall in turnout since 1992.
Since the resignation of Thatcher in 1990, the Conservative and Labour parties have reached a consensus on several key issues. This post-Thatcher consensus has meant there is less real choice between the main parties.	Labour shifted moved further to the left under Brown, Miliband and then Corbyn, making a much clearer distinction between the two main parties.
The growth in issues and parties has made elections less clear cut and more difficult to understand.	People tend to cast their vote on the one or two issues that mean the most to them, so the fact that there are more issues is not relevant.
Sleaze and a negative culture spread by the media have turned people away from politics.	Scandals and sleaze have both existed in politics for many years. Turnout was not damaged by the scandal of the Profumo affair in the 1960s and was still at 71.4% in 1997, after 5 years of sleaze reporting.

Key term

Social capital The theory that politics requires cultural and moral resources to engage the people and make them feel part of society. As such, citizens have certain responsibilities and duties to make society work effectively.

Perhaps the real reason for the decline in turnout is the perception of lack of choice, or a deeply unappetising choice, which has existed since 1992:

- It was clear that Labour was going to win big in 1997 and the Conservatives were so mired in sleaze it was unlikely they would mount a serious challenge.
- In 2001, Tony Blair was still hugely popular and the Conservatives remained deeply divided over the issue of Europe, which would explain the all-time low of 59% turnout.
- Between 2001 and 2005, Blair had become tainted and distrusted, and was leading an increasingly fractious Labour Party as it approached the 2005 general election. Meanwhile, the Conservative Party remained deeply divided over Europe and had ousted the unpopular Iain Duncan Smith as leader in 2003, only to replace him with the slightly less unpopular Michael Howard, who led them into the 2005 general election.
- There was a more competitive election contest in 2010, which might explain the 4% jump in turnout, but the choice appeared to be between an unpopular Labour prime minister (Gordon Brown) and a Conservative Party that remained unpopular and divided.
- In 2015 the election promised to be close and exciting, yet turnout reached only 66%. This time an increasingly unpopular prime minister (David Cameron) and chancellor (George Osborne) led a divided party against an embattled and unpopular opposition leader (Ed Miliband).
- In 2017 turnout fears persisted over the competence of both main party leaders, with real concerns of May's style and Corbyn's ideology and competence. Issues, rather than the leaders, drove an increase in turnout, but not to the levels of 1992.

Debate

Are politicians to blame for declining turnout?

Yes
- They have failed to inspire the public.
- Scandals and corruption have turned people away from politics.
- Negative campaigning and adversarial politics have alienated many people.

No
- If the public are not happy with what is on offer, they need to make their voices heard, not stay silent.
- The media are responsible for undermining respect for politics in the UK.
- Low turnout reflects social and generational changes that politicians can do little about.

Activity

What is the main role of political parties? Is it to promote the interests of their core membership, or is it to win elections by appealing to as many groups as possible?

Explaining voter choice

Social factors may play a part in the decision-making process for people, but when a person votes, they do so as an individual and have to make their decision based on what is important to them. There are, broadly, three key theories which explain how individuals make their electoral choices:
- rational choice theory
- issue voting
- economic or valence issues

Rational choice theory

Rational choice theory assumes that voters will make a rational, or logical, judgement based on what is in their own best interests. In an ideal version, voters will be fully informed about the various options and will choose the option that is best for them. By aggregating these views, the winning verdict will reflect what is best for society as a whole. The assumption here is that a voter will conduct a cost/benefit analysis of all options and make their choice accordingly.

Issue voting

Where issue voting takes place, voters place one issue above all others and cast their vote based on that issue. They judge a party or candidate by their position on the issue and choose the one that most closely reflects their own opinion. This can mean they vote for a candidate whose other policies would be to their detriment.

Economic or valence issues

A valence issue is one where voters share a common preference (i.e. the desire for the country to be economically prosperous). In this theory, everyone wants a prosperous and successful economy, so no one will vote against a candidate who promises to improve the economy. Instead, they cast their vote based on who they believe is best placed to deliver a strong and successful economy. This idea is known as **governing competency**. Politicians will be rewarded if they deliver a strong economy but will be punished at the polls if the economy fails.

Factors affecting individual voting

The rise of partisan dealignment has seen a growing trend for voters to think more individualistically about their votes, using the models noted above. This means that a range of factors other than party loyalty have become more important:

- **Policies.** Voters consider the policies presented in the party manifestos and make a decision based on which set of policies suits them best. This is rational choice theory in action.
- **Key issues.** Party campaigns increasingly focus on a clear message about one issue they think will win them the election because voters increasingly cast their vote based on the issue that is most important to them.
- **Performance in office.** Using the economic and valence issues theory, voters tend to simplify the election into a referendum on the current government. If the economy does well, the government is rewarded with another term; if the economy does badly, the government is removed and the opposition is given a chance to govern.
- **Leadership.** The role of the leader has become increasingly important since Harold Wilson's time in office, and voters often take the view that they are selecting a prime minister rather than voting for a party or an MP. As a result, leaders must convince voters that they can be trusted to deliver and are capable of running the country, and they must deliver all this through a likable and engaging media presence.
- **Image.** Beyond the leadership issues, voters will make their choice based on their perception of the party's image, which is connected to issue voting.
- **Tactical voting.** Due to the nature of the first-past-the-post (FPTP) electoral system, many voters use **tactical voting** to determine their choice. If their preferred candidate is unlikely to win the seat, the voter will vote for their next favoured candidate if they think they have more chance of success. This is often done to try to prevent the candidate of the least favoured party from winning the seat.

The role of the party leader

There has always been a focus on the image of the party leader, but it was less pronounced back in 1945, when Winston Churchill is reported to have described Clement Attlee as 'a modest man, [with] so much to be modest about' while Margaret Thatcher described him as 'all substance and no show'. Yet, Attlee and Labour won a landslide majority against the more charismatic, and seemingly popular, Churchill. It would seem to suggest that rational choice theory played a role in that election, with voters choosing the manifesto that would provide them with the best quality of life in the postwar world. Since then, the role of the party leader seems to have become far more important in terms of general elections.

Party leaders — Nick Clegg, Ed Miliband and David Cameron — on the campaign trail in the 2015 general election

UK Government and Politics for AS/A-level

Key term

Spatial leadership A style of leadership where the prime minister relies on his or her own inner circle of advisers, rather than cabinet.

With the rise of **spatial leadership** in the UK, voters increasingly make their choice based on party leadership and who would be best placed to be prime minister. As a result, the personality and image of the party leader can play a significant role in determining voting behaviour. The role of the party leader is to:

- inspire the party activists
- appear prime ministerial
- have a positive media presence
- appear strong in leading the party and, if elected, the nation

Indeed, the media increasingly focus on the character and image of the party leader above all other considerations because it is far easier to report on a single person than on a range of figures or policies (see Table 11.8).

Synoptic links

The serving prime minister enjoys a distinct advantage over potential rivals. With the exercise of the royal prerogative, spatial leadership and the media focus, prime ministers are regularly given the opportunity to present themselves as strong national leaders and to gain the confidence of the public.

Table 11.8 Public perceptions of party leaders in elections

Date	The successful party leader	The unsuccessful party leader
1964	Harold Wilson, presenting himself as a man of the people, who preferred tinned salmon to expensive smoked salmon...	...defeated the former peer and aristocratic Sir Alec Douglas-Home.
1983	Margaret Thatcher, who appeared as a strong, nationalistic leader after victory in the Falklands War...	...defeated Michael Foot, who was considered scruffy, and was particularly criticised for wearing a 'donkey jacket' (an untailored work jacket) when laying a wreath on Remembrance Sunday.
1992	John Major, a calm and reassuring figure, who was polite and gentlemanly...	...defeated Neil Kinnock, who had been labelled the 'Welsh windbag'.
1997	The young, charismatic and media savvy Tony Blair...	...defeated the 'straw man' or 'grey man' John Major, who was considered to be weak and boring.
2010	A smartly presented, reassuring and young David Cameron...	...defeated the dour, taciturn and 'dithering' Gordon Brown.
2015	After 5 years of showing himself capable of being prime minister, David Cameron...	...defeated Ed Miliband, who suffered from a poor media presence and images of having 'stabbed his brother in the back' in the Labour Party leadership election.
2017	The austere and arrogant May ran a poor campaign and lost seats, but defeated...	...the ideological Corbyn who made gains but still suffered from party divisions and concerns of his competence.

The Sean Bean/Mr Bean divide

In a 2014 ComRes poll, respondents were asked who would play Nigel Farage in a film. The most popular result was Rowan Atkinson in his Mr Bean persona, with Sean Bean coming in at a mere 8%. However, when the respondents were broken down by party, UKIP voters put Sean Bean top, with Daniel Craig a popular second or third choice. This effectively demonstrates partisan perceptions of party leaders. For non-UKIP supporters, Farage is seen as the buffoonish, selfish and comedic Mr Bean. For UKIP supporters, he is seen as a rugged and heroic English icon, taking on the forces of evil.

Question

Look at the current party leaders in the UK. For each, evaluate whether they are a help or hindrance to their party.

Are party leaders the main reason for a party's electoral fortunes?

Yes
- A strong leader will inspire confidence from floating voters.
- A strong performance will motivate the core voters and enthuse activists.
- A leader can maintain party discipline to ensure a unified party during an election campaign.

No
- People vote for their local MP, not for the prime minister.
- Other factors, such as major events that have affected public opinion (e.g. the Iraq War or the 2008 financial crash), are far more important.
- Core supporters will remain loyal despite the leadership.

Voting trends across elections

The Conservative Party's, 'Labour isn't working' poster for the 1979 general election

The 1979 general election

Background

After a narrow victory under Harold Wilson in October 1974, Labour had seen its majority disappear and its leader replaced by James Callaghan. By 1979, a vote of no confidence triggered an early election.

There were a number of other key issues at the time:
- How would the economic decline of the UK affect the vote?
- What impact would growing trade union strife have on the result?
- Would the New Right policies of the Conservatives alienate voters?
- Would the public vote for a party with a female leader?
- How would the Liberals fare after the Lib–Lab pact, agreed in 1977?
- Would the Labour Party be damaged by its extreme left component?

Key policies

The Labour Party focused on its ability to deal with the trade unions and the experience of its leader, James Callaghan. It adopted a moderate financial course and kept the left silent.

The Conservative Party focused on 'Labour isn't working' and insisted that Britain could be better. It proposed the right to buy scheme in housing and promised tax cuts.

The campaign

More than in any previous election, the mass media played a prominent role in the way the campaigns unfolded:

- Press conferences were timed to provide stories for the midday news.
- Afternoon walkabouts by leaders were designed to coincide with the early evening news.
- Major speeches were timed to catch the evening news.

Following polls that showed the public did not like an adversarial model of politics, the leaders of the two main parties avoided making attacks on each other. Callaghan referred to Thatcher simply as 'the leader of the Conservative Party' and the Conservatives toned down the insult-laden style of their broadcasts following criticism of the first one.

Despite this, the campaign was more presidential than ever, with most broadcast media focused on the personalities and attitudes of the two main leaders. This raised the question of the 'Thatcher factor' — whether her gender and personality would cause voter resentment under prolonged exposure.

The Thatcher factor did seem to be significant, as regular comparisons of the two leaders seemed to show potential voters were put off from voting for the Conservatives and the party lost some of its lead in the polls over the course of the campaign. When compared to Callaghan, Thatcher was considered to be:

- less experienced
- less in touch with ordinary people
- more extreme
- more condescending

These factors were compounded by the simple fact that she was not a man.

Labour and the Conservatives deliberately kept the radical wings of the parties silent. The New Right spokesperson, Sir Keith Joseph, and the leaders of the radical left, Tony Benn and Michael Foot, played little part in the campaign and were rarely to be heard. In this way, both parties concentrated on a low-key campaign that focused on the centre ground of politics, offering little real distinction other than the style of leadership.

Such a low-key campaign was 'won' by James Callaghan, whom voters preferred to Thatcher as their leader, but Labour had started a long way back in the polls and it was the Conservatives who won the election.

Impact

While the campaign led to a tighter election than the early polls had suggested, the result was a decisive rejection of Labour and a clear victory for the Conservatives (see Table 11.9).

Table 11.9 1979 election results (the Conservatives won a majority of 43 seats)

Party	Seats	Win/loss	Share of vote
Conservative	339	+62	43.9%
Labour	269	−50	37.0%
Liberal	11	−2	13.8%
Plaid Cymru	2	−1	0.4%
SNP	2	−9	1.6%
Other	12	0	3.3%

The campaign was dull and uninspiring. The fight for the middle ground offered little effective choice and the 1983 election saw both parties, Labour much more so, move further to their extreme wings.

The Conservative policies of right to buy and tax cuts were certainly popular ones and may have helped win over the C2 class vote. However, most voters appear not have favoured tax cuts at the expense of cuts to public spending. Policies were generally second to the mood for change following the 'Winter of Discontent', a period of widespread strike action during 1978–79.

Opinion polls may have played a role in the eventual outcome of the election — the closing gap between the two parties encouraged Labour supporters while the Conservatives became increasingly concerned about their policies. The closing gap may also have helped boost turnout for the Conservatives.

By focusing so heavily on the two major party leaders, 1979 set the trend by which future general elections would be judged as presidential-style contests rather than a choice between parties. The orchestration of the media and the focus on media image set the standard for future elections.

How did people vote?

The pattern of voting by location, class, gender, age and race in 1979 is shown in Table 11.10.

Table 11.10 Voting by location, class, gender, age and race, 1979

Geography	All areas swung towards the Conservatives, but the swing was much more pronounced in southern Britain.
Class	The Conservatives remained dominant with the AB and C1 voters. Labour won the C2 and DE vote but the Conservatives gained swings of 11% and 9% with these groups.
Gender	Men were evenly split between the two main parties. Women showed a slight preference for the Conservatives.
Age	Labour won the 18–24 age group. The Conservatives won across all other groups. Labour's support declined most among voters aged 35–54. The majority of Liberal support came from the 35–54 age group.
Race	Lack of data for black and minority ethnic (BME) voting in 1979 (under 5% of the population and not considered by parties or polling organisations).

The 1997 general election

Background

After a surprise victory in 1992, John Major's Conservative Party became intensely divided by the issue of the European Union. The Labour Party had seen leader Neil Kinnock replaced by John Smith in 1992. Smith died in office in 1994 and was replaced by Tony Blair, as Labour shifted to the right.

There were a number of other key issues at the time:

■ How would the economic crisis and being ejected from the European Exchange Rate Mechanism (ERM) affect the economic reputation of the Conservatives?
■ Would Blair's 'Third Way' appeal to enough moderate voters while still enthusing the traditional left?
■ What impact would the legacy of sleaze have on the election?
■ Would the Liberal Democrats make a breakthrough to become a major party?
■ How might tensions over Europe affect Conservative voters?

Key policies

Leading Conservatives wanted to focus on economic recovery, but internal divisions and the presence of the Referendum Party meant the issue of Europe dominated the Conservative campaign, leaving Labour free to present its 'Third Way' economic policy.

Labour focused on reassurances about the economy and five specific pledges: to cut class sizes, to introduce a fast-track punishment system for young offenders, to cut NHS waiting lists, to get 250,000 unemployed under 25-year-olds into work, and to cut VAT on heating and not raise income tax.

The Liberal Democrats focused on democratic reforms to create greater equality.

The campaign

The 1997 campaign was to be a 6-week ordeal, longer than the 31-day average of campaigns since 1959. John Major hoped this would put pressure on Tony Blair and expose divisions within the Labour Party.

The campaigns of the two major parties focused on the leaders, touring marginal seats on campaign buses and planes. The manifestos reflected the themes of the parties:

■ Conservatives 'You can only be sure with the Conservatives'
■ Labour 'Because Britain deserves better'
■ Liberal Democrats 'Make the difference'

Labour ran a strict, disciplined campaign from Millbank Media Centre, run by Tony Blair, Gordon Brown, Peter Mandelson, Alistair Campbell and Philip Gould. The Conservatives highlighted the dangers of Blair and the Labour Party restoring power and influence to the trade unions and Blair not being trustworthy.

Sleaze, referring to the record of sex scandals and financial corruption among Conservative MPs, became a dominant issue in the campaign.

The issues of devolution and the Northern Ireland peace process also played a minor role in the campaign, with Labour promising to promote decentralisation and make the UK more democratic, while

A Conservative Party poster for the 1997 general election depicted Labour candidate Tony Blair with a pair of demonic red eyes

the Conservatives warned that these reforms, particularly devolution, would be a disaster for the UK. With 3 days to go in the campaign, they announced they had '72 hours to save the Union'.

Impact

The 1997 election marked a turning point in British elections and in British politics as a whole. After years of sleaze, a generally negative campaign drew high levels of cynicism towards politicians of all parties.

People saw little difference between the main parties on policies, leading to a rise in **disillusion and apathy**. A drawn-out campaign and opinion polls relentlessly pointing towards a substantial Labour win also engendered a sense of apathy.

The media focus on sleaze contributed to the rise in apathy, while the disciplined messages meant popular party figures sounded like robots.

Ultimately, the election campaign did little to change the result (see Table 11.11) as there is widespread belief that the financial recession of 1992 guaranteed that the Conservatives would not be returned to power. However, 1997 saw an enormous leap in disciplined, media-focused electioneering and a rise in US-style partisan claim and counter-claim advertising, which brought a more negative and confrontational style of campaigning to the UK.

> **Key term**
>
> **Disillusion and apathy** A process of disengagement with politics, leading to a decline in political activity, particularly in voting.

Table 11.11 1997 election results (Labour won a majority of 179 seats)

Party	Seats	Win/loss	Share of vote
Conservative	165	−171	30.7%
Labour	418	+147	43.2%
Liberal Democrats	46	+26	16.8%
Plaid Cymru	4	0	0.5%
SNP	6	+3	2.0%
Other	20	+3	6.8%

How did people vote?

The pattern of voting by location, class, gender, age and race in 1997 is shown in Table 11.12.

Table 11.12 Voting by location, class, gender, age and race, 1997

Geography	Labour gained votes across all regions, bucking the trend towards a Conservative south and Labour north. The Conservatives were wiped out in Scotland and Wales and reduced to 11 in London, becoming a party of the English suburbs and shires. The Liberal Democrats were evenly spread, but established a stronghold in the southwest.
Class	Labour gained support across all classes, with the largest gains being in the C1 (+19%) and C2 (+15%) groups.
Gender	Labour closed the gender gap with men and women equally likely to support them. There were only minimal differences between gender votes for any party.
Age	The Conservatives remained dominant among the voters aged 65+, but Labour won decisively among all other age groups.
Race	Labour beat the Conservatives among white voters, gaining 43% of the white vote, along with 70% of BME votes. The Conservatives won 32% of the white vote and 18% of BME votes. The Liberal Democrats received greater support from white voters, with 18% of the white vote and 9% of BME votes.

The 2010 general election

Background

Gordon Brown had inherited the office of prime minister in 2007, but decided against calling a snap election. He may well have won in 2007, but 2008 saw the greatest financial recession since the Great Depression of the 1930s.

There were a number of key issues at the time:

- How damaging would the recession be to the Labour Party?
- Had David Cameron done enough to detoxify the Conservatives?
- What role would the first-ever UK leaders' debates have in the campaign?
- What role would UKIP and other minor parties play in the election?

Key policies

The Conservatives focused on saving the NHS and on the need to save the economy through better management and efficiency savings.

Labour focused on Gordon Brown's economic management and action in preventing a worse economic collapse.

The Liberal Democrats focused on striking a compromise between the two main parties.

The campaign

This general election campaign saw the introduction of the first televised leaders' debates in the UK. The performance of Nick Clegg in the first debate raised his personal profile and led to genuine three-party reporting across the press, as well as the catchphrase 'I agree with Nick', from Gordon Brown. The debates continued the growing presidential-style contest of recent election campaigns.

Other traditional aspects of campaigning, including early-morning press conferences, launch initiatives, challenges to other parties, set-piece broadcast interviews and party political broadcasts, were marginalised as the media focus concentrated on the leaders and the debates.

The financial crisis meant there was little any party could do in terms of eye-catching policies, as all acknowledged cuts would need to be made and there was little money to spend.

Media support swung decisively behind the Conservatives, with only the *Mirror* and *Sunday Mirror* backing Labour.

The Conservatives benefited from greater financial resources, spending more than four times as much as Labour during the campaign. Labour had to cut its spending by two-thirds from 2005, so was less able to carry out polling and advertising. Instead, it relied on a larger number of committed activists and a grassroots campaign.

The campaign saw the first major use of the internet, with online reactions to debates, a clear web presence, online fundraising and independent viral campaigns. Social media played a clear role in the campaign, though not necessarily a decisive one. It made it more difficult for the parties to control the message being delivered and reported.

Debate

Were the televised leaders' debates important in the 2010 election campaign?

Yes
- They raised the profile of Nick Clegg.
- David Cameron lost vital support.
- They became the main 'event' of the election campaign and concentrated media attention.

No
- Shifts in the polls were marginal after the debates.
- They do not appear to have altered the result of the election.
- The second and third debates made little impact and few headlines.

Impact

The election result confirmed that Britain now had a multiparty political system (see Table 11.13).

Table 11.13 2010 election results (the Conservatives were 19 seats short of a majority; the Conservative–Liberal Democrat coalition had a majority of 78 seats)

Party	Seats	Win/loss	Share of vote
Conservative	307	+109	36.1%
Labour	258	−98	29.0%
Liberal Democrats	57	−5	23.0%
Plaid Cymru	3	+1	0.4%
SNP	6	0	1.7%
Other	19	−3	9.6%

The prominence of the television debates during the campaign meant it would be difficult to avoid holding them in the future.

Unlike in previous elections, the campaign played an important role in the eventual outcome. Liberal Democrat support rose by 3–4% while Conservative support fell by 2–3%. This was enough to prevent the Conservatives from gaining a clear majority.

Nick Clegg's increased media presence meant he was seen as a credible deputy prime minister and that the Liberal Democrats were a viable party of government, leading to acceptance of the UK's first peacetime coalition in 70 years.

How did people vote?

The pattern of voting by location, class, gender, age and race in 2010 is shown in Table 11.14.

Table 11.14 Voting by location, class, gender, age and race, 2010

Geography	Labour gained votes in Scotland, but lost them across England and Wales. The Conservatives gained votes in southern England, mainly those lost in 1997.
Class	The Conservatives saw strong swings from the C1 and C2 class categories. Labour gained a 10% swing from the DE category.
Gender	Men showed a slight preference for the Conservatives. Women tended to favour Labour and the Liberal Democrats.
Age	Labour narrowly won the 18–24 age group, though support was evenly divided across all three parties. The Conservatives won all other age groups, most decisively with voters aged 65+.
Race	The Conservatives mostly won among white voters, with 38% of the white vote and 16% of the BME vote. Labour was heavily supported by BME voters, with 68% of the BME vote, but only 28% of the white vote. The Liberal Democrats were the most equal party, with 24% of white votes and 20% of BME votes.

The 2017 general election

Background

Having repeatedly stated that there would be no early election, people were surprised when Theresa May announced on 18 April 2017 that she would be calling an early general election in order to provide a mandate to deal with Brexit. Despite the Fixed Term Parliament Act, May succeeded because Labour backed the calling of the early election. The key issues included:

- Were the polls accurate and would the Conservatives gain a landslide majority?
- Would this be an election dominated by Brexit and questions of leadership, or something else?
- What role would the smaller parties, particularly UKIP, play in this election?
- Was this a gamble worth taking?

Key policies

Although mostly focused on Brexit, the Conservatives continued with policies relating to austerity with promises to protect the NHS, but making cuts to other services and major reforms in education.

Labour announced a number of polices that would improve welfare provision and increased investment, while pledging to abolish university tuition fees and introduce four new bank holidays.

The Liberal Democrats under Tim Farron focused on the type of Brexit, fighting for a second referendum after the negotiations, while also offering a series of social reforms to be funded by increases in taxation as well as potential cuts.

UKIP focused on ensuring the Conservatives would commit to a hard Brexit with no backsliding, while the SNP promised to fight for Scotland's interests in the Brexit negotiations, and the potential for another independence referendum after the negotiations.

The campaign

With the surprise announcement, the first weeks of the campaign were relatively quiet, with many party activists already focusing on the local council elections and regional mayoral elections taking place in early May. At the start, the Conservatives held a dominant led in the opinion polls over Labour.

Much was made of the leadership debates. Theresa May stated from the beginning that she would not be participating in any head-to-head debates, claiming she would rather be meeting voters and that she had already debated with Jeremy Corbyn regularly at PMQs. Initially, Corbyn also pulled out of the debates because May was not participating, leaving the first debate a rather flat affair. However, for the second leadership debate on 31 May, Corbyn announced that he would attend, and Amber Rudd stood in for May. While the other leaders attacked Theresa May for not attending, Corbyn was able to present himself as a contrast to her and suggest he was more prime ministerial.

The campaign was also marked by a number of policy missteps by the Conservatives, as decisions were taken by May's top advisers, Fiona

Hill and Nick Timothy, with Philip Hammond being largely marginalised. The 'Dementia Tax' triggered an embarrassing U-turn within 24 hours of the manifesto launch, while commitments to grammar schools and the removal of the triple lock on pensions alienated some of the core voters.

Liberal Democrat leader Tim Farron was forced to deal with his faith as attacks were made in the early days on his position on gay rights, while Labour's Diane Abbot had a series of media blunders where she forgot key pieces of information. During the campaign though, Corbyn was seen repeatedly addressing large, enthusiastic crowds, while May was seen speaking to small groups in closed locations.

In a final twist, two terrorist attacks took place in the two weeks before the election, one at a concert in Manchester and the other at Borough Market in London. Usually such an event would have played to the strengths of the Conservatives on law and order, but questions were raised about cuts to police services and the failure of the Home Office to deal with suspects before the attacks. Although Diane Abbot had misspoken over police numbers, she had been calling for increases. When compared to the Conservative cuts to policing, these events undermined confidence in Theresa May's leadership skills and the poll lead was further reduced.

Impact

The election appeared to suggest a return to traditional two-party politics. Both the Conservatives and Labour increased their share of the vote, by 5.5% and 9.5% respectively, mostly at the expense of UKIP and other small parties (see Table 11.15).

Table 11.15 2017 election results (a hung parliament)

Party	Seats	Win/loss	Share of vote
Conservative	318	−13	42.4%
Labour	262	+30	40%
Liberal Democrats	12	+4	7.4%
Plaid Cymru	4	+1	0.5%
SNP	35	−21	3%
Other	19	−1	6.7%

Despite gaining 42.4% of the vote, almost 6% more than David Cameron had in 2015, Theresa May lost 13 seats, resulting in a hung parliament for the second time in seven years. May pledged to carry on with support from the DUP who had 10 seats, but her position as leader of the Conservatives and as prime minister had been severely weakened, especially after the tragedy of the Grenfell tower fire a week later.

By gaining 30 seats and 40% of the vote, Jeremy Corbyn secured his place as Labour leader and silenced many of the critics who had been expecting a 1983 style 'wipeout'. The number of votes he achieved were more than that won by Tony Blair in 2005.

UKIP's share of the vote fell from 12.6% to 1.8% and leader Paul Nuttall resigned as a result. The Liberal Democrats did gain four seats, but their vote fell by 0.5%, which, along with challenges to his faith, led to the resignation of Tim Farron.

In Scotland, a unionist revival took place, led by the Conservatives. Labour and the Liberal Democrats also gained seats from the SNP, so although they remained the largest party, their total fell to 35 seats.

How did people vote?

The pattern of voting by location, class and gender in 2017 is considered below. At the time of writing, information about voting by race was not available.

Table 11.16 Voting by location, class, gender, age and race, 2017

Geography	Rural England remains predominantly Conservative, but Labour gained in some areas, notably in Canterbury and Ipswich in the south east. Labour remained strong in the urban centres and continued to gain strength in London. The SNP fell back in Scotland, with the most gains there coming from the Conservatives, but Labour and the Liberal Democrats also. gaining as an anti-nationalist backlash emerged. The Liberal Democrats gained in London, Scotland and Bath, but lost their seats in Wales and Yorkshire. UKIP were wiped out nationally.
Class	The Conservatives made rapid gains among the C2 and DE categories while Labour gained votes among the AB and C1 groups, meaning that the class divisions were minimal.
Gender	Female voters broke evenly for the Conservatives and Labour, but the male vote leant towards the Conservatives by 6%.
Age	A clear division was shown, with a person 9% more likely to vote Conservative for every ten years they age, with the turning point being 47. In this election the young came out in greater force. Although still the lowest group to turn out, their increase in turnout was significant and predominantly went to Labour.

The role of the media in politics

The media include broadcasting, publishing and the internet as a means of communication.

Print media

- **Broadsheet media.** Usually seen as 'highbrow', these deal with weighty political debates and present information in a measured, if partisan, way.
- **Tabloid media.** These are populist newspapers which focus more on sensation and entertainment.
- **Magazines.** These can provide an important check and help to inform high-level debates as political and satirical magazines produce detailed reports on political activity and scrutinise the work of politicians.

Radio media

- **News headlines.** Every radio station has to give regular news broadcasts, usually on the hour. These are basic, informative headlines that present information without analysis or bias.
- **Commercial radio.** There are a number of talk radio stations designed to engage in political discussion and debate.

- **BBC radio.** This has many platforms for political discussion, with a number of flagship political programmes which interview and challenge politicians and public perceptions, as well as phone-in shows to encourage political debate.

TV media

- **News broadcasts.** All terrestrial channels are obliged to have regular and impartial news broadcasts, which occur at set times and for a set duration.
- **Party political broadcasts.** These are 5-minute broadcasts that occur at set times, usually after a news broadcast, across the channels. There are regulations to ensure that all parties are given a fair and equal chance to influence public opinion.
- **News channels.** These provide 24-hour news coverage which can drive political events by raising public awareness and 'hyping' events to make them appear more serious than they are.
- **Political programming.** This involves extended interviews and discussion of political issues, allowing the public to engage and sometimes participate.

Online media

- **Opinion polls.** Online polls are conducted online with greater frequency and they are cheaper to run than traditional polls.
- **Blogs.** These provide sources of information and a forum for discussion about political issues.
- **Twitter.** The platform can provide an informal poll to assess the popularity of an issue or the performance of politicians. It can also provide a forum for political debate.
- **Campaigning.** Parties will use viral videos, social media and other tools to test ideas and messages before committing to traditional media. They might also use it as a source of unregulated campaigning.
- **Websites.** Parties and politicians have their own websites which provide a means to find out about policies, raise issues and donate to the party.

Key term

Opinion poll A survey of public opinion from a sample of the population at a given moment. They are often used to determine the expected results of an election.

Opinion polls

The role of **opinion polls** has increased considerably since the 1970s. Parties, think-tanks, interested individuals and the media all commission a variety of opinion polls to try to work out how the respective parties are faring. These polls are often used to test key policies, leadership performance and the success of a campaign. Opinion polls are also used by the media as a starting point for political discussion and reporting.

When they are done well, polls can be a useful tool to help parties tailor their policies and messages to target key demographics and ensure they appeal to voters' concerns. When they are done badly, polls can misrepresent public opinion and affect the way in which people vote.

The role of the polls in the 2015 general election

In 2015, opinion polls tended to show Labour and the Conservatives in a tight race. This drove media speculation about the possibility of a Miliband government and greater scrutiny of Labour as a possible party of government, rather than focusing on the track record of the Conservative–Liberal Democrat coalition government. The polls also suggested a hung parliament, with speculation that a Miliband government might form a coalition with the SNP or that a Conservative government might form a coalition with UKIP.

Possible effects

- Some voters may have employed tactical voting by voting for the Conservatives instead of UKIP in order to prevent a Labour–SNP coalition.
- Many Liberal Democrat voters may have voted for the Conservatives as the lesser of two evils due to concerns about Ed Miliband, the SNP and UKIP.

- Conservatives may have been motivated to turn out to vote by fear of a Labour victory.
- Labour voting may have been depressed because supporters thought that the party was going to be victorious.
- People may have been more willing to vote for UKIP and the SNP in the belief they might become parties of government.

The polls certainly got the predictions wrong, overestimating the Labour vote and underestimating the Conservative vote. This was thought to be due to a reliance on online polling, which tends to be done by younger voters, who favour Labour, at the expense of traditional polling, which would have been more representative of the population.

Questions

- The polls also got it wrong in 1992. Do some research into why this happened and the effect it had on the election and then make a comparison with the 2015 election.
- Given the notable failures of the polls in the 2015 general election, the EU referendum and the 2016 US presidential election, should the results of polls continue to be made public during political campaigns?
- Explain how opinion polls may affect the way in which people vote.

The changing role of the media

The role of the media has traditionally been to:
- report accurately on political events
- provide a commentary on political events and policies
- act as a check and scrutinise the government of the day
- investigate controversies and bring them to public attention
- educate the public on major issues and explain the potential impact of the various options available
- provide a forum for public debate and discussion, and act as a bridge between the electorate and the elected

As we have seen, the media play quite a different role in politics today (see Table 11.17) and there have been many criticisms of the changes to this role:
- The press and online sources have become overly partisan and mock and ridicule rather than providing informed debate.
- They have created a national mood of cynicism towards politics and politicians by their focus on scandal and corruption.

- The focus on leaders and personalities has turned politicians into celebrities, instead of focusing on their roles as public servants with a job to do.
- The media have made entertainment out of politics.
- The focus on crises rather than concerns has led to sensationalism and helped create a negative public view of the world.
- The relentless pressure of 24-hour news means the media create stories and issues, and give minor issues more prominence than they warrant.
- The rise of online media platforms has led to to partisan and uninformed debate being presented as fact, causing the parties and the mainstream media to lose control of the agenda. This has resulted in a more partisan, opinion-orientated and susceptible electorate who are more superficially aware, but less engaged in the issues.

Table 11.17 Have the media influenced election results?

Event	Yes, it did influence the result	No, it did not influence the result
1979: 'Crisis, what crisis?' A headline in the *Sun* newspaper in relation to the 'Winter of Discontent'	Although he never actually said it, this headline suggested James Callaghan was out of touch with ordinary voters and swung opinion against the formerly popular prime minister.	Opinion polls showed Callaghan as Labour's strongest asset and he was generally ahead of Thatcher throughout the election campaign.
1992: 'We're alright' A claim made repeatedly by Neil Kinnock at a rally in Sheffield	Television pictures showing Neil Kinnock as triumphalist a week before the election alienated some voters and caused some Labour voters to be more apathetic.	Happening a week before the election, it is unlikely that this, on its own, had the impact required to explain the different levels of support between the opinion polls and the election results.
1997: The *Sun* switches support from the Conservatives to Labour	After Tony Blair met with Rupert Murdoch, the *Sun* (and much of the rest of the press) declared support for Labour, leading to many voters switching their allegiance.	The press was simply reacting to the prevailing mood of the time, reflected in the polls, which was clearly swinging towards Labour.
2010: 'I agree with Nick' A statement made repeatedly by Gordon Brown and David Cameron during the first TV leaders' debate.	The performance of Nick Clegg in the TV debates raised his profile at the expense of David Cameron's, resulting in a hung parliament.	The Liberal Democrats only increased their share of the vote by 1% and actually lost seats in the election.
2010: MPs' expenses scandal exposed by the *Daily Telegraph* following a freedom of information request	The expenses scandal undermined the reputation of all MPs and led to many losing their seats and the Labour government being rejected at the polls.	Despite this cynicism, turnout was 4% higher than in 2005 and Labour were set to lose anyway after the financial collapse of 2008.
2015: TV leaders' debate	The TV debate caused issues for all the participants, apart from Nicola Sturgeon. Ed Miliband's fall from the stage and over-excited 'Hell yes, I'm tough enough' made him appear less prime ministerial than David Cameron.	Opinion polls suggest the debate made no real difference to voting intentions, merely confirming existing impressions of the leaders.
2017 Televised leaders' debate	Theresa May's refusal to participate became a means of attacking her and a potential weakness. After Jeremy Corbyn participated in the seven-way debate and performed better than expected, Labour improved in credibility.	May went on to win more votes than Cameron had in 2010 or 2015. Corbyn still lost and third-party performers who did well saw no improvement in their vote shares.

What role have the media played between elections?

War reporting

The jingoistic and patriotic reporting of the Falklands War helped create the impression of Thatcher as the 'Iron Lady' and helped swing public opinion towards her.

Sleaze

During the 1992 parliament, the media reported on a number of sex and corruption scandals that afflicted the Conservative Party. This led to the party being associated with the term 'sleaze' and fed an impression of the Conservatives as 'the nasty party' and one that had abused its time in power. This helped swing public opinion toward the anti-sleaze Tony Blair and his 1997 campaign that 'things can only get better'.

'Bliar'

The BBC reporting and resulting press coverage about a 'dodgy dossier' and 'sexing up' the case for war in Iraq became a political scandal and resulted in the death of weapons inspector David Kelly. Although the Hutton Inquiry exonerated the government, it fed the impression of Blair as a liar and a 'poodle' of President Bush, fundamentally damaging his reputation.

Expenses

In 2009, the *Daily Telegraph* used a freedom of information request to obtain the records of MPs' expenses. The newspaper then revealed details of wrongful claims and outright abuses by MPs and peers, including a £1,645 claim for a duck house in a garden. This created a mood of cynicism and distrust in politics and all politicians.

The EU

The EU usually ranks fairly low down their list of priorities whenever voters have been surveyed. However, press reporting (usually against the EU) has made the issue more prominent with politicians than it needed to be. Furthermore, the press successfully began to link the issue of the EU to immigration, an issue that did rank highly with many voters. UKIP adopted this strategy and it explains why pressure to hold an in/out referendum mounted under media pressure.

Satire

Perhaps more than anything, the rise in political satire since the 1960s has coincided with a decline in the reputation of politicians. Programmes like *That Was The Week That Was* began openly mocking politicians and stage shows like *Beyond the Fringe* presented mocking impressions of prime minister Harold Macmillan. This began to undermine the prestige with which politicians were regarded.

Into the twenty-first century, shows like *Have I Got News For You*, *Mock the Week* and *The Thick of It* have continued to parody politics and politicians, at their best providing scrutiny and checks on politicians, at their worst feeding a mood of cynicism towards politics. Politicians themselves have tried to engage with these developing media formats, with many politicians appearing on shows like *Have I Got News for You* in order to raise their public profile and engage with the electorate.

Other politicians have tried to use the appeal of social media in the same way, with Ed Miliband being interviewed by Russell Brand on his YouTube channel 'The Trews'. While this may have raised Miliband's profile with younger voters and those who follow Brand, it caused some loss of credibility and was mocked on more traditional media programmes. With the young being less likely to turn out to vote, social media has so far only provided limited success for politicians hoping to increase electoral support.

What you should know

- How people vote is a complex issue, with many different ways in which people can make up their minds. Class, gender, age, ethnicity and geography all play a significant role in determining how a person may vote, and parties will seek to 'win' these groups, rather than the whole electorate.
- Who votes is perhaps the most important aspect in explaining electoral successes and failures. The young, the poor and black and other ethnic minority groups are the least likely to vote, while older, white and more prosperous citizens are more likely to vote — which explains why successful parties tend to tailor their message to these groups.
- The party leader has taken on a far more prominent role in political elections in recent years. This has coincided with a rise in presidential-style politics and spatial leadership.
- Four general election case studies have shown the key issues, key contests and key voting information. You should know the links between these elections and how they differed, leading to a comparative understanding of them.
- The media play an increasingly important role in politics and election campaigns. They shape political discussion and may be able to influence the outcome of elections.
- Beyond elections, the media hold political figures to account and act as a check on government but they have also played a role in undermining the reputation of politics in the UK.

UK/US comparison

Voting behaviour and the role of the media

- US politics is broken down into similar groups of class, race and gender, with those from poorer backgrounds, racial minorities and women tending to favour the Democrats in recent years, while poorer, white and male voters tend to vote Republican. Geography is a more prominent factor, owing to the federal nature of elections, the existence of the Electoral College and the fact that regions tend to be more homogeneous within themselves and distinct from other areas.
- The US president has always been elected separately to Congress, so considerations of presidentialism have existed for many years. The fact that the president is elected separately means voters have the option to 'split their ticket', i.e. vote for one party for the president and another for the legislature.
- The USA has a formal electoral cycle over a 2-year period, which means people are always campaigning, and this is exploited by the media. There are few national newspapers and most news is local in focus, with party conventions and presidential debates being exceptional as genuinely national political events. Politicians are also free to purchase political advertising, leading to rising costs in electoral cycles.
- Opinion polls are used extensively in the USA to test policies and to move public opinion. Their use and sophistication is far beyond that in the UK and politicians will coordinate events and announcements in order to gain a 'bounce' in the polls.

Further reading

Butler, D. and Kavanagh, D. (1979) *The British General Election of 1979*, Macmillan.

Butler, D. and Kavanagh, D. (1997) *The British General Election of 1997*, Palgrave Macmillan.

Cowley, P. and Ford, R. (2014) *Sex, Lies and the Ballot Box: 50 things you need to know about British elections*, Biteback.

Cowley, P. and Ford, R. (2016) *More Sex, Lies and the Ballot Box: Another 50 things you need to know about British elections*, Biteback.

Cowley, P. and Kavanagh, D. (2010) *The British General Election of 2010*, Palgrave Macmillan.

Cowley, P. and Kavanagh, D. (2015) *The British General Election of 2015*, Palgrave Macmillan.

Denver, D., Carman, C. and Johns, R. (2012) *Elections and Voters in Britain*, Palgrave.

Electoral Commission: www.electoralcommission.org.uk

Ipsos MORI: www.tinyurl.com/j6k3d9y

UK Parliament: www.parliament.uk/topics/Elections.htm

Exam focus

Short-answer questions

1 Explain, with examples, class voting.

2 Explain, with examples, the role of televised debates in elections.

3 Explain and analyse three ways in which the media have affected the outcome of UK general elections.

4 Explain and analyse three theories for explaining how people cast their votes.

Mid-length questions

1 Describe the main features of voting turnout since 1992 in UK general elections.

2 Describe the main functions of opinion polls in general election campaigns.

3 Analyse and evaluate the role of party leaders in fighting general elections.

4 Analyse and evaluate the reasons for declining voter turnout in the UK.

Essay questions

1 Evaluate the view that elections are lost by governments rather than won by the opposition. You should make reference to at least one pre-1997 election, the 1997 election and at least one post-1997 election.

2 Evaluate how far the behaviour of the British electorate has altered since the 1950s.

3 Analyse and evaluate the argument that the media shape public opinion and voting intentions.

4 'Media support is crucial for achieving success in general elections.' Analyse and evaluate this statement, making reference to at least three general elections.

Chapter 12

Political parties

Key questions answered
- What is a political party and what roles do parties perform in the UK?
- What types of political party operate in the UK?
- Is there a two-party system in the UK?
- What are the origins of the main UK political parties, how have they developed, and how has this shaped their current policies?
- How are the main UK political parties structured and organised?
- How are the main UK political parties funded and why is party funding so controversial?

On 24 June 2016, in the wake of the EU referendum, David Cameron announced his intention to stand down as prime minister and Conservative leader. In most western democracies, the resignation of a politician of such importance would result in an election or, at the very least, the promotion of an elected deputy in anticipation of just such an eventuality, but something very different happened in this instance.

The UK prime minister holds office not on the basis of any personal mandate won through the ballot box, but by virtue of the fact that they lead a political party capable of commanding the confidence of the House of Commons. Thus Cameron's resignation statement, far from precipitating a general election, resulted in nothing more or less than a contest to become the next leader of the Conservative Party, and Theresa May's victory in that contest saw her take possession of the keys to No. 10 as well as the mantle of Tory leader.

The UK operates under a parliamentary system of government, as opposed to a presidential system, and it is impossible to understand how the machinery of central government works without developing an appreciation of the pivotal part played by political parties within that system.

Political parties play a pivotal role in UK government

What is a political party?

A political party is a group of like-minded individuals who seek to realise their shared goals by fielding candidates at elections and thereby securing election to public office. Most mainstream UK parties ultimately aim to emerge victorious at a general election, however distant that goal might appear at a given point in time. In this respect, parties differ significantly from pressure groups, for while some pressure groups employ electoral candidacy as a means of raising public awareness of their chosen cause, they generally have little interest in, or prospect of, being elected to office.

Manifestos and mandates

A political party uses its **manifesto** to set out the policies it would seek to pass into law if elected to office, and so the party that is returned to power at Westminster in the wake of a general election is said to have earned an electoral **mandate** — the right to implement its stated policies. This is because popular support for the winning party at the ballot box is taken, rightly or wrongly, as support for the manifesto that the party presented to voters during the election campaign. Crucially, the **Salisbury Doctrine** holds that the unelected House of Lords should not, at second reading, oppose any bill that was included in the governing party's manifesto at the time of the general election.

The implementation of the first stage of Lords reform is a good example of how the electoral mandate works in practice. In its 1997 general election manifesto, the Labour Party promised to remove the rights of hereditary peers to sit and vote in the House of Lords. The party's landslide victory in the election therefore handed the party a strong mandate to fulfil this first stage of Lords reform, and it duly delivered with the House of Lords Act 1999.

Issues relating to party manifestos and the doctrine of the mandate are also discussed in Chapter 5 and Chapter 11. The former also addresses the Salisbury Doctrine.

Key terms

Mandate The right of the governing party to pursue the policies it sets out in its general election manifesto.

Manifesto A pre-election policy document in which a party sets out a series of policy pledges and legislative proposals that it plans to enact if returned to office.

Salisbury Doctrine The convention that the House of Lords does not block or try to wreck legislation that was promised in the manifesto of the governing party.

In focus

Salisbury Doctrine

A constitutional convention under which the House of Lords should not, at second reading, block a government bill that is seeking to deliver on a manifesto pledge. The origins of the doctrine lie in the idea of the mandate developed by Conservative prime minister Lord Salisbury in the late nineteenth century — that general election victory gives the governing party the authority to implement the programme it presented to the electorate. The Salisbury Doctrine then developed in the 1940s as an acceptance that the unelected Lords should not frustrate the will of the elected Commons. It is said to extend to any bill appearing in the government's programme for the session.

In focus

Manifesto

A pre-election policy document in which a party sets out a series of policy pledges and legislative proposals that it plans to enact if returned to office. The latter years of the twentieth century saw party leaders taking direct control of the process of drafting the election manifesto. In 1992, the Conservative leader John Major famously declared that the party's manifesto was 'all me'.

In focus

Mandate

The right of the governing party to pursue the policies it sets out in its general election manifesto. The mandate gives the governing party the authority to pursue its stated policies, without the need to go back to voters for further approval — such as through a referendum. Crucially, the mandate does not require the government to deliver on its manifesto promises or prevent it from drafting proposals that were not included in its manifesto.

Does the concept of an electoral mandate make sense?

Yes

- The franchise is widely held and there is a high level of individual voter registration.
- The first-past-the-post electoral system usually results in a single-party government, so it follows that the victors should have the right to implement their stated policies.
- Each party's manifesto is readily available to voters ahead of polling day, both in print and electronic form.
- Digested summaries of the main policies of each party are disseminated by the mainstream media. Televised leaders' debates at the last two general elections have seen the leaders of the parties questioned on their main policies.

No

- The low turnout at recent general elections means that the winning party can hardly claim to have secured a convincing mandate.
- Coalition governments such as that seen in the wake of the 2010 general election mean that two or more parties must agree a compromise programme for which no single party has a mandate.
- Most voters pay little attention to party manifestos, whether in full or digested form. Voting behaviour is more about long-term factors or personalities than it is about policy detail.
- The concept of the mandate is flawed because it is impossible for voters to cast a ballot for or against a given party on the basis of a single policy.

Roles of political parties in the UK

Political parties in the UK perform five main roles:

- providing representation
- encouraging political engagement and facilitating political participation
- engaging in political recruitment
- formulating policy
- providing stable government

Representation

Traditionally, parties were said to represent the views of their members. This was certainly true in an age of mass-membership parties, when parties and voters were clearly divided along class lines. Partisan and class dealignment, accompanied by the rise of centrist 'catch-all' parties, can be said to have undermined this primary role.

Political engagement and participation

By making the wider citizenry aware of the issues of the day, parties perform an educative function that, by its very nature, encourages political engagement. Parties further promote political participation by encouraging citizens to engage with the democratic process and giving them the opportunity to exercise power within their chosen party. The quality of participation afforded to members is shaped largely by the extent to which political parties are themselves internally democratic.

Political recruitment

Parties assess the qualities of those seeking election to public office, casting aside those who are, for whatever reason, considered unsuitable. Parties also give those who will ultimately become the nation's leaders an opportunity to serve a form of political apprenticeship at a local level before 'graduating' to high office.

Policy formulation

Parties discuss and develop policy proposals before presenting them to voters in a single coherent programme (their manifesto). It is argued that this process is likely to result in a more considered, joined-up style of government than that which might emerge in the absence of political parties.

Stable government

Without parties, it is argued, the House of Commons would simply be a gathering of individuals, driven by their personal goals and political ambitions. Parties present the voters with a clear choice, while also providing order following the general election — by allowing a single party to form a government and secure the safe passage of its legislative proposals through the Commons.

Distinguish between

Political parties and pressure groups

Political parties
- Political parties tend to offer a broad portfolio of policies, informed by a guiding ideology.
- The main UK political parties have open membership structures and are therefore inclusive.
- Political parties contest elections with a view to securing control of governmental power.
- The main UK parties are highly organised and offer their members an input into key decisions through formalised rules and procedures.

Pressure groups
- Pressure groups generally pursue a narrower cause or sectional interest.
- Many pressure groups — particularly sectional groups — are more exclusive in their membership.
- Those pressure groups that field candidates in elections generally do so simply as a means of raising their own profile — or to encourage candidates representing the mainstream parties to adjust their policies for fear of losing votes.
- Even the larger, more established pressure groups are often dominated by a small leading clique; few pressure groups display high levels of internal democracy.

Types of political party in the UK

Mainstream parties

In the modern era, UK politics has been dominated by three main national political parties: the Conservative Party, which emerged from the Tory group within parliament in the mid-nineteenth century; the Labour Party, formed by trade unions and socialist organisations at the start of the twentieth century; and the Liberal Democrats, which came into being as a result of the merger between the Liberal Party and the Social Democratic Party (SDP) in 1988.

Minority or 'niche' parties

Nationalist parties

Nationalist parties look to nurture the shared cultural identity and language of those indigenous to a given geographical area — whether a 'nation', as in the case of the Scottish National Party (SNP), or a region, as in the case of Mebyon Kernow (The Party for Cornwall). While some nationalist parties campaign for full independence for their region or nation (e.g. the SNP), others may have more modest goals (e.g. Plaid Cymru in Wales). Although always much smaller than Plaid Cymru or the SNP, the British National Party (BNP) differs from most other nationalist parties in that it campaigns in support of the way of life and values that it claims are common to all indigenous UK peoples. However, having achieved some electoral success in the early part of the twenty-first century, the party had been reduced to a single local councillor and just 500 members by 2016.

Single-issue parties

Recent years have seen a rise in the number of single-issue parties contesting elections in the UK. In some cases, these parties offer a wide-ranging programme of policies rooted in a particular ideological perspective (e.g. the Green Party). In other cases, they campaign on a particular issue (e.g. UKIP on the European Union), or even a specific policy (e.g. the ProLife Alliance on abortion). Recent elections have also seen the rise of local single-issue parties such as the Independent Kidderminster Hospital and Health Concern Party, whose candidate Dr Richard Taylor won the Wyre Forest constituency at the 2001 and 2005 general elections. In many cases, such single-issue or ideological parties blur the boundary between political parties and pressure groups, as their primary goal is to raise awareness of a particular issue as opposed to winning an election and/or securing power. UKIP can be seen as a case in point.

Activity

Using the material provided in Table 12.1 as well as your own research, what do the figures provided tell us about the electoral impact of these four minority parties, when compared to mainstream parties such as Labour and the Conservatives? In what ways could the figures presented in the table be considered misleading?

Table 12.1 Larger minority parties in Britain, 2016

	SNP	Plaid Cymru	Green	UKIP
Membership	120,000	8,273	55,000	39,000
MPs	54	3	1	1
Lords	0	1	1	3
Regional assembly members	63	11	8	8
MEPs	2	1	3	20
Local councillors	405	171	177	492

Source: membership data from House of Commons Library, *Briefing Paper: Membership of UK political parties* (www.tinyurl.com/zy6j8mt)

UKIP after BREXIT

In 2016, Paul Nuttall was elected leader of the UK Independence Party, replacing Nigel Farage. The 39-year-old Member of the European Parliament, who served as UKIP's deputy leader for 6 years, won 62.6% of support among party members.

He promised to 'put the great back into Britain' and force the government to 'give us a real Brexit'. It was UKIP's second leadership election in a year, after previous winner Diane James quit after 18 days in the role. Mr Farage acted as interim leader while the second leadership race took place.

In his acceptance speech, Mr Nuttall said: 'The country needs a strong UKIP more than ever before. If UKIP is to be an electoral force, there will be an impetus on [the Prime Minister] Theresa May, and her government, to give us a real Brexit.' He added: 'I want to replace the Labour Party and make UKIP the patriotic voice of working people … speaking the language of ordinary working people. We're going to move into the areas the Labour Party has

Paul Nuttall was elected leader of UKIP in 2016

neglected. We will be focusing on the issues that really matter to working-class people on doorsteps — immigration, crime, defence, foreign aid, ensuring that British people are put to the top of the queue in the job market' (www.tinyurl.com/glqjtxo).

Questions
- Explain why UKIP could be seen more as a pressure group than a regular political party.
- Using the extract above and knowledge gained from your own research, explain why and how UKIP attempted to reposition itself in the wake of the 2016 EU referendum.

The UK party system

Dominant-party system Where a number of parties exist but only one holds government power, e.g. in Japan under the Liberal Democratic-Party between 1955 and 1993. Some argue that the UK party system has, at times, resembled a dominant-party system — with the Conservatives in office 1979–97 and Labour in power 1997–2010.

Multiparty system Where many parties compete for power and the government consists of a series of coalitions formed by different combinations of parties, e.g. in Italy between 1945 and 1993.

Single-party system Where one party dominates, bans other parties and exercises total control over candidacy at elections — where elections occur at all, e.g. in Nazi Germany or the Democratic People's Republic of Korea (North Korea).

Two-party system Where two fairly equally matched parties compete for power at elections and others have little realistic chance of breaking their duopoly.

Britain has traditionally operated under a **two-party system**. While there have been times when a period of domination by a single party has led onlookers to herald the emergence of a **dominant-party system**, the UK has never witnessed a **single-party system**. Similarly, although the rise of the Liberal Democrats and a range of other smaller parties in the early part of the twenty-first century led some to suggest that the UK was morphing into a **multiparty system**, most still regard it as conforming broadly to the two-party model.

Does the UK now have a multiparty system?

Yes

- In the 2015 general election, 13.5% of UK voters (and 61% of Scottish voters) backed parties other than the 'big two'.
- In some parts of the UK, such as Scotland, there is genuine multiparty competition for elected office.
- Although parties such as UKIP, the Green Party and the BNP have struggled to secure parliamentary representation at Westminster, they have achieved success in second-order elections.
- Any party that was able to mobilise non-voters would stand a chance of winning the election — in the 2015 general election, that was 33.8% of registered voters.

No

- The Labour and Conservative Parties are the only parties that have a realistic chance of forming a government or being the senior partner in a coalition at Westminster.
- Even in 2015, Labour and the Conservatives secured 67.2% of the popular vote (up 2.1% from 2010), winning 86.5% of the 650 seats contested.
- The success of parties such as the BNP at second-order elections has proved fleeting. The Green Party has failed to add to its single Commons seat. UKIP was widely seen as a spent force by the end of 2016.
- Of the parties that contested seats across mainland Britain in 2015, the Liberal Democrats (in third place) finished with 22.5% of the vote and 224 seats behind Labour (in second place).

Key term

Political spectrum A device by which different political standpoints can be mapped across one axis or more, as a way of demonstrating their ideological position in relation to one another.

The political spectrum

Party ideology in the UK has generally been discussed in terms of the simple left–right **political spectrum** (see Figure 12.1) that emerged in revolutionary France at the end of the eighteenth century. In modern usage, those on the extreme left of the political spectrum are said to favour some form of communal existence, with all property being held collectively as opposed to individually, while moderate left-wingers accept capitalism but favour greater government intervention in the economy and a more comprehensive welfare state. In contrast, those on the right are said to favour private enterprise over state provision, resulting in a process that the former Conservative prime minister Margaret Thatcher described as 'rolling back the frontiers of the state'.

Figure 12.1 The left–right political spectrum

In the UK, where the extreme ideologies of communism (on the left) and fascism (on the right) have never really taken hold, the debate over the direction of government policy has generally centred on the battle between socialists and conservatives. However, all three of the main British parties are better seen as 'broad churches', each comprising members of various different political shades.

Activity

The website **www.politicalcompass.org** allows you to position yourself on the political spectrum by answering a series of questions about how you feel about different aspects of policy. Go to the site, click on the 'Take the test' link, answer the questions and see where you are placed on the spectrum.

The three main political parties in the UK

Before the Great Reform Act of 1832, UK parties existed not as mass-membership organisations with formal structures outside of parliament, but as groups of like-minded individuals within the legislature. These groups were bound together by shared ideals, friendship or family ties. With electoral reform came the need to organise in order to mobilise the growing electorate. It was at this point that UK political parties as we know them today began to emerge.

The 1832 Great Reform Act, which extended the franchise, is discussed in Chapter 3 as an example of a piece of statute law that is of historical importance in constitutional terms.

The Conservative Party

The Conservative Party emerged from the Tory Party in the 1830s, with many dating its birth to Robert Peel's Tamworth Manifesto in 1834. In the twentieth century, the party was in office (either alone or in coalition) for a total of 67 years and enjoyed two extended periods in office:

- 1951–64 under Winston Churchill, Anthony Eden, Harold Macmillan and Alec Douglas-Home
- 1979–97 under Margaret Thatcher and then John Major

One-nation conservatism

For most of the twentieth century, the Conservative Party was truly conservative in ideology: that is, rooted in pragmatism and a belief in gradual improvements founded on experience and existing institutions. This was a form of collectivist or **paternalist conservatism** which favoured pluralism and social inclusion and held that, while authority should be centralised, the state should be benevolent and care for the neediest.

The proponents of this form of **conservatism**, now commonly referred to as 'one-nation Tories', were committed to:

- slow, gradual change — 'evolution', not 'revolution'
- a Keynesian mixed economy — with significant state intervention, where necessary
- support for a universal welfare state
- internationalism and increasing European integration

Thatcherism

The late 1970s and early 1980s saw the rise of a new form of liberal or libertarian conservatism on both sides of the Atlantic. Dubbed the 'New Right', this movement combined a belief in **monetarism**, free market economics and deregulation (an approach commonly referred to as **neo-liberalism**) with a more orthodox conservative approach in the sphere of social policy, such as support for the traditional family unit and more traditional views on sexual orientation. The US president Ronald Reagan (1981–89) and UK prime minister Margaret Thatcher (1979–90) were key figures in this movement — the latter to such an extent that this broad approach has become known simply as

Activity

Table 12.2 provides a snapshot of some of the factions that existed in the Conservative Party in 2016. Using the material provided and your own research, draw up a table listing the main Conservative Party factions that exist today. Briefly explain what each faction stands for and identify at least one, named individual who could be said to be part of that faction.

Thatcherism in the UK. The advent of Thatcherism marked the death of the **postwar consensus** and the rise of a more **adversarial politics**.

Supporters of this approach, known as Thatcherites, favoured the importance of the individual over the needs of society as a whole. Thatcherism offered a radical agenda including policies such as:

- deregulation in the field of business
- privatisation of publicly- owned industries
- statutory limits on the power of trade unions
- a smaller state ('rolling back the frontiers of the state') and more limited state intervention in the economy
- a greater emphasis on national sovereignty
- more limited state welfare provision (a lower 'safety net')

Thatcher referred to those who were not prepared to sign up to this agenda, in many cases the old one-nation Tories, as 'wets'. Committed Thatcherites were referred to as 'dries', with Thatcher's most loyal acolytes dubbed 'ultra dry'.

Synoptic links

Adversarial politics and Prime Minister's Question Time (PMQs)

Prime Minister's Question Time, which takes place each Wednesday in the House of Commons, is often seen as an example of the kind of adversarial, 'yah-boo', politics that characterised UK party politics in the 1970s and 1980s. This is also discussed in Chapter 5 and Chapter 6.

Intra-party squabbles

The factional infighting that came to the fore as a result of this shift in direction under Thatcher led to formal challenges to her leadership of the party in 1989 (Anthony Meyer) and 1990 (Michael Heseltine). Though the latter led to Thatcher's resignation in November 1990, the leaders who followed on from her — John Major, William Hague, Iain Duncan Smith, Michael Howard and David Cameron — often struggled to command the full confidence of the entire parliamentary party due to internal party factions and personal rivalries.

In the 1990s, Philip Norton identified seven broad and overlapping factions within the parliamentary Conservative Party. By 2013, Richard Kelly was able to identify three broad ideological strands (see Table 12.2).

Table 12.2 Conservative Party factions, 2016

Ideological strand		Groups and individuals	
Pre-Thatcherite (one-nation Tory)		Tory Reform Group	Kenneth Clarke Nicholas Soames
Thatcherite		Conservative Voice Bruges Group	John Redwood Liam Fox
Post-Thatcherite	Red Tory	ResPublica (think-tank)	Philip Blond Iain Duncan Smith Jesse Norman
	Liberal Conservatism	Bright Blue (think-tank) Free Enterprise Group	Boris Johnson Nick Boles

Distinguish between

One-nation conservatism and Thatcherism

One-nation conservatism
- It takes a pragmatic approach.
- It advocates incremental change.
- It is paternalistic.
- It favours a mixed economy.

Thatcherism
- It is dogmatic.
- It advocates radical change.
- It is individualistic.
- It favours a free-market economy.

When David Cameron was elected as party leader in 2006 he was widely referred to as the 'heir to Blair'

The Conservatives under David Cameron

David Cameron's election as party leader in 2006, in the wake of three successive general election defeats for the Conservatives, was widely seen as analogous to the kind of epiphany that the Labour Party had experienced a decade earlier under Tony Blair. Indeed, Cameron was himself widely referred to as the 'heir to Blair'.

Cameron initially sought to lead the Conservatives away from those areas of policy over which the party was deeply divided (e.g. Europe) and towards those where it could gain electoral advantage (e.g. the environment). He recognised the extent to which the party had come to be regarded as unelectable — or the 'nasty party', as Theresa May had put it back in 2002 — and set about 'detoxifying' the Conservative brand. The desire was reflected in the Conservatives' 2010 general election pledge to fix 'broken Britain'.

Locating David Cameron and his supporters on the political spectrum

Some dubbed Cameron's Conservatives the 'New Tories' or, as Cameron himself put it on at least one occasion, 'liberal Conservatives'. Back in 2008, Richard Kelly offered three possible early judgements on Cameron's conservatism:
- first, that it represented a 'flagrant capitulation to New Labour'
- second, that it should be seen as a 'subtle continuation of Thatcherism'
- third, that it amounted to little more than 'shameless opportunism'

While there were elements of truth in all three of these judgements, it was the last that presented the most enduring obstacle. Cameron's promise of an in/out referendum on the EU ahead of the 2015 general election was certainly seen as evidence of such opportunism, with the party internally divided on the issue and facing a challenge from UKIP in its electoral heartlands.

The substance of policy

Although David Cameron's Conservative Party issued a swathe of policy proposals in the run-up to the 2010 general election, the party's manifesto favoured style over substance. For example, the early talk of replacing the Human Rights Act 1998 with a new UK Bill of Rights appeared without further elaboration in the party's 2010 manifesto. Even in the wake of the 2010 general election, it remained unclear as to how Cameron intended to reconcile (or triangulate) his desire to adopt traditionally liberal positions on the environment and social welfare with his commitment to pursue the

Thatcherite agenda of 'rolling back the frontiers of the state'. Moreover, the need to keep the party's Liberal Democrat coalition partners engaged made it difficult for the Conservatives to deliver even on those very few explicit promises that they had made in the run-up to the 2010 general election.

The 2015 general election and beyond

While the Conservatives in coalition (2010–15) could be forgiven for not delivering on some of their more radical policy pledges, it was perhaps more surprising that they did not attempt to make more substantive changes after being returned to office as a single-party government in 2015. The party had, after all, set out a number of significant proposals in its election manifesto.

The decision to hold the EU referendum so early in the parliament meant that cabinet colleagues would find it hard to work together towards policy goals in the conventional way. The result of the referendum, leading to Cameron's resignation as prime minister and replacement by Theresa May, also limited the effective working of the government. With the triggering of the early election in 2017, the opportunities for the Conservative government to achieve many of its policies was severely limited.

Case study

Conservative policies under Theresa May

Although much of Theresa May's time in office has been focused on the issue of Brexit, her early initiatives and policies in the Conservative Party manifesto of 2017 show a marked shift away from the policies of David Cameron.

Economically, May pledged to end austerity and focus on the issues of the 'just about managing' (Jams) group. There was a commitment to raising the personal tax allowance, ruling out a rise in VAT and extending the target deadline for balancing the budget to 2025. However, such aims were undermined by a pledge to cut corporation tax and a review of business rates which had hit many small businesses.

Controversially, the 2017 manifesto stated a policy to means-test winter fuel allowances and take into account people's assets (notably houses) when determining the costs they would need to pay for elderly care. Labour and the media soon labelled this a 'dementia tax', and the prime minister announced a seeming U-turn within 24 hours, stating that the total amount would be capped. Furthermore, the manifesto pledged to remove the triple lock on pensions, which raised further concerns with elderly voters.

In education, May planned to allow for the reintroduction of grammar schools. This was controversial with many Conservative backbenchers. However, the education policy that was more prominent with voters was the plan to replace free school lunches with free school breakfasts as a cost-saving measure, with many activists, including chef and campaigner Jamie Oliver, condemning the move.

In environmental policies, support for fracking and only one mention of air pollution showed that the environment was not a major priority for May, building on her abolition of the Department of Energy and Climate Change, while creating two new departments for dealing with Brexit: the Department for Exiting the European Union and the Department for International Trade.

Questions
- Using the material above and your own research, produce a table outlining the main policy differences between May and Cameron.
- Explain how far Brexit was the dominant feature of the Conservative manifesto in 2017.

Although Theresa May set out a number of significant proposals beyond the issue of Brexit in the 2017 manifesto (see case study) it was always likely that the issue of Brexit would dominate the government's agenda for the full parliamentary term, regardless of the result. However, by losing the majority and being forced to operate as a minority government, with the support of the DUP, Theresa May was forced to drop many of her more controversial policies, particularly those that were believed to have cost their party outright victory in the election.

The Labour Party

The Labour Party was created at the start of the twentieth century. Although the Independent Labour Party, the Fabians and the Social Democratic Federation were involved in forming the Labour Representation Committee in 1900, it is important not to underestimate the role of the Trades Union Congress (TUC). In 1900, 94% of the Labour Representation Committee's affiliated membership was from the unions and in the 1990s they still controlled around 80% of the votes at party conferences and provided a similar proportion of the party's annual income.

The Labour Party was formed to represent the working classes at a time when the franchise had not yet been extended to such groups. The decision to give all men over 21 the right to vote in 1918 provided the Labour Party with the potential base of support necessary to launch a serious electoral challenge.

The party's origins in the unions and socialist societies of the late nineteenth and early twentieth centuries meant that it originally pursued an agenda centred on **socialism**.

In the nineteenth century, socialism was often seen as similar to communism. In the UK, socialism was closely associated with the Labour Party, from the party's creation at the start of the twentieth century through to the emergence of New Labour under Tony Blair in the 1990s.

Broadly speaking, socialism can be subdivided into two distinct strands:

- revisionist (or reformist) socialism, which looks to improve capitalism (e.g. **social democracy**)
- revolutionary (or fundamentalist) socialism, which aims to abolish capitalism and bring all property into common ownership (e.g. Marxist communism)

The 1918 constitution

The extension of the franchise to all adult men in 1918 coincided with the adoption of the new Labour Party constitution. Clause IV of that constitution (see the case study on page 323) provided a clear commitment to public ownership of key industries and the redistribution of wealth.

Labour factions

Despite its left-wing origins, the party was home to a number of ideological factions by the 1970s. For example, the Labour prime minister James Callaghan (1976–79) and those on the right of the party took the view that public sector pay demands had to be resisted, whereas those on the left (e.g. Michael Foot and Tony Benn) still favoured greater wealth redistribution.

Key terms

Social democracy A political ideology that accepts the basic premise of capitalism while advocating a more equitable distribution of wealth along the lines favoured by all socialists.

Socialism A political ideology advocating greater equality and the redistribution of wealth. Socialists are suspicious of capitalism. They favour greater government intervention, in both economic and social policy.

Key terms

New Labour A term that characterises the party that emerged to fight the 1997 general election following a process of party modernisation completed by Tony Blair. Blair first used the phrase 'New Labour' when addressing the Labour Party conference as party leader in 1994. Labour's modernisation programme began under Neil Kinnock, following the party's landslide defeat at the 1983 general election. It involved a less powerful role for the trade unions and a rebranding exercise designed to make the party more appealing to middle-class voters. In ideological terms, the New Labour project was characterised by the concept of **triangulation** and the **Third Way**.

Old Labour A term that characterises the Labour Party prior to the modernisation programme begun by Neil Kinnock in 1983 and completed by Tony Blair. It refers to the party's historic commitment to socialism and its links with socialist societies, trade unions and the old working class.

Third Way An ideological position said to exist between conventional socialism and mainstream capitalism, closely associated with Tony Blair and New Labour, and also referred to as the 'middle way'.

Triangulation The process of melding together core Labour Party principles and values, such as the party's commitment to greater social justice, with the lessons learnt from Thatcherism. It was closely associated with New Labour and the notion of a Third Way.

Labour's defeat in the 1979 general election, in the wake of the period of industrial unrest known as the 'Winter of Discontent', saw those on the left gain control of the party under the leadership of Michael Foot. Foot led Labour into the 1983 general election with one of the most left-wing manifestos in the party's history. It included commitments to state control of all major industries, tighter regulation of business, enhanced workers' rights, support for unilateral nuclear disarmament and a withdrawal from NATO. At the time dubbed 'the longest suicide note in history' by the Labour MP Gerald Kaufman, the manifesto was seen as a key factor in the Conservative Party's landslide victory. Indeed, the manifesto was so left-wing in its approach that the Conservatives ran an advertisement in the *Daily Mirror* newspaper carrying the tagline 'Like your manifesto, Comrade', drawing parallels between key clauses in Labour's programme and the provisions of the Communist Manifesto.

Old Labour versus New Labour

Although the Labour Party was formed to represent the working classes, changes in the class and occupational structure of the nation since the 1960s, together with the general election defeats of 1979, 1983 and 1987, saw the party looking to broaden its appeal beyond this core support.

Case study

Clause IV of the Labour Party constitution

Original 1918 text:

> ...to secure for the workers by hand or by brain the full fruits of their industry and the most equitable distribution thereof that may be possible upon the basis of the common ownership of the means of production...

Reworded 1995 text:

> [We] work for a dynamic economy, serving the public interest, in which the enterprise of the market and the rigour of competition are joined with the forces of partnership and cooperation to produce the wealth the nation needs and the opportunity for all to work and prosper, with a thriving private sector and high-quality public services.

Questions
- Assess the extent to which the 'new' Clause IV, adopted in 1995, represented a significant departure from the one agreed in 1918.
- Explain why the Labour Party under Tony Blair felt the need to make this change.
- Study the material on Jeremy Corbyn's policy positions that appears later in this chapter. In what ways might Corbyn be trying to 'reset' the Labour Party to the time before the change to Clause IV?

Old Labour and New Labour

Old Labour

- It is dogmatic.
- It is predominantly the party of the working class.
- It is interventionist.
- It favours public sector provision.
- It advocates social justice.
- It supports universal welfare.

New Labour

- It takes a pragmatic approach.
- It markets itself as a catch-all party, not limited to the working class.
- It favours a market economy.
- It favours public–private partnerships.
- It advocates social inclusion.
- It supports targeted welfare.

This process of outreach, started by leaders such as Neil Kinnock (1983–92) and John Smith (1992–94), is most closely associated with the leadership of Tony Blair (1994–2007). Under Blair, the party was rebranded as **New Labour** (with the term **Old Labour** describing what had come before) and the iconic Clause IV of the party's written constitution was controversially reworded. Some critics accused Blair and other Labour modernisers of abandoning the socialist principles upon which the party had been founded.

Labour under Gordon Brown

Gordon Brown's accession as Labour leader in June 2007 was greeted with optimism by those on the left who felt that his commitment to the concept of **social justice** was greater than that of his predecessor, Tony Blair.

As chancellor, Brown had favoured deregulation and a light touch approach to economic management. As prime minister, he was forced to nationalise a number of high-street banks, while overseeing an apparent return to the 'tax and spend' approach of Old Labour. New Labour's hard-fought reputation for economic competence was ultimately surrendered, along with much of the political capital that the former chancellor had accrued during his decade in charge at the Treasury.

Even in the field of constitutional reform, where Brown had been widely expected to take the lead, the Constitutional Renewal Bill (2008) and the Constitutional Reform and Governance Act (2010) largely failed to fulfil expectations.

Labour under Ed Miliband

Even the most ardent former Blairites, such as the former foreign secretary, David Miliband, were keen to distance themselves from the New Labour tag in the wake of the Labour Party's defeat at the 2010 general election. 'New Labour is not the future', Miliband acknowledged, 'I'm interested now in Next Labour' (*Observer*, 16 May 2010). However, the question of precisely what 'Next Labour' might mean dogged the party's efforts to regroup under the leadership of the Miliband's younger brother, Ed.

Dubbed 'Red Ed' by the media, due in large part to the fact that his narrow victory over his brother in the election to become Labour leader had relied so heavily on the backing of the trade unions, Ed Miliband struggled to establish a coalition of voters large enough to carry the party back into office in 2015.

The result at that election, a sweeping defeat for the party, led to a period of introspection not entirely dissimilar to that which came in the wake of Labour's defeat to the Conservatives back in 1983. For those on the right of the party, the reversal had resulted from Miliband abandoning the formula that had served the party so well under Blair. For those on the left, Miliband's defeat was evidence of the essential bankruptcy at the heart of the New Labour model; a sign that the party should return to its base and embrace socialism once more.

Labour under Jeremy Corbyn

Jeremy Corbyn's ideological positioning made it difficult for him to command the support of his fellow Labour MPs

The election of Jeremy Corbyn as Labour leader in September 2015 came as something of a surprise to those outside of the Westminster bubble. Corbyn, a committed socialist from the left of the party and a serial backbench rebel of epic proportions during the New Labour era, had only made it on to the ballot paper because a number of fellow MPs felt that the existing field lacked the necessary ideological breadth. Although Corbyn's victory in the membership ballot that followed was made easier by changes to the rules which allowed registered supporters of the party, as well as members, to vote, the scale of Corbyn's win (with 59.5% of first preferences) was impressive nonetheless.

Corbyn's ideological positioning and track record as a rebellious backbencher made it difficult for him to either demand or command the support or loyalty of his fellow Labour MPs. His re-election as leader in September 2016, in the wake of a vote of no confidence among the Parliamentary Labour Party (PLP) and a botched leadership challenge, offered the prospect of a more polarised political landscape in the run-up to the 2020 general election. The challenge for a leader so long on the backbenches in opposition mode, in relation to both the Conservatives and some of those within his own party, was to articulate a positive vision capable of garnering support among the wider electorate. Corbyn's vision, however, as stated on his website (www.jeremyforlabour.com), appeared to look back towards the kinds of policies that the party had pursued pre-New Labour, in the 1970s and early 1980s:

- full employment and an economy that works for all
- a secure homes guarantee
- security at work
- secure our NHS and social care
- a national education service open to all
- action to secure our environment
- put the public back into our economy and services
- cut income and wealth inequality
- action to secure an equal society
- peace and justice at the heart of foreign policy

Case study

Labour Party factions in 2016

Since Jeremy Corbyn became leader of the Labour Party in 2015, the party has become more divided than ever. Jon Cruddas, the party's former policy chief, who has produced a report entitled 'Why Labour lost in 2015 and how it can win again', has accused the party of becoming 'dangerously out of touch with the electorate and…unwilling to acknowledge this growing estrangement'. Factions, old and new, continue to divide the party and its supporters. What are the main factions?

- Momentum
- Saving Labour
- Labour for the Common Good
- Consensus
- Progress Labour First

- Socialist Workers Party
- Stop the War Coalition
- Labour Together
- Open Labour

Source: adapted from E. Kilheeney (2016) 'Labour Party factions', *Politics Review*, Vol. 26, No. 3, pp. 16–17

Questions

- Using the material provided above and your own research, produce a summary table showing the main Labour Party factions that existed in 2016.
- Include a summary of the views of each faction along with examples, where available, of key individuals who could be said to sit in each faction.

The Liberal Democrats

The Liberal Democrats were formed in 1988 with the merger of the Liberal Party and the Social Democratic Party (SDP). The Liberal Party had been the main party of government in the early twentieth century but was a distant third by the 1960s, rarely polling more than 10% of the vote. The SDP, in contrast, had been formed as a result of the decision of four leading politicians to leave the Labour Party in 1981. Roy Jenkins, David Owen, Bill Rodgers and Shirley Williams felt that Labour had come under the control of hard-line left-wingers following the defeat of James Callaghan's moderate Labour administration in 1979.

This **'Gang of Four'**, as they were known, launched the SDP with their 1981 Limehouse Declaration. With the Labour Party in disarray, the SDP formed an electoral alliance with the Liberals (the **SDP–Liberal Alliance**) in 1983, securing 26% of the popular vote, yet gaining only

Key terms

'Gang of Four' Referring collectively to Bill Rodgers, Roy Jenkins, Shirley Williams and David Owen. Believing that the party had fallen under the control of a left-wing clique led by Michael Foot in the wake of Labour's defeat at the 1979 general election, these four former Labour ministers left the party in 1981 to from the Social Democratic Party (SDP).

SDP–Liberal Alliance An electoral alliance between SDP and the Liberal Party that was in place at the time of the 1983 and 1987 general elections. The alliance won 26.0% of the vote (23 seats) in 1983 and 23.1% of the vote (22 seats) in 1987. The two parties merged in 1988 to form the Liberal Democrats.

23 seats in parliament. Following a similarly disappointing return for the alliance in 1987, the parties merged in 1988 to form the Social and Liberal Democrats and Paddy Ashdown was elected party leader. The following year the party was renamed the Liberal Democrats (or Lib Dems for short).

While Conservatives traditionally emphasise the role of society in shaping individuals, **liberalism** places a greater emphasis on the importance of the individual. Traditionally, liberals favoured a society formed of free, autonomous individuals of equal worth.

In focus

Liberalism

Although liberalism is often referred to as a single ideology, it is possible to identify a number of different strands — the most obvious being classical liberalism and progressive (or new) liberalism.

Classical liberalism, which emerged in the nineteenth century, is an early form of liberalism favouring minimal state intervention. Classical liberals stress the importance of freedom, toleration and equality. They believe that self-reliance and self-improvement have a bigger part to play than the state in improving the lives of those from less privileged backgrounds. Some of the classical liberal agenda was adopted by the Thatcherite New Right from the later 1970s, resulting in them being referred to as neo-liberals.

Progressive (or new) liberalism is a more compassionate form of liberalism that sees the need for some regulation of the market as well as the provision of basic welfare. It was originally advanced by writers such as T. H. Green and L. T. Hobhouse. Progressive liberalism later developed into the mixed economy supported by John Maynard Keynes and William Beveridge. This second, more progressive form of liberalism — with its emphasis on reform, individual rights and a mixed economy — provided the ideological foundation for all of the liberal centre parties of the second half of the twentieth century, and most recently the Liberal Democrats.

Nick Clegg, leader of the Liberal Democrats from 2007 to 2015, at the launch of the Liberal Democrat manifesto for the 2015 general election

The Liberal Democrats under Nick Clegg

From 2007, under the leadership of Nick Clegg, the Liberal Democrats developed a programme for government that included more orthodox Liberal Democrat policies on issues such as constitutional reform and the protection of civil liberties, alongside other pledges that appeared to challenge the very tenets upon which the party had been founded; not least by offering the prospect of significant tax cuts, if elected. This repositioning on tax marked the triumph of the 'Orange Book' liberals over the social liberals, while also making the possibility of a coalition with the Conservatives in 2010 more conceivable (see Table 12.3).

Table 12.3 Key Liberal Democrat factions after 2010

Ideological strand	Positions	Key individuals
Orange Book liberals	Draw on 'classical liberalism' Influenced by the neo-liberalism of Milton Friedman and others Endorse Thatcherite economics	Nick Clegg Ed Davey David Laws
Social liberals	Draw on the 'new' or progressive liberalism of Keynes and Beveridge Reject Thatcherite economics	Tim Farron Simon Hughes

The party policies in 2017

The surprise calling of the 2017 general election caught out many of the party organisers, and policies were slow in being produced as a result. Theresa May had hoped to make it a 'Brexit' election with the central theme being who was best suited to lead the negotiations, her or Jeremy Corbyn. However, by pledging to support the UK's withdrawal from the EU, Corbyn effectively nullified this as a central issue and the resulting focus on other parties showed increasing divisions between the main parties and attitudes to austerity after nearly a decade had passed since the financial crash.

The Conservatives planned to make a number of tax cuts, by cutting corporation tax, raising the personal allowance and pledging to maintain rates of VAT while achieving a balanced budget by 2025. Labour, however, promised to introduce a £250 billion stimulus package over 10 years, increase corporation tax and increase the top rate of tax to 50p in the pound for those earning above £80,000, while the Liberal Democrats pledged to balance day-to-day spending by raising income tax for everyone by 1p in the pound, using this to fund £100 billion investment in infrastructure.

In welfare, the Conservatives showed a marked difference from the other parties, with plans to remove the triple lock on pensions, means-test the winter fuel allowance and adult social care by considering people's homes and other assets. While the Liberal Democrats did favour the withdrawal of winter fuel payments for wealthy pensioners, they, like Labour, committed to maintain the triple lock on pensions and to review and reverse the cuts to universal tax credits. Labour also committed to raising employment and support allowances by £30 per week as well as increasing the carer's allowance by £11 per week and reinstating housing benefits for the under-21s.

On health, all three parties committed to raising spending, the Liberal Democrats by the introduction of an extra 1p on all income tax bands, ring-fenced for the NHS, while the Conservatives pledged to raise investment in the NHS by £8 billion by 2022/23 and Labour pledged to raise investment by £30 billion in the same timeframe.

In education, the Conservatives and Liberal Democrats were committed to maintaining student tuition fees, which Labour was set to abolish. The Liberal Democrats and Conservatives also agreed to increase the overall schools budget in England, by £7 and £4 billion respectively. However, both Labour and the Liberal Democrats opposed the introduction of new grammar schools and both opposed the Conservative plan to replace free school lunches with free school breakfasts, while Labour also committed increasing the amount of free childcare to 30 hours a week.

The policies that stuck out to most voters were (in order of importance) the 'dementia tax', the replacement of free school lunches with breakfasts, the abolition of tuition fees and Labour's proposal for four new bank holidays. This became an election more about welfare and social provision than a 'Brexit' election. It shows that clear ideological divisions have opened up again between the main parties.

Table 12.4 Highlights from the 2015 party manifestos

Policy area	Conservative Party	Labour Party	Liberal Democrats
The economy	Eliminate the deficit and return to an overall surplus by the end of the parliament Raise personal tax allowance to £12,500 and 40% tax threshold to £50,000 Legislate to keep people working 30 hours on minimum wage out of income tax No rise in VAT or National Insurance contributions Expand apprenticeships	Balance the books by cutting the deficit every year, with a surplus on the current budget and national debt falling in the next parliament Raise minimum wage to over £8 an hour by 2019 Reintroduce the 50% top rate of income tax for people earning over £150,000, and the 10% starting rate End 'non-domiciled' tax status No rise in VAT, National Insurance or income tax rates Expand apprenticeships	Deal with deficit by 2017/18 through spending cuts and tax rises Raise the income tax threshold to £12,500 £14bn from tax rises on corporations and the wealthy Increase tax charges to 'non-domiciled' residents Raise £1bn from extra corporation tax on banking sector Expand apprenticeships
Home affairs	Aim to keep annual net migration in tens of thousands Limit EU migrants' access to benefits and social housing Introduce Extremism Disruption Orders for those who 'spread poison' A new law on victims' rights	1,000 new border staff Cap on non-EU workers Two-year wait before EU migrants can claim out-of-work benefits Scrap police and crime commissioners Create commissioner on domestic and sexual abuse Overhaul the anti-terrorist 'Prevent' programme Establish a victims' law	Scrap police and crime commissioners End imprisonment for possessing drugs for personal use Restore full border checks New claimants with poor English to attend language courses to get jobseeker's allowance
Education	Protect school funding per pupil Create at least a further 500 free schools in England by 2020 30 hours per week free childcare for working parents of 3- and 4-year-olds	Index link budget for 0–19-year-olds Cut university tuition fees to £6,000 a year Guarantee primary school childcare from 8 a.m. to 6 p.m. Cap class sizes at 30 for 5-, 6- and 7-year-olds	Guarantee qualified teachers A core curriculum including sex education Ring-fenced education budget for 2–19-year-olds
Health	Increase NHS spending in England by at least £8bn above inflation over the next 5 years Seven-day access to GPs by 2020 and same-day appointments for over-75s when needed Improve access to mental health treatments Integrate health and social care	£2.5bn extra funding for the NHS 20,000 more nurses, 3,000 midwives and 8,000 GPs Repeal the Health and Social Care Act Limit the profit private firms can make from the NHS to 5% Integrate health and social care	Increase NHS funding in real terms by at least £8bn a year by 2020 £3.5bn extra for mental health care Integrate health and social care budgets
The environment	Protect the environment and green belt in the planning system Spend more than £3bn by 2020 to improve the environment Phase out subsidies for new onshore wind farms Invest £500m to make most cars and vans zero emission by 2050	Freeze energy bills until 2017 and give energy regulator new powers to cut bills this winter Reduce carbon emissions generated during electricity production to zero by 2030 Prioritise flood prevention End the badger cull	Double renewable electricity by 2020 Aim to decarbonise the power sector by 2030, leading to a zero-carbon Britain by 2050 Plant 750,000 trees/year Charge for plastic bags
Foreign and security	Replace Trident with four submarines to maintain continuous at-sea nuclear deterrent A comprehensive strategy to defeat Islamic State Hold an in/out referendum on Britain's renegotiated EU membership by 2017 Scrap Human Rights Act and replace with a British Bill of Rights	A minimum, credible, independent nuclear deterrent Strategic Security and Defence Review Make it illegal to discriminate against or abuse members of the Armed Forces No transfer of powers from Britain to the EU without an in/out referendum. Reform the EU's Common Agricultural Policy	End continuous at-sea nuclear deterrent Help service personnel and veterans with mental health problems Integrate defence and security spending Remain in the EU an in/out referendum if there is a plan for 'material transfer of sovereignty' from the UK

Policy area	Conservative Party	Labour Party	Liberal Democrats
Constitutional reform	Devolve further powers to Scottish Parliament and Welsh Assembly Introduce 'English votes for English laws' in the House of Commons Reduce the number of MPs in parliament Equalise the size of parliamentary constituencies	Home Rule Bill to give extra powers to Scotland Set up a people-led Constitutional Convention Replace the House of Lords with an elected senate Votes for 16- and 17-year-olds	Devolve further powers to Scotland and Wales Bring in votes for 16-year-olds, and the single transferable vote system Reform the House of Lords Cap annual political donations at £10,000 per person

Although the election of Jeremy Corbyn as Labour leader appeared to offer the possibility of a return to a more adversarial form of UK party politics, it is probably too early for us to make a judgement on the question of whether or not we are seeing a more general drift back towards once-entrenched ideological positions. In a sense, that is a judgement that will need to wait until the 2020 general election, when the wider citizenry will have the opportunity to issue their verdict on Corbyn's efforts to reposition the Labour Party.

Debate

Have recent years witnessed the 'end of ideology'?

Yes

- The three main parties are all essentially social democratic in nature. They are concerned with making piecemeal changes to the current arrangements as opposed to imposing an ideological model.
- The ideological wings of each of the three main parties have been marginalised.
- There are significant overlaps in the stated policies of the three main parties.
- Parties that once appeared fundamentally opposed to one another were able to enter into coalition in 2010.
- There is an increased emphasis on presentation and personality over substance.

No

- The three main UK parties still have distinct ideological traditions and a committed core support that strongly identifies with such traditions.
- The ideological dividing lines became more apparent in the wake of the global financial crisis.
- The election of Jeremy Corbyn as Labour leader in 2015 offered the prospect of a return to a style of ideologically polarised politics not seen since the early 1980s.
- The rise of smaller ideological and single-issue parties and pressure groups suggests that ideology still matters to a significant proportion of the electorate.

The structure and organisation of the three main UK parties

Local and national level

Labour Party

Those who join the Labour Party are assigned to a local branch — the lowest level of the party organisation. Branches select candidates for local elections and send delegates to the General Committee of the Constituency Labour Party (CLP). The CLP organises the party at constituency level. It takes the lead in local and national election campaigns and plays a part in selecting candidates for parliamentary elections, although the extension of one member, one vote (OMOV) has diminished the role of constituency party leaders in relation to regular members.

The National Executive Committee (NEC) is the main national organ of the Labour Party. It enforces party discipline, ensures the smooth running of the party, has the final say on the selection of parliamentary candidates, and oversees the preparation of policy proposals. Although the annual conference was once the party's sovereign policy-making body, its role diminished somewhat in the 1990s.

Conservative Party

The Conservative Party has a similar structure to the Labour Party at the local level. Branches corresponding to local council wards operate below the constituency-level Conservative Associations (CA). The CAs play a key role in organising the party at grassroots level and planning election campaigns. As with the Labour Party, however, the CAs no longer have a free rein in selecting parliamentary candidates.

The national party is organised around the Conservative Campaign Headquarters (CCHQ) at Millbank, Westminster. The party's headquarters were previously referred to as Conservative Central Office (CCO).

Liberal Democrats

As a party, the Liberal Democrats are organised along federal lines. Separate national parties in England, Scotland and Wales operate with a fair degree of autonomy within their own geographical jurisdictions — and a series of regional parties exist under each national party. In the absence of a separate 'English Parliament' (or 'English Assembly') to mirror those institutions in Scotland and Wales, the English Liberal Democrats are governed by the English Council Executive. This body comprises the representatives of all 11 English regional Liberal Democrat parties. At the UK level, the Liberal Democrats are governed by a number of federal institutions that were traditionally coordinated by the Federal Executive. However, the party's 2016 autumn conference opted to replace this executive with a new Federal Board — a body that would shape the strategic direction of the party and oversee the work of the party's other federal committees.

UK parties sitting in the European Parliament

UK members of the European Parliament (MEPs) sit in a number of transnational groups in the chamber as opposed to a single UK block. Following the UK elections to the European Parliament in 2014, the 19 Conservative MEPs sat with the European Conservatives and Reformists (ECR) group, the 20 Labour MEPs sat with the Progressive Alliance of Socialists and Democrats (PASD), and the single Liberal Democrat MEP sat with the Alliance of Liberals and Democrats for Europe (ALDE).

Internal party democracy

As political parties seek to exercise control over our democratic institutions, it is only proper for commentators to question the extent to which parties are themselves internally democratic. This means measuring

Distinguish between

Ordinary party members and ordinary Members of Parliament

Ordinary party members
- These are individual members of a party.
- They form the rank-and-file, grassroots membership.
- They are paid-up party members who do not hold senior positions within their chosen party.

Ordinary Members of Parliament
- These are elected Members of Parliament (also known as backbenchers).
- They do not hold front-bench responsibilities as government ministers, shadow ministers or party spokespersons.
- Although every MP will be a paid-up member of his or her chosen party, when thinking about ordinary party members you should focus on regular party members, rather than the influence of backbenchers.

Table 12.5 Membership of the three main British political parties, 2016

Party	Membership
Labour Party	515,000
Conservative Party	149,800
Liberal Democrats	76,000

Source: House of Commons Library, *Briefing Paper: Membership of UK political parties* (www.tinyurl.com/zy6j8mt)

the extent to which rank-and-file members have genuine power within a given political party. Three processes are commonly considered when assessing how internally democratic a political party is:
- the way in which leaders are chosen
- the way in which candidates for parliamentary elections are selected
- the way in which party policy is formulated

Choosing and removing party leaders

All three of the main UK parties now operate a two-stage system that places the ultimate responsibility for electing the party leader directly into the hands of grassroots party members (or members and registered supporters in the case of the Labour Party).

Conservative Party
- Conservative MPs vote in a series of ballots designed to narrow the field of leadership candidates down to two.
- Party members vote on a one member, one vote (OMOV) basis to decide which of these two candidates becomes party leader.

Labour Party
- Candidates must secure the nomination of 15% of the Parliamentary Labour Party (PLP) to qualify for the ballot.
- Party members and registered supports vote on a one member, one vote basis under an alternative vote system.

Liberal Democrats
- Candidates must secure the nomination of 20 local parties or 200 party members to qualify for the ballot.
- Party members vote on a one member, one vote basis under an alternative vote system.

Choosing parliamentary candidates

All three major parties have traditionally employed a three-stage process to select parliamentary candidates:
- First, hopefuls must get their names on to a centrally vetted, approved list of prospective candidates.

- Second, the local party draws up a shortlist from those approved candidates.
- Third, constituency party members vote for their preferred candidate, whether in person at a meeting or by postal ballot.

In recent years, Labour and the Conservatives have looked to widen the pool from which prospective parliamentary candidates are chosen. The Conservative Party experimented with public **hustings**, **open primaries** and **priority lists (A-lists)**, while the Labour Party pioneered the use of **all-women shortlists** (see the case study).

Case study

All-women shortlists

The Labour Party's practice of employing women-only shortlists existed in its original form between 1993 and 1996. Although it was briefly outlawed under the Sex Discrimination Act in 1996, the government subsequently amended the legislation to allow such lists. This exemption to anti-discrimination legislation was subsequently enshrined in the Equality Act 2010.

The use of all-women shortlists in many safe Labour seats contributed to the significant increase in the number of

women MPs returned to parliament at the 1997 general election. However, such shortlists have proven controversial — not least because they serve to discriminate against suitably able and qualified male candidates. At the 2005 general election, the independent candidate Peter Law was elected to represent the constituency of Blaenau Gwent, having been prevented from seeking selection as the official Labour Party candidate by the party's imposition of an all-women shortlist.

Questions
- Outline the case in favour of using all-women shortlists.
- Why is the use of such all-women shortlists so controversial?

Establishing party policy

Until the late 1990s, Conservative Party policy was largely determined by its leader. Although the leader was expected to canvass the views of senior colleagues on the front benches, the 1922 Committee, party elders and the grassroots membership, it was an unashamedly top-down process. As John Major famously said of the party's 1992 general election manifesto, 'It was all me.' The establishment of a national party Policy Forum as part of William Hague's 'Fresh Future' initiative in 1998 appeared to allow for grassroots participation in the process but the initiative was short-lived. The party's 2010 general election manifesto was said to have been written entirely by David Cameron, Oliver Letwin and Steve Hilton (Cameron's director of strategy), while Jo Johnson MP (younger brother of Boris Johnson) was said to have been behind the drafting of the 2015 manifesto.

The Labour Party conferences of the past were genuine policy-making events but from 1997 the party adopted a 2-year policy-making cycle. The National Policy Forum appointed policy commissions to make proposals which were then formalised in the National Executive Committee, before passing to the party conference for approval. Although this process helped the party to avoid the kinds of nasty surprises and public shows of disunity that had characterised earlier party conferences, such reforms could be said to have reduced the party conference to little more than a rubber stamp for policies agreed elsewhere. Ed Miliband, who later succeeded Gordon Brown as Labour leader, was widely credited with having drafted the party's 2010 general election manifesto, and the 2015 document was supposedly drafted by a team comprising academics such as Jonathan Rutherford, MPs including Jon Cruddas, and Marc Sears — Miliband's long-time friend and speech-writer.

Though the Liberal Democrats' federal structure once led commentators to argue that they were the most democratic of the three main parties in terms of policy making, the party leadership's influence over the Federal Policy Committee has also allowed it to steer policy, at least to a degree.

Political party funding in the UK

The changing basis of party funding

Most political parties receive income in the form of membership subscriptions. Until the 1990s, however, the lion's share of Labour Party funding came from fees paid by trade unions and other affiliated organisations, while the Conservative Party was said to be bankrolled by wealthy business interests.

The decline of UK political parties as mass-member organisations in the 1980s and 1990s had an adverse impact on party finances. Efforts to reduce the influence of trade unions within the Labour Party, under Neil Kinnock, John Smith and Tony Blair, also resulted in falling revenues. Such developments led parties to seek donations from wealthy individuals such as Bernie Ecclestone and Lord Sainsbury for Labour, and Sir Paul Getty and Stuart Wheeler for the Conservatives, though Wheeler later defected to UKIP — becoming the party's treasurer.

Controversy and regulation

The rise of large individual donations to political parties in the 1990s led to the perception that access or political influence could be bought. For example, some felt that Bernie Ecclestone's £1 million donation to the Labour Party in 1997 may have prompted the subsequent delay in the introduction of the ban on tobacco advertising in Formula 1 motor racing. Such controversy inevitably led to calls for regulation.

Political Parties, Elections and Referendums Act (PPERA) 2000

The PPERA (2000) imposed an overall limit on party spending in general election campaigns (£30,000 per constituency), established additional spending limits for elections to devolved bodies and the European Parliament, and required parties to declare all donations over £5,000 to the Electoral Commission. In so doing, the Act sought to make parties less reliant on wealthy individual backers.

Political Parties and Elections Act (PPEA) 2009

The PPEA (2009) built upon the regulations established under the PPERA: imposing tighter regulations on spending by candidates in the run-up to an election, allowing the Electoral Commission to investigate cases and impose fines, restricting donations from non-UK residents and reducing the thresholds for the declaration of donations.

Cranborne money Funds paid to opposition parties in the House of Lords in order to help them cover their administrative costs and thereby provide for proper scrutiny of the government. In 2014–15, the Labour Party received £572,717 in Cranborne money.

Short money Funds paid to opposition parties in order to help them cover their administrative costs and thereby provide for proper scrutiny of the government. It is available to all opposition parties that win at least two seats — or win a single seat while also securing over 150,000 votes nationally — at a general election. In 2014–15, the Labour Party received a total of £6,684,794 in Short money, which included £777,538 to support the work of the Leader of the Opposition.

State funding of political parties

The 2007 Phillips Report, *Strengthening Democracy: Fair and Sustainable Funding for Political Parties,* concluded that one way forward might be greater state funding for UK political parties, perhaps through some form of 'pence-per-voter' or 'pence-per-member' funding formula.

Although the case in favour of the comprehensive funding of UK political parties is still widely contested, it is worth remembering that public funds have long been in place in the form of the Policy Development Grants (PDGs) established under Section 12 of the PPERA, **Short money** and **Cranborne money**. The PDGs are particularly significant as they are available not only to the main opposition parties but also as a share of an annual pot of £2m to any party that has two or more sitting MPs taking the oath of allegiance (see Table 12.6). Parties also receive subsidies in respect of their television broadcasts and help with their postage costs during election campaigns.

Table 12.6 Policy Development Grants, 2015–16

Party	Value of grants
Conservative Party	£359,478
Democratic Unionist Party	£137,929
Labour Party	£359,478
Liberal Democrats	£359,478
Plaid Cymru	£132,553
Scottish National Party	£153,676
Social Democratic and Labour Party	£137,929
UK Independence Party (UKIP)	£359,478
Ulster Unionist Party	N/A
Total	£2,000,000

Source: House of Commons Library, *Briefing Paper: Political party funding: sources and regulations* (www.tinyurl.com/h6qywot)

Debate

Should political parties be state-funded?

Yes
- If parties are not funded by taxpayers, they will be funded by wealthy individuals and interest groups.
- State funding would allow politicians to focus on representing their constituents rather than courting potential donors.
- Parties such as the Liberal Democrats could compete on an equal financial footing because funding would be based entirely on membership or electoral performance.

No
- Taxpayers should not be expected to bankroll parties that they oppose.
- Politicians could become isolated from real-world issues if they are denied access from interest groups.
- Parties will always have unequal resources, even if state funding is introduced — not least because there will be differences in membership levels, and human and material resources.

Has the reformed system worked?

Although the new regulations have made party funding more transparent, there have been significant teething problems — not least the attempts by parties to circumvent the PPERA's regulation of donations by encouraging supporters to offer the party long-term, low-interest 'loans'. It was this tactic, and the inducements supposedly offered to secure such lines of credit, that gave rise to the 'loans for peerages' scandal during Labour's time in office (1997–2010). Although the police investigation into that scandal ultimately ended without any prosecutions being brought, the issue of party funding is still controversial, as seen in the efforts to address the status of donors not registered as UK taxpayers under the PPEA. Many considered this measure to be aimed squarely at individuals such as the long-term Conservative Party backer and party deputy chairman Lord Ashcroft, whose tax status provoked debate and controversy until March 2010, when he finally revealed that he did not pay UK tax on his overseas earnings. It is telling that even in 2015, when the Labour Party's membership enjoyed an unprecedented upsurge, membership fees only accounted for 19% of the party's overall annual income (see Figure 12.2).

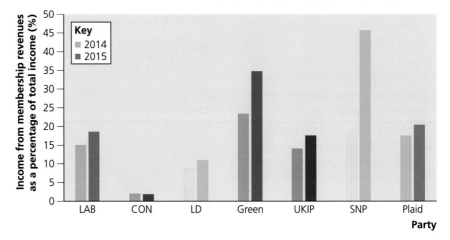

Source: House of Commons Library, *Briefing Paper: Membership of UK political parties* (www.tinyurl.com/zy6j8mt)

Figure 12.2 Income from membership revenues as a percentage of total income, by party, 2014 and 2015

Statutory regulation and public funds aside, it is clear that the main UK political parties still receive considerable sums in the form of donations at key points in the electoral cycle. It is clear also that the wealthy individual backers that the PPERA sought to identify have not been put off by the prospect of losing their anonymity. Although the scale of donations to the main parties is obviously greatly reduced when there is no general election in prospect, the sums flowing into the parties' coffers in such years are significant nonetheless (see Table 12.7).

Table 12.7 Donations to UK parties in the first quarter of 2016

Beneficiary	Number and total value of donations
All parties	568 donations totalling £14,384,737
Conservative Party	269 donations totalling £6,751,948
Labour Party	150 donations totalling £5,489,345
Liberal Democrats	79 donations totalling £766,119

Source: House of Commons Library, *Briefing Paper: Political party funding: sources and regulations* (www.tinyurl.com/h6qywot)

Party funding: where to from here?

While all parties appear to accept that 'big money' in the form of donations should be removed from politics, few at Westminster believe that voters enduring an extended period of austerity could easily be convinced of the need for greater state funding of political parties at taxpayers' expense. Moreover, while the Labour Party would be happy to impose tougher restrictions on individual donations, the Conservatives would only accept such an overt attack on their own income streams if similar restrictions were placed on Labour's trade union backers. Thus further reform of party funding, like reform to the House of Lords, appears to have arrived at a natural impasse.

What you should know

- A political party is a group of like-minded individuals who come together with the aim of realising their shared goals by fielding candidates at elections and thereby securing election to public office.
- Parties differ from pressure groups in that the latter would normally only contest elections as a means of raising the profile of their chosen cause or interest, as opposed to having a genuine desire to be returned to office.
- Although smaller niche parties of all types have made great strides in recent years, in terms of both votes won and candidates elected, the UK is still generally characterised as a two-party system.
- The main UK political parties are highly hierarchical organisations comprising a number of different organisational levels, from local and constituency parties to the national party level. The MEPs elected to represent the main UK parties in the European Parliament sit in transnational ideological groupings as opposed to a single national group.
- The emergence of New Right thinking in the 1970s and the Thatcherite revolution of the 1980s marked the end of the postwar consensus, with the two main UK parties adopting more ideologically coherent positions.
- The Conservatives under Margaret Thatcher pursued a neo-liberal agenda whereas the Labour Party under Michael Foot campaigned in the 1983 general election on the basis of an orthodox left-wing manifesto that was later described as 'the longest suicide note in history'.
- Under the leadership of Neil Kinnock, John Smith and Tony Blair, the Labour Party sought to reposition itself on the political spectrum and broaden its appeal beyond traditional Labour voters. This effort to triangulate traditional Labour values and approaches with the lessons learnt from Thatcherism resulted in the emergence of New Labour.
- New Labour rejected the 'tax and spend' approach of previous Labour administrations in favour of establishing partnerships between the public and private sectors and creating internal markets within public services as a way of improving efficiency.
- In response to three consecutive general election defeats (between 1997 and 2005), David Cameron sought to 'detoxify' the Conservative brand by campaigning on issues such as the environment and social inclusion.
- Some argue that the convergence of the three main parties on the centre ground has led to the 'end of ideology'. There were more similarities than differences between the manifestos published by the three main parties at the time of the 2015 general election.
- Party funding has proven a contentious issue in recent years as the revenue generated from membership subscriptions has declined and the main parties have become increasingly reliant on donations from wealthy individuals.
- Attempts to reform party finance under the PPERA (2000) and the PPEA (2009) have addressed some of the main areas of concern, although many commentators still argue in favour of the introduction of a more comprehensive system of state funding of parties than exists at present.

Political parties

- The USA, like the UK, is generally characterised as a two-party system. Vacant seats aside, all 435 members of the House of Representatives were either Democrats or Republicans in 2016, along with 98 of 100 US Senators. Every president since 1853 has been either a Democrat or a Republican.

- While one would expect a Conservative Association in Surrey to stand by the same broad programme of policies as one in Yorkshire, many commentators speak of the USA as having 50 party systems or 100 distinctive parties (i.e. two per state). This is because the differences between Democrats (or between Republicans) in different states can be more significant than the differences between the official party platforms of the Democrats and Republicans nationally: in other words, there may be more differences within the parties than between them.

- While some niche parties in the UK are permanent, most minor (or third) parties in the USA are short-lived. Indeed, many might be seen as pressure groups employing electoral candidacy as a means of raising awareness of and support for their cause or sectional interest, as opposed to true political parties.

- US political parties have traditionally been more decentralised in their organisation than their UK counterparts. The main US parties have no party leader as such, and the national parties have a far more limited role outside of elections than their UK equivalents.

- Candidate selection in the UK remains largely controlled by political parties but the introduction of primary elections in most US states has seen this power transferred to regular voters.

- The traditional left–right political spectrum is less useful when discussing US politics because the two main parties are both regarded as right of centre. Instead, commentators tend to describe policies and parties as being 'more liberal' or 'more conservative'.

- UK political parties were once seen as broadly ideological in character but the two main US parties have always been regarded as broad churches or 'big tents'. While the UK is said to have undergone a period of ideological convergence in recent years, with the rise of catch-all parties, US parties have become more ideologically coherent and distinctive, as seen in the 2016 presidential election campaign.

- The 1974 Federal Election Campaign Act (FECA) — amended by subsequent legislation and moderated by rulings by the US Supreme Court — established a form of state funding of elections and regulated donations to candidates and parties. Despite this, campaign finance remains just as controversial an issue in the USA as it is in the UK.

Further reading

Bale, T. (2017) 'How socialist is the Labour Party?', *Politics Review*, Vol. 26, No. 3, pp. 6–9.

Goodwin, M. (2015) 'The UKIP and SNP insurgency during the 2015 general election', *Politics Review*, Vol. 25, No. 1, pp. 12–15.

Heywood, A. (2016) 'Corbynism: the strange rebirth of UK socialism?', *Politics Review*, Vol. 25, No. 4, pp. 2–5.

Kilheeney, E. (2017) 'How does Theresa May's government differ from David Cameron's?' *Politics Review*, Vol. 26, No. 3, pp. 16–17.

McNaughton, E. and Magee, E. (2017) 'Cameron as prime minister: a verdict', *Politics Review*, Vol. 26, No. 4, pp. 20–23.

Quinn, T. (2015) 'The UK party system: a two-party or a multi-party system?', *Politics Review*, Vol. 24, No. 3, pp. 26–30.

Exam-style questions

Short-answer questions

1 Explain, with examples, the role of party manifestos in general elections.

2 Explain, with examples, the meaning of a 'two-party' system.

3 Explain and analyse three Thatcherite policies.

4 Explain and analyse three factions of the modern Labour Party.

Mid-length questions

1 Describe the main features of one-nation conservatism.

2 Describe the main functions of political parties.

3 Analyse and evaluate the arguments in favour of state-based party funding.

4 Analyse and evaluate the arguments that suggest Britain is a multiparty system.

Essay questions

1 Evaluate how far the Labour Party has remained true to its traditional principles.

2 Evaluate how far the modern Conservative Party may be described as a 'one-nation' party.

3 Analyse and evaluate the criticisms of the major political parties.

4 'The two-party system is over in Britain.' How far do you agree with this statement?

Index

Page numbers in **bold** refer to key term definitions